The Politics of State Expansion

The Politics of State Expansion

War, State and Society in Twentieth-Century Britain

James E. Cronin

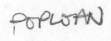

London and New York 3627

First published 1991
by Routledge
11 New Fetter Lane, London EC4P 4EE

Simultaneously published in the USA and Canada
by Routledge
a division of Routledge, Chapman and Hall, Inc.
29 West 35th Street, New York, NY 10001

Typeset in 10/12pt Garamond, Linotron 202
Disk conversion by Witwell Ltd, Merseyside
Printed in England by T. J. Press Ltd, Padstow, Cornwall

British Library Cataloguing in Publication Data
Cronin, James E.
  The politics of state expansion: war, state and society
  in twentieth-century Britain.
  1. Great Britain. Society. Role of state, history
  I. Title
  361.650941

Library of Congress Cataloging in Publication Data
Cronin, James E.
    The politics of state expansion : war, state, and society in
  twentieth-century Britain / James E. Cronin.
      p. cm.
    1. Great Britain–Politics and government–20th century.
  2. Bureaucracy–Great Britain–History–20th century. 3. Great
  Britain–Economic policy. 4. Great Britain–Social policy.
  5. Politics and war–History–20th century. 6. Welfare state–
  History–20th century. I. Title.
  JN309.C76   1991
  941.082–dc20

ISBN 0-415-03623-2

To my parents, Lenora and Jim Cronin
and to their granddaughters, Rebecca and Johanna.

Contents

Preface

The expansion of the state is one of the grand themes of twentieth-century British history. Strangely, however, the process has for the most part escaped serious analysis. It has often been noted, but ordinarily it is treated as one of those background factors that we recognize but do not pause to interpret. The purpose of this book is to focus directly on this transformation and to see what forces and interests shaped it, propelled it forward, delayed, deflected or occasionally reversed it.

These questions lie at the intersection of the distinct histories of public policy and of administration, and in formulating answers to them I have drawn heavily upon the extensive literatures in both of these fields. I have not written a history of social and economic policy, or a study of bureaucracy, but I have learned a great deal from scholars who have. Hopefully, the notes will serve to acknowledge most of my specific borrowings, but my broader indebtedness needs to be recorded separately.

So, too, does my gratitude to the institutions and colleagues who have materially assisted this effort. My research was initially supported by a generous and timely fellowship from the German Marshall Fund of the United States; subsequent grants from the Graduate School at Boston College have allowed me to finish. The Center for the Study of Industrial Societies at the University of Chicago provided an extremely pleasant and yet serious place to work during much of 1985-6; and the Minda de Gunzburg Center for European Studies at Harvard has since 1987 brought me into contact with an unusually productive and stimulating group of scholars, many of whom share my interest in citizenship, the state and public policy. At a less formal level a quite large number of individuals helped me in diverse ways. Several read and criticized the grant proposal with which I solicited funds for research; several others read early papers on the topic or drafts of chapters; still others pointed me to sources or allowed me access to their unpublished work; and some just talked about the project. Among these were Paul Addison, Ed Amenta, Peter Baldwin, Richard Chapman, Gary Cross, Michael Dintenfass, John Foster, Bentley Gilbert, John Gillis, Hugh Heclo, Carol Heim, Sandy Jencks, Paul Johnson, Paul Kennedy, Jane Lewis, Charles Maier, Michael Mann, Andrew

McDonald, Keith Middlemas, Ralph Miliband, Jim Obelkevich, Leo Panitch, Harold Perkin, Fran Piven, Richard Price, Neil Rollings, Jon Schneer, Bill Schwarz, Jim Tomlinson, Noel Whiteside, Jay Winter, Karel Williams and Chris Wrigley. I am especially grateful for the opportunity to present my ideas and, at the time, very meagre evidence for them, to seminars at the Center for European Studies at Harvard, the Center for Studies of Social Change at the New School for Social Research, the Center for the Study of Industrial Societies at the University of Chicago, the History Departments of New York University and the University of Illinois at Urbana and the Center for Social History at Carnegie–Mellon and the University of Pittsburgh; and I want to thank Peter Hall, Chuck Tilly, Herrick Chapman and Bob Scally for arranging these occasions. Chuck Tilly also invited me to submit a working paper on the British state and the Second World War to the Committee on States and Social Structures of the Social Science Research Council. Writing that paper forced me to think seriously about the themes that now dominate chapters eight and nine, and defending it made me think hard about the entire book. I would also like to thank Mark Kishlansky and Ted Cook, who asked me to co-ordinate a special issue of the *Journal of British Studies*. That gave me the chance to write an essay adumbrating many of the broad themes argued throughout this book.

I feel I have incurred debts to many others whose contributions have not been especially tangible but whose friendship has made me happy while writing it. I have in mind my old friends from Wisconsin – Gene Eisman, Carole Shammas, Darryl Holter, Bob Schwartz, Margaret Atherton, Margo Anderson, Reg Horsman, Marc Levine, Ron Ross and Terry Radtke; and my new friends at Boston College – Larry Wolff, Paul Breines, Alan Rogers, Kevin O'Neill, Clairemarie Fisher O'Leary, Robin Fleming and Paul Spagnoli. Bob Moeller, Pat Thane and Peter Weiler have not only been good friends, but have also read the penultimate draft of the entire book. Their criticisms have undoubtedly made the book better, though I'm sure it would be still better if I'd taken more of their suggestions.

My greatest debts are, of course, to my family. This book is dedicated to my parents and to my children, Johanna and Rebecca, whose love and approval I crave and who therefore constitute in some basic sense my ultimate audience. The other person whose love I need and whose judgment I care deeply about is Mary Cronin. She has lived through the birth of this book with grace and tolerance and offered insightful criticisms at critical stages of research and writing. During that time she has often borne more than her share of our joint responsibilities, but nevertheless managed to achieve more professionally than I could ever imagine. I owe her much, and want everyone to know it.

Chapter 1

Introduction: The politics of state expansion in twentieth-century Britain

Just where to set the boundaries between state and society has become perhaps the most central and certainly the most contentious question in late twentieth-century British politics. Of course, the precise relationship between the individual and the collective, between the market and the polity, has been a perennial concern in modern society. Recently, however, the sustained growth of government, of public provision and of state involvement in the economy seems to have disturbed previously established boundaries by extending the sphere of the state. For nearly a quarter of a century after the Second World War the boundaries of the state – measured by some in terms of tax rates, by others in terms of the share of national income spent by government, by still others in terms of the extent of government interference in the market – were roughly stable and broadly accepted.[1] But during the 1970s and early 1980s the state seemed to have broken through those admittedly arbitrary limits and became once more the centre of intense controversy. Like most issues in contemporary politics, the argument over the state has been conducted with little reference to the past and with even less knowledge of it. It has been nevertheless an intrinsically historical argument, for the discourse about the state's proper role in contemporary society has been largely a discussion about whether its sphere of action has changed and how it might be transformed yet again.

It would seem essential, then, to reassess the process by which the state grew over the course of the present century and came to occupy such a prominent place in the nation's social and political life. A reassessment conceived at a time when the state's role is a matter of intense controversy should also lead to an account that is less complacent about outcomes than many previous analyses and more aware of the fiscal and bureaucratic implications of state growth. Historians of economic and social policy have provided many detailed and highly useful studies of particular innovations in specific areas where the state has chosen to act upon society.[2] They have produced fewer analyses of the broad range of the state's efforts, however, and virtually no account that links policy with the structure and funding of the state itself. The aim of this book is to offer such an account by bringing together the too often separate histories of policy-making, of administrative evolution and of public finance.

Constructing such an integrated view of the past has almost as many difficulties as advantages. The hope is that the proliferation of solid mono-graphic research in each of these areas can minimize the difficulties and provide the grounding for a broader analysis. As to merits, chief among them must surely be the possibility of comprehending the historical growth of the state in a new, more coherent fashion, in a manner that makes it clear how, for example, the adoption of beneficial social programmes has depended on developments in the government's taxing capacity that had little to do with the desire for social reform; how the use of new techniques of economic planning had to wait upon administrative changes that would only be made under pressure of war; how bureaucratic politics reinforced, or occasionally under-mined, party alignments and how central the politics of taxation were to the ebb and flow of Parliamentary politics; and how much easier it was, after 1945, to gain rhetorical acceptance of the goal of full employment than to put in place the means to make it a reality. An account of this sort should also be more interesting than older analyses, less preoccupied with lists of pro-grammes and more aware of the forces opposed to policy innovation and its bureaucratic and fiscal accompaniments, and in the end more fully appreciative of what it was that supporters of the welfare state achieved.

Reassessing the process of growth requires as a first step getting a handle on its pace and dimensions and fashioning a set of questions appropriate to the pattern of growth. The expansion of the state during the twentieth century was a curious phenomenon. Looked at from a distance, it appears to have been steady, inexorable and massive. Viewed more closely, it was much more fitful and uneven, a discontinuous process whose ultimate outcome was the sum of a rather idiosyncratic combination of discrete, and often quite contradictory, short-term trends. In the aggregate, both the level of public expenditure and the size of the state apparatus grew substantially. Nevertheless, for many years growth was quite modest. Between 1900 and 1913, for example, expenditure adjusted for inflation grew by just 1 per cent; from 1920 to 1934 it grew by just 8.5 per cent. Real per capita expenditure actually declined by 9 per cent during the years 1900–13 and grew by merely 1.5 per cent over the years from 1920 through 1934. In fact, very much the greater part of the twentieth-century increase in expenditure occurred during periods of rearmament or war. In 1913, government spending equalled 12 per cent of national income. This rose spectacularly to 52 per cent in 1918, then fell back and stabilized at about a quarter of the national product, roughly double the prewar standard. Only with rearmament after 1935 did the proportion begin to increase again, to 35 per cent in 1939 and to a massive 74 per cent at the peak of war mobilization in 1943. By 1946 it had already receded to just over half and by 1950 it was down to 39 per cent, where it again stabilized until the 1960s. From 1913 to the 1950s, then, it had grown from about an eighth to approximately 40 per cent of the national product, but almost all of that increase was concentrated in years marked by war or preparation for war.[3]

Other indices of state expansion followed slightly different paths, but they, too, have displayed considerable irregularities. The curve of spending on social services from 1900 to 1955 rose more steadily than did aggregate spending, for example, but it nevertheless registered sharp inflections around both wars. The course of public employment manifested a similarly uneven pattern of growth. Thus, while it is true that from 1901 to 1971 the share of public employees in the working population grew from 5.8 per cent to 22.7 per cent, it is also the case that for most of the intervening years the share remained stable. Between 1911 and 1921, for instance, it jumped from 7 per cent to 10 per cent, and as of 1938 was still only 9.9 per cent. The proportion leapt forward again to 14.5 per cent by 1951, but was just under that as late as 1961.[4] Even more interesting has been the failure of military expenditure to rise consistently. Despite the emergence in the 1880s and 1890s of something like a modern "military-industrial complex," restraints on spending for weapons and for soldiers remained strong. Moreover, neither the Boer War nor the First World War managed to break the historic resistance to sustained, large-scale military expenditure in Britain. After both, therefore, spending on arms fell dramatically.[5] Only with the rearmament of the 1950s, undertaken largely at the urging of the United States, was this aversion to military spending overcome within the counsels of the state. So even when broken down by category, the tendencies for the British state to expand would seem to have been surprisingly weak in periods other than those marked by war, its imminence or aftermath.

Nor was there a separate history of policy innovations and legislative intervention that, while not costing much, nevertheless would indicate a more consistent tendency for the state to encroach upon civil society. British governments did not always adopt the most expensive forms of social provision – e.g., with national insurance – but generally innovations coincided with increases in expenditure. Only very rarely did Britain get involved in more passive sorts of public policies, e.g., regulation, and even less often did it rely upon relatively unobtrusive, self-enforcing mechanisms for effecting its will. On the contrary, the preference for setting up boards, commissions and tribunals meant that most policy initiatives were administratively visible and typically carried relatively significant price tags.

In sum, the appearance of fitful progress toward a larger state in twentieth-century Britain would seem not to be a mere statistical artifact, but a reflection of the historical process itself. What, if anything, does this "irregular time pattern" suggest about the process of state expansion? Surely it casts doubt upon the conventional understanding of what is routine and what is exceptional in the history of state expansion. Reading certain neo-conservative writers on the state would lead one to expect to discover in the historical record a constant tendency for expansion, checked only by periodic outbursts of the citizenry refusing to pay for it.[6] The "normal" pattern seems to have been quite different. The regular workings of British politics have not generated a particularly strong and sustained tendency to augment the state's power or to fill its coffers. On the contrary, for long stretches of time those who have sought to restrict the size and the scope of the state seem to have been able to keep government growth firmly in check. Of course, any attempt to label one pattern or period normal and another abnormal is questionable. Still, using the terms in this instance would have at least heuristic value. Most theories of state growth do not, after all, predict such discontinuities and irregularities; and those that do recognize them have not provided a sufficient explanation.[7] More pragmatically, if there is a justification for regarding any moment as "abnormal" in the life of states, it would seem to apply to those moments when the state's very existence has been threatened in what, in the present century, has been a series of "total wars." Yet it was precisely in those moments and, until recently, only in those moments, that the twentieth-century British state has expanded on a significant scale.[8]

It is perhaps necessary, therefore, to turn around the question typically asked about state expansion. Instead of inquiring into the forces that have pushed the state to expand, it would presumably be at least as helpful to know what has held it back. The question is made still more interesting, and more difficult to answer, when those factors that have regularly been adduced to explain government growth are taken into account. The steady growth of working-class power, the logic of bureaucratic aggrandizement or at least of incremental budgeting, the logical progression from social discovery to social reform and, perhaps most important, the process by which the meaning of democratic citizenship has broadened to encompass social and economic, as well as political, rights have undoubtedly imparted an upward bias to the trend of state activity.[9] So, too, did the process through which collectivist ideas and values gradually encroached upon and eventually prevailed over individualist beliefs within the political culture, a process put into reverse only recently. Given all this, the forces impeding state expansion must have been strong indeed in order to hold growth in check for so very long, and for that reason alone merit attention.

THE RESISTANCE TO STATE EXPANSION

Measuring the resistance to state expansion is not a simple task. Precisely because the questions asked about the state have for so long been informed by a sense of its inevitable tendency to grow, knowledge about resistances to state expansion is limited. Interest groups that pitted themselves against the welfare state have tended to be written off as mere political relics, while thinkers who opposed the state's assumption of greater responsibility have been seen as uncritical prisoners of orthodoxy and hence intellectually barren. The chapters that follow will seek, if not to rehabilitate the interests and institutions that held back the expansion of the state, at least to restore them to the centre of the conflicts over public policy. Recasting the problem in this fashion will reveal two factors as having been primarily responsible for limiting the expansion of the state: the anti-state logic embedded in the politics of taxation and the self-denying tendencies inherent in the unique structure of the British state.

Nothing has been more pivotal in British political life throughout the nineteenth and twentieth centuries than taxation, but scholars have not seriously integrated the history of taxation into the history of politics and the state.[10] What has been missed in particular is the way the politics of taxation has operated to make it very difficult for those seeking to expand revenues to prevail. Beyond the difficulty of raising taxes, the administrative structure of the British state would seem also to have been quite inhospitable to those seeking to lay hold of the organs of central power in order to use them for social reform. A major part of the reason is that at the centre of bureaucratic power in Britain has been the Treasury, which in the nineteenth century enshrined as its guiding principle a fundamentally negative view of the state's role in society and subsequently adopted a more or less "permanent posture of menace and rejection" towards attempts to augment the state.[11] Proponents of greater state activity have therefore been confronted simultaneously with the need to convince the public and the politicians to favour their proposals, with the task of finding a way to pay for them, and with the difficulty of overcoming frequently fierce bureaucratic resistance. This has been a formidable challenge that has given rise to a powerful inertial logic that regularly frustrated efforts to expand the British state. The creation of the fiscal and administrative capacity necessary for social reform has been, in fact, much more difficult than the creation of a political consensus on the virtues of reform.[12]

Not that it was ever easy to reach agreement on reform itself. Over the course of the twentieth century, the main interest pressing a reformist politics based on an expanded state has been the organized labour movement. But labour's politics have never been monolithic and labour's has never been the sole voice urging reform. Upper-class reformers and philanthropists, feminists and women's organizations, groups specifically concerned with education, with pensions and old age or with children, and professional organizations of doctors, teachers and social workers have all made major contributions to the debate on the proper role of the state and social provision. These advocates, or opponents, of reform have seldom spoken with unanimity, but rather have pursued different, if often overlapping, agendas. Inevitably, their impact has varied over time and from one issue to another. Philanthropists, especially those represented by the Charity Organization Society, were primarily concerned with poor relief; feminists have been more active and effective on family policy and issues surrounding maternal and child welfare; doctors have been critical in the evolution of health care; teachers on education. Not infrequently, these groups and interests have found themselves either opposed by labour or in an uneasy alliance with its representatives.

As the best organized and most consistent source of support for expanded social provision, the Labour party and the unions had to be part of any successful coalition. Their support was not easily obtained, however, for the labour movement jealously guarded the prerogatives of its members. Unions and friendly societies had evolved their own means of coping with unemployment, sickness and old age and were reluctant to acquiesce in initiatives that might jeopardize the fiscal basis of these efforts or break the link they provided with the membership. The unions were especially resistant to proposals that might interfere with bargains struck in the labour market – e.g., proposals for family allowances or schemes for decasualizing dockwork. The state itself, moreover, elicited distrust and hostility from labour. The unions were first brought together behind the incipient Labour party to counter a series of legal attacks. Long after these were reversed, the Trades Union Congress and the Labour party remained wary of the intentions of a government they did not control and a bureaucracy staffed by their social superiors. Gradually, the ambivalence towards the state would be overcome, and by the end of the Second World War the representatives of the workers would become the most uncritical advocates of collectivist policies administered by the central state. Until that transformation occurred, and until a majority coalition for greater state intervention had been created, however, the constraints on the state proved almost insurmountable. Even then, success was only possible because the anti-state biases of the politics of taxation and the structure of the state machine were put in abeyance by the need to wage war.

TAXES AND THE STATE

Getting taxation up to the level required to fund the modern, "Keynesian welfare state" proved especially complicated. The nation's previous tax history combined with the changing character of its political system and the structure of its economy to strengthen the routine resistance to high taxes. During the eighteenth century, the British state had grown stronger by increasing its revenues from customs and excise.[13] When augmented by the proceeds of income tax imposed during the Napoleonic Wars, they provided the government with the most productive tax system in the world. The coming of peace prompted a reversion to the earlier pattern, as income tax was abolished and replaced in effect by the Corn Laws. After 1815, however, the tendency was for taxes on trade to be lowered or eliminated and for government to rely on increases accruing from economic growth or on the income tax, reimposed at a modest level in 1842. By 1846, the tax structure had shifted from a reliance upon indirect taxes on trade and consumption to a more even balance between direct and indirect taxes. The free trade policies in place after 1846, and the tax structure that accompanied them, provided the framework of public finance that allowed Britain to become the world's leading economic power during the next half century.

The historic commitment to free trade precluded any quick and easy recourse to indirect taxes as a means of financing the twentieth-century state. There was debate, of course, and the bulk of the Conservative party would follow Joseph Chamberlain into the pro-tariff camp after the Boer War signalled the need for much higher taxes. Support for tariffs would persist among Unionists, and especially among manufacturers, into the interwar years and would in fact triumph at the height of the depression in 1932. But it was never likely that tariffs would be raised high enough or quickly enough to provide the revenues that would be needed by the state either for defence or social reform. Attention turned inevitably to direct taxation to provide the fiscal underpinnings of the expanding state. To be effective, though, direct taxes on income and inheritance would have also to be graduated so as to tap the wealth accumulated in the higher reaches of the social order. The modern British "tax state" would thus come to be built on a major increase in progressive taxation.[14]

Putting together a political coalition powerful enough to bring about a substantial rise in progressive taxation would prove very difficult. Ironically, nineteenth-century Conservatives had feared that widening the franchise would lead directly to confiscatory tax policies, but in practice it turned out to be very hard to extract higher taxes from Britain's increasingly democratic political system. The emerging polity, with its mass parties and highly mobilized interests, was so structured as to privilege the opposition to taxation and to limit the effectiveness of those seeking to expand the fiscal capacity of the state. A number of features of the British state and its system of representation contributed to this anti-tax bias. At the most basic level, the process by which taxation has been imposed made the raising of taxes a rare event. The process goes on at national level on an annual basis: indeed, the spring budget has served for most of this century as the key event in the calendar of central government activity. Taxes therefore cannot typically be increased automatically or unobtrusively. Rather, the setting of taxes is accompanied by close scrutiny and elicits from interested parties intense, more or less continual, mobilization and lobbying at the national level.

Not surprisingly, it has been bankers, merchants, industrialists and other upper- and upper-middle-class groups who have been most successful at this sort of politics. The unions and the even more disorganized and haphazard organizations of the poor or other groups likely to want to see taxes and spending increase have been much less effective in this arena. The organizational bases of the unions and of the Labour party have been highly localized and fragmented and were cobbled together around labour market or workplace issues. Influencing policy at the centre, especially budgetary policy, has been extremely difficult. The organizational linkages of elites, however, have been broader in scope, more stable and far more capable of sustaining an effective presence at Westminster and Whitehall.

The input of those arrayed against taxes has also counted more heavily with officials than has that of the proponents of higher taxes. Outwardly, officials at the Board of Inland Revenue and at the Treasury have maintained a scrupulously neutral stance towards interests seeking to influence the making of tax policy: they do not give away secret information and they will receive deputations from both sides. The records of both departments are replete with the minutes of meetings held with representatives of commerce, manufacturing, labour, farmers, landlords and accountants. Ministers and officials may not respond equally to the concerns and complaints of business and of the unions, but they do listen to both. However, there has long existed a more fundamental and indeed prior link between officials and the upper and middle classes. From 1842 until the introduction of the PAYE (pay-as-you-earn) system a century later, liability to income tax was almost exclusively an upper- and middle-class phenomenon. To pay income tax was virtually a badge of class status and the term "taxpayers" became almost synonymous with the middle and upper classes. Paying tax was what made the middle classes into full citizens and, judging from the high rates of compliance, it was a duty discharged proudly and publicly. Voluntary compliance was essential if income tax was to be administered cheaply and profitably. Officials thus came to feel that success depended on the goodwill of the taxpayers and were reluctant to impose obligations that might stimulate avoidance. Over time both the Treasury and the Inland Revenue became increasingly protective towards taxpayers and tended to take their interests into account whether formally expressed or not. Bureaucratic self-interest thus reinforced the class instincts of officials, who would all have come from taxpaying families, and made them sympathetic to the desire to keep tax rates low.

The structural asymmetry in the political clout of those ordinarily on either side of the battle over taxes, and in the receptivity of officials to their concerns, was accentuated by yet another structural feature of the British political economy: the unusual predominance of financial interests concentrated in the City of London.[15] One of the peculiarities of Britain's economic history has been the separation of manufacturing industry from commerce and finance. Manufacturing was for a very long time provincially based, both in its financing and in its production; commerce and banking, on the other hand, have long been centred almost exclusively in London and oriented in their activities towards the world market. The largest fortunes have consistently been made in the financial and commercial sectors, and the City has always been more powerful socially and politically than industry.[16] The City, moreover, has consistently had privileged access to the state by means of its intimate connections with the Bank of England and the Treasury. That access was used regularly to shape financial policy. The City did not share with small business or manufacturing their antipathy to virtually all taxes; they were more responsible than that. Nor did the financial community have much use for tariffs, as many industrialists did. Rather, they favoured taxes sufficient to keep the budget in rough balance but little more, and were eager to keep taxes earmarked for specific purposes – the sinking fund was the favourite – thus denying government the flexibility to divert revenues from one purpose to another. This overall approach to taxation dominated the thinking and discourse over tax policy at Westminster and in Whitehall. Its practical consequence was an unrelenting pressure for debt reduction that never allowed for the permanent lowering of tax rates so longed for by the middle and upper classes. The steady pressure of taxes, however, kept taxpayers and their political defenders organized and vigilant, ready to move quickly into action to oppose higher taxation.

The nature of British Conservatism also discouraged higher taxes. Historically, Conservatives in Britain have exhibited highly ambivalent attitudes towards the state. To many Tories, the state was anathema, and so were the taxes and the reforms that they identified with the state. An equally large number, and undoubtedly the more articulate of Conservatives, viewed the state more favourably. They saw the state as essentially theirs and hence found it hard to regard it as a wholly alien growth; more specifically, they projected upon the state the task of paternalistically integrating the lower orders into society. Theirs was the vision of Disraeli, and later of Joseph Chamberlain and of Harold Macmillan, and until recently it was the vision that exerted a rhetorical domination within the party.[17]

If government involved merely or primarily the translation of political ideas into policies, this ambivalence might well have led Conservatives to raise taxes and to expand services in response to perceived social need. It did not, however, for in the course of acquiring and holding a mass base, the Tories came to be held together by a shared opposition to progressive taxation. The process was extremely complex, but what seems to have happened is that the Conservatives entered twentieth-century politics as an aristocratic and rather anachronistic political formation. Their late nineteenth-century efforts to acquire a middle-class base had been only partially successful, their courting of the emerging working-class electorate even less so. Conservatism's ties to business, both to manufacturing and to the City, were also weak, although the dissolution of the links that previously bound businessmen to the Liberals provided them with a great opportunity. Between 1900 and the early 1920s, the party managed to rally behind its banners large sections of business and of the urban middle classes.[18] Doing so necessitated certain commitments. Winning the support of industry, for instance, meant supporting tariffs, both as protection against imports and as a source of revenue. Actually having to implement a tariff policy would have alienated much of the City – and even threatening to do so drove many potential supporters temporarily back to the Liberals in 1906. But for the most part the Conservatives were able to maintain their support for tariffs as an electoral pledge and as a hypothetical alternative to progressive taxes on land and income without having to endure the opprobrium that would have come from imposing them.

So while the tariff policy undoubtedly cost votes in the short term, it also increased support for the Conservatives among key constituents and arrayed the Tories against the main practical mechanism for enlarging the compass of state activity – progressive taxation. The manner in which the urban (and increasingly suburban) middle and lower-middle classes were brought behind the party also reinforced the predisposition against progressive taxation. The modest expansion of the state in the late nineteenth century had taken the form primarily of an expansion of spending by municipal authorities. This spending was financed out of local rates and produced a genuine crisis in the fiscal affairs of local government. The middle and lower-middle classes emerged from the crisis highly organized and overwhelmingly opposed to higher taxes. In some cities, organizations of ratepayers or "municipal reformers" formed the backbone of local Conservative support and organization.[19] Enrolling these opponents of "municipal socialism" into the ranks of Conservatism meant adopting their attitudes toward taxes and spending.

The relationship between the Conservative party and its mass base, who largely defined themselves either as businessmen or ratepayers, prevented the party's leadership from adopting policies that might otherwise have flowed naturally from their paternalist outlook. That relationship, moreover, was highly unstable and Conservatives were regularly called upon to reaffirm their opposition to taxes and their commitment to economy. The link between Conservatives and businessmen, for example, was repeatedly threatened with disruption. The period just after the First World War, for example, witnessed a widespread mobilization of business opinion against waste in government and against high postwar rates of taxation. Businessmen again found their voices in 1930–1 and helped to create the climate that produced the crisis of August, 1931. The discontent of businessmen over the government's unwillingness to confront the unions has also erupted periodically since the mid-1950s, with serious political consequences. The close relationship between Conservatism and the middle classes has likewise been punctuated by a series of middle-class "revolts." Middle-class ratepayers threatened, for instance, to carry the attack on expenditure in the early 1930s much further, into local government in particular, than the Conservative party wanted. Middle-class *ressentiment* over rationing and physical controls between 1947 and 1951 was more deeply felt and hence less easily assuaged than the more tactical concerns of the Conservative leadership. Tory leaders were also taken aback by the revolt of the middle class of the late 1950s, prompting Harold Macmillan's famous query about the middle classes: "I am always hearing about the Middle Classes," Macmillan wrote to the head of the Conservative Research Department. "What is it they really want? Can you put it down on a sheet of notepaper, and I will see whether we can give it to them."[20] The latest revolt of the middle classes went by the name of "Thatcherism." Of course, neither businessmen nor the middle classes have had since the 1920s any real alternative to the Conservatives, for the Liberals were seldom a viable option and Labour was what they feared. Still, they could be more or less forthcoming with funds and enthusiasm, they could abstain from voting or, in extreme cases, throw their votes away on a third party. In a closely balanced electoral system, even such minor acts of disloyalty could matter and sufficed to keep Conservatives true to their anti-tax stance.

The Conservatives, of course, did not by themselves constitute the entire political universe, and they could not dictate the platforms of other parties. Nevertheless, the especially pronounced resistance to taxation embedded in the very basis of modern Conservatism must surely have compounded the other difficulties in the way of increasing taxes. Labour could therefore be assured of incurring the opprobrium of the Tories as well as of the organized interests of business and the City for any breach of financial orthodoxy; and the Liberals, despite their identification with progressive taxation between 1906 and 1914 and despite Lloyd George's flirtation with Keynes in the late 1920s, were prompted by the extent of opposition to taxation to rally behind the banner of orthodoxy most of the time. In sum, then, the political context in which tax policy has been made in Britain has served primarily to constrain the expansion of government.

BRITAIN'S PECULIAR STATE

The other major constraint upon state expansion has been the nature of British central government. No government can expand and undertake new responsibilities without changing its bureaucratic shape and size. In Britain, this has meant that virtually every innovation in public policy has represented a challenge to the existing machinery of government, to the pre-eminent role of the Treasury within it and to the principle of "Treasury control." The need to couple the implementation of new policies with the restructuring of government has meant that most advocates of collectivist policies have also been advocates of "administrative reform" and that moments of rapid policy innovation have witnessed bitter contention over the state. The basic question confronting reformers has been whether and, if so, how to transform or dismantle the system of "Treasury control." These efforts and arguments clustered around the two world wars, when the role of the Treasury was most open to doubt and alteration.

The unique role of the Treasury in British government has often been noted, but "Treasury control" is ordinarily understood as if it were a timeless, enduring practice. The reality is much more interesting, for the influence of the Treasury on the state has been based only partly on structural features. It has also been based to a considerable extent on the willingness of politicians to submit to the workings of these structures; and that, of course, could vary. Underpinning the Treasury's power has been its role as the co-ordinating department within the civil service and its close working relationship with the Bank of England and the financial markets in the City. On paper, the Treasury was responsible for the functioning of the civil service from the 1870s and its control over the preparation of the budget had long given Treasury officials a supervisory role over the scope of other departments' activity. Despite these controls, the practice of administration before 1914 remained highly variegated, the state riddled with protected niches and inefficient departments, with little or no detailed co-ordination by the Treasury or anyone else. Until 1914, "Treasury control" was thus restricted mainly to the habit of saying no.[21]

Even if its supervision and control over departments was incomplete before 1914, the Treasury's influence in the higher counsels of the state was very great indeed. That influence derived largely from its involvement in the financing of government. The Treasury had the job of raising the funds needed by the state through the sale of government securities. The process deeply implicated the Treasury in the workings of the City and the maintenance of the gold standard. Inevitably, there was a convergence of views on the part of the Treasury, the Bank and the City – a consensus that could be presented rhetorically as deriving from the apolitical dictates of the market. The Treasury would thus claim that its advice to the government represented not merely its preference but the irresistible logic of world financial markets. Backed up in this way, the input of the Treasury was hard to ignore.

The Great War shook up this comfortable system dramatically.[22] Government was forced to expand massively in order to mobilize the nation for war: at the top, new structures of control, like the War Cabinet and the Cabinet Secretariat, were called into existence; lower down, a vast array of new departments, boards, commissions and advisory committees was established. This created an administrative problem of co-ordination that was further complicated by three novel political developments. First, the suspension of currency convertibility during the war removed that powerful and seemingly impersonal constraint upon government activity – the prewar gold standard. Second, the new ministries and agencies represented alternative sources of power and advice to that of the Treasury and often developed close ties to the interests they were supposed to superintend. They tended, therefore, to serve as their advocates within the state and as proponents of greater intervention or expenditure on their behalf. This was completely at odds with the traditions of British administration and the practice of "Treasury control." Third, the restoration of the old relationship between state and society was further complicated by changes in the system of parties. The political crisis of 1916 had led to a fracturing of the once mighty Liberal party into a group led by Asquith and a faction that Lloyd George took into the wartime coalition. The fragmentation of the Liberals, together with the atrophy of Conservative organization and its lack of a distinct presence so long as it remained hitched to Lloyd George's coalition, created new political space for Labour and the opportunity for a major political realignment. The election of 1918 produced an enormous majority for the coalition, but did little to revive either the Conservatives or the Liberals. The "forces of order," absorbed or at least implicated in Lloyd George's government, thus lacked a viable mass party that could guarantee popular backing for the tasks of postwar stabilization. Within the coalition the Conservatives were clearly dominant, but the Cabinet was presided over by a charismatic leader who, before the war, had shown himself more than willing to depart from Treasury orthodoxy. Worse still, the major opposition to Lloyd George after 1918 was the Labour party, which was committed not only to a greater role for the state but to a "capital levy" to pay for it.

These circumstances guaranteed that the stabilization of postwar politics would require considerable time and effort, and that a key component of the process would be a reshaping of the party system and a revitalization of the Conservatives as the main bulwark against socialism and state expansion. But the instability of the party alignments just after the war prompted those seeking to restrain the state to work outside the parties as well. The "Anti-Waste" campaign launched in the Rothermere press and echoed by a large section of the middle classes and of business was one example; the related demand for committees of businessmen to examine state expenditure – resulting, for example, in the appointment of the Geddes Committee in 1921 – was another. Institutionally, stabilization would also require reorganization within the state. This took the form of a sustained effort to reimpose "Treasury control" of the bureaucracy in an even stricter fashion than before the war and to back that up by returning to something like the prewar gold standard.

The battle over the conditions of postwar stabilization was fought out with a good deal of bitterness from 1916 to 1926. The outcome was a more or less unqualified victory for orthodoxy and retrenchment, and for the Treasury, which managed to sell itself as the only mechanism capable of bringing order out of administrative chaos and to claim that, in performing that function, it was implementing many of the reforms proposed by the Haldane Committee on the Machinery of Government. But the Treasury never gave up its old role of financial watchdog, paring down estimates, sabotaging proposals for state expansion and generally taming departmental appetites. In doing so, it won support from all those seeking to restrain the autonomous growth of the state and to ensure that even a future Labour government would encounter resistance to its plans. The series of manoeuvres by which this was accomplished began with the appointment during the war of the Bradbury Committee on government organization and of the Cunliffe Committee on the currency; it continued through the official designation of the Permanent Secretary to the Treasury as the Head of the Civil Service in 1919; and it climaxed, after several intermediate victories, in the return to gold in 1925. By that time, the initiatives of postwar had been checked, their proponents largely driven from government and even, in some cases, their departments abolished. Orthodoxy was to remain firmly in control of social and economic policy throughout the interwar period.

Despite repeated calls for policies to deal with the depression, the role of central government stood largely unaltered from the early 1920s through the 1930s. The onset of war in 1939, however, ushered in a second and more successful era of reform. Mobilization for war not only called for an end to administration guided by parsimony, but produced a general critique of the way government had been conducted between the wars. A surprising amount of the criticism aimed directly at Chamberlain and the "appeasers" hit indirectly at the civil service and the Treasury's control over it. Appeasement was seen as the work, not only of Chamberlain and the "guilty men" around him, but of the political and bureaucratic establishment.[23] Particular anger was directed at the aloofness and exclusiveness of the civil service, especially of the Foreign Office and the Treasury, and the latter's reluctance to spend money on defence. This current of criticism was pervasive and put officials very much on the defensive, forcing them to take seriously the complaints and proposed remedies of outsiders like Cripps and Laski and of groups like Political and Economic Planning and to co-operate in two exhaustive inquiries into administrative practice and possibilities for reform.[24]

Equally important, the prosecution of the war went on largely outside the direction of the Treasury. For much of the war, the Chancellor was excluded from the War Cabinet and even the Treasury's innovative work on war finance, including Keynes' famous budget paper of 1941, was not central to the planning of the war effort. Instead, wartime planning was accomplished by means of the so-called Manpower Budget, crafted in the first instance by the Ministry of Labour under Ernest Bevin, in a process that sought to match available physical resources, primarily labour, with military and civilian needs. This bypassing of the Treasury would continue after the war, as the responsibility for domestic affairs under the Labour governments came to be vested in the Lord President's Committee, chaired by Herbert Morrison, and the job of economic planning shared between various interdepartmental committees, the Economic Section located in the Cabinet Office and, from 1947, the Central Economic Planning Staff in but not quite of the Treasury. Bureaucratically, these arrangements were rather messy, and over the long term impossible to maintain. But for some years the system worked, and its success allowed an essential hiatus during which the Treasury was not allowed to dominate the workings of government and much of the welfare state was brought into being.

THE CONTRADICTIONS OF THE "POSTWAR SETTLEMENT"

It required, then, two world wars to convince the public and policy-makers to increase taxes enough to maintain the level of social provision envisioned in the postwar welfare state and to break the control of the Treasury over the state itself. In the absence of war, the logic of tax politics and of "Treasury control" prevented all but the smallest moves towards the interventionist welfare state. Neither the adjournment of the normal politics of taxation nor the escape from "Treasury control" during the Second World War were to be permanent, however. The Treasury would regain much of its power after 1947, and from 1951 the Conservatives would seek to reassert the steady downward pressure on taxation characteristic of British politics prior to 1939. But the terms on which the old logics were re-established in the 1950s reduced their effectiveness. The postwar settlement, worked out between 1945 and 1955–6, was built upon the commitment of both major parties to maintain full employment and the array of entitlements left in place by the Attlee governments.[25] That commitment was reinforced by the close electoral balance between Labour and the Conservatives and underlined by the organized strength of the unions. Indeed, the power of the unions forced governments of the left and the right to concede the unions' claim to speak for the working class, to engage in corporatist bargaining or at least consultation with the unions over critical matters of economic and social policy, and to avoid tampering with the two key tenets of the "postwar settlement."

The need for politicians and bureaucrats to acquiesce in the commitments implied in the postwar settlement was made more palatable by the "Keynesian revolution" in economic theory and policy-making.[26] There is still, of course, considerable controversy over the details of the transformation of economic thinking that occurred from the 1930s to the 1950s. It is by no means clear, for example, just when policy-makers adopted Keynesian styles of economic management. The Labour governments of 1945–51 contained many converts to Keynes, but the understanding of its top leaders and the mechanisms used to steer the economy remained to some extent pre-Keynesian. Nor is it easy to specify the precise impact of Keynesian policy on postwar economic performance.[27] The dramatic effect of Keynesian theory upon the political culture would seem to be far less debatable, however, for the simplified Keynesian message – that deficits were not disastrous, that spending by government stimulated the entire economy and thus was not inimical to growth, and that taxes, interest rates and other parameters of economic policy could and should be manipulated to socially desirable ends – drastically altered political discourse. Before the war, opponents of taxes and spending were able to restrict the terms of political argument and to make all sorts of options seem virtually unthinkable. The effect of the "Keynesian revolution" was to open up the range of strategic options. Even when the Conservatives were returned to office and the Treasury restored to its superordinate status within the bureaucracy, therefore, the sense of what government could do and what policy should be about remained broader and more open-ended than before 1939.

The agreement to maintain full employment and social services, sustained by Keynesian optimism, made it politically very difficult for the Treasury or the Conservative party fully to indulge their shared passions for cuts in expenditure and taxation. Spending cuts threatened both the level of services and demand, which jeopardized full employment; while excessive tax cuts would make it more difficult to pay for social programmes or defence and might also fuel inflation. Thus, the political commitments of the postwar settlement precluded easy recourse to the social and economic policies of the era before 1939. On the other hand, the historical preferences of the Treasury, the Conservatives and the banking and business communities for free markets and against state intervention would ensure that the postwar state was not given the authority or the capacity to manage the economy effectively, to stimulate growth or to raise the funds necessary to pay for adequate levels of social services. Labour had sought during the 1940s to restructure the state and to give it the fiscal and administrative capacity to make good on the promises of postwar reconstruction, but it had failed to institutionalize the necessary changes. After 1951, Conservatives worked with higher civil servants to remove physical controls over the economy, to rule out more interventionist economic policies, to subordinate planning to the dictates of sound finance and to lower taxes, thus denying to the state the policy devices that might have been used to guarantee fulfilment of the commitments taken on between 1945 and 1955.

The critical flaw in the postwar settlement therefore was that it left in place a much expanded set of public commitments without the means to make them into reality. The historic incapacity of the British state persisted into the era of big government and the welfare state, giving rise to a steadily widening gap between the demands placed on the state and its ability to meet them.[28] The state was expected in particular to fulfil the promises of the welfare state without raising taxes. As a result, politicians and officials spent endless time trying to find ways to contain public expenditure, none of which were especially successful. Economic growth seemed, for a time, to offer a way around the fiscal impasse, but the state did not possess the tools to ensure that it would continue. Politicians discovered "growth" in the late 1950s, and governments thereafter sought frantically to engineer it.[29] New institutions – the National Economic Development Council (NEDDY), supplemented later on by a series of little "Neddies" for different industries – were established; new departments were created – the Department of Economic Affairs during Harold Wilson's first government – and old ones renamed – the Ministry of Labour became at various moments the Department of Employment or Employment and Productivity – with the aim of overcoming bureaucratic lethargy; and a wide array of costly policies adopted. But growth proved elusive, and the gap between what was promised and what was achieved became wider, its increasing visibility seriously eroding the credibility of government.[30] The state's repeated interventions in the economy, whether undertaken on behalf of growth, for or against mergers or to control wages, came in practice to constitute a pattern of multiple and cumulative failure. Its typically *ad hoc* initiatives merely substituted for more serious and long-term policies and were seldom sustained or strongly enforced. They were justified rhetorically, moreover, by means of a discourse that exaggerated the state's capacity, encouraged expectations that could not be satisfied and hence virtually ensured failure and invited blame.

Policy failures ultimately undermined support for interventionist economic policies and for social provision, but not before the level of expenditure and taxation had grown substantially. The expanded commitments taken on by government after the war and the political balance that forced continued adherence to them prevented either the reimposition of "Treasury control" or prolonged Conservative rule from putting effective limits on expenditure and taxation. This weakening of the traditional constraints combined, especially after 1960, with a set of economic and demographic changes to push up spending and revenues. The result was a sustained tendency for the state to grow from the late 1950s – slowly at first, but then more rapidly until, by the 1970s, the expansion of public programmes and budgets and the acceleration of inflation caused a sharp reaction against the state. When coupled with the government's inability to control the economy, the apparently uncontrolled growth of the state allowed those who had never fully accepted the broadened definition of citizenship and the state's social and economic functions embedded in the postwar settlement finally to break faith with the commitments to full employment and to the welfare state. That break took the form of a triumph, within Conservatism, of the anti-state politics represented by Mrs Thatcher, and within the polity more broadly, of the collapse of an effective opposition and of any viable alternative to Conservative hegemony. The results are with us still. The purpose of this book is not to dissect those results or offer remedies, but to clarify how they came to be. Understanding, it is hoped, will produce not complacency or resignation, but a more realistic sense of what is involved in expanding the state and making it serve the interests of ordinary people.

Chapter 2

The Victorian inheritance

The mid-Victorian state was a modest, and only moderately democratic, affair. It was modest both in its size and in what it set out to do. There was no pretence that government could do much on its own to remedy or compensate for social ills and no party in the land had a serious programme of state intervention. This minimalist character of the state was underpinned by the constraints of Gladstonian finance and reinforced by its inaccessibility. Political participation was the preserve of a distinct minority, less than 15 per cent of the male population even after 1832. The Second Reform Act of 1867 widened the franchise further, to about 35 per cent of men, but political citizenship continued to be denied to the majority of men and all women. Participation would increase gradually after 1867, as successive reforms brought working-class men, middle-class women, and finally all women into the formal political system.[1]

The effects of democratization upon public policy remained unclear, however. It was widely thought at the time that democracy would lead directly to increased state intervention in society. Joseph Chamberlain, the most disruptive force in late nineteenth-century politics, both predicted and welcomed the prospect:

> When Government represented only the authority of the Crown or the views of a particular class, I can understand that it was the first duty of men who valued their freedom to restrict its authority and to limit its expenditure. But all that is changed. Now Government is the organised expression of the wishes and the wants of the people, and under these circumstances let us cease to regard it with suspicion . . . Now it is our business to extend its functions, and to see in what way its operations can be usefully enlarged.[2]

The expansion of the state would in fact prove more difficult and controversial than Chamberlain imagined, and a considerable period of time would have to elapse before the democratic polity produced a popular mandate for collectivist economic and social policies. The limitations of the Victorian state seem to have imposed corresponding limits upon the sense of what was politically possible and appropriate and of what could legitimately be asked of the state. Even after the political system became more open, therefore, the demands placed upon the state's rulers remained highly circumscribed. The constraints on the nineteenth-century state were thus deeply embedded. They were acceptable to the nation's dominant interests and support for them was diffused throughout the political culture, reflected in the outlook and pro-grammes of the major parties and reinforced institutionally by the structure of the state machinery. The absence of more ambitious efforts to direct the economy or compensate for the victims of the market was seldom lamented. It resulted, in fact, from decisions taken very consciously over the course of the century and aimed at shielding the state from society and the social order from the state. It was not founded on ignorance or a want of sympathy but upon deliberate choices aimed at putting into place a political economy premised on a sharp distinction between the public and the private and on a belief in the superiority of market outcomes and the perverse consequences of state intervention. That political economy was institutionalized by 1850, and was hard to alter thereafter.

What is perhaps most striking about the British state at mid-century was its strength and legitimacy.[3] From about 1795 to the 1840s governments were much embattled, confronted by unprecedented social and economic problems and by reform movements fuelled, at least in part, by those problems. It managed, however, to fend off these challenges with judicious concessions and timely shifts in policy. The result was a state that commanded greater authority than anyone would have predicted in the 1830s and 1840s. That authority had been augmented in some curious ways in the three decades before 1850. The so-called "nineteenth-century revolution in government" created a series of mechanisms by which the central state could make its decisions locally effective. Equally significant was the manner in which the relations between state and society were recast during this era of economic restructuring. In some fields, like health and sanitation, factory inspection and, of course, the police, the state became more directly involved and responsible. At the same time, however, the state shed responsibilities in a number of spheres and strove to replace administrative discretion with the workings of the market – e.g., in the labour market and in trade policy. This retreat from direct involvement in the details of economic and social life probably strengthened the overall authority of the state, for it made the state less vulnerable to claims for it to do what it could not in fact easily accomplish.[4]

The state also achieved a measure of fiscal independence that was to be a continued and unambiguous source of strength: "In fiscal terms the state had by 1851 . . . come to terms with the tax system and the debt."[5] The enormous liabilities incurred during the French and Napoleonic Wars had severely compromised the autonomy of the state by reducing its ability to respond quickly and effectively to military and political changes. The extent of indebtedness, and the dire measures used to deal with it, were also a direct cause of unrest, for they seemed to confirm the critique of British politics so effectively summarized by the notion of "Old Corruption." Hence the successful handling of the debt and the imposition of fiscal responsibility were part of a larger process by which Old Corruption was replaced by a reformed and more legitimate state. That the debt could be largely redeemed over the very same period during which protection, with its assured and substantial revenues, was abolished was a major achievement and a critical step in the process of building a modern state.[6] Putting the state's finances on a secure footing strengthened the authority of the state by disentangling it from the "interests" bound up with the creation and servicing of its debts. The method by which fiscal probity was restored, moreover, recast the relationship between the state and its citizens. With the substitution of a modest income tax for various indirect levies, the state became less tied to particular "interests," more responsible to the broader class of taxpayers. Income tax itself helped to define the class of income taxpayers, whose self-interested vigilance would reinforce subsequent efforts to enforce economy in government. Ultimately, of course, income tax would be transformed into a progressive levy that would play a critical role in financing the expanded state of the mid-twentieth century. Before 1900, however, the politics of income tax constituted a brake upon the expansion of revenues and programmes.

The origins of income tax thus long preceded the twentieth-century rise in state revenues and expenditures which it made possible. It had been adopted in the first instance as a temporary supplement to existing, primarily indirect, taxes. It is a commonplace in tax history that, prior to the modern period, the most effective sorts of taxes were indirect. So long as wealth was held in land and income calculated largely in physical terms, it was hard to tax either wealth or income directly. It was, on the other hand, much easier to tax goods in motion – as they were being bought, sold or transported. Britain was quintessentially a trading nation and most of its economic activity was mediated through the market and exposed to taxation, making it possible for the state to extract quite large revenues from customs and excise during the eighteenth century. The result was that during the Napoleonic Wars the British paid nearly three times the taxes the French did, most of them indirect. This was done, moreover, in a far less painful and politically explosive fashion than in France, even if the system was no more equitable.[7] This capacity to tax was a critical factor behind Britain's rise to commercial and colonial pre-eminence and its ability to lead the resistance to Napoleon.[8]

Nevertheless, the Napoleonic Wars required still more revenue, and the state was forced both to borrow extensively and, in 1799, to impose a tax of 10 per cent on incomes above £200.[9] Income tax was highly unpopular, however, for it was regarded not merely as a levy on the wealthy but also as highly invasive – "inquisitorial" even, in its administration. It was in fact repealed in 1802, only to be reimposed in 1803, but then once again "removed with indecent haste and with little regard for a fair balance of taxation, in 1816."[10] Repeal of the income tax, coupled with the imposition of new duties on corn,

created a highly regressive and class-based system of taxation whose distributional impact was made still more adverse by the fact that so much
revenue – 60 per cent between 1820 and 1850 – went to pay interest on the
enormous national debt inherited from the wars. Taxation served as a huge
system of transfer payments, taking money from consumers and traders and
giving it to the rentiers who held the bulk of the debt. This arrangement was
almost as unpopular as income tax, and added fuel to the considerable unrest
that gripped the nation in the two decades leading up to 1848.

It did not prompt a quick return to direct taxes, however. Though there was
a widespread belief that Pitt's failure to tax more heavily during the wars was a
major mistake, there was little support for reimposing income tax. That would
come only in 1842, when Peel reinstated the tax to compensate for the
revenues being lost through the movement away from protection. Peel was
driven to income tax by several years of red ink, caused by massive economic
distress and by wars in the east – the Opium Wars and the Afghan War in
particular. Support was garnered by labelling the tax temporary and by
coupling it with reductions elsewhere. Whatever Peel himself may have
thought, even members of his government believed that the tax would not last.
Lord Ashburton could not conceive otherwise: "It would be next to insupportable to live in a country where such a tax were permanent." Politically, it was
the link between income tax and progress toward free trade that proved
decisive: as one historian has argued, "Tariff reform and a new corn law were
. . . the two wings . . . of the income tax."[11]

In retrospect, Peel's decision was the key event in Victorian tax history, but
it by no means settled the argument about the proper form or level of taxation.
This proved extremely controversial, for tax questions were intimately bound
up with broader issues of representation and of the very shape of the polity.
Within this discourse income tax occupied a curious position. Radicals such as
Cobden and the Financial Reform Association wanted the government to rely
almost entirely on direct taxes, partly on grounds of equity but mostly in the
hope that this would produce pressure for retrenchment. Gladstone was
sympathetic to the broad aims of this policy, though more cautious in
application. He was himself particularly concerned to link taxation with
citizenship, arguing in 1859 "that it is desirable in a high degree, where it can
be effected, to connect the possession of the franchise with the payment in
taxes." Gladstone's plan to fix the exemption limit at £100 was thus calculated
precisely to align payment of income tax with political participation, for that
figure was thought at the time to constitute, as Gladstone himself explained,
"the dividing line . . . between the educated and the labouring parts of the
community." In Gladstone's thinking, liability to tax would inspire a sense of
fiscal responsibility and the proper discharge of that liability would be the
prerequisite for citizenship. Full membership in the polity would be restricted
to "a self-taxing class of income-tax paying electors." Inevitably, this coupling
of taxpaying and political participation endowed the paying of taxes with

moral worth and civic duty, and in consequence helped to reconcile middle-class opinion to the increasing likelihood that income tax would be permanent.[12]

The process of making the tax acceptable to the middle and upper classes also required the removal of those aspects of income tax that were deemed unfair. What made it unfair was, of course, a matter of dispute. Many thought the tax in any form was unjust, and it was to them that the argument about its passing character was directed. To most others, however, the major point of contention was over the incidence of the tax on different kinds of incomes. Should so-called precarious incomes, earned by skill and industry, be taxed at the same rate as stable incomes derived, but not in any sense "earned," by ownership of land or capital? It was widely conceded that they should not be, and that there should instead be some sort of "differentiation" between earned and unearned income. Despite this consensus, reform along these lines was hard to achieve. To those who sought ultimately to remove the tax, it made little sense to reform it, for doing so would make its burden less odious. Lightening the burden on earned income, moreover, meant simultaneously increasing that borne by unearned income – by the landed and propertied. It proved politically impossible to generate support for such thorough-going differentiation. Rather, Gladstone introduced in 1853 an allowance for life assurance premiums, on the theory that insurance premiums were the mechanism by which those with precarious incomes provided for the future and that the amount of such premiums represented a proper discount on earned income.[13] The solution was by no means ideal, but it served to make the tax just that much more acceptable, at least in the short term. Over the longer term, habit, fiscal need and the absence of an alternative gradually made income tax into a permanent part of the revenue apparatus.

The project of gaining acceptance of income tax – "to consolidate support to the income tax," in Gladstone's phrase – was still nearly always accompanied by promises to do away with it, which Gladstone himself reiterated in 1853 and even in 1874. It proceeded nevertheless and with help from both parties. Tolerance for income tax was thus further increased by the decision of the Tory Chancellor Northcote to raise the exemption limit to £150 in 1876. His aim was to eliminate or lessen the income tax liabilities of nearly half a million middle-class taxpayers who, it was hoped, would repay the Conservatives with their votes. The indirect effect was to make income tax less onerous, less controversial and less likely to be repealed. Even so, acceptance would probably not have been so universal had rates not remained quite low and had the middle classes not been regularly reassured that expenditure was being kept to a minimum. The role of the income tax within the Victorian tax system was therefore to augment revenues slightly but to put clear limits upon the activities of the state.[14]

The state's strength and aloofness would also be increased by its successful escape from responsibility for the regulation of labour and of the food supply.

During the French Wars the government had become deeply involved in guaranteeing the provision of food; and bulk purchases, warehousing and controlled distribution were maintained for several years after the end of the wars and the adoption of agricultural protection. The repeal of the Corn Laws three decades later was the final act in the retreat from responsibility for provisioning the populace, but *de facto* responsibility had disappeared long before. The attack on the old poor law was a critical step, for it took aim specifically at a system – Speenhamland – which had linked the granting of relief to the price of food. The New Poor Law was designed simultaneously to remove from the state a paternalistic obligation for ensuring subsistence and to create a free, national labour market. However intrusive the means – the granting of relief only through workhouses and all the moral policing that entailed – the objective was to lessen the state's responsibility for the well-being of its citizens. Poor Law reform exposed the British state to sharp criticism from opposite directions: it could be attacked for abandoning its historic responsibilities towards the poor or for the nastiness of its recent interventions. It was the intrusiveness of the state's actions in the 1830s that most roused the antipathy of the poor and their defenders, but the government's innovations were in fact aimed at limiting the state's role in social and economic affairs. The reforms of the 1830s, particularly the New Poor Law, thus need to be set in the context of a protracted effort to reshape the state, the effect of which was to make the British state more aloof from domestic interests and less engaged in the daily functioning of economy and society. This effort was capped by the repeal of the Corn Laws, by which time the main features of the *laissez-faire* state were established. Resistance to intervention would continue after 1848 and the role of the "Benthamite" reformers, who had been so prominent in the policy initiatives of previous decades, would be much diminished.[15]

The Northcote–Trevelyan Report of 1854 was aimed, at least in part, at keeping such programmatic enthusiasts out of administration and replacing them with generalists whose loyalty would be to the state as a whole and to the taxpayers, rather than to any specific policy or department. Its proposals would also, as Gladstone argued, "strengthen and multiply the ties between the higher classes and the possession of administrative power." In particular, the plan to separate the "intellectual" from the "mechanical" in the work of officials would "open to the highly educated class a career and give them a command over all the higher parts of the civil service, which up to this time they have never enjoyed." The report produced no immediate revolution in administration, but it helped to further the trend toward a centralized administration dominated by the Treasury and presided over by a self-conscious intellectual elite, drawn from the upper classes and trained at Oxford and Cambridge. Gladstone's meritocratic reforms in the selection process began to make these principles operative, and ensured that the state was insulated from experts and enthusiasts as well as from representatives of the lower orders.[16]

It was this *laissez-faire* state to which political actors were increasingly forced to respond from mid-century, and whose limits structured political discourse and mobilization. The political settlement bargained out in the 1840s removed key issues of social and economic affairs from politics, and served to keep them off the political agenda for close to half a century: "Social policy was believed to have been 'taken out of politics' by the Poor Law of 1834 in much the same way as monetary and commercial policy had supposedly been taken out of politics by the Bank Charter Act of 1844 and the repeal of the Corn Laws in 1846." [17] Of course, there were *de facto* social and economic policies that resulted from the partly conscious and partly unconscious workings of the state, but the attempt to banish social and economic questions from politics was highly successful until at least the 1890s. Their inability to place issues on the political agenda limited what ordinary people could expect from the state and hence what they would ask of it. Their efforts were thus displaced to other arenas and to strategies not oriented to the state. The much-vaunted voluntarism of the Victorian era was in large measure rooted in this sense of political incapacity. Working-class organization was particularly constrained by the new arrangements between state and society. No popular movement of the late nineteenth century could stand comparison with those movements, especially Chartism, that had flowered before 1850. Chartism, for example, had managed to enrol behind its banners artisans from old but reasonably stable industries, workers from declining trades and in small communities, and also a good number of workers in the newer industries. It spanned the nation, was directed at the centre of national political power and was marked by a rhetoric that clearly manifested its national and political orientation. After 1850, by contrast, working people organized themselves by trade, by occupation and by locality. They seldom put together broader movements or coalitions and put very few demands upon the state. [18]

These more restricted efforts were, not surprisingly, more practically effective than the earlier, grander mobilizations of the 1830s and 1840s, and the generation of leaders who pioneered these new movements evolved an outlook that made a strategic virtue out of the limits upon their action. "Three themes," it has been argued, "dominated the consciousness of mid-Victorian labour: independence and respectability, sectionalism and localism . . . Independence and respectability expressed both class pride and social acceptance; sectional organization . . . was the only sure way of securing the protection for independence; and localism . . . provided the focus for collective identity or solidarity." [19] Thus the voluntarist, anti-statist orientation adopted by British trade unions between 1850 and 1914, an attitude that appears inexplicably odd to those who expect workers or trade unions to be spontaneously socialist in politics, was rooted in what was deemed possible in the 1850s and 1860s. So, too, were the tenacious efforts of skilled workers and their unions to seize and hold control of the shopfloor and the local labour market. It might not be possible to remake the world or to challenge the power of capital nationally, but workers could contest that power at the point of production or in the local community.

To the extent that the institutions created by working people – the unions, the co-operatives, the clubs, friendly societies and so on – were infused with the ideology of independence and respectability and structured to engage in sectional, highly localized activities, the constraints upon them became more and more internalized. Particularly damaging were the notions of gender and of social need upon which the concepts of independence and respectability seem to have been premised. Trade unionists committed themselves, as early as Chartism, to the idea of the "family wage" and used it to buttress the claim for higher wages for working men. The needs of women and children were in this way subsumed under those of men, and attempts to sort out and meet those needs separately were viewed with a lack of enthusiasm and, at times, hostility by men and their unions. Since social reformers in the late nineteenth century were frequently women and since they typically focused their concerns on the fate of women and children and since, for ideological, practical or merely tactical reasons, they tended to frame their plans for reform around women's and children's needs, they often found a disappointing lack of support among trade unionists.[20]

The prevailing Victorian context of limited state responsibility and minimal social provision shaped the emerging institutions of the labour movement in other ways as well. Many unions, for example, doubled as friendly societies and provided various kinds of insurance for their members. This involvement meant that they were quite resistant to proposals for state-sponsored insurance which might threaten the viability of union efforts or the relationship between the unions and their members. Insurance was, of course, only one of many services that, in the absence of decent incomes or adequate social provision, working people had somehow to provide for themselves. They responded by building a distinct and surprisingly well-developed "working-class economy' whose successes, limited as they inevitably were, dampened support for more wholesale structural reform undertaken by the state.[21]
Working-class organizations, most importantly the friendly societies and the unions, thus remained at best only vaguely collectivist in their politics, and certainly not socialist, however collective the ethos which later came to permeate their rhetoric.

This non-socialist stance has often been seen as a sign of the immaturity of the labour movement, a sign of a lack of growth and development within the working class. It is perhaps better understood, however, as a rational response to the limited opportunities created by the structure of state power. Those limits were reflected clearly in the major collective mobilizations occurring after 1850, particularly in the agitation for reform leading to the 1867 Reform Act and in the upsurge of strike militancy in 1889–90. There is no doubt that popular pressure added critical weight to the movement for suffrage reform and that in the process of mobilizing for reform a national network of working-class organizations came together. But the effort was also constrained in decisive ways: participation was largely confined to those skilled workers already organized by trade and the movement gave no spur to the organization of the less skilled. It also lacked a programme for making use of the expanded franchise to effect social reforms. There was a strong feeling that working men deserved the right to vote and the citizenship that embodied, but there was little sense that citizenship might involve social rights as well. There was therefore little effort to think through what a reformed government should do or what a reformed state would look like. The Reform Act was in fact followed by the election of a government, Gladstone's great reforming administration, committed to making the state more efficient and still more aloof from society, a government anxious to secure its independence from the ties of patronage, corruption and debt. Organized workers, moreover, were forced to devote the better part of their political energies after 1867 to protecting their independence from the state and its regulation. They had in particular to fend off the attack on unions prompted by the "Sheffield outrages" and to seek legislative immunity from employer reprisals over the use of the strike.[22]

The narrow bounds within which mass movements operated were demonstrated again in 1889–90. Those years witnessed an explosion of strikes, an impressive wave of organization among the less skilled – like the dockers, the match girls and the gas-workers – and the emergence of the so-called "new unionism." "New unionists" were more militant than their predecessors, favoured a more inclusive strategy of organizing and tended to be more radical politically – some of them, like Tom Mann, going on to become leaders in the emerging socialist movements of the 1890s. The movement remained largely apolitical, however, and placed few demands upon the state. The state in turn largely stayed away from the agitation. The aims of the strikes and their leaders were overwhelmingly industrial, and had to do with economic issues and the right to organize. Of course, the very notion of a "new unionism" represented a break with the past and hence went beyond the accepted boundaries of industrial relations, but this novelty was probably an inevitable concomitant of the extension of union organization.[23]

If there was an innovation in the rhetoric and outlook of labour during the upsurge of the "new unionism," it came in the demand for eight hours. The debate over how to achieve the eight-hour day, however, itself indicates the bounds within which working-class leaders felt they were acting. The more militant "new unionists" insisted upon a legal eight-hour day; their opponents argued that to legislate hours would be a sign of weakness and dependency and thus antithetical to their traditions of independence. "New unionists" did not disagree with the point, but argued that without state aid the employers were too strong and could not be forced to accept shorter hours. The sense that workers needed the state's support to balance the employers' strength became even more widespread within the labour movement as the initial gains of 1889–90 began to be taken back in a nasty counter-offensive by the employers in the early 1890s. But it was not until it appeared that the employers themselves had succeeded in enrolling the state on their side, with the series of anti-labour court decisions that culminated in Taff Vale, that a significant number of trade unionists were convinced to take political action by forming the Labour Representation Committee. Even then, their aims remained largely defensive: to beat back the employers' legal attack and to restore the legal immunities of trade unions. There was, to be sure, a growing socialist movement trying to inject a broader vision into trade union politics; and, having taken the first tentative steps towards independent political represen- tation, the unions and the newly created Labour Representation Committee placed themselves on a path that would lead them to take quite unexpected positions. But that was still to come.[24]

Through the end of the century, therefore, the limitations of the mid-Victorian state continued to discourage political actors, inside and outside the formal polity, from voicing demands for policies that would involve an expansion of the state's sphere of activity. Since these limitations tended to be widely accepted and adhered to by both parties, they took the form primarily of ideological constraints, as a restricted sense of the appropriate boundaries of political action. Political argument in late nineteenth-century Britain was very inhospitable to demands for state action. W.L. Burn put the matter well some time ago: "Although the idea of a coherent and dominant *laissez-faire* philosophy cannot be maintained, there was a well-used set of *laissez-faire* clichés which possessed emotional appeal: the administrator had no cor- responding set of collectivist clichés to help him."[25] Despite Dicey's rather alarmist claims, the progress of collectivism was slow and halting in the late nineteenth century; and further progress waited upon, among other things, a transformation of political discourse. That would come slowly, primarily as a result of the reworking of Liberal social theory. As recent research on Liberal social theory testifies, however, the breakthrough to collectivism required not merely the philosophical work of T.H. Green and his disciples, but also the popular concern with poverty and its remedies that began with Henry George in 1881 and continued with the investigative work of Booth and Rowntree and, perhaps most important, the confrontation with socialism. It would require, too, the linking of programmes of reform with proposals for paying for it, proposals that long eluded even the most advanced Liberals.[26]

There was also an institutional context underpinning "the extraordinary tenacity with which mid-nineteenth-century principles and practices survived."[27] A closely articulated network of interests helped to keep social concerns off the political agenda in the second half of the nineteenth century. The powerful complex encompassing the Treasury, the Bank of England and the City of London had become deeply committed to the *laissez-faire* state and had developed a compelling case linking the nation's economic well-being to the principles of free trade and "sound finance."[28] Moreover, the evolution of the British economy after 1850 seemed to have confirmed that argument.[29] To advocate an alternative would mean conflict with these institutions and, typically, political defeat. It would also presuppose the prising apart of the links between the City, the Bank and the Treasury, the building up of other departments and the restructuring of the relation between the Treasury and the rest of the state apparatus. Institutional development of this sort was quite out of the question in the second half of the nineteenth century, however, and as late as 1900 the bureaucratic capacity for undertaking new initiatives in social and economic policy was still utterly lacking. Despite some incremental growth in the size of the bureaucracy over the second half of the nineteenth century, the British state remained small in 1900, and those sections of the administration connected with home affairs especially underdeveloped. Nor does the state appear particularly well developed even when those sections responsible for administering the empire are included, for the passion for economy was at least as strongly felt in matters concerning empire as in domestic issues. As a proportion of national product, for example, government expenditure actually fell from 12 per cent in 1850 to 9 per cent in 1890. By 1900, the South African War had pushed that figure up to 15 per cent, but after the war it fell back again, to under 13 per cent by 1910.[30]

The fiscal capacity of the state remained equally limited, and purposely so. It had been a cornerstone of Gladstonian finance that income tax should eventually be abolished, and even the imperatives of war and empire did not tempt policy-makers toward an extension of direct taxation. The Crimean War, for example, proved much more expensive than anticipated, but did not produce a substantial increase in income tax. Gladstone raised the rate from 7d to 1s 2d and Cornewall Lewis pushed it up by 2d more, but this was still well below the rate that had prevailed during the wars with France. As a result, nearly half of the war expenditure incurred during the Crimean conflict was met by borrowing. Particularly striking was the clear class reasoning behind the wartime resistance to income tax. It was well understood by mid-century that the ultimate burden of loans financed by indirect taxation fell upon the poor and that paying for war by a substantial increase in income tax would place the burden on the more well-to-do. To Gladstone, however, reliance on income tax would be "less just," and other methods of war finance would spread the burden more "fairly among the different classes of the community." The movement toward direct, and potentially more equitable, taxation begun in 1842 had therefore gone as far as was politically feasible by the 1850s. Not until the 1880s would it become possible to move more decisively towards direct taxes, and even then progress would occur largely by indirection.[31]

The social compromise over taxes worked out in the 1850s continued to serve as the framework within which tax policy was made through the last half of the nineteenth century. Thus, the two major issues around which controversy had revolved in the 1850s and 1860s, differentiation and graduation, remained unresolved at the turn of the century; and even the fiction that income tax was temporary was not fully put to rest until after 1900. Lord

Salisbury had predicted in 1860 that "the question of the incidence of taxation is in truth . . . the field upon which the contending classes of this generation will do battle," but it was not until Salisbury himself had left the political stage in 1902 that the struggle would be truly joined. Nevertheless, within this basically stable framework there were the beginnings of change late in the century. In particular, the continued increase in public expenditure led to a broad recognition of the need for further revenues and this in turn made progressive taxes seem more attractive. For most of the century a conscious policy of imposing direct and graduated taxes had been "beyond the pale" of normal political debate. Its first real entry onto the political agenda came with Chamberlain's radical programme of 1885, which proclaimed to the electorate that "a direct progressive tax on income and property is the lever to which we shall look for social reform." Graduation continued to fascinate policy-makers desperate for revenue, including Randolph Churchill and even Goschen, and Sir William Harcourt took a modest step towards progressivity with the introduction of a new scale of graduated death duties in 1894. On a theoretical level, moreover, economists and experts in public finance began to express support for progression and to abandon their earlier faith in the nostrums of Adam Smith. Despite these changes, the framework within which taxation was debated stayed very much within the terms elaborated by Gladstone, Disraeli and their mid-Victorian colleagues.[32]

There were thus very few who in 1900 envisioned a drastic reform of the tax system, fewer still who would have proposed increases of the order that proved necessary after 1906, and virtually none who would have been bold enough to propose the degree of graduation imposed by 1914. Only the year after his imposition of new and increased death duties Harcourt had declared that, "in the growth of expenditure of this country you have very nearly reached the limits of tolerable taxation." He was wrong, of course, but no more wrong than the great majority of his contemporaries, who could in no way foresee the dramatic transformation of tax policy that would be wrought in the years after 1900. Progressive taxation remained highly controversial at the turn of the century; indeed, only in 1907 did Asquith concede that the income tax itself had become "a permanent and integral part of the financial system." It was thus not until the defeat of protection in 1905 and the subsequent introduction of differentiation (between earned and unearned income) and graduation (by means of exemptions and super-tax) that the state came to possess a tool for extracting a significant share of the national wealth. Only then could proposals for a comprehensive programme of social reform get even a hearing within the charmed circles of British "high politics."[33]

Prior to 1900, then, the limited capacity of central government served to circumscribe political debate and the mobilization of interests around demands for collective redress of private grievances. Perhaps the most compelling example was the absence of a set of demands, and of a political movement behind them, for dealing with the depression of 1873–96. Economic historians have long debated whether the notion of a "Great Depression" is a very accurate description of the contradictory tendencies of the British economy in these years, but contemporaries were in little doubt about the matter. There was an undeniable crisis in the rural economy, affecting landlords, farmers and labourers. The profits of industrialists suffered as well, and workers faced recurring bouts of heavy unemployment and declining money wages. If real wages were moving ahead – as they must have in view of the steadily falling price of food – it was nevertheless a form of progress that many would have preferred to trade in for the promise of steady work.

There were responses to distress, of course. There was agitation among the unemployed, including riots in London – actions which produced a brief outpouring of charity and, more importantly, led to the Chamberlain Circular of 15 March 1886 urging local government to provide temporary work for the unemployed. At the level of party politics Chamberlain's radical programme of 1885 constituted a recognition of heightened economic difficulties; and there was the growing reaction against free trade within both parties. There was also, to be sure, the Irish land war. More broadly, one might interpret the upsurge in imperial sentiment as a displaced demand for a countercyclical economic policy. But overall it is the lack of a strong political response to the depression that is most noteworthy, particularly in comparison with developments in Germany, France or the United States. It is true that, during precisely these years, the first steps were taken toward the creation of a genuinely mass-based party system. The secret ballot was introduced in the early 1870s, there was legislation to reduce corrupt practices in the early 1880s, and there was the suffrage extension and redistricting of the mid-1880s. The new conditions of party competition led both parties to expand organization in the constituencies and to encourage the setting up of extra-Parliamentary groupings, like the National Liberal Federation and the Primrose League, to rally support for the party. This democratization of the forms of politics had, however, minimal impact upon its content, and party programmes and political discourse were surprisingly little affected. The Liberals were more and more forced to rely upon working-class votes, but not until after 1900 would these brute facts of electoral sociology be translated into policy. Prior to that, the best the Liberals could come up with was the Newcastle programme of 1891, with its focus upon Irish Home Rule, Church disestablishment in Wales and Scotland, temperance, the abolition of plural voting, land reform and allotments and other worthy, but in social terms very limited, causes.[34]

Probably the only arena in which there were significant, and somewhat successful, efforts to extend state activity was in local government. For much of the nineteenth century the initiative in social policy had rested with the localities, even if they had to be prodded regularly by the centre, and social legislation had often been framed in permissive terms, allowing local government to undertake various sorts of functions and providing some aid in doing so. The Chamberlain Circular, for example, had been issued through the Local

Government Board and it was assumed that local government was the appropriate mechanism for assisting the unemployed. With the reforms of local government in 1888, 1894 and 1899, and particularly with the setting up of the London County Council, local authorities tended to become both more representative and more active. In London, for example, the "Progressive" coalition undertook to provide better relief and social services and made moves towards municipal trading. This incipient "municipal socialism" soon ran into difficulties, however, as it confronted the fiscal limits of the late Victorian state. Local finances became increasingly strained, and officials turned to the centre to restructure the basis of local taxation. The increase in rates prompted strong resistance from the middle classes who, still numerically predominant within the local electorate, began to organize themselves as ratepayers. In that role they became the backbone of Conservative resurgence in the urban areas, capturing the London County Council in 1907, and councils in Sheffield, Nottingham and Leicester in 1908. The recourse to local initiatives in social policy thus turned out to have limits as tough and narrow as those that circumscribed national efforts.[35]

All this would change after 1900, as the state itself expanded, as the demands put upon it grew, and as political argument and party platforms were transformed. The constraints upon government were somehow loosened and the logic of democratic citizenship, with its collectivist tendencies, slowly came to prevail over the complex of beliefs, practices and institutions that had previously held the state's activities in check. The process owed little to the internal development of the state machine, however. It was propelled, on the contrary, by a series of qualitative transformations in the relationship between state and society prompted by war and the dictates of war mobilization. The first stimulus was the Boer War; rather more powerful stimuli were imparted by the two world wars. War-making would therefore prove central to dissolving the constraints upon state expansion.

The role of the state and its agencies was more ambivalent. While the expansion of the state after 1900 contributed significantly to the demand for still greater state responsibility, the actual institutions of the state manifested no marked tendency to grow. Before 1914, in fact, bureaucratic conservatism was predominant. There were three main locations within the late Victorian state from which bureaucratic innovation might have emerged: the Home Office, the Board of Trade and the Local Government Board. None of them, however, succeeded in breaking free of Treasury control and the conventions of limited government. The Home Office was very much preoccupied with "law and order" and with supervising the establishment of prisons and the development of police forces. Its responsibility for industrial regulation, exercised through the Factory Inspectorate, received far less attention and achieved a great deal less. The most significant innovation with which it was associated prior to 1914 was the Children Act of 1908, the so-called "Children's Charter."[36] The Act gave children a new legal status and protection by creating a separate juvenile justice system and reorganized the care of children dependent on the state. From an administrative point of view, however, the Act mainly called for an increase in inspection, registration and enforcement, activities that did not require a major departure from the historic practices of the Home Office.[37]

Within the Board of Trade the most dynamic section was undoubtedly the Labour Department, which pioneered the collection of data and the formulation of policy for dealing with strikes and lockouts. Labour statistics began to be collected in 1886, and the Board intervened successfully in the strikes of coal miners in 1893 and of boot and shoemakers in 1895. The 1896 Conciliation Act regularized the department's role as a mediator and encouraged the spread of the practice. Between 1900 and 1914 more of the Board's efforts were spent adjudicating industrial disputes than in any other direction. This was perhaps one reason behind the effort by industrialists to have the Board's position altered and to have it made into a ministry of "commerce and industry," in which role it could serve as an advocate for the nation's business. Still more social and economic functions were added to the Board's duties under Lloyd George and Churchill from 1906. The Board was placed in charge of the new Labour Exchanges in 1909 and it was made responsible for the unemployment section of the National Insurance Act of 1911. The administration of the Trade Boards, set up in 1909 to regulate wages and conditions in the "sweated trades," was also given to the Board. By 1914, therefore, the state's main efforts to control the labour market were concentrated within the Board of Trade. With the war, those functions grew in importance and were transferred to the new Ministry of Labour created in 1916. The Board of Trade served, therefore, as a major vehicle through which the government approached social and economic problems. But it seldom initiated new policies: the Labour Department was typically starved of funds by the Treasury and kept on a very short leash. The Board became the administrative home of the state's new industrial relations policies largely by accident and the default of other departments – because Lloyd George and Churchill happened to be at its head and because the logical department for undertaking these initiatives, the Local Government Board, was neither willing nor equipped to do so.[38]

On administrative grounds the most likely source of policy innovation before the war should have been the Local Government Board, which dealt not only with local authorities but with the Poor Law. It was thus organically linked to the most dynamic and flexible level of government and responsible for the state's main effort at social policy. But the Local Government Board was hampered by its history, structure and personnel. The Board had its origins in the amalgamation in 1871 of the Medical Department of the Privy Council, the Local Government Act Office within the Home Office and the Poor Law Board. The new department was explicitly structured to minimize the influence of "experts" in health. Its legalistic style of work derived largely from its role in supervising, registering and inspecting the work of local authorities, and its structure was based primarily on the administrative system designed for the Poor Law. The bias against experts and advocacy was intensified after 1876, with the departure of Sir John Simon and the internal reorganization that followed, and with the continued appointment of "generalist" administrators who brought very little vision to their work and who quickly became "dependent for their interpretation of issues on internal written records and departmental wisdom" of a highly conventional sort.[39]

The Local Government Board was thus unable to overcome the ideological principles informing the Poor Law or the inertia that resulted from the conflicting jurisdictions, mandates and interests of local government. The Board's deference towards this "local possessive pluralism," as one scholar has labelled it, was extremely debilitating and prevented it from taking advantage of the opportunities opened up by the reform of local government. The reshaping of local government after 1888 thus allowed considerable activism at the level of urban government, but it left in place the existing structure of interests and did nothing to resolve the local fiscal crisis. The Local Government Board, moreover, was pressed as hard by representatives of the rural areas, anxious to keep down rates and restrict spending, as by those seeking to expand the fiscal capacity of the local state. The Local Taxation Committee, set up in 1869, enrolled urban ratepayers behind the regressive tax politics of rural landowners and farmers and put intense pressure on central government to deny local government the power to increase its revenues. By 1900, the Local Government Board had therefore come to be seen more as an obstacle to social reform than as an instrument for its realization. With the appointment of John Burns as President under the Liberals, its negative reputation was secured. If there were any doubt, it was removed by the performance of the Board's representatives before the Royal Commission on the Poor Law. However varied and flexible the Board's practice, its officials argued before the Commission for a return to the principles of 1834 and against any serious reorganization of the administration of the Poor Law. Nor was the Board reinvigorated by the opportunities opened up by the Housing and Town Planning Act of 1908. Instead, the Act was administered in the same legalistic spirit as most previous legislation, and its impact was similarly rather minimal. Institutional conservatism simply overwhelmed all other options within the Local Government Board.[40]

The backwardness of the Local Government Board in policy innovation stands in strong contrast to the achievements of the Board of Education, from which a surprising amount of innovation sprang. The Board itself was created only in 1899 and had a much narrower remit than the Local Government Board. Moreover, religious controversies surrounded and complicated its efforts to restructure education, and by its earliest initiatives the department forfeited the goodwill of labour. The labour movement was not unreasonably opposed to the subsidizing of religion by the Act of 1902 and also to the narrowing of options for working-class youths implied in the increased separation between primary and secondary education. Despite these initial disadvantages, however, the Board of Education managed after 1902 to put into place an effective system of local administration and to capture a steady flow of local revenues. Onto this emerging structure of local education authorities was grafted an increasing array of public health and welfare functions, as the Board became involved in the provision of school meals in 1906, in medical inspection in 1907 and in youth employment in 1911. By the end of the Great War the sectarian controversies over the 1902 bill had become a distant memory, and what remained was a large measure of political support for the expanded provision of primary and secondary education and of social services linked to the schools. The Board was thus able to put up a quite effective resistance to the cuts in education proposed by the infamous Geddes Committee in 1921.[41]

Still, the extent to which a welfare state could be built around an aggrandizing education department was strictly limited; nor could the Board of Trade's interventions be extended much beyond the labour market. Indeed, the activism characteristic of these two departments should be read as a signal of the overall lack of initiative within the late Victorian and Edwardian state. The most notable feature of public policy after 1870 was, in fact, "the slowing down of growth." There was some "further expansion of numbers and elaboration of procedures," but the "general picture is of a bureaucracy gently ossifying, concerning itself primarily with pushing out again the paper that came in."[42]

The quiescence of the late Victorian state owed a great deal, of course, to the efforts of the Treasury to limit the financial commitments of government. The Treasury's control over expenditure ultimately derived from Parliament's historic responsibility for taxation, but took on its modern form more recently. Departmental estimates had begun to pass through the Treasury in the 1820s, but more formal control by the Treasury had to wait until the passage of the Exchequer and Audits Department Act of 1866. The Act put in place the systematic review of expenditure by the Comptroller and Auditor-General, who became close allies of the Treasury, and prompted the Treasury to issue the famous minute of April, 1868, requiring that explicit sanction was required for any increase in expenditure. Strengthened by the extremely able recruits brought into the department after 1870, the Treasury and its top officials – Lingen, Welby, Hamilton, Murray and Chalmers – proceeded to impose this largely negative mandate upon the spending departments. Its method, however, was less to intrude upon existing practices and more to discourage innovations and accompanying requests for increased expenditure. As the Chancellor of the Exchequer, G. J. Goschen, explained in 1887, "The first object of the Treasury must be to throw the departments on their defence, and to compel them to give strong reasons for any increased expenditure, and to explain how they have come to have to demand it. This control alone contributes to make the departments careful in what they put forward."[43]

There was considerable debate after 1870 as to whether the Treasury's power to veto, or at least to make difficult, proposals for new expenditure added up to a sufficient guarantee of economy. The Playfair Commission came out for stronger measures of control in 1875 and the Ridley Commission on the Civil Service (1887–90) urged still greater clout for the Treasury. Treasury officials themselves seemed unsure of their authority and effectiveness: at times they proclaimed Treasury control nearly complete, at other moments saw it as seriously deficient. The essential problem was that the control exercised by the Treasury effectively limited innovation, but did little to eliminate inefficiency in the routine functioning of departments. The goal of creating a unified civil service, with pay and conditions comparable across departments and similar methods of organization applied throughout the government, thus remained elusive. This failure was to prove a source of considerable discontent within the civil service and was a major consideration behind the appointment of yet another Royal Commission (the MacDonnell Commission, 1912–13) just before the war.[44]

Perhaps the most serious consequence of this essentially negative type of control was that it tended to pit the Treasury and the Chancellor against the spending departments and their representatives in Cabinet. Innovations in social and economic policy were sufficiently rare in the late nineteenth century to ensure that those which were implemented enjoyed fairly broad political support. Hence, Treasury resistance to the necessary expenditure – on education, for example – was correctly seen as impeding the policies adopted by the government as a whole. Officials at the Treasury insisted that their control did not alter policy, but the claim was difficult to sustain.[45] And precisely because the Treasury's objections did involve policy, it was not uncommon for disputes to be adjudicated within Cabinet. In that arena, moreover, the Treasury enjoyed indifferent success: a small department could be bullied but a large, prestigious one could not easily be denied. The services were particularly effective in resisting the Treasury's drive for economy. Cabinet had always been the court to which a department could appeal a negative judgment from the Treasury, but the nature of Treasury control in the late nineteenth and early twentieth centuries ensured that it was appealed to more regularly than a smoothly functioning system of Treasury domination would have permitted. Had the Treasury more effectively policed the agenda of Cabinet and intervened at an earlier stage in the formulation of policy, objectionable innovations might have been blocked before ministers had committed themselves; but the Treasury did not obtain such leverage until after the First World War.

By implicating Cabinet ministers in disputes between the Exchequer and the departments, the exercise of control over expenditure also lowered the status of the Treasury and encouraged further criticism. The classic case was the critique launched by Lord Salisbury in the Queen's speech of January, 1900. Salisbury had long resented the Treasury's reluctance to spend for defence and for empire, and the government's exposed and embattled position in southern

Africa seemed to demonstrate the dire consequences of such misplaced parsimony. By 1899, Salisbury had concluded that the "position given in our system to the Treasury" was both "very peculiar . . . and . . . very galling to other departments." "Because every policy at every step requires money," he explained privately to Michael Hicks-Beach, the Chancellor, "the Treasury can veto everything." The Prime Minister delivered his public rebuke shortly after this, elaborating on how the Treasury "has the power of the purse, and by exercising the power of the purse it claims a voice in all decisions of administrative authority and policy. I think," he concluded, "that much delay and many doubtful resolutions have been the result of the peculiar position which, through many generations, the Treasury has occupied." [46]

Little came of Salisbury's criticism of the Treasury. There was a flurry of debate in the press and another internal reorganization, but the outlines of Treasury control remained.[47] In the years after the Boer War, the Treasury even increased its supervision of military expenditure.[48] Still, Salisbury's attack illustrated the limitations of the Treasury's effectiveness. The Treasury's primarily negative control allowed it to discourage and deflect innovation, but it did not possess the administrative capacity to shape policy in a more thorough fashion. Its position depended therefore in large part upon the support it received from ministers and from Parliament. The identification of the Treasury with economy combined with the broad political consensus in favour of lower taxes and spending to ensure that its position was endorsed by most serious politicians most of the time. After 1900, however, the Victorian budgetary consensus began to break down, demands for more state intervention began to find a place on the agenda of high politics and a series of enterprising politicians, Lloyd George and Winston Churchill in particular, decided that reform and innovation could advance their political fortunes. When that happened, the Treasury's relatively weak institutional position was exposed and, in crucial instances, overwhelmed. The Treasury did largely succeed in preventing policy initiatives from emerging from within the state itself, but they were unable to block proposals that came from outside – from the effective entry of the working class into the system of representation and from the impact of war upon the politics of taxation.

Chapter 3

Labour and the demand for state expansion, 1890–1918

When nineteenth-century liberals searched for reasons not to enfranchise the lower orders, they most often hit upon the argument that, given the right to vote, workers would elect governments pledged to redistribution at the expense of property. A cursory look at the political history of the twentieth century suggests that they were not entirely deluded. Indeed, the three most salient facts about political development since 1900 are surely related: the democratization of the political system allowed, it would seem, for the emergence of the working class as a distinct and visible claimant to political power; and the working-class presence within the polity seems to have stimulated the enormous extension of the social and economic role of the state. Just how redistributive the policies of this enlarged state have been remains a matter of some dispute, but property has certainly had to pay something – a bit more ransom, as Joseph Chamberlain would have said – for social stability.

The coincidence between the rise of the working class and the creation of the welfare state has led many to argue that it was the enfranchisement of the working class, with its vast pool of grievances crying out for redress, that created the political demand for welfare.[1] In Britain, however, there was a considerable time lag between enfranchisement – which can be dated as early as 1867 or as late as 1918 – and the creation of an electoral majority committed to the welfare state. Two related factors account for this delay: the inability of workers as a class to secure an effective voice within the party system inherited from the nineteenth century; and the ambivalence of working-class institutions, and presumably workers themselves, towards the state and public provision. The two impediments would be overcome simultaneously, but slowly.

The clearest evidence of popular suspicion and resentment of state welfare comes from before the First World War, when working-class organizations manifested a notable lack of enthusiasm for the social reforms initiated by the Liberals.[2] The best-known examples were pensions and unemployment insurance, measures that were supported only with marked reluctance and serious reservations. The debate over pensions had a long history that was bound up closely with the continuing discourse over poverty and the Poor Law. The depression of the 1870s and 1880s opened a new phase in this discussion through which it became clear to many that "pauperism" in old age demanded remedies separate from the Poor Law. The clergyman William Blackley floated a scheme for old age pensions as early as 1878, and in 1882 founded the National Providence League to push for its adoption. Much more politically serious were two plans proposed in 1891. On 2 April Joseph Chamberlain delivered a speech in Portsmouth advocating contributory pensions and proceeded to form the so-called Committee of 100, a group of MPs committed to pensions. In November, Charles Booth presented a paper to the Statistical Society arguing for a non-contributory plan financed by general taxation. All of these plans were opposed by the major working-class institutions involved in the provision of relief: the friendly societies.[3]

Throughout the nineteenth century, membership in friendly societies was very popular and by 1900 over four million workers belonged to one or more of the thousands of societies. Typically, friendly societies offered sick pay, some medical care and death benefits. They did not provide pensions, but the line between sick pay for aging members and old age pensions was often blurred. For many workers, the friendly societies were the main defence against the poverty of old age, and the societies knew that alternative provision, if it were to be financed by contributions, would compete for the limited funds as well as the loyalty of their members. The most powerful societies – the Manchester Unity of Odd Fellows, the Ancient Order of Foresters and the Hearts of Oak – therefore lobbied hard against the first wave of proposals for pensions. Chamberlain immediately conceded their right to be consulted and began discussions with representatives of the National Conference of Friendly Societies in March, 1892. At its meeting the following year, however, the conference rejected his plan. Booth's more expensive proposal fared even less well and was denounced by an official of the Foresters as "a form of universal pauperization."[4] The various proposals for pensions continued to be a focus of debate throughout the 1890s, but by 1898 the failure of the advocates of pensions to win support from either the Royal Commission on the Aged Poor (the Aberdare Commission) or the Treasury Committee on Old Age Pensions (the Rothschild Committee) seemed to indicate the enduring strength of the interests arrayed against state-sponsored pensions.[5]

Over the next decade, however, support for pensions became more widespread, the interests opposed to pensions were mollified or won over and the fiscal constraints that had previously made Booth's scheme, for example, "beyond the range of the possible," were largely overcome. The result was the Old Age Pensions Act of 1908. The change in the attitude of labour was critical, as the friendly societies came to recognize that their increasing financial problems would be eased considerably if all workers, or at least their members, were awarded state-financed pensions. By 1902 the National Conference had come out in favour of a state-financed pension of 5s per week. Even before that, there was evidence of growing working-class support for pensions. The National Committee of Organized Labour . . . on Old Age Pensions had been founded in 1899 and had quickly secured the support of the Trades Union Congress and, in 1901, of the co-operative societies as well. The Labour Representation Committee was also quite firmly committed to pensions, as were its Parliamentary spokesmen. Their demands became more insistent after 1906, as did those of the Trades Union Congress. Of course, they wanted pensions to be more generous, to be granted at an earlier age and to be more broadly available than those provided by the Liberal scheme. Still, it appears that the increased working-class presence in Parliament after 1906, reinforced by the by-elections at Durham and Colne Valley in 1907 and coupled with the more consistent support for pensions among working-class organizations and their leaders, helped to push the Liberals to develop even their modest plan for pensions.[6]

The formulation of the National Insurance Bill of 1911 – the second great achievement of Liberal social reform – also elicited an ambivalent reaction from working-class organizations. The bill had two parts, one providing unemployment insurance and the other health insurance. Insurance against unemployment was less controversial, although there was suspicion that labour exchanges would be used to recruit blacklegs, resistance to the contributory principle and doubt about the fairness of a flat-rate contribution for workers with varying incomes. Neither the unions nor the friendly societies felt their interests were seriously threatened, however, and most of the debate took the form of questioning whether the Liberal measure was the best that could be expected in the circumstances. In this questioning the Social Democratic Federation and the Fabians took the lead but, backed up by strong support from the Trades Union Congress, Ramsay MacDonald was able to carry the majority of the Labour party on behalf of the bill.[7]

The provision of health insurance was another matter altogether. Large numbers of workers depended for health care and sick pay upon the friendly societies. The takeover of such functions by the state could threaten the societies' very existence. Inevitably, therefore, the societies reacted by seeking to become the instruments through which the state scheme would be handled. This would allow them to capture a considerable subsidy from the state, to reinforce their relationship with their members by making them more dependent on the services offered by the societies and also to enrol many more workers into their ranks. They sought as well to keep the state from offering the sorts of benefits which they saw themselves as already providing. A particularly striking example was widows' and orphans' benefits, which could be seen as competing with the death benefits offered by friendly societies and which the latter therefore tended to oppose. These were, in fact, removed from the insurance plan. Friendly society lobbying was not always so successful, however, for they were in competition with the private insurance companies who were eager to be involved in the scheme and commanded far greater resources. The societies sought to have the private companies excluded from participation, but in the end they were allowed in, as was any trade union that set itself up under the very liberal rules for becoming an "approved society."

The friendly societies thus managed to secure their own privileged position only by accepting a plan that gave the same rights to their competitors. It was a worthwhile compromise nevertheless, for the societies got the subsidy that came with the administration of health insurance and maintained their position as intermediaries between their members and the benefits provided by the state.[8]

Working-class ambivalence toward the state's initiatives in social policy was not limited to pensions and national insurance. Workers reacted with scepticism or hostility to the first steps taken towards compulsory education, to many of the early housing schemes, which seemed more effective in removing than replacing working-class accommodation, to restrictions on the working hours of children, to the appointment of health visitors and, of course, to the Poor Law. Many clearly felt that, as one of their number put it, "social reform means 'police'," or at best the unwanted intrusion of middle-class reformers. Such complaints suggest both the origins and depth of working-class hesitancy towards the state's initiatives. Before 1914, social reform was aimed at workers and seldom framed by or for them and hardly ever administered by their representatives. Policies were often justified by reference to the pathologies of working-class life, culture and institutions and structured in opposition to them. The passion for reform that grew out of the Boer War and the fears of physical degeneration that it provoked were linked directly to a critique of working-class women and the working-class family. Even the most ardent reformers shaped their proposals – on health insurance, for example – so as to prevent malingering and other behaviours which the middle classes were so ready to see as characteristic of those they sought to help.[9]

Not only were workers the objects of reform, rather than its architects, but they were also too weakly organized before the war to aspire to a more activist role on the national level. Labour was a small party, able to exert pressure but not control, in Parliament. Working-class organization was, moreover, very much rooted in the localities and much more capable of being mobilized in local than in national contexts. Trades councils, local Labour parties and unions could make an impact on the municipal level that was not possible nationally. In tacit recognition of this, socialists in the SDF and the ILP and labour activists more generally held out much more hope for progress at the municipal than the national level and were much more favourably disposed towards initiatives that could be undertaken locally. In this they were no doubt aided by the reform of local administration of 1888 and the more democratic local franchise. Equally important, some of the issues which most directly touched upon working-class interests could be affected directly by local political activity. The Poor Law, for example, was administered by boards of guardians elected locally, and local officials had considerable discretion over questions of housing, local public works and the wages and conditions of local authority employees. There were thus more opportunities and greater rewards for local political activity on the part of labour.

Labour responded to this particular structure of opportunity by focusing their efforts at the local level, where they registered some notable successes.[10] The effect was not only to provide labour representatives with their first real experience of government, but also to make local government more significant. As Ramsay MacDonald argued, the period when labour entered the local polity became "the most fruitful period . . . in local government . . . we have ever experienced." Working through the trades councils, Independent Labour Parties or incipient labour parties, socialist activists across Britain became involved in local politics and began to offer voters an alternative to the hegemony of Liberal or Conservative interests. Perhaps the most impressive record was compiled in London where, despite the weakness of trade union organization, labour joined with radical Liberals under the "Progressive" banner and dominated the new London County Council from 1889 to 1907. They campaigned not only on the well-known "social" issues of housing and sanitary reform but also on the more clearly "economic" questions of unemployment, sweated labour and the eight-hour day. "Progressives" naturally fought as well for public provision and control over gas and water, electricity and public transportation. The increased role of municipal government in providing these services also created unprecedented opportunities for public intervention in labour markets. Labour and its allies insisted on inserting "fair wages and conditions" clauses in municipal contracts; worked for better pay and conditions for municipal employees; argued for the direct employment of labour by local authorities; and even attempted to carry out public works countercyclically – i.e., to increase building by local governments during years of unusually high unemployment or to undertake such work during the winter months that bore so harshly on casual workers.[11]

When these efforts met with success, they ran the risk of submerging working-class interests under the leadership of the more "advanced" Liberals – as happened in London. But they also led to the emergence of theories and strategies for labour centred upon the importance of local politics. Representatives of labour recognized early on that local government was more democratic and accessible than national government and urged that it be made more so. They began simultaneously to demand that reform programmes proposed and adopted at Westminster be locally administered and democratically controlled. Perhaps even more important, the alliance politics pioneered in labour's prewar work in the localities helped to shape the broader electoral strategy adopted by the national party after 1918. As MacDonald wrote before the war, "Socialism is no class movement . . . It is not the rule of the working class; it is the organization of the community." Hence, as he saw the matter, "one of the most significant facts of the times is the conversion of the intellectual middle class to socialism." The possibilities offered to the labour movement by local politics thus played a critical role in shaping Labour's vision of the state and in convincing the party that the prospects for social reform were worth fighting for. The national state, by contrast, offered few openings to the labour movement. It was remote, notoriously hard to influence and had a record of hostility to organized labour. The spur to the formation of the Labour Representation Committee had been in fact a series of adverse legal decisions that threatened the ability of workers to organize unions and bargain effectively with employers. The party's immediate task, then, was to enter Parliament as the representative of the organized workers and to defend the autonomy of the organizations – the friendly societies, the co-ops, but especially the trade unions – built by those workers. The aim was largely defensive, and making use of the state for a more positive programme of reform was a distant prospect at best.[12]

What was being defended was not merely a set of self-interested institutions but a particular strategy of working-class advance. At the core of that strategy was a belief in independent organization, collective provision and trade union bargaining. Working people would organize themselves for savings, consumption and for their own recreation and social life; and they would also organize at the workplace for improved wages and better working conditions. Within such a strategic orientation state aid was not essential; and given the state's demonstrated antipathy it was best to keep it at some remove from issues affecting the working class. Its effectiveness would be measured primarily by success at wage bargaining. With decent wages, in fact, it would be unnecessary for the state to get involved in pensions or insurance against unemployment and sickness. As MacDonald argued in 1911, "If the employer pays proper wages . . . then we do not want charity and we do not want assistance at all . . . the prime consideration of everyone who is concerned in raising the status of the working classes is the amount of wages the working class get." The Ancient Order of Foresters had been arguing a similar position since at least 1895, when they asserted that "The aim of the working class ought to be to bring about economic conditions in which there should be no need for distribution of state alms. The establishment of a great scheme of state pensions would legalize and stamp as a permanent feature of our social life the chronic poverty of the age." [13]

By a similar logic, it was more important to demand public action to secure the "right to work" than to improve the terms on which those out of work would be maintained. Labour displayed little hesitancy in advocating local action to provide work for the unemployed. Indeed, MacDonald went so far as to argue that "The political demands of socialism cannot be understood better than by a study of the concept of the 'Right to Work'." Labour's "right to work" campaign was instrumental in securing passage of the Unemployed Workmen's Act (1905) and, when that bill's limitations became visible, in pressuring the Liberal government for a so-called Right to Work Bill, first introduced in 1907. The Right to Work Bill proposed numerous devices, from labour exchanges to emigration to reforestation to public works, through which to combat unemployment. More important, it proclaimed that workers had a right to work or to be maintained at rates comparable to union wages; it imposed upon government the duty to provide such work or maintenance; and proposed the establishment of a central committee on unemployment to supervise the task. Financial support would come from local rates and from taxes collected at the centre, while administrative control would remain largely with the local authority. The bill was anathema to large sections of the Liberal party and particularly offensive to John Burns at the Local Government Board. It was easily defeated in Parliament in 1908, but Labour continued its formal support of the bill until 1911 and beyond.[14]

Work and wages remained at the centre of working-class visions of how to achieve social and economic progress. Essential to that strategy was collective organization, especially at work but also outside of it through friendly societies and co-ops. Organizing was difficult, of course, but British workers were particularly adept at it and managed before 1914 to weave together an impressive array of formal and informal institutions in the workplaces and urban spaces which it occupied and made its own. Alternative strategies, involving a greater reliance on the state and public provision, would not only fail to utilize this peculiar strength of the British working class but could easily be seen as threatening these organizational underpinnings of working-class progress. Ambivalence towards the social interventions of the state and the Liberal reformers was thus more or less inevitable.

The privileging of work and wages within working-class politics had its costs, however. The struggle for regular work at good wages became for many a struggle for the employment of adult men at wages sufficient to support a family. The process by which the needs of working-class women and children came to be subsumed under those of adult, male trade unionists was complex and protracted, stretching back at least through the Chartist period. The impetus to define work as the domain of men and to confine women to the home and reproduction was not confined to the working class, of course. It was central to broader conceptions of gender relations in the nineteenth century, conceptions reflected and concretized in a changing division of labour within industry and made devastatingly effective by a conjuncture of shifting technologies and exclusionary practices. The increasingly marginal position of women in the labour market presumably further encouraged men in the tactical use of exclusionary rhetoric – in arguments, for instance, about the need to protect women and children at work or about the necessity of a family wage for male workers – and it is likely that such rhetoric was also deeply felt by many men in the trade union movement. Buying into that view placed serious limits upon working-class politics. It encouraged the separation of social policy questions from those of wages and the tendency to regard welfare as something for women, the old and the weak. Women, unable to participate fully in national politics and ignored on the great national issues of war and peace and taxation, were much more active in local politics and specifically in the politics of social and moral reform. Inequities of citizenship led to a "feminization of reform," producing highly gendered responses to reform.[15]

The desire to raise the pay and status of the male breadwinner also diminished the zeal with which men assisted the organization of women. Prior to the First World War trade unionism among women was largely confined to textiles, and even there the unions were dominated by the men. Elsewhere trade unionists tended to look upon the organization of women as more of a threat than a benefit. In matters of social policy, moreover, the distinct needs of women and children were slighted in favour of those of men, especially when they might have threatened the institutions created by men. The entire conception of national insurance, for example, was based upon two premises: that the way to improve working-class welfare was to enable the man to keep working; and that the main threat posed by sickness was not to the health but to the employability of workers. The health of the family was within this framework a distinctly secondary concern. Lloyd George was particularly committed to this conception, but it was one from which trade unionists did not typically dissent. Most important, however, the notion that the needs of working women and the working-class family could be dealt with adequately by providing work and wages for men involved a serious underestimation of the scope of need. An impoverished sense of need led to a restricted vision of what was desirable and politically feasible and helped to reinforce the limitations of the political programme around which Labour and the unions were active.[16]

LABOUR'S GREAT TRANSFORMATION, 1914–18

The relative weakness of working-class organization before the war, especially of the unions and the Labour party, and the attenuated nature of their vision of what it was possible to achieve through the state, were closely connected. In particular, their often defensive stance towards possible encroachments by the state upon their domains of quasi-social provision were prompted as much by a sense of the futility of broader, more inclusive strategies as by sectional interest. With the First World War, these constraints were to a considerable extent removed: unions grew enormously and seemed to put into the workers' hands the destiny of the nation; the Labour party was able by luck and effective leadership to move into the political space opened up by the disintegration of the Liberals and became suddenly a viable contender for power; and the state itself took on the capacity to serve as a genuine agent of social reconstruction. The material underpinnings of Labour's approach towards the state and its potential thus began to shift. In consequence, both the party and the unions came to adopt a vision of social transformation that accorded a much greater role to the national state.

The change in outlook was closely connected to the enhanced social presence and organizational clout of the working class.[17] Its consequences were visible in union organization, in industrial conflict and in politics. In 1914, for example, just over 300,000 workers went out on strike; in 1918, close to a million did;

and in 1919–20 the average was two million per year. Industrial strength and militancy translated more or less directly into increased support for the Labour party. Labour and the unions thus emerged from the war much stronger than in 1914. With greater strength came more self-confidence and a broader view of what was politically possible and of what could be demanded of the state.

The reorientation of perspectives on the state was not to be easy, uniform or unambiguous, however. The war had caused a growth in state power that was both fascinating and frightening. Thus Lloyd George unabashedly asserted that "a perfectly democratic State has . . . the right to commandeer every resource, every power, life, limb, wealth and everything else for the interest of the state," and his decisive actions at the Ministry of Munitions, and later as Prime Minister, gave proof that the government was prepared to exercise that right. Inevitably, the cost of its exercise would fall heavily upon the workers. Mobilization for war was more extensive than ever before, and working people were the primary objects of that unprecedented effort to move men into battle and to provide them with food, clothing and weapons. It was workers who made up the bulk of the recruits, workers who would produce the materiel with which to outfit the troops, and the deprivations of the war economy would disproportionately affect working-class families. Like most others, workers rallied to the nation's cause at the beginning of the war, but as the impact of mobilization and, of course, the losses of war itself came increasingly to be felt, working people and their representatives grew restive. The war, it was clear, was being fought on the backs of the working class and the state's power was being deployed to mobilize their efforts and resources. It seemed that "Government control during the war was managed by private interests" and that the sacrifices made necessary by the war were not being shared out equitably.[18]

The government's handling of two specific issues provided particular evidence for such criticisms. Very soon after the outbreak of war the government decided that the flow of arms would be greatly facilitated if unions agreed not to strike and to suspend their rules over shopfloor practices. To this end Lloyd George negotiated the famous Treasury Agreement of March, 1915; shortly thereafter, the Munitions Act made into law what had previously been a set of voluntary restrictions on trade unions. The Act was used to carry through a policy of dilution, by which skilled male workers were replaced by less skilled men or by women in certain jobs. Dilution produced considerable resentment and a sharp confrontation on Clydeside and became a major spur to the development of the wartime shop stewards' movement. Even if its effects were seldom as draconian as critics contended, it nevertheless symbolized the way state power could be utilized against workers and the direction which state intervention could possibly take. The experience of the Munitions Act and dilution coloured in particular the popular reaction to conscription. As the government moved toward compulsory military service during 1915–16, unionists detected not merely a plan to recruit more soldiers but a desire to control labour by introducing what they referred to as "industrial conscription." [19]

The control of manpower was therefore one crucial area of state activity which prompted negative reaction from workers. The lack of control over prices was another. The government's groping effort to mobilize the economy did not result in effective control over prices and for two years prices ran way ahead of wages, which were held back by the suspension of normal collective bargaining. Between 1914 and 1916 real wages dropped by about a sixth. Price increases were concentrated, moreover, on the key items of working-class consumption – food, fuel and housing. By 1915, the state had become convinced of the need to intervene in the housing market and rents were frozen, but other prices continued to rise. When the Commissioners on Industrial Unrest toured working-class districts in 1917, they found that the major concern was inflation, especially in the cost of food. This patently economic grievance, however, had taken on a political form, for it led logically to a critique of "exploitation, profiteering and bad distribution" and to the broader view "that a portion of the community is exploiting the national crisis for profit." [20] Out of such a critique came anger at the state and demands that it impose an equality of sacrifice upon all classes.

The expansion of the state during the war therefore gave workers and their leaders real cause for complaint. But it also strengthened workers in relation to the employers and to the government. The co-operation of workers was essential to war production and that could only be obtained by dealing with the unions. Employers were thus forced to treat the unions as legitimate representatives of the workers and union officials were put on a wide array of committees and advisory bodies dealing with production, the distribution of food and fuel, and with relief. Within industry and within the counsels of the state, therefore, the status of the unions was much enhanced. The process was highly controversial, for it implicated officials in government decisions and probably distanced them from at least some of their more militant members. The net effect, however, was extremely beneficial to the collective organization of workers and it was directly reflected in union membership figures, which doubled between 1914 and 1920. [21]

The strengthening of the industrial side of the labour movement was accompanied by complex changes in Labour's political fortunes. For the first couple of years the party truce masked any dramatic shifts that might have been occurring in political allegiance, but in the last two years of the war Labour was transformed into a major contender for power. It came out of the war with a new constitution, with a new organizational structure and with a set of rhetorical commitments that effectively distinguished the party from its political competitors. These changes provided the party with the strategic and programmatic resources with which to take advantage of the opportunities opened up by the widening of the franchise and the split among the Liberals. Backed up by the finances and industrial clout of the unions, Labour was prepared by the end of the war to make a decisive entry into the British polity armed with a broadly collectivist outlook.[22]

Labour came to its new programme and structure gradually. The first signs of change came early in 1916, when the threat of conscription prompted a rethinking of the terms on which working-class co-operation in the war effort had been purchased. A critical role in this rethinking was played by the War Emergency Workers' National Committee, which had been set up in 1914 and which initially adopted an approach in keeping with the prewar focus upon work and wages. They were concerned in particular to minimize the consequences of mobilization which, it was assumed, would put many out of work and disrupt the flow of income to working-class families. Their needs should be met by special state provision outside the normal workings of the Poor Law. The committee put particular emphasis on dependants' allowances. As the war progressed, the WEWNC became more concerned with workers as consumers and echoed in official circles the popular complaints about prices and distribution. The prospect of conscription pushed the committee in a new direction. In February, 1916 they produced a "Memorandum on Labour after the War" and urged the Trades Union Congress, the Labour party and the General Federation of Trade Unions to call a meeting to respond to the government's initiative. After some manoeuvring, the TUC summoned a special congress for 30 June 1916 which called for the "conscription of riches." Coupled at first with more specific proposals for dealing with prices and for making sure that conscription was not abused by employers or the government, the demand for the "conscription of riches" soon came to occupy the central place in Labour's emerging programme. The slogan gained wide currency in the summer of 1916 and it was formally adopted by the Trades Union Congress in September, 1916 and given more precise shape during 1917.[23]

What made the "conscription of riches" campaign so important was not merely its appropriateness to the context of wartime mobilization and its accompanying conscription of men, but also its implications for state control of the economy. The demand facilitated a rapid progression, intellectual and political, from the relatively innocuous notion of equality of sacrifice to the much more dangerous idea that wealth should be seized to pay for the war and private industry taken over to guarantee its efficient contribution to the war effort. That progression produced a growing consensus within the labour movement behind a collectivist rhetoric of social reform and ultimately gave rise to Clause IV, the socialist commitment embedded in Labour's 1918 constitution.

That commitment was sufficiently imprecise as to remain open to many diverse interpretations. To many trade union leaders it probably meant rather little, and its adoption by the Labour party did nothing to diminish their effective domination of the party apparatus. To others, in particular to those middle-class socialists outside the trade unions who were now invited to sign up as individual members of the party, it presumably meant a great deal more. Whether it betokened a broader commitment to socialism among the working class is very difficult to judge, if only because consciousness of this sort is so fleeting and so dependent on the precise language in which it is expressed. It did signal, however, a heightened sense of what it was possible for the state to provide and hence reasonable for working people to demand.[24]

Labour's conversion to socialism was, of course, notoriously incomplete. Many unions remained suspicious of the state and were eager after the war to resume bargaining with employers unaided and, so far as they were concerned, unimpeded by the state.[25] Perhaps more significant was the relative absence in Labour's thinking of a clear notion of how its programmatic commitments would be implemented by the state. Labour made little contribution to the widespread debate over the shape of the state after the war. Some unions had cherished the hope that the new Ministry of Labour would give workers a new voice in government and others expected great things from the Ministry of Reconstruction. In both cases they would be disappointed, as the Treasury and the Cabinet oversaw the taming of the one and the destruction of the other, but in neither instance did Labour have much to say.[26] Labour's leaders were more concerned with the issue of whether Labour was "fit to govern" than with how they would actually utilize the state to their ends. When MacDonald turned his attention to the probable shape of a future Labour Cabinet, he was most concerned with how Labour would run the Foreign Office and the armed forces but quite complacent about the management of domestic affairs. He apparently foresaw few difficulties in the way of changing the state into an agency of social transformation.[27] The Webbs, of course, were active behind the scenes in discussing the reform of the administrative machine, and Beatrice Webb's membership on the Haldane Committee on the Machinery of Government gave the pair of them privileged access to the most serious examination of the state and its functions undertaken in half a century.[28] Neither her presence on the committee nor the judicious nature of its report, however, could guarantee it a decent hearing from the government or from Labour. Its recommendations were thus largely ignored and the battle over the shape of the postwar state was fought primarily on the terrain of economy. Labour, though committed formally to statist solutions and to an ambitious scheme of taxation by means of a capital levy, did little to counter the ensuing campaign against the state.[29]

In short, Labour's approach to the realities of state power and to the difficulties involved in making public policy was partial and incomplete even at the end of the First World War. Both the party and the unions did seem to be learning quickly; unfortunately for them, however, the issues with which they were grappling during and just after the war proved not to be the questions that would dominate the period of peace. Indeed, the lessons learned during the war turned out to be of dubious relevance to the postwar world; and the largely economic problems that would confront, and confound, policy-makers of all parties between the wars would require yet further transformations and rethinkings about the proper role of the state in the provision of social services and in the direction of the economy.

Chapter 4

War and the creation of the modern tax state

The state's ability to extract resources from its subjects, or citizens, has varied a great deal over time; and different sorts of taxes have proved to be more or less effective instruments for that task. Over the course of the twentieth century the main fiscal tool used to expand revenues in Britain has been the income tax. The preference for income tax is not difficult to explain: it falls directly upon the wealth of individuals; it has been at least mildly progressive and for this reason politically acceptable, if not exactly popular; and it is highly flexible and efficient. As of 1900, however, there was no particular reason to believe that the state would come to rely so heavily upon income tax, nor that the tax itself would become an especially progressive levy. And there were certainly few who would have ventured to predict the enormous sums it would eventually raise. The historical effort to fund the expansion of the state since 1900 thus largely devolves into the history of income tax and its role in the budget of the state.

Though the income tax was firmly in place by the turn of the century, there was little indication prior to the Boer War that it would be transformed or expanded, and the logic of Victorian tax politics ensured that there would be strong resistance to any effort to do so. Between 1900 and 1914, however, the political context of tax policy-making altered enormously. The Boer War and the demands for increased defence expenditures made it essential to find new sources of revenue. The critical re-examination of the state of Britain and its population that was prompted by the war lent greater urgency to the search for revenue, as the need for the state to undertake some programme of reform became common political currency. Equally widely accepted was the sense of a mounting crisis of local finance, leading municipal leaders to undertake an intensive effort to obtain relief from central government. The major parties began to diverge over how the state should respond and how its interventions should be funded. Politics became much more polarized and the late nineteenth-century consensus on financial policy was called into question. Liberals and Unionists increasingly defined themselves in terms of distinct and opposed sets of policies linking social reform and taxation, and this redefinition of the existing poles of the political spectrum also provided the first, but highly critical, opening within which Labour began to define itself. In sum, the fiscal crisis prised open the confines of British politics and reshaped the outlook and orientation of the main political actors. As politics changed, so did the framework of parties and interests governing the making of tax policy and so did the discourse within which they debated and decided. Not surprisingly, the expanded framework produced new and different, and highly contentious, outcomes. Attention needs to be paid, therefore, both to the policy results and to the new logic of tax politics from which they emerged.

The fiscal crisis of the early twentieth century is reasonably well known, though its dimensions are seldom fully appreciated. It sprang from three, interrelated sources that combined to place fiscal issues high on the political agenda. The most visible pressure for increased taxes came from the demand for state intervention to bring about reform. From the 1880s "advanced" thinkers had argued forcefully against *laissez-faire* prescriptions for state inactivity, and with considerable effectiveness after 1900. Reform required revenue and the rethinking of the relation between state and society led inevitably to the exploration of new avenues of taxation. Reform and higher taxes did not find a ready political home in the party system of the 1890s and early 1900s, however. The Liberals should have been inclined, temperamentally and electorally, to respond favourably, but the legacy of Gladstonian finance was a powerful inhibitor. The Liberal Imperialists under Lord Rosebery tended to be intellectually receptive, but they rallied around "efficiency" not reform, and the resistance to structural change implied in that choice was characteristic. Their proposals were marked "by moderation," they "were seeking a minimum." Still, their refusal to rule out tax increases did weaken the resistance to higher taxes: Haldane, for example, argued in 1902 that the country had not yet "exhausted the resources of civilization in respect of income tax." The Liberal Imperialists did not, however, succeed in linking progressive taxation and social reform in a compelling vision. Nor, prior to 1906, did other Liberals.[1]

The Conservatives offered no more hospitable an environment. The rhetoric of Randolph Churchill and Joseph Chamberlain, so audible in the 1880s, was heard only faintly in the 1890s. The Unionists were led by Salisbury, who was deeply resistant to spending money on reform. "However much you may desire to benefit your neighbour," he cautioned, "do not benefit him by taking money out of the pockets of another man." Salisbury owed his political ascendancy largely to the question of Home Rule, and the Unionist coalition he led was a very poor vehicle for any particularly expansive vision of reform. Chamberlain certainly found himself unable to put it to such use and Salisbury, anxious not to "alarm the interests" that stood behind the Conservative party, was determined not to try.[2]

Despite the widespread discussion of social reform, then, reformist policies did not fit well within either major party prior to 1900. Between 1900 and 1906, however, the interest in reform became much greater and the parties more receptive. A key factor was surely the founding of the Labour Representation Committee. Labour was itself primarily a defensive formation, established to protect the rights of trade unions and to promote a vaguely defined independent labour interest. But the creation of a distinct Labour party signalled the growing size and increasing autonomy of the working-class electoral presence. Recognition of that presence prompted both Liberals and Unionists to take reform seriously as a means of attracting or retaining working-class voters. If the prospect of Labour pushed many politicians toward reform out of fear, others were moved by national and imperial sentiments aroused by the Boer War. The difficulties of the Boer War – in the field, in the recruiting and mobilization of troops, and in its diplomatic consequences – provoked a national crisis of confidence. The crisis involved doubts about the quality of the British race and of British institutions, particularly its military institutions. It led to calls for change that managed to forge a novel link between the case for social reform and the needs of empire and nation. Imperialists like Chamberlain had attempted such rhetorical connections before, but they were not credible until military disaster could be tied directly to poverty, ill health and their consequences.[3]

So the call for reform became much more insistent after 1900, and came to assume a practical dimension. Only the means of financing it were lacking. But there were other claims on finances besides reform, claims which reinforced the urgency of fiscal issues while threatening to overwhelm the claims of reform. The most irresistible were military. Spending on the army and navy had turned sharply upward in the 1890s in response to the German naval challenge and it was the issue of increased funding for the navy that actually forced Gladstone's retirement in 1894. Ordinary defence expenditure grew by over £8 million from 1890 to 1895, by another £20 million by 1905 and by yet another £28 million, to a total of £91.3 million, by 1913. During the Boer War, of course, the sums needed had increased even more. Overall, then, rising defence expenditure imparted a steady upward pressure on spending and hence upon taxes, a pressure which politicians found hard to resist. Politicians were confronted as well with demands to relieve the tax burden on local property. Much of the prior expansion of social provision and of spending on infrastructure had been carried out by local government, and much of the cost placed on rates. Just who paid local rates, and hence their distributional impact, was much debated. Rates were levied in the first instance on property, but whether they ultimately fell on the landowner or occupier and whether they increased rents or depressed property values and profits were matters of intense dispute. What was not in dispute was that they were steadily increasing and that these increases were highly controversial, provoking recurring ratepayers" revolts with widespread support. Discontent over rates mounted still more after 1888, for the reform of local government led to a further expansion in the role of local authorities and further increases in rates. Between 1890 and 1905 the share of local spending in total government expenditure increased from 38 per cent to just over 50 per cent, from £51 million to £128 million. The crisis in local finance became a crisis in local politics, and the new organs of local government arenas of mobilization and polarization. Local leaders of both parties put pressure on national leaders to do something to relieve local rates, and both parties were forced to come to terms with the issue.[4]

The conjuncture of local and "imperial" fiscal problems immensely complicated the solution to either set of problems, and forced all parties and factions to rethink their financial policies. It was not enough to reform national finances, and it was not possible to lighten local burdens without taking on new burdens at the centre. The political exigencies of local politics might not mesh neatly with those of national politics, moreover, and the protection of interests at one level might preclude the development of an effective policy at another. The resolution of the multi-faceted Edwardian fiscal crisis therefore entailed a reshaping of political beliefs, alignments and constituencies at national and local levels. It was almost inevitable that an early casualty of the fiscal crisis would be the Gladstonian consensus on finance and that this would accentuate party political differences. It was likely, too, that there should have been a great deal of confusion and fluidity in the discourse over fiscal policy.[5] Support for Gladstonian-style retrenchment, for example, was evident within both parties: Unionist free traders and the more moderate among the Liberal Imperialists, for example, shared a roughly similar vision and for a time appeared likely to coalesce. There were also embarrassing similarities between Fabian calls for Exchequer grants in aid of local authorities and Conservative policy, despite the deeper compatibility between socialist and "advanced" Liberal views. The main lines of argument became clarified between 1902 and 1906, by which date two major alternatives confronted one other. The Unionists rallied around a policy of tariffs on food and manufactured goods, to be used for protection, for imperial unity and for revenue, and of the utilization of that revenue to fund expanded defence needs and selected policies of social reform and to relieve ratepayers through subsidies. The Liberals maintained their allegiance to free trade but came to accept the need to complement free trade finance by raising large sums of money from direct, graduated taxes – such as income tax, sur-tax and death duties – from progressive local taxes on land, and from taxes on vice and luxury – e.g., licence fees and taxes on liquor and tobacco. The two alternatives were starkly opposed: they implied vastly different approaches to political economy and to the nation's economic future, and they were intended to generate opposed and distinct, if putatively overlapping, coalitions of interests and constituencies. Both aimed to be "popular" and to be fiscally effective; beyond that, they had little in common.[6]

Behind the Liberal alternative were a cluster of principles that had deep roots in the party's past and a series of calculations about the adjustment of those principles to the political and economic realities of the twentieth century. The most important principle was the commitment to free trade and the opposition to protection. Protection was identified with the Corn Laws, with the aristocracy whose sectional advantages they were meant to protect, and hence with the corrupt old regime. It was also linked to militarism, a connection reinforced by the duty temporarily imposed on corn during the Boer War. Free trade, on the other hand, was rhetorically coupled with peace, internationalism and economic growth. Free trade could be said to have produced prosperity and created a fair field on which various interests could compete. Over the years, moreover, Britain had evolved into the open centre of the world economy, and empire and free trade had seemed to go happily together. The most prosperous sectors of the economy were, of course, finance and trade, but even manufacturers had found the net effects of free trade beneficial. The City and the older, staple industries had, then, either positively embraced free trade or at least come to accept it; and the City in particular had waxed powerful and profitable under the free trade regime. The fiscal policy of the Liberals was designed to preserve that open international economy and with it the ties between the Liberals and those interests that had done well out of it. In addition, the increasing reliance of the Liberals upon working-class support made them sensitive to the argument that indirect taxes fell most heavily on the poor. Herbert Samuel, for instance, estimated in 1902 that the poorer classes paid a greater portion of their incomes in indirect taxes than the middle classes did in direct and indirect taxes combined. The desire to woo working-class voters in this way reinforced Liberals" principled objections to indirect taxes.[7]

But the aversion to protection carried heavy fiscal consequences. It was the decision to move toward free trade and the attendant loss of revenues that had compelled Peel's reimposition of the income tax, and continued progress towards free trade had meant the sacrifice – the "wanton sacrifice," according to Sir Robert Giffen – of other sources of revenue.[8] By 1900, therefore, there were few possible devices for raising additional revenue. The main possibility was the income tax, but that required explicit Parliamentary approval through the annual budget, and proposals to raise income tax had a way of provoking debate and eliciting the mobilization of interests. The Liberals' need to raise additional money within a free trade framework nevertheless drove them to resort to income tax and to other taxes on wealth, in particular landed wealth. The focus on land was, of course, especially attractive to Liberals, for it promised a means both of financing reform and of attacking inherited privilege. Land taxes also seemed to offer a way out of the dilemmas of local finance, for if land itself were taxed more, ratepayers might be taxed less. Indeed, "In the Liberal search for new sources of revenue, land, and notably urban land, exercised a magnetic attraction."[9]

The movement to tax land had been given an enormous boost in the 1880s by the writings and speeches of Henry George and his single-tax movement. The influence of Henry George on early British socialism has been noted often, but his influence among Liberals was at least as great. George built upon notions already current, and rooted in Ricardo and J.S. Mill, about the "unearned increment" and hence the justice of taxing land values. The value of land, it was argued, was socially produced, and the accident of ownership should not prevent the acquisition by society of that value. Taxation of land values would have a number of important, positive consequences: it would remove or lessen taxes on capital or property or trade and thus stimulate economic activity; it would reduce the incentive of landowners to hold land off the market until rising prices made its development profitable and therefore stimulate the building of houses, factories and shops; and it would redistribute wealth. The radicalism inherent in the taxation of land values made moderate Liberals shy away from the policy for as long as possible, but the crisis of local rates put a definite limit on that avoidance. Local rates and cries for relief both mounted from 1888 and the Unionists responded by grants-in-aid to local authorities. Between 1887 and 1892 they doubled the amount of national revenues assigned to localities from £4 to £8 million, distributed to both rural and urban areas. In 1896 the Conservatives put forward an Agricultural Land Rating Bill that was again aimed at relieving rates with Exchequer grants, this time exclusively in the countryside. Even worse, as one Conservative MP candidly admitted, "No one has denied . . . that the Rating Act was in relief of the landlord and not of the tenant." The outcry from urban leaders, and from the Liberals, led to the appointment of a Royal Commission on Local Taxation, which was to keep the issue of local taxation on the political agenda until it reported in 1901, and beyond. From 1903, the Liberals were forced to commit themselves to land taxes for fear that the tariff reformers would effectively link protection with the relief of ratepayers. As the radical C.P. Trevelyan expained in October, 1903, "The Liberal position would be rather pathetic if Mr. Chamberlain came forward with a great scheme for the relief of rates as a compensation for his food-taxation." Subsequently, the combination of political, and more purely fiscal, concerns served to maintain and even intensify the Liberals' interest in land taxes and led them to incorporate a new series of taxes on land in the famous budgets of 1909–10 and 1913–14.[10]

The prospective yield of various impositions on the landlords was never entirely clear and Liberals had to increase other taxes as well. They turned to taxes on income and inheritance, and proposed to make them heavier and more progressive. Increased death duties had already been imposed in 1894, and there were few political or administrative difficulties in raising them still further, as Lloyd George would do in 1909–10. Reforming the income tax and enhancing its yield were more difficult propositions, as the decades of debate over the issues of differentiation and graduation had demonstrated. But it had become increasingly clear that "the sheet-anchor of future Liberal finance should be a further development of the principle of graduation applied to the income tax so as to place an increasing share of the burden upon the upper portion of the incomes of the wealthy."[11] For that to happen, it was necessary for Liberals "to show," as Leo Chiozza Money attempted, "that the income tax could be so amended that, so far from being counted an obnoxious impost, it would be regarded as a just and proper instrument of taxation." [12]

Upon returning to office in 1906, the Liberals therefore appointed a committee under Sir Charles Dilke to inquire into the feasibility of differentiating between earned and unearned income and of graduating the impost. The committee pronounced both to be feasible, and Asquith proceeded to incorporate a different rate for earned versus unearned income in 1907. Graduation, too, would be introduced subsequently by means of super-tax, but the Liberals took care to ensure that it would fall overwhelmingly on the wealthy. Super-tax was imposed on incomes above £2,000, and many of those with incomes below that would actually be relieved of tax by more generous allowances. The Liberal proposals were thus calibrated very precisely to exempt the middle and lower-middle classes from increased direct taxation and there is some evidence that, even after the increases of 1909–14, the majority of taxpayers were less heavily taxed than before. [13]

The key to the Liberals' proposals regarding taxes on land, inheritance and income was their understanding of class and the class basis of their appeal. "In Britain, tax politics is class politics," a recent history of taxation concludes, and the behaviour of the Liberals before 1914 was no exception. [14] But the Liberals also raised a substantial amount of revenue from taxes on luxuries and liquor licences. They were able thereby to satisfy some of their supporters' antipathy towards "the trade" in liquor and concern for temperance and moral reform. In 1912–13 the new or increased duties on spirits, tobacco, gasoline, car and liquor licences yielded more than the increases or new impositions on estate duties and almost as much as those on income tax and super-tax combined. [15] So class was not all that mattered, but it was none the less central to the Liberal solution to the fiscal crisis.

The principles and political calculations underlying the Unionist alternative were equally complex, and shaped just as much by considerations of class and economic interest. At the centre was Chamberlain's plan for tariff reform. The commitment to tariffs evoked memories of protection and of the Corn Laws and in that sense was as rooted in British fiscal history as the Liberal stance, but in the first decade of the twentieth century it was the plan for tariff reform which seemed new, exciting and potentially disruptive to established notions and policies. Tariff reform implied not merely a new means of raising money but a new vision of the economy and the state and of the relationship between the national state, the national economy and the empire. As a policy it spoke to vague fears of national decline and to the specific problems of British industry. Tariff reformers, keenly aware of the competitive weakness of British industry, saw a need for the state to involve itself directly in providing markets for British products, both by excluding competing goods from the home market and by creating a structured and systematic preference for British goods in empire markets. Behind protection, Conservatives hoped, could be united both urban and rural property, the historic agricultural base of Tory support and the industrial base they sought to win. [16]

Tariff reform would also solve the state's fiscal crisis in a manner more in keeping with the traditional Tory predisposition in favour of indirect taxes. Conservatives had opposed the shift towards direct taxation from 1842 onwards, and had argued instead for "broadening the base" of taxation so that it would "touch lightly" at a variety of points within the economy and in society, thus raising revenues with the least difficulty. They recognized that the trend of Liberal finance had involved a forfeiting of various levers for extracting taxes indirectly from the populace, and they sensed intuitively that the narrower the range of taxes, the more likely it was that the remaining taxes would be increased on those most able to pay them. So their concern for a balance between direct and indirect taxation masked a more basic concern to deflect attention from accumulations of inherited, especially landed, wealth as possible sources of revenue. Tariffs, in this sense, were a defence against direct, progressive taxes.

It was also hoped that tariffs would raise sufficient revenue to relieve local ratepayers through vastly expanded Exchequer grants. Both parties vied for the allegiance of ratepayers, but Conservatives had a long history of arguing for relief of local rates. In the late 1840s Disraeli had made the relief of local rates a critical part of his fiscal appeal, using the prospect of lower rates as a means of reconciling the landed interests to the loss of duties on corn. The appeal to ratepayers was thus virtually built into the political programme of the modern Conservative party from the beginning; so, too, was the need for some source of "imperial" taxation that would allow a lessening of "local burdens." [17] Tariffs were the answer.

The Unionist stance on local taxation grew naturally, then, out of its historic commitments to the land and to the landed classes. But just as Liberal policy towards the land was given a contemporary twist after 1900, so the Conservative approach was adapted to new political needs and opportunities as well. The Conservatives had long disdained active involvement in local politics and had never been in much sympathy with the claims of those who wished to expand the activities or capacities of local authorities. During the 1880s franchise reform and the restructuring of local government combined to force Conservatives to take local politics more seriously, however. It also afforded them new electoral possibilities. The resistance of ratepayers to increasing taxation provided fertile ground for the cultivation of Conservative sentiment, and the movements of ratepayers offered in addition a means of recruiting and organizing local activists.

It was in London that the new, ratepayers' Conservatism emerged most clearly and effectively. Control of the London County Council was captured at first by the Liberals, led by Lord Rosebery, who headed a "Progressive" alliance of Liberals, Fabians and other reformers who proceeded to make London a showcase of aggressive local government. The Conservatives fought back under the "Moderate" label, but not very effectively until the mid-1890s. Various attempts were made to organize the Conservative forces in London politics: there was the short-lived London Ratepayers' Defence League, founded in 1891 but dead by 1892; the London League, whose brief existence in 1892 was unknown to most Londoners; and finally in 1894 the London Municipal Society, founded with Lord Salisbury's reluctant support. The London Municipal Society represented a crystallization of the ratepayers' interest behind the banner of Conservatism. Rebellions of ratepayers had, of course, been a recurring feature of nineteenth-century local politics, but they were notoriously short-lived and did not produce any sustained advantage for either of the major national parties. That changed in 1895, when the London Municipal Society helped the Moderates to stem the Progressive tide in London. In 1907, after years of agitation against municipal trading and rising rates, the Conservatives actually captured control of the London County Council. Between 1900 and 1914 ratepayers' organizations on the London model sprang up across Britain. Organizational control of these movements was always contested: the Anti-Socialist Union and the Liberty and Property Defence League, for example, both aimed to give leadership to the resistance to the mounting political threat to property and wealth. However, as *The Times* of 19 January 1909 concluded, "The London Municipal Society appears to be the most completely armed of all the anti-socialist organizations, in spite of its nominally local sphere of operations." It was in fact largely by leading the resistance to local taxation that the Conservatives acquired a mass electoral base in the early twentieth century. Acquiring that base reinforced the Conservatives in their opposition to direct taxes and in their commitment to tariffs.[18]

Unionist support for tariffs served a dual purpose. Positively, it offered an imperialist and interventionist solution to Britain's problems. It aimed to promote prosperity and to create jobs, and was intended to appeal to the working class and to those industries that were not doing well out of free trade.[19] It promised, too, revenue with which to fund social reform, an additional lure to the working class. At the same time tariffs were the main means devised by Conservatives for avoiding direct taxation both locally and nationally. Every penny raised through tariffs would be a penny saved in rates or income tax. The problem for Conservatives was that the positive and negative aspects of their commitment to tariffs were continually in conflict and, more important, were seen as such by voters and rivals. The contradictory motives behind the tariff campaign were evident from the beginning, and Chamberlain himself failed to transcend them. During 1903–4, therefore, the campaign for tariff reform stressed its effect on imperial unity, and its potential for supporting social reform was not emphasized. There was a brief moment in 1908–9 when the more "constructive" effects of tariffs were emphasized, but this emphasis was overwhelmed in the resistance to the People's Budget, which demonstrated very clearly that what Unionists were most concerned with was avoiding the taxation of the well-to-do.[20] In the end, this ambivalence doomed the movement for tariff reform and guaranteed the triumph of free trade finance, with its reliance on the progressive income tax. The ambivalence was no mere tactical mistake, however, for it reflected the needs and social basis of Unionism. Indeed, tariff reform served the essential function for Conservatives of providing them with a seemingly positive answer to the fiscal crisis of 1900–14 while arraying most of the nation's large and small property-owners behind their cause. It may not have contributed significantly to the solution of the fiscal problem, but it laid the basis for subsequent Conservative strength.[21]

The triumph of Liberal finance was not simply a victory over the Unionist alternative, however, for the Liberal policy had also to overcome a good deal of institutional resistance from the Treasury and the Board of Inland Revenue. Resistance was particularly strong just after 1900, when the dimensions of the fiscal crisis were only beginning to be understood. Official attitudes towards tax policy were never wholly negative: the Treasury and the Inland Revenue recognized that the fiscal health of the state and their own position within it were dependent on their ability to tax effectively. The Treasury could discharge its responsibility for the sale of government securities only if the state's credit was deemed worthy by the City of London, and both the City and the Treasury developed a set of very high standards against which to measure worthiness.[22] The Treasury thus developed a strong interest in the viability of the tax system that paralleled its interest in controlling expenditure. One consequence of that interest was a marked reluctance to tamper with the nation's fiscal system. Both the Treasury and the Board of Inland Revenue had evolved a quaintly protective attitude towards the taxpayer and spoke up readily on his behalf. Henry Primrose, Chairman of the Inland Revenue, was especially adept, for example, at imagining himself in the role of the beleaguered taxpayer and voicing his putative grievances. Thus in 1903 he asked rhetorically how anyone could advocate a graduated income tax: "Is it conceivable that in this country some 15,000 of the most powerful of the community would tolerate tamely such an inquisition into their private affairs as would be inevitable with a system of progressive Income Tax? Or would any reasonable person wish to subject them to such an inquisition, if he realized that little or no profit to the community could result from it?" Primrose claimed to be merely echoing Alfred Milner, his predecessor, in suggesting that "the indirect injury done to the Revenue in the long run" would "outweigh the meagre pecuniary results" which graduation would produce in the short run.[23] Primrose's argument depended, of course, on his calculation of the yield of a super-tax, and his estimate was notoriously low. But the argument was also partially self-fulfilling, for if the Revenue pronounced progression unworkable, were they not also in a position to make it so in practice?

Such expert opinion was thus very hard to counter, for it successfully confused the question of what was desirable with what was deemed practical by those who were in a position to know. It was necessary, therefore, for advocates of progressive taxation to show that fiscal reform was indeed practical and would generate substantial revenue. The Dilke Committee of 1906 was forced, in fact, to reject explicitly the advice it received from Primrose, Bernard Mallet and other representatives of the Inland Revenue and to seek advice from outsiders, like Leo Chiozza Money, to demonstrate the feasibility of graduation and differentiation. It would fall to Lloyd George as Chancellor to show beyond a doubt that these tax changes could also be profitable. But both points had to be proved against the wisdom and wishes of those who had held the senior posts at the Inland Revenue and the Treasury when the fiscal debate began.[24]

What made it possible to overcome such resistance? The personality of Lloyd George was a key factor, for he had little patience with bureaucratic obstruction and an overriding political will. He managed as Chancellor to find or bring in a cluster of less senior officials – for example, William Clark, who came with him from the Board of Trade, William Blain, who had prepared an important Treasury paper on the feasibility of super-tax for the Select Committee of 1906, and John Bradbury, upon whom Lloyd George was forced to rely after Blain's untimely death in December, 1908 – who were willing to undertake the staff work necessary to make details of tax reform into legislation. Lloyd George's task was made easier by the retirements of E.W. Hamilton at the Treasury and Primrose at the Board of Inland Revenue, and by the appointment of Robert Chalmers to head the Treasury. So changes in personnel and the force of personality had some effect in forcing through a new fiscal policy.

Surely more important, however, was the peculiar political conjuncture. What made the moment so peculiar were the dimensions of the fiscal crisis itself and the Unionist response. The fiscal crisis emerged not merely, or primarily, from the excesses of expenditure for domestic purposes, although such expenditures were growing. Rather, they grew directly out of war and defence spending. This meant that large sections of moderate, even Conservative, opinion were led to recognize that the crisis was genuine. Still worse for advocates of economy, it was impossible to solve the financial difficulties by borrowing. Already before the Boer War the government had resorted to borrowing for its defence build-up; after the war and its attendant increases in both taxes and borrowing, it was widely felt that further loans would threaten the state's fiscal viability and impair its ability to raise funds in event of a real emergency. Thus Hamilton of the Treasury warned in 1905, "It is bad enough to embark on war with an impaired Field-Gun; but it is almost worse to embark on it with an impaired credit." [25] The continued decline in consols after 1906 prevented the government from resorting to borrowing for the duration of the Edwardian fiscal crisis and made it imperative for both parties and for policy-makers, even at the Treasury and the Inland Revenue, to think new thoughts about how to pay for government.[26]

In rethinking government finance there were really only two possible alternatives: free trade, coupled with direct and graduated taxes, or tariffs. The Conservative decision to opt for tariffs meant that the case for an alternative to free trade and direct taxes would get a thorough hearing, but it meant, too, that both poles in Edwardian political discourse accepted the need for enhanced revenue. An increase in taxation, in other words, became almost inevitable politically, and debate was focused on the relative merits of the two alternatives. The alternatives, moreover, were presented as packages of interrelated policies that fitted together rather closely. It was not possible to prise them apart and, in so doing, to arrive at some minimalist compromise, or at least it proved impossible to that particular generation of politicians. Another generation with a different set of formative experiences and beliefs might have been capable of striking a compromise over taxes. Certainly, the generations that lived through the Great War, the depression of the 1930s and the war against Hitler would be much more capable of envisioning a permanently expanded state and of tolerating a much-enhanced burden of taxation. In retrospect, however, what seems most remarkable about the generation of leaders who sought to deal with the prewar crisis was how far they had themselves travelled from Victorian orthodoxies and how imaginative were their responses to the novel needs of the state. The Liberals, heir to the Gladstonian tradition of *laissez-faire* and economy in government, came to advocate quite drastic infringements on the rights of property and to the possession of wealth; while the Conservatives, in the advocacy of tariffs, had come around to proposing a drastic reorientation in the economic life of the nation. Neither alternative bespeaks a lack of imagination.

The outcome of the prewar struggles over taxation, however, also suggests the limits of the rethinking of the political economy and of the system of party allegiances within which it took place. The Liberals, for example, found it necessary to shape their financial policies so as to ensure that the majority of middle-class taxpayers would pay no more in tax than before. After the implementation of old age pensions, moreover, they were unable to put in place further social reforms without imposing a significant share of the cost on working people. The limits upon the Unionists were even more serious. Ideally, the espousal of tariffs was meant to allow for the possibility of social reform and hence for an appeal to the working class. But the link between the two policies was always tenuous. As Richard Jebb, an ardent advocate of tariffs and social reform, admitted in 1912, "we were running a Radical policy in the name of Conservatism . . . . We did it in good faith, but it was a fraud all the same." The contradiction became especially evident and politically crippling after 1909, when Lloyd George provoked the Unionists into a defence of the land and the Lords, a defence that turned tariff reform into a thinly veiled rationale for reaction across the board. Even so, the victory of Liberal, free trade finance – registered in the elections of 1910 – was a narrow one, and nothing about the resolution of the prewar tax crisis implied that more revenues, or further instalments of reform, would be easily come by.[27]

The prewar tax battles determined the contours of the tax system and structured the options available to government during and after the war. The choice of direct over indirect taxes, and the narrowing of the range of possible taxes that implied, had thus already been made in 1906 and ratified in 1910. By 1914, the share of tax revenues generated by direct taxes stood at 60 per cent, up from about half at the turn of the century.[28] Among those direct taxes the income tax, newly differentiated and slightly graduated, had begun to play the dominant role, even if the recent budget battles had focused rhetorically upon land. These distinctive features of the tax system would be accentuated during the Great War. The huge sums needed to fight the war were raised primarily by direct taxes. As a contemporary analyst noted, "One of the most striking features of the British tax program was the small number of sources from which the increased revenue was drawn. More than half . . . came from the income and excess profits taxes." [29] The increases were indeed staggering: the standard rate of income tax was boosted from 1s 2d in the pound to 6s in the budget of 1918–19, and the number of persons who paid income tax more than tripled. Rates of super-tax were comparably increased and liability broadened, resulting in an increase in its yield from £3.3 million in 1913–14 to £35.5 million in 1918–19; while excess profits tax was raising £284 million by 1918–19, or 36 per cent of total revenues. The net effect was to raise the share of revenues from direct taxes to 80 per cent in 1918.[30]

There was relatively little resistance to higher taxes during the war. If anything, there was a widespread belief that taxation, which covered about a quarter of the cost of the war, should have been greater and that government should have borrowed less. But it became obvious as the war progressed that the struggle over taxes had been adjourned, not ended, and that the question of how to pay for the long-term costs of the war would dominate the agenda of postwar politics. That agenda, moreover, would have on it an innovative proposal which, if enacted, would have further accentuated the progressive character of the existing tax system and provided the postwar state with substantial new revenues. It was the proposal for a capital levy. The plan for a levy on capital or, as it was sometimes referred to, on war wealth, was apparently first broached by Leo Chiozza Money. It entered into the debate about the prosecution of the war largely through the efforts of the War Emergency Workers' National Committee, whose "Conscription of Riches" campaign pressured the Trades Union Congress and the Labour party into support for a radical fiscal policy. In June, 1916 a TUC Special Congress endorsed the idea, and it was given a more detailed, programmatic shape by the appearance of *How To Pay for the War*, written by Sidney Webb and published by the Fabian Research Department in July, 1916. The TUC reaffirmed its support at its meeting in September, 1916 and again at Blackpool in 1917. Representatives of the TUC, the Labour party and the WEWNC pushed hard for the capital levy at a meeting with Bonar Law on 14 November 1917. Whether out of an absence of forethought or an excess of dissembling, Bonar Law had proclaimed himself "significantly sympathetic" to the proposal. His remarks were reported in the *New Statesman* on 17

November and at that moment the capital levy came onto the agenda of high politics. It would remain there for the next decade and would largely structure the discourse on debt and taxation.[31]

While the proposal for a capital levy originated from within the labour movement and was of enormous political benefit to the Labour party, it also managed for a period of time to transcend its origins and to garner support from officials, politicians and voters generally unsympathetic to the claims and pretensions of the working class. The plan for a capital levy may well have been Labour's first truly original and creative contribution to fiscal and economic policy. Earlier demands for nationalization were never especially practical and never captured the public imagination. Before the war, moreover, Labour's fiscal policies differed little from those of the more advanced Liberals. But the notion of a capital levy went well beyond what the advocates of Liberal finance would countenance. To Labour a capital levy was not only a means of paying for the war. It was also potentially "a demand for the public ownership and control of all the most vital sectors of the economy," a demand that met with a surprisingly broad and favourable response.[32]

The plan for a levy on capital began as a rather imprecise idea for getting hold of "accumulated wealth" for purposes of war finance. In Sidney Webb's hands it became part of a much larger programme of permanent financial reform. That programme involved an expansion of the activities of the post office and an extension of public ownership into several new fields, such as railway and canal transport, coal and insurance, all of which would be expected to generate substantial revenues. These would be coupled with a "revolution in the income tax." Unlike the Treasury officials, who myopically but cleverly insisted that postwar budgets should be shrunk back to prewar dimensions, Webb assumed that "Peace, in fact, will call for a revenue of two and a half times the pre-war figure." He recognized, too, that "only by means of the Income Tax (including as it now does the Supertax) can our richer neighbour, who is manifestly a much more fit subject for taxation than ourselves, be made annually to contribute to the Exchequer anything like proportionately to his undeserved wealth." Webb proposed doubling the rate of income tax from 5s to 10s in the pound. More generous exemptions for families would mean that those with lower incomes would feel little increase, but the tax would be more steeply graduated with super-tax beginning at £1000 and rising steadily thereafter. The net effect would be that the total regular exactions from the better off would be quite substantial. This would not be enough to free the nation from the tyranny of servicing the national debt, however, and for that a "perfectly herculean repayment of debt" was not merely called for, but should be considered "literally a part of National Defence." To effect that would require "*once for all*, a lump sum contribution – a Special War Levy – of 10 per cent of the capital value of all private property."[33]

How To Pay for the War gave shape to the demand for the "conscription of riches" and embedded the capital levy in a broader programme of socialist

advance. As such, it marked a major advance in the theoretical and programmatic sophistication of the labour movement. By late 1917, however, it
became clear that the demand for a capital levy had an appeal far broader than
the normal constituency of working-class politics. Inevitably, the capital levy
came to be defended as a separate policy in and of itself. The most articulate
defence came from F.W. Pethick Lawrence, who premised his advocacy on the
inevitability of some "heroic" effort at debt reduction: "So cogent will prove
the hard logic of facts," he wrote in 1918, "that it is almost certain, in my
opinion, that whatever government is in power when the war is over, a levy on
capital will have to be resorted to." The precise amount to be raised by a levy,
Pethick Lawrence sensibly claimed, would depend upon the amount of debt
one wished to wipe out. He estimated that an average levy of 38 per cent –
which would in practice be graduated from an assessment of approximately 9
per cent on a capital of £1000 to a rate of 26 per cent at £10,000, 44 per cent at
£100,000 and 62 per cent at £1 million – would eliminate all of the debt. Lesser
levies would reduce a smaller portion of the debt. Pethick Lawrence assumed,
or at least argued, that all of the proceeds from the capital levy would go
towards reduction of the national debt and would hence lower debt service
charges. This would make possible a substantial reduction in the rate of income
tax. The complete elimination of the debt would allow the postwar tax rate to
be cut in half. The contrast with Webb, who envisioned a doubling of tax rates
after the war in addition to the capital levy, is clear. Already by 1918, it seems,
the capital levy had been shorn of at least some of its more radical
implications.[34]

Despite the concession to lower rates of income tax, even Pethick
Lawrence's tame version of the capital levy had disturbing implications. Most
important was its potential for advancing state ownership. Despite claims that
the capital levy would not diminish wealth, but merely redistribute it, it was
obvious that it would place a much greater share of the nation's wealth at the
disposal of the state, enough, as Pethick Lawrence suggested, so "as to make
the [state's] assets greater than or more nearly equal to its liabilities." The
transfer of wealth, moreover, would not for the most part take place in cash,
but rather in capital – in consols, war loan and other government securities, in
foreign and colonial securities, in shares in railways, ships, banks, insurance
companies and armaments firms, as well as trustee securities, other high-
quality stocks and bonds and certain sorts of landholdings. With the payment
of the capital levy, one official warned, the "state would become for the time
being a shareholder in all the limited liability undertakings in the country, a
partner in all the private enterprises and a part owner of all real property."
The effect of the capital levy would therefore be to give the government a
direct, material interest in major parts of the economy. This would facilitate
schemes for the nationalization of such industries as the railways and
armaments and would provide the government with leverage even in banking
and insurance. Whatever the ultimate disposal of these assets – and no

immediate selling off would be possible, for this would lower their value –
there would be substantial time and scope for the exercise of government
control over the economy.[35]

The capital levy had, therefore, quite dramatic implications both for the
distribution of wealth and for the role of the state – implications that
guaranteed the plan's ultimate defeat. That defeat was to be an essential part of
the broader conservative stabilization constructed in the immediate postwar
period. The boldness of the capital levy and the strength of its appeal testify,
however, to the near-revolutionary effect of the Great War upon the state,
upon public finances and upon the political system. They indicate as well the
dimensions of the task confronting those who wished to see the state shrunk
back to its prewar boundaries. And they point even more clearly to the pivotal
role that finance would play in the project of reshaping the relations between
state and society after the war.

Chapter 5

The state in war and reconstruction

WAR AND THE TRANSFORMATION OF THE STATE

War is the ultimate test of the state and, judging from the number of historic states that did not survive the Great War intact, it was a particularly arduous test. It was a new kind of war that employed new weapons and tactics, called for larger armies and required the systematic mobilization of domestic resources in order to supply and arm those military forces. It placed novel demands upon the state and forced a quick abandonment of "business as usual."[1] Meeting those demands meant a suspension of the normal workings of politics; in Britain, that meant the suspension of the two characteristic features of politics whose logic typically worked to block the expansion of the state. The constraints placed on policy innovation by the politics of taxation and by the predominance of the Treasury were effectively removed for the duration of the war and for some time after that. Neither the need to finance the war nor the compulsion to account carefully for funds spent on its prosecution would be allowed to dominate policy-making during 1914–18.

Freed from the normal constraints, the state grew enormously. The direction and extent of expansion were largely dictated by the need for manpower and for materiel and by the economic adjustments required to provide these. Theories about the proper sphere of public responsibility had little to do with the actual practice of state control. Rapidly, however, ideas about what the state could and should do began to alter in response to the changing reality of state power. The most visible transformation occurred in the thinking of the Labour party and the trade unions, who elaborated a much more collectivist programme during the war. Others also began to take the state more seriously and to develop plans to use or to frustrate its new capacity for social and economic intervention. Political discourse was transformed and a range of proposals for state action found a place on the political agenda. As a distinguished group of Conservatives put it in retrospect, "The war period shattered preconceived economic notions, removed irremovable barriers, and created new and undreamt of solutions."[2] Just what turn this discourse would take, and which proposals would remain on the agenda and, in some cases, be implemented would depend primarily on the political strength of their advocates. This, too, was altered by the war. War and mobilization disturbed the balance of political power between classes, interests and parties, allowing new groups to obtain representation within the charmed circle that largely determined public policy.

Before the war, the debate over the proper limits of state responsibility was dominated by a narrow group of political actors whose bargaining produced few innovations. The institutional complex of the Treasury, the Bank of England and the City was especially powerful, their vision of public finance and the limited state largely unchallenged. The preferences of voters may have been less consistently opposed to innovation, but their preferences were aggregated by parties whose organizational bases gave particular weight to propertied interests and whose programmes only grudgingly acknowledged social and economic need. Increasingly manufacturers saw their interests as best served by the Unionists, but the historic attachment of capital to Liberalism and to free trade left its mark on both the politics of business and the social orientation of the Liberals. The working class was, of course, the social presence looming threateningly over this fundamentally bourgeois system of representation, but its impact was indirect. Liberals and Conservatives both saw the need to compete for working-class votes and sought ways to adjust their programmes and rhetoric to that end. Adaptation was limited, however, by the parties'' prior links with middle- and upper-class interests and outlooks. Workers in any case had little input into the process and registered their opinions obliquely – through the collective organizations they had built, through the fledgling Labour party, through their votes and through industrial conflict.

The Great War shattered this system of representation and of policy-making. Within the state the Treasury lost control over finance and over the size and shape of the bureaucracy, and by dint of that the entire complex of Treasury, Bank and City became merely one of several competing centres of power. Party alignments also ceased to provide an adequate representation of interest or opinion. Asquith's government was able to carry on with Irish support for the first year of the war and opposition was muted by the "party truce" and by a genuine enthusiasm for the cause. The Conservatives took a further step towards eliminating party conflict by agreeing in May, 1915 to serve in a coalition under Asquith. The coalition continued until December, 1916 when it was replaced by a reconstructed Cabinet largely staffed by Unionists but led by Lloyd George. The combined effect of the electoral truce and years of coalition rule was an atrophy of debate and of party allegiance, compounded after 1916 by the open split among the Liberals. The Conservatives remained trapped in the negativism of 1910–14, and prevented by participation in the coalition from responding to the opportunity presented by the difficulties besetting the Liberals. Hence, the most visible consequence of the wartime transformation of politics was the rise of the Labour party, which began to fill up the political space vacated by the more progressive Liberals by positioning itself as the "people's" party. Less obvious, but perhaps as important, was the diversion of political activity from the normal channels of party competition into "direct action" or bargaining by organized interests within and against the state. The unions came to wield considerable power, and business became more organized and articulate. During the war, moreover, the state bureaucracy was itself transformed. Government expanded by incorporating representatives of business and labour and numerous technical experts and advocates. As Beatrice Webb commented in 1914, "The government is calling to its aid innumerable Committees – everyone who has any kind of reputation as a social reformer is on some Committee or other.' Gradually, the state itself therefore came to speak not with one voice, dominated by the Treasury and its orthodoxies, but with distinct voices, rival departmental agendas and divergent programmes. With the appointment of official committees to plan reconstruction in 1916 and 1917 and the creation, in July, 1917 of a separate Ministry of Reconstruction, the government gave formal sanction and encouragement to the wartime proliferation of proposals for increased state intervention in economy and society.[3]

The Ministry of Reconstruction would prove a keen disappointment to those who saw its work as ushering in a new era of reform. So, too, would the Ministry of Labour, set up with high hopes in late 1916. Still, the existence of these distinct centres of innovation within the machinery of government was testimony to the dramatic changes that had taken place in the British polity. The war had destroyed the fiscal and conceptual constraints on state expansion, had displaced the institutional embodiments of bureaucratic conservatism from the centre of policy-making and had given new clout to interests long excluded from high politics. The debate over the proper role of the state after the war would thus be fought out within a transformed political arena, and its outcome would remain very much in doubt for several years. By the mid-1920s, it would become clear that the postwar settlement had been achieved largely on terms favourable to the Treasury, the bankers and those who paid for government rather than those who might have benefited from its increased activity. It was a victory, however, that was achieved only slowly and painfully. To understand its roots, it is necessary to review briefly how the war changed the balance of power between the major competing interests – workers, employers and the state – and how the coming of peace altered that balance yet again.[4]

The most obvious point to make about the impact of the war upon workers, employers and the state was that it was extremely contradictory. In terms of living standards and conditions at work, the war was a very mixed affair for workers; in terms of political and industrial clout, it brought about immense gains. For businessmen, on the other hand, the political and economic effects were largely reversed: profits increased enormously, but politically businessmen were placed very much on the defensive. The war had an equally ambiguous impact upon the state itself, for while it greatly expanded its social and economic reach, it also increased the demands and expectations placed upon the state. The war thus made the state's successful functioning more dependent than ever before upon its ability to secure the consent of key groups in civil society. On balance, it would seem that the sum of economic and social changes stimulated by the war enhanced the cohesiveness and collective clout of working people more than that of other interests or of the state itself. It was undoubtedly this new-found strength that underlay the novel aggressiveness and self-confidence displayed by working men and women from 1917. This strength was manifested politically in the development of the Labour party, which grew in numbers, became increasingly well organized locally and elaborated a more thoughtful and appealing programme in the later stages of the war. Its industrial manifestation was even more impressive, as British workers launched the most massive wave of strikes and organizing in their history, largely in defiance of their officials. Labour therefore confronted the challenge of shaping the postwar order with vast new reserves of strength. Unfortunately, its greatest assets were those that could be deployed at the point of production and through "direct action," and it was far less effective at the level of national politics and party competition, which was the arena in which the contours of the postwar settlement were mostly fought out. Still, the Labour party and the unions could not be ignored even at this more exalted level of policy-making.

Employers were better positioned to influence high political deliberations, but they were by no means able to dominate the process. For employers, the war had brought both good news and bad. The good news was that business was booming and profits were up, the bad news was that the war brought with it a decisive reorientation in the relationship between business and the state. Before 1914, employers had virtually free rein inside their shops. They may have had difficulty exercising effective control over their skilled workers, but that was due not to interference from outside but to the structural weaknesses of British industry. With the coming of war, this freedom was sharply curtailed. As the dimensions of the effort needed to win the war gradually became clear to those in authority, they realized the necessity of a sustained and strenuous effort to direct the nation's material resources towards war production. This implied controls over labour, over the allocation of raw materials and over prices. Making these controls politically acceptable required that politicians also exert controls over businessmen's profits and their relations with workers.[5]

The imposition of controls proved difficult and politically explosive. The major difficulty was the absence of any mechanism to undertake the detailed supervision of economic activity. Government made good this lack by cobbling together an apparatus of control made up largely of those with expertise in the industries affected. This meant primarily businessmen, who constituted the primary membership of the District Armaments Committees set up in various regions.[6] Trade unionists were also called upon for government service, though more often than not they were involved in such things as the distribution of food and other necessities. However, they were also called upon to bargain away, for the duration of the war, shopfloor privileges and the right to strike. This they did in the famous Treasury Agreement of 1915, and the leaders of the unions spent much of the rest of the war trying to deliver on the promises made at that moment. As the spread of the "shop stewards" movement" and the mounting record of strikes suggest, they were largely unable to do so. On the contrary, the apparent co-option of the union officials pushed "rank-and-file" discontent into forms that were, if not quite revolutionary in their impact, at least very hard to control; and it arrayed ordinary workers behind more radical leaders who in normal times might have had rather more difficulty obtaining such a large following.

The authority of union officials was undermined in part by the widespread belief that businessmen were profiting tremendously during the war and that government intervention consistently favoured the interests of employers. Even well-placed officials felt that the government, led by Lloyd George at the Ministry of Munitions, had conjured up a quite justified antipathy among the workers. As Robert Morant explained in 1916, "the workers . . . are convinced that Ll-G [Lloyd George] is filled with vindictiveness against them and is trying to arrive at compulsory powers (via conscription) for smashing their industrial possibilities." This was ironic, for businessmen believed that the state sought to diminish their control. Whether or not their perceptions were entirely accurate, they felt that within the counsels of the state "The workmen's interests are paramount, and the masters" entirely neglected." As evidence they could point to the ready access of the Trades Union Congress to government ministers, the state's readiness to give in to demands for wage increases, for rent control and for restrictions on profits, the growth of union membership and the waxing power of the shop stewards and, perhaps most galling of all, the government's insistence that employers recognize and bargain with the unions.[7]

In response, businessmen developed a marked hostility to the state and its interventions and proceeded at the same time to create several political organizations reflecting this stance. The historic lack of concentration within British industry was reflected in its extreme political fragmentation prior to 1914. Employers had entered the war disorganized and had little time to get organized before the onset of serious government intervention. When that moment arrived, they felt themselves at a considerable disadvantage, particularly compared with the apparent strength of the unions. The perceived imbalance prompted repeated efforts, encouraged by government, to put together a national organization of businessmen. After considerable bargaining, the Federation of British Industries emerged in 1916 as the "peak organization" of British business. Even then, numerous employers and employers" associations, particularly the Engineering Employers' Federation, contested the FBI's right to speak on behalf of industry, especially on questions of industrial relations. The dispute led to the creation in 1919 of the National Conference of Employers' Organizations, which claimed sole responsibility for dealing with labour. Together, the formation of the FBI and the NCEO represented a real augmentation of the potential political clout of business. They did not manage to overcome the disunity characteristic of British industry, nor allow it to speak with a unified voice, but they did serve to magnify its volume in the strident debates about the shape of the postwar political economy and the role of the state within it.[8]

The organization of business had been stimulated in part by the need to deal with an expanding, mobilizing state. The vastly increased state machine created problems of control within the government as well. The imperatives of war production forced policy-makers to abandon the strict accounting of prewar and not to be deterred by cost. The War Office and the Admiralty were allowed to commit funds without prior approval and the new departments set up during the war, often run by outsiders from the business community, were built up rapidly and without the usual attention to organization and economy. As the Bradbury Committee on the Staffing of Government Offices subsequently explained, "During the war, general authorities have been given to many departments to appoint staffs at their discretion within wide limits." In consequence, "The permanent Civil Servants for the first time in their lives could settle their arrangements without reference to the Treasury. The business men, on the other hand, could settle their arrangements without reference to the need for paying their own way." The classic example was the Ministry of Munitions which, set up in June, 1915 with Lloyd George at its head, largely escaped traditional controls on personnel and procurement and even developed its own labour and welfare policies. The Ministry of Munitions was in fact virtually forced to innovate. It had to work closely with industry, and so Lloyd George recruited directly from business: by July, 1915 he boasted of having taken on "at least 90 men of first class business experience." It had also to assemble an enormous clerical staff at headquarters that by 1918 amounted to over 25,000. Given the shortage of male clerks, over 60 per cent of the staff were women. The high proportion of women employed directly in the ministry was replicated in the munitions factories. The ministry responded by the appointment of welfare officers and the elaboration of new welfare policies. All of this was new, and little of it met with Treasury approval.[9]

Munitions was the first major new department created during the war, but not the last. Lloyd George's coalition quickly set up separate ministries for labour, food, shipping and air. These departments were not entirely novel creations: Labour was hived off from Trade; and under Asquith there had been committees to co-ordinate food, shipping and air. Still, departmental status was not without bureaucratic meaning and the proliferation of state agencies allowed for further state expansion and enormously complicated the co-ordination of policy. Inevitably, therefore, the expansion of state control and of the state itself was accompanied by efforts towards integration and centralization. The Cabinet Secretariat, which had its origins in the secretariat for the Committee on Imperial Defence, grew under Maurice Hankey into a highly efficient office for handling the business of the Cabinet as a whole and, in particular, of the War Cabinet. Lloyd George also created his own small band of advisors, his "garden suburb," upon whose judgment he often relied.[10]

Neither device, however, was adequate to overcome the widespread feeling that the expanding government machine was out of control. As William Beveridge complained in 1917, "Not only the last Government, but the whole of the Civil Service is out of office." [11] The Treasury and its officials were particularly upset at the massive growth of the bureaucracy and at the financial expedients by which it had occurred, and never acquiesced in their loss of control. Nor did Parliamentary critics of bureaucracy, who demanded greater accountability, especially from the War Office and the Ministry of Munitions. During 1917–18 the Treasury began a protracted effort to re-establish control. Its objectives were furthered by the appointment in 1918 of a committee on the civil service to be chaired by John Bradbury, who ensured that it would endorse a return to economy and strict control of expenditure. The committee surveyed almost the entire array of departments and found them typically wanting in efficiency. The War Office and the Admiralty came in for strong criticism, though the new departments like pensions, food and national service elicited the strongest expressions of opprobrium. Predictably, the Committee recommended "that full Treasury control over the staffing of the Public Service should be resumed." [12] The famous Haldane Committee on the Machinery of Government also echoed the call for greater co-ordination by the Treasury.[13] For as long as the war went on these attempts to enforce the prewar standards of fiscal prudence were bound to fail, but after the signing of the armistice the dictates of orthodoxy would begin to make themselves felt again.

By the end of the war, therefore, there had arisen a new state in Britain, enlarged by the novel tasks imposed upon it and entangled in society and economy to an unprecedented degree. Reviewing the wartime growth of the state, an official account described how "In common with all belligerents . . . this country has, since August, 1914 moved steadily along the road of an ever-extending State control of industry . . . As the military struggle developed in scope and intensity . . . section after section of industry was taken over . . . The process of extending State control, taking over more works and applying it to an always widening range of products, continued unbroken right up to the end of 1916." With the change of government in December, 1916 the advance of state control went several steps further and 1917 turned out to be "the year in which State control was extended until it covered not only national activities directly affecting the military effort but every section of industry – production, transport and manufacture." By the end of the war, twelve new departments and 160 new boards and commissions had been set up; and the number of civilians employed by the central government had increased by over half a million – from under 325,000 in 1914 to better than 850,000 in 1918. The limited state was but a memory.[14]

It was to prove a very enticing memory and not a few officials and politicians would spend the decade after the war trying to recreate the reality upon which it was based. To others, however, the new state was a sign of progress and there could be no going back. The War Cabinet itself regarded the expansion of government as a display of virtue and resolve: "These developments," they wrote, "have been the result of the determination of the people to leave nothing undone which could contribute to the winning of the war. None the less," they happily proceeded, "they are bound to produce lasting and far-reaching effects on the social and economic life of the community." The practical advance of collectivism had been accompanied, in fact, by the elaboration of a compelling discourse of community and citizenship. The War Cabinet, for example, was moved to argue that "the organic life of the community has been strengthened" by the extension of state intervention. The rhetoric surrounding the Ministry of Reconstruction struck the same chords and was premised upon the notion that the changes brought about by the war were but a starting point for further reform: "It is indeed becoming more and more apparent that reconstruction is not so much a question of rebuilding society as it was before the war, but of moulding a better world out of the social and economic conditions which have come into being during the war." [15]

THE POLITICS OF RECONSTRUCTION

The government itself was thus deeply ambivalent about its future, and the self-denying propensity of the prewar state was not much in evidence. The changed character of the state ensured that the question of its role in society and economy would be central to postwar stabilization, and it likewise guaranteed that the debate would be contentious and its outcome uncertain. For not only was the state less monolithic than before, but the system of political representation was more open to influences that had been excluded prior to 1914. Not all the new political forces were equally powerful and effective, however, for they came out of the war with different capacities and the peculiar conditions of postwar altered the resources available to various interests yet further. The agenda of politics also changed decisively with the end of the war, and the plans and programmes worked out during the war were no longer appropriate. Labour was particularly adversely affected. The unions were much more powerful industrially, but they were largely unable to project their industrial clout into politics. Their industrial strength, moreover, would last only as long as the demand for labour remained strong. When that collapsed in 1920, the ability of unions to battle employers was seriously undercut. Unemployment also confounded the Labour party, whose 1918 programme was not well suited to a period of retrenchment. The shift from wartime economic boom to postwar depression thus gravely weakened the industrial and political clout of working people.

Business and banking also suffered economically, but were strengthened politically by postwar developments. The short boom that followed the war encouraged a wave of investment, most notably in the older staple industries. When the boom collapsed, industrialists found themselves burdened with excessive capacity, large debts and higher wage bills. Their reaction was to cut employment and wages, thereby threatening most of the gains extracted by workers during 1917–19. The employers met considerable resistance in their efforts, but in the prolonged battle with the unions they also had the advantage of their new-found collective strength. Together with the collapse in the market for labour and selective intervention by the state, the employers prevailed in their confrontations with the unions. The experience of war had also provided the background for a change in the structure of banking, reflected in a rash of bank amalgamations that climaxed in 1917–18. Banking emerged from the process far more concentrated than before, and also rather more deeply implicated in domestic industry than had been the case before 1914. The bankers' interests were thereby implicated in the employers' efforts to shed workers and lower wages, and the clout of the banking community was, if anything, increased by its restructuring.[16]

The position of the Bank of England was also strengthened. In the early stages of the war the Bank had lost ground to the Treasury in the management of internal and external finance and had been forced to acquiesce in a variety of distasteful financial expedients. The Bank had also suffered from the personal idiosyncrasies of its Governor, Lord Cunliffe – "an exceptionally assertive brow-beating type" who was thought by some to have become, by 1918, "a dangerous and insane colleague."[17] Cunliffe quarrelled with Reginald McKenna and Bonar Law, who succeeded Lloyd George as Chancellor, and by the spring of 1918 had been removed from office. Virtually his last act, however, was to chair the currency committee which began the process of restoring orthodoxy and the Bank's authority. The Cunliffe Committee reviewed the financial history of the war and recommended that the country return to the principles of the prewar gold standard "at the earliest possible date." For that to happen, the committee argued, "It is essential that as soon as possible the State should not only live within its income but should begin to reduce its indebtedness." This endorsement of orthodoxy represented a rejection of all serious plans for reconstruction and gave a clear lead to the City to resist the continued expansion of the state. The restoration of the gold standard may not have been in the objective interests of manufacturing, let alone that of the nation as a whole, but in 1918 there was a broad consensus in the business community on the need to return to gold in order to revive trade and industry as well as to shore up Britain's position in world finance. Implied in the commitment to gold was, of course, a set of highly restrictive fiscal policies whose impact would become especially oppressive with the trade depression of the early 1920s and would prompt manufacturers to break with the bankers over the priority accorded to debt reduction in public finance. Still, the main postwar response of industry and finance, of big business and small, was to mobilize against expenditure and against the state.[18]

Out of the war, therefore, there began to emerge a consensus among bankers, manufacturers and men of commerce that the state should be shrunk back to its former size, spending cut and taxes drastically reduced. This anti-state sentiment, this "widespread organic resistance to change," was shared by much of the middle class, who felt oppressed by taxation and by high prices and who viewed the novel pretensions of labour with apprehension.[19] They responded with expressions of anger over waste and extravagance and with grassroots organization against rates, taxes and the encroachments of the state. Perhaps the most visible manifestation of middle-class *ressentiment* was the foundation in May, 1919 of the Middle Classes Union. "When Capital and Labour went to Downing Street," a leading spokesman complained, "they were invited into the parlour at once, and soon had the government kowtowing and touching its cap to them." The goal of the new organization was to right the balance by creating a "movement which would bring to bear upon the Government the just and due influence which ought to belong to the middle classes."[20] The middle classes were active as ratepayers, as supporters of the Anti-Waste campaign waged by the press, and even as volunteer strike-breakers. Theirs was hardly a co-ordinated movement, and the confused character of party politics forced it to take even more unusual forms than might otherwise have been the case, but it added considerable social weight to the resistance to reconstuction, reform and the expansion of the state.[21]

The economic context of postwar thus shifted yet again the relative strength of those arrayed for and against an enlarged role for the state. During the war events had conspired to expand the state directly and to give greater representation to those seeking its further growth; after the war the economic crisis eroded the industrial clout of labour, toughened the resistance of the middle and upper classes and privileged the input of traditional, particularly financial, interests. The outcome of the postwar stabilization would largely be determined by the new social and political balance in place by late 1920. It was fought out between 1920 and 1926 on several different levels, though the most dramatic confrontations took place within industry and culminated in the defeat of the General Strike in 1926. Less riveting but equally consequential battles were joined over monetary policy leading to the return to gold in 1925, a discussion closed to the many but also of enormous import.[22]

Rather larger numbers of ordinary citizens were engaged in the reshaping of party alignments, though much of the action was confined to a very small elite of politicians and political journalists.[23] So long as Lloyd George was secure as the head of the coalition government and the *de facto* leader of the "anti-socialist front," the scope for party politics was limited. The Conservatives thus found themselves in the anomalous position of numerical dominance but political weakness; and their supporters became extremely restive from early 1921. They finally rid themselves of Lloyd George in 1922 and politics began to flow in normal channels once again. Even so, the Conservatives were regularly troubled by revolts, or rumours of revolts, from discontented ratepayers or industrialists who had difficulty fully trusting the Tory leadership. The troubles besetting the Liberals were even more daunting, and the party continued its slide to impotence throughout the 1920s.[24] It remained the political home, however, for an important segment of opinion that, but for their distaste of workers, might have been added to the forces supporting a more activist state and more enlightened social and economic policies. Labour, of course, continued to grow, but it was still a long way from being able to hold power on its own. In party political terms, therefore, stability could only be achieved by making Conservative hegemony the norm and by keeping Labour on a short leash.

· There were also more direct battles over taxes and over the shape and control of the state. The debate over taxes was especially complicated, for the proponents of orthodoxy faced simultaneous challenges from two different directions. The middle classes, businessmen especially, were driven to demand lower taxes regardless of the dictates of fiscal responsibility or the consequences for the state's credit. Labour and the unions, by contrast, wanted to guarantee the state's creditworthiness by getting control of the nation's wealth through the capital levy. These were highly unorthodox proposals. Orthodoxy was represented, of course, by the Treasury and its allies in the City. For the City and the Treasury the questions of the debt and the level of expenditure were closely connected with the broader issue of Britain's position in the international economy. Before the war London was the world's leading financial centre, but the war rendered that status quite precarious. In particular, the suspension of the gold standard meant that the future role of sterling as the world's leading currency was very much in doubt; so, as a corollary, was the future prosperity of the City. The abandonment of the gold standard had domestic implications as well. Before the war currency convertibility guaranteed fiscal rectitude; and movements of money served both to signal the response of financial markets to government policy and actually to force governments to follow fiscally responsible courses of action. With the gold standard in abeyance, there was no automatic check on spending.

This was deeply worrying to officials at the Treasury, who had also lost their institutional capacity to control government expenditure, and to the City. There were thus powerful interests behind the decision to return to gold as soon as possible. It would prove impossible to do this prior to 1925, however, for it required a prolonged deflation to bring British prices close enough to American ones to allow for convertibility. In the meantime, it was essential to restore the nation's credit by balancing the budget. That could only be done by keeping taxes high, for expenditure had grown enormously during the war. 'Notoriously war begets extravagance,' R.G. Hawtrey would claim in retrospect, but just how much war had increased expenditure was at first little understood.[25] By 1917–18, though, it was becoming clear that the war had imposed upon Britain not merely a much heavier tax load but an enormous weight of debt, which would make it impossible to reduce taxation for the foreseeable future. The prospect of continued high taxes provoked a renewed interest in taxation, and again called into question many of the issues that seemed settled by 1914 and placed at the top of the agenda of high politics the question of who was to pay for the long-term costs of the war. The size of the debt was in fact enormous by contemporary and historic standards. Taxation during 1914–18 covered only a quarter of the costs of war. Critics of government finance pointed out with justice that an earlier recognition of the demands of total war and a readier resort to taxing the wealthy would have left less of a debt. The government could claim on its behalf that no one understood the dimensions of the war or its likely final cost and that they had pushed progressive taxes to levels higher than anyone had thought possible before 1914. In either case, there was no disputing the figures at the end of the war: the total national debt had swelled from £650 million to over £7800 million, an amount roughly equivalent to the cumulative deficit on the wartime budgets of over £7000 million. Interest on the debt, which had been only £18.7 million in 1913, skyrocketed to more than £320 million in 1920 and would remain at about £300 million for the next decade. Throughout the 1920s debt service consumed over 20 per cent of government expenditure and approximately 5 per cent of GNP. Paying for the war debt was not the only reason for continued high levels of taxation, however. In addition to the debt, the government had to find the money for war pensions totalling £105 million in 1920, decreasing over the decade to about half that level. Expenditure on social services had also roughly doubled between 1913 and the postwar era. It had taken about a third of government spending in 1913, was shrunk back to less than 10 per cent during the war, but would recover to just over a third (of a total budget that was twice as large as prewar) in the 1920s. Virtually every other category of government expenditure increased proportionally as well, ensuring that total spending after 1918 would never amount to less than a quarter of GNP.[26]

The pressures pushing up spending after the war were thus very strong. They would also prove extremely resilient, even in the face of sustained efforts to contain them. The Treasury, for its part, was determined not to allow the wartime increases in spending to become permanent. They insisted on regarding the increased expenditure as exceptional and temporary and continued after the war to budget for what they termed the "normal year," defined basically in terms of the level of taxation and expenditure prevailing in 1914. The Treasury in this way set as their goal the restoration of prewar levels of government activity and social provision and set themselves against further innovations in policy. They also began immediately to sound the alarm over increased expenditure. In July, 1919 Otto Niemeyer of the Treasury warned that the combined costs of war debts and coalition promises would bankrupt the state and urged in response a public campaign for economy. "It is very commonly held," he claimed, "that the enormous financial effort of the war proves that we can continue to spend on a very large scale without serious damage, or even with advantage." That misconception had quickly to be countered.[27]

The requirement to educate the populace to the need for economy was itself sufficient reason for making sure that increases in expenditure were covered by increases in taxation. Treasury officials continued to believe, as had Gladstone, in "the educative effect of direct taxation placed on as large a part of the community as possible." The Board of Inland Revenue held that such a policy was rooted in the national character: as they saw it, "What may be called the 'Tax psychology' of Anglo-Saxon countries, particularly in Britain, differs markedly from that of Latin countries . . . The Anglo-Saxon wants, as a general rule, to know what taxes he is paying. The Latin does not; he prefers to have them served as powder in the jam." The political consequence of keeping before the Anglo-Saxon public its bill for state services was supposed to be a resolution to reduce both the services and the bill. It was essential, then, not to disguise the extent of indebtedness or the taxes needed to meet it. The appointment of the Royal Commission on the Income Tax in 1919–20, with its mandate to rationalize the tax without giving up any revenues, made it clear that the government shared the outlook of its officials. They assumed that taxes would be maintained at a high level and hoped to find a system that would be based on "the best possible scale for fitting the burden to the back." [28]

The search for a system that would bear the vastly increased burden of postwar taxation was difficult, but preferable to the alternative. The alternative, of course, was borrowing – which was not only anathema to the Treasury, the Inland Revenue and the City, but which also threatened the stabilization programme centred on the return to gold. Sir Basil Blackett of the Treasury put the case forcefully in 1922: "Most of the economic and social ills of today . . . are in large part due to the inability or unwillingness of foreign Governments to meet their expenditure out of taxation . . . It would come as a terrible shock to the world to see Great Britain budgeting for a deficit." The economic effects would be both a "serious loss of credit" for the government and difficulties "for the London Market." "The political dangers of borrowing to cover ordinary expenditure" would be as devastating as the economic effects, Blackett warned: "Once admit that expenditure can proceed without relative taxation and the floodgates are opened. Why not reduce income tax to the pre-War level and make good the loss out of the newly-found gold mine?" "The ultimate end of the new system," he concluded, "is so clearly either a confiscatory levy on capital or a repudiation of the Government's internal debt . . . that the Labour extremists could hardly wish for better." [29]

The Treasury and the City would therefore coalesce behind a set of policies that included a relatively high level of taxation and "dear money," the net effect of which was a sustained lowering of prices and a slowdown of economic activity. The resulting deflation, however, was disastrous for British manufacturers – simultaneously reducing demand and increasing the burden of their debts. The political consequence was a considerable increase in the tension between industry and the City, and that antagonism carried over from monetary to fiscal policy. Repeatedly, representatives of industry would be led to protest the high rates of postwar taxation. In so doing they placed themselves in opposition to the policies of the Treasury and the City, both of which favoured the continuation of reasonably high rates of taxation so as to maintain fiscal responsibility and restore investor confidence. Businessmen were sufficiently upset to propose, if it were necessary to lower taxes, the suspension of the sinking fund, whose status was sacrosanct to orthodox opinion. On the other side the Bank of England and various City interests were moved to propose increases in income tax and super-tax to meet the crisis. An April, 1920 memo from Montagu Norman to the Chancellor called for temporarily imposing super-tax on lower incomes and increasing the standard rate. The City's willingness to sacrifice the interests of business and the middle class is striking testimony to the panic prompted by the postwar financial crisis and to the self-interested and fragmented responses to which it gave rise.[30]

WHO WILL PAY?

The early postwar years were thus marked by frantic efforts of interested groups to escape from the increased tax burdens or to shift them onto others. Businessmen were especially active, partly because of their increased liabilities but partly because they were much better organized than before the war. Not infrequently they caused embarrassment to their traditional allies in the Conservative party. Thus Sir Leslie Scott, Conservative MP and Solicitor General, was forced to fight a by-election in 1922 during which, as he complained to the Chancellor, Sir Robert Horne, he was attacked on issues of "economy" by local Conservative activists. They had been organized, it turned out, by the Federation of British Industries (FBI) and the Association of British Chambers of Commerce (ABCC), who called in March, 1922 for demonstrations to demand "a substantial reduction of Taxation."[31] Businessmen also besieged the Chancellor, especially in the period just before the budget, with deputations from the FBI, the Chambers of Commerce, the National Union of Manufacturers and a variety of self-styled defenders of the taxpayer. They argued vehemently for economy and against taxation, coupling these broad statements with detailed complaints about specific forms of tax. The excess profits duty elicited a particular antipathy.[32]

Not all such claims were well received by the government. Austen Chamberlain, for example, was noticeably irritated by the demands put forward by the National Union of Manufacturers at their meeting of 19 May

1920, and told them curtly that "I can always get suggestions from Deputations to tax somebody else, I have not asked for that." Nor did he wish to hear any more about the excess profits tax: he dared the NUM to "upset the Government if you can" but he would not be moved to repeal it. It would be hard to regard such an encounter as a success, but even rather testy meetings such as this must have been of some benefit to businessmen. They served to signal officials as to the limits of their toleration for taxes and both the Treasury and the Inland Revenue were highly sensitive to the potential of tax resistance. Officials, in fact, argued repeatedly against levies that might be resented and avoided by taxpayers. Thus the Inland Revenue seems to have been convinced by late 1920, presumably by groups like the NUM, that "The present hostility of business men towards the Excess Profits Duty and the uncertainty of its duration must, it is suggested, greatly aggravate the inherent defects of the tax." [33]

Most meetings, it seems, went more smoothly than the one on 19 May 1920, and successive Chancellors seem to have become very adept at telling deputations what they wanted to hear. Churchill was especially good at echoing businessmen's concern for economy. Officials also developed a sense of whose complaints needed to be taken seriously. By the mid-1920s, for example, they knew that representations from the FBI were of inherently greater moment than those from the Chambers of Commerce, and they were presumably even less likely to take heed of the complaints of such fringe groups as the Middle Classes Union (later the Income Tax Payers Society) or the League to Enforce Economy.[34] What is most striking overall about official attitudes, however, is the contrast between the solicitous approach taken by officials towards the taxpayer in general and towards businessmen in their capacity as taxpayers and their rather unsympathetic stance toward industry as a particular sector of the economy.

This contrast was revealed most clearly in the debate in the early 1920s on the impact of taxes upon the economy. Merchants and manufacturers claimed repeatedly that high tax levels dampened economic activity. As one businessman put it in September, 1921, "the heavy burden of direct taxation . . . was rapidly crushing out the commercial life of the trading and manufacturing community." The "grinding nature of existing taxation," he went on, "stifled enterprise, drove capital from the country and made the life of the manufacturer and trader almost intolerable." [35] To most businessmen such claims were self-evidently true and there was no need to adduce evidence from beyond their own experience. There was a parallel debate of a somewhat more theoretical nature on whether Britain had exhausted its "taxable capacity." Reginald McKenna, a strong advocate of reduced taxation, admitted that it was difficult to determine the precise limit to which taxes could be pushed, but felt that, as of 1922, "We cannot shut our eyes to the signs that our present taxation has probably exceeded this limit." [36] The argument over "taxable capacity" had a considerable impact on public opinion, helping to reshape the debate over tax policy. As the Cabinet Committee on Taxation realized, "the continual reference of speakers and writers to the subject [of taxable capacity] is probably influencing the public mind against new forms of taxation." The effect outside Cabinet was noticeable as well. Philip Snowden, for example, felt the need to trim Labour's proposals for taxation and expenditure to fit within the estimates set out by McKenna, all the while protesting that this limit "by no means exhausts the taxable capacity of the country." [37]

Sir Robert Horne, Chancellor of the Exchequer during 1921–2, was even more impressed and found himself in considerable sympathy with business claims for relief. He was struck, too, by the apparent coincidence of high taxation and industrial depression. He asked his officials to investigate alternative sources of revenue and to report on the burden of taxation to industry. They produced a remarkable document, "Industry and the Weight of Taxation," that was quite dismissive of the businessmen's case. The officials maintained that income tax might possibly slow the rate at which industry expanded, but would not produce a decline in economic activity. High rates of tax would, of course, reduce savings somewhat, but this would likely be offset by a "counter-current, for by diminishing personal spending power it inevitably stimulates a large number of individuals to new and greater earning activities in order that they may not lose their present and prospective standards of living and saving." Nor, they concluded, did taxes have a serious effect on prices, for "Prices are determined by forces quite independent of, and exclusive of, taxation." "It is a common delusion of business men that they can and do add Income Tax to their costs, but on examination it invariably appears that it is not in fact done." Rather, prices were set by competition. Even the taxation used to service the national debt does not disappear but instead "returns to the community as war loan repayment and interest, and . . . is available for the service of industrial capital requirements." In sum, the report concluded that "the common talk of taxation of industry is full of fallacies." Officials were particularly unimpressed by the claim that taxation reduced incentive and led to a " 'de-energizing' of enterprise": as R.G. Hawtrey wrote at the time, "it is hardly plausible to suppose that people *usually* prefer to escape Income Tax by escaping income." [38]

One reason for the resistance of the Treasury and the Inland Revenue to the arguments from business was that they led directly to proposals to shift the tax burden towards indirect taxes and hence onto the shoulders of others. The agitation over taxable capacity and taxation's ill effects upon the economy had in fact convinced Horne of the desirability of reducing income tax and substituting various indirect taxes to make up for the lost revenue. Horne's request to officials to study the impact of taxation on industry had been coupled with a request for advice on the feasibility of introducing or increasing other taxes: including taxes on "semi-luxuries" like liquor, tobacco, entertainments and betting and genuine luxuries like furs; on foodstuffs like tea, sugar and skimmed milk; on bicycles and matches; as well as more general taxes on advertising, on "turnover," on auction sales and on tourism. Officials at the Treasury and the Inland Revenue were highly suspicious of Horne's zeal for replacing direct with indirect, "fancy" taxes and could see little more than "a selfish claim for its individual interest" behind the economic arguments put forward by industry.[39]

The identification of virtually all of "industry" as an "individual interest" is a telling reminder of industry's enduring lack of clout within the counsels of the state even after the formation of two new national organizations of business, the FBI and the NCEO. This disjunction between industry and the state was, of course, almost a structural feature of the British polity, a feature with a recurring impact on tax policy. It would manifest itself repeatedly between the wars in the form of an unwillingness on the part of the Treasury to support proposals to use tax benefits to stimulate industrial investment. Such uses, officials routinely argued, were inherently discriminatory and as such would undermine the fairness of the tax system.[40] The indifference of the Treasury and the Inland Revenue to industry, as opposed to the "taxpaying classes" in general, would be demonstrated again in the debates before the Colwyn Committee on National Debt and Taxation, which sat between March, 1924 and November, 1926. The arguments developed by officials in response to Horne's initiative of 1921–2 were refined and restated with considerable force to the committee. W.H. Coates of the Inland Revenue, for example, began his testimony by claiming the sanction of economic theory for the position taken by officials: there were, he said, two views on the question of the incidence of taxation, "the one consistent with the main body of economic doctrine, and the other instinctive to ordinary business men." As in 1922, the instincts of the businessmen were wrong. On the impact of taxes on consumer prices, for instance, Coates had "been unable to find any reasonable evidence in support of the business man's view." Nor was he inclined to believe "that the existing rate of income taxation has a harmful effect upon the supply of permanent capital" or acted "as a deterrent to saving generally or to enterprise." Instead, as Lord Bradbury went on to point out, "repayment of debt out of Income Tax probably stimulates saving." The committee's report was drafted largely by Sir Josiah Stamp who, despite a business background, shared the officials" contempt for "business instinct." Not surprisingly, it concluded that it would "be difficult to maintain the view that as a whole the enterprise of the wealthy business man is seriously damaged" by existing high rates of income tax. Equally unsurprising was the hostile reception accorded to the Colwyn Report by businessmen, who felt utterly betrayed by the official lack of sympathy for their plight.[41]

If the complaints and counterproposals of businessmen could not force a shift in tax policy, it might well be assumed that the demands of labour would have had even less effect. But in fact the postwar strength of labour, both as a party and as an industrial movement, made a considerable impact on tax policy. Fear of working-class hostility was largely responsible for preventing governments from relying more heavily upon indirect taxes to fund the war and the postwar debt. Working-class unrest during the war had been directed overwhelmingly at the rising prices that accompanied war mobilization, and the containment of that unrest involved the government in setting prices and rents and ensuring the distribution of necessities. Indirect taxes, especially on food, would counteract those policies by raising prices and might well intensify discontent. Workers' resistance to taxes on consumption was, of course, merely an extension of the Liberal opposition to protection, but working-class organizations were extremely active during the war in arguing against any taxes, including increased insurance contributions, that would fall upon the workers. The head of the boilermakers wrote to Lloyd George in 1917, for example, "to warn the Government that we are prepared to meet with drastic action, any further taxation of the working class." Such threats managed in November, 1917 to extract from Bonar Law, the then Chancellor, a promise not to impose further taxes on the workers. In a revealing monologue, Law explained: "as a matter of prophecy I would venture to say this, that the political conditions which prevail in this country will be of such a nature that the burden of this [wartime] taxation is not likely to fall on the wage earners as long as there is wealth which can be made to pay it; that is my own view. I think there is little danger from your point of view, of the great bulk of it not continuing to be paid in the same way as the war itself is being paid for." The Labour party and the TUC continued to argue against the taxation of working people throughout the 1920s, and the fear of what higher prices would do to industrial relations was at least one major factor in predisposing officials to reject business proposals for higher indirect taxes in 1922.[42]

Not only was the labour movement capable of shielding its own from the imposition of further taxation, it also came very close to succeeding in having the greater portion of the cost of the war shifted onto the upper classes by means of the capital levy. Its viability and popularity were indicated by the virulent opposition it provoked among businessmen and the wealthy. They understood that it was directed against them as a class, and they reacted in a united fashion against it. On this issue the City and industry collaborated, and capital spoke with one voice. Delegation after delegation of businessmen visited the Chancellor and the Prime Minister and made clear their opposition. As the Select Committee on the Increase of Wealth (War) conceded, "the tax is strongly opposed by the financial and commercial world." The press was equally hostile, with numerous spokesmen for capital emerging full of reasons why the capital levy was unworkable and, if made feasible by some clever bureaucrats, nevertheless evil. The most consistent argument focused on the promise that the levy would not be repeated. As one writer argued insightfully in 1918, "If a levy is justifiable to pay for killing Germans, why not also to save British children and their parents by giving them a healthy environment? Peace has her emergencies no less than war. The greatest happiness of the greatest number would cover a multitude of levies."[43] In a more popular vein *The Economist* of 3 August 1918 had recourse to a sexual analogy: "There have been women who never had an affair of gallantry. There never was a woman who had only one." The returns on a second or third or later capital levy, in short, would prove too great a temptation for future governments. And in the short term, capital did not want even a first attempt at confiscation.

Inland Revenue officials were particularly moved by the scale and intensity of business opposition. They remembered how taxpayer resistance had frustrated the assessment of the Land Value Duties and feared that "the Department entrusted with . . . [implementing the Capital Levy] might be brought down by organized opposition fastening on every legal technicality." They worried, too, about the reaction of the City and its impact on the government's continued ability to borrow: "So long as the City believes (either rightly or wrongly) that the scheme represents the end of the world . . . the City atmosphere might easily induce, upon the announcement of a heavy Capital Levy, such a landslide in capital values and such a hold up of credit as would constitute a national disaster." More precisely, such a reaction would make it impractical to impose a levy "while the Government is desiring to borrow on any scale." Officials at the Inland Revenue thus took it upon themselves to protect the taxpayers by stressing the enormous administrative costs of the levy and and by consistently underestimating its possible returns. To officials at the Inland Revenue, moreover, the taxpayers' interests encompassed far more than a certain level of taxation; they involved as well a set of norms and relationships governing the imposition and collection of taxes. In a curiously revealing report on the capital levy in France, the Board boasted in 1919 of the advanced and scientific character of the tax system in Britain. A capital levy might not be "unnatural in France where the development of scientific taxation has been retarded," but in Britain, which "has possessed a scientific Income Tax for upwards of a century," it would be a step backwards. As the Inland Revenue saw it, "A General Property Tax as a main tax represents historically an early, even a primitive, stage in the evolution of direct taxation, while the Income Tax represents its final stage." Among other virtues, the British system of direct taxation was based upon a history of co-operation between officials and taxpayers. This would be jeopardized by a capital levy that would require a new set of assessments carried out by, as the Board put it, "an army of highly trained officials, backed up by another army of expert valuers' and by yet "another army of officials . . . [who would] . . . arrange the transfers of assets" from the taxpayers to the state.[44]

The Inland Revenue therefore needed no prompting from taxpayers to oppose the capital levy. As early as 1917 the Board's two top officials, Nott-Bower and Fisher, explained to the Chancellor that "We find it difficult to conceive any advantage to the State from the substitution of this cumbrous proposal for the existing system of taxing property and income," certainly nothing that could outweigh the losses that would result from the insecurity and dislocation created by a capital levy. At this point, it seems, the Inland Revenue hoped to make do with increases in death duties to fund the debt and ordinary expenditure after the war and were a long way from contemplating the sort of radical tax policy implied in the capital levy. By 1919, however, the Inland Revenue had been forced by continued public interest in the levy and by its own investigations to conclude that the capital levy was indeed technically feasible. Even then, of course, they claimed it would generate only £1000 million and that the effort required to get that amount would surpass "in difficulty any previous effort at taxation." They also hinted at the possibility of massive taxpayer resistance and warned of its consequences: "No tax of this magnitude could be effectively imposed unless it were accepted by the great majority of taxpayers as a fair though onerous burden." Since it would appear that the officials at the Inland Revenue did not themselves regard the capital levy as a "fair" imposition, it was unlikely that taxpayers would be convinced of its fairness.[45]

The heartfelt resistance of business to the capital levy, particularly as it percolated through the Conservative party and sympathetic sections of the bureaucracy, would ultimately prevail and prevent the imposition of the tax. But it would take a decade to put the proposal to rest. The main reason for that delay was the surprising sympathy with which the demand for a capital levy was met on the part of at least some politicians, many economists and even certain Treasury officials. There was, for example, considerable support for the capital levy among economists: Keynes, Dalton, Pigou and Edgeworth, among others, thought it a good idea. Had economists as a group enjoyed more status as government advisors during this period, or had they more ready access to policy-making, their support might have made more of a difference. As it was, the support for the capital levy among economists was of rather less political consequence than was the more ambivalent, and unexpected, support given the notion by politicians and Treasury officials. What attracted some officials, particularly at the Treasury, was the prospect of using the levy to re-establish the state's credit on a firm basis. Traditionally, the Treasury and the banking community had a close, indeed symbiotic, relationship. During the war, however, the terms of that relationship had shifted decisively in the banks' favour. The government was forced to borrow funds on increasingly bad terms, whose effects would be felt in budgets for a long time to come. Reducing the debt could restore the bargaining position of the Treasury vis-à-vis the banks and, by dint of that, the Treasury's dominant role within the state: as one recent study has suggested, "Only by reducing the floating debt, and thus denying the banks the power they exercised over Treasury bills, could the Treasury regain greater control of the economy." The capital levy therefore appealed to many officials on quite traditional grounds.[46]

Of course, the prospect of a confiscatory levy was not intrinsically appealing to the Treasury, nor were its political implications. But a levy was a powerful device for raising revenue that exerted a considerable attraction on desperate officials. The Treasury tended, as a result, to be torn between distaste for the radicalism of the capital levy and its "socialist parentage" and grudging respect for its fiscal potential. In this they mirrored the ambivalence of politicians like Bonar Law who, for instance, wished that the capital levy "could be looked upon simply as a fiscal measure without the prejudice involved in it by the fact that the Labour Party are putting it forward for the express purpose if not of confiscating capital at least of making it pay for every kind of social reform." The reaction of Bradbury at the Treasury was equally tortured. Asked to comment on the feasibility of a capital levy as a fiscal measure, Bradbury wrote apologetically to Austen Chamberlain that "I am afraid the memorandum reads rather like an argument in favour of a capital levy – for which of course," he went on, "the present time is not opportune." However distasteful an imposition it might prove to be, officials were forced to concede, as Stanley Baldwin would subsequently admit, that the "Capital Levy is a perfectly legitimate form of taxation." To grant the legitimacy of the capital levy was to acknowledge that the proposal to impose it had somehow got onto the political agenda. That was no mean feat, and probably could not have happened had the political establishment as a whole – in particular the leaders of the Conservative party and officials at the Treasury – rejected it out of hand. But they hesitated, wavered and, in effect, refused to rule it out of practical consideration. This surprising openness combined with the strong support for a capital levy from Labour and from the public more broadly to force policy-makers to give it serious consideration. The capital levy remained central to the discussion of taxation throughout the 1920s, dominated the election of 1922 and was critical in pushing Stanley Baldwin to opt for tariffs as an alternative.[47]

Getting onto the agenda of high politics did not mean that the capital levy would be put into effect. It was, in its essence, a threat to the security of capital and it would indeed have represented a dangerous precedent. As the social unrest that greeted the war's end ebbed in 1920, so, too, did support for the capital levy, though even as late as March, 1920 at least some Treasury officials remained open to the idea of a levy and saw it as possibly aiding their efforts at deflation. The Select Committee on War Wealth Duties, chaired by the Liberal Sir William Pearce, delivered a split verdict later in the spring, but support was slipping away. Businessmen continued to lobby hard against the levy, as did Conservative Central Office. In April the Governor of the Bank of England, Montagu Norman, weighed in on the same side, urging instead a higher standard rate of tax and the extension of super-tax liability further down the income scale. By June, Sir Josiah Stamp had switched over into opposition, and the Cabinet were moved to reject the proposal. Austen Chamberlain summarized the key consideration when he said, "I confess I fear the unreasoning fear of the City." Bonar Law gave voice to the same concerns, but expressed them more politically: "You cannot neglect the supporters of the Government, and they are also the people on whom the permanent commercial prosperity of the country depends."[48]

By 1921, the Liberals had also come out against the levy and joined in opposing what was increasingly seen as a Labour plan. Labour continued to press for a levy and took its case to the country in 1922. Though the party increased its vote, the election returned a Conservative government led by Bonar Law. Defeat convinced some Labour leaders – Clynes and Snowden in particular – to downplay the demand for a capital levy, and Baldwin's decision to fight the 1923 election on tariffs diverted attention away from Labour's commitment to the capital levy.[49] The Labour government of 1924, with only minority support in the House of Commons, obviously was unable to proceed with such a controversial measure as the capital levy and instead set up the Colwyn Committee. For the next three years the debate was largely contained within the discussions in and around that committee.

The appointment of the Colwyn Committee therefore served several purposes. It provided a forum within which to air the grievances that had surrounded tax policy since the war while it allowed governments to put off any serious changes. Its appointment signalled the winding down of the bitter debates about taxation that had marked the immediate postwar years; and its judicious report, published in 1927, marked the stabilization of the tax system inherited from the war. The committee listened sympathetically to the complaints of merchants and industrialists about the excessive burden of tax, but ultimately rejected the "common sense" of businessmen on the economic impact of taxes. Having concluded that the existing burden of debt and taxation was not unbearable, moreover, it made little sense to support a massive new tax such as the capital levy. Not surprisingly, the committee found the case for the capital levy unconvincing. A minority report, signed by the Labour representatives on the committee, also backed away slightly and called not for a capital levy but for a graduated sur-tax on unearned incomes above £500. This proposal was subsequently written into Labour's programme and effectively replaced the call for a capital levy.[50]

The Colwyn Committee thus largely confirmed the existing structure of the taxation. By the time its report appeared in 1927, approximately 2.2 million persons were liable to tax at the standard rate which, having reached 6s in the pound in the early 1920s, was down to 4s. Of these about 100,000 were also assessed super-tax or surtax rising from 9d in the pound for incomes between £500 and £1000 to 6s in the pound for incomes above £30,000. These rates raised nearly £450 million and swelled the proportion of direct taxes in the overall sum of government revenues. The ratio of direct to indirect taxes had stabilized at around 65:35, ensuring that the British state would continue to be funded in a manner that was mildly progressive but that, in keeping the cost of government firmly in front of the taxpayer and spreading the burden broadly among the middle classes, guaranteed that proposals for greater taxation and expenditure would elicit powerful resistance. So would proposals to alter the structure of taxation, for by the mid-1920s all of the major proposals for changing the shape of the tax system had been rejected: the capital levy had been defeated; neither the arguments of the bankers for higher income taxes nor of businessmen for lower direct and higher indirect taxes had been successful; and tariffs, the Conservatives" main alternative to the existing levels of direct taxation, had also met with defeat, at least for the moment.[51]

RESHAPING THE STATE

The battle over taxes was paralleled by, and often intertwined with, the struggle over the shape and direction of the state machine. Within the state stabilization would mean the restoration of Treasury control and the enforcement of rigid economy, which presupposed the taming of wayward agencies and officials within the bureaucracy and the abandonment of the social reforms promised during the war. The main stratagem used by Treasury officials to block reform was to emphasize its cost and the country's dire financial predicament. They persisted, for example, in calculating the budget on the principle of the "normal year," which made all reasonable estimates of expenditure appear massively profligate. They sought also to dramatize the indebtedness of the government and its impending fiscal crisis. In July, 1919, for example, Austen Chamberlain circulated a memo predicting bankruptcy if the Coalition's pledges were carried out and urging the government to initiate a propaganda campaign on the need for economy: "only persistent explanation, particularly outside Parliament . . . can bring the financial facts home to the minds of ordinary citizens." The fears expressed by the Treasury did not stop all proposals for reform in 1919 or 1920. Coalition plans for the creation of a new Ministry of Health went ahead, the government proposed an ambitious scheme for house building in March, 1919 and pushed through a major extension of benefits in the Unemployment Insurance Bill of August, 1920. Pensions were also increased, as were teachers' salaries. These initiatives scarcely fulfilled the promises of 1918, but they were more than the Treasury had wanted.[52]

Before orthodoxy and economy could triumph over reconstruction, however, the bureaucracy itself had to be brought into line. The recommendations of the Bradbury Committee for a reimposition of Treasury control were embodied in a set of changes implemented during 1919–20. The Treasury was reorganized into three divisions concerned with finance, supply and establishments, each headed by a controller who reported to the Permanent Secretary. The innovative aspect of the new structure was the prominence it gave to establishments work, i.e., to the Treasury's supervision of the civil service. At the same time, the Treasury's top official was designated as "Official Head of the Civil Service." Shortly after, the Treasury obtained substantial control of the Cabinet agenda. To enforce this policing of political discourse, the Treasury was allowed to appoint a member of the Cabinet Office, who understood his job to be "to keep a special watch on all proposals for new expenditure and to make sure that the Chancellor of the Exchequer had had sufficient time to pronounce on their financial implications before they were submitted to the Cabinet for decision." The new rules for the handling of government business were promulgated in January, 1920 and reaffirmed at regular intervals thereafter.[53]

Making the new system work would be the responsibility primarily of Sir Warren Fisher, who took over the direction of the Treasury in October, 1919. Even before taking office, Fisher wrote to Lloyd George arguing that it was necessary to eliminate entire departments and drastically reduce the staffs of those that remained. The fundamental problem, as he saw it, was not "swollen Civil Service establishments" but rather policy. The public had become accustomed to consuming services "at a price below their cost – the difference being made up by the Exchequer." During the war they had come to depend on subsidies for coal, for the railways and even for bread. From the provision of these goods and services the Treasury should "therefore dissociate entirely." Departments created for the duration of the war should also be "wound up as rapidly as possible and *not continued*." Most important, however, was the need for a large-scale reduction in the spending of the permanent departments. As Fisher explained, "I am clear that no further enquiries or orders [urging economy] will be of any use, and I would suggest that the Cabinet should commission (say) three men to go – *with unlimited executive powers* – and purge them on the spot. The peccant Departments are few in number and will probably be found to be the Air Ministry, Pensions, . . . Labour, Munitions . . . War Office, Admiralty, Board of Agriculture, Ministry of Food, Board of Trade." He proceeded to suggest the possible membership of such a committee and concluded confidently that, "They need not take long over the job." [54]

In fact, it took some years before Fisher's goals were realized. Critically important was the onset of depression in 1920, which allowed the government to back off from its commitments to reconstruction. The housing programme was the most visible casualty of the straitened economic circumstances. Addison's plan to build half a million new houses was probably never realistic, for its success depended on initiative and financial support coming from local government, on convincing private builders to forgo more lucrative commercial jobs, on overcoming the scarcity of building materials and on coaxing more workers in the building trades. But Treasury parsimony helped ensure that it would fail. As early as 1918 the Cunliffe Committee had warned that the housing plans being discussed by the government would cost too much and the Treasury consistently resisted the necessary expenditure. In November, 1919 the Exchequer was forced to come up with money to subsidize the work of private builders, but after that funds became much tighter. The Treasury imposed unfavourable terms on local authorities offering housing bonds and higher interest rates forced up the cost of borrowing generally. The Chancellor, Austen Chamberlain, continued to oppose the programme and exaggerated its cost. In December, 1920 the Lords rejected a Health Bill that would have given local authorities more powers over housing, and in February, 1921 the government put a cap of £15 million on housing expenditure. Addison, the minister in charge of housing, was sacrificed the following summer. By early

1921, therefore, the Treasury and the Chancellor had put an effective stop to the effort to create "homes fit for heroes to live in."

The pressure for economy also led to the dismantling of the economic controls with which the government had fought the war and the disbanding of the new, war-related, departments. Reconstruction had been eliminated in June, 1919; several other departments – including munitions, shipping and food – were wound up in 1921. The newly-independent Ministry of Labour continued, if embattled; the Board of Trade soldiered on with much less to do; the Board of Education worked steadily to implement the policy goals adopted in 1918; and the Ministry of Health oversaw the incremental growth of provision for health and the more fitful development of housing while seeking consistently to limit the liabilities of central government. They were all hampered by inadequate funding, however. The Ministry of Transport, created in 1919 when it seemed that the railways might well be nationalized and would need, in any event, to be controlled, had much less to do after their return to private ownership in 1921. It remained in existence to supervise canals, harbours, trams and the like, and increasingly to deal with roads and motor cars – an ironic transformation of its original mission. By 1921, there were few sources of innovation and independence within the administration.[55]

The scope for innovation was narrowed still further with the appointment of the Geddes Committee on National Expenditure in August, 1921. The committee had its origins both inside and outside the government. It was becoming increasingly clear to officials and ministers that further reductions in spending would require draconian cuts which would directly affect policy. Making such cuts would require support outside the government and even outside Parliament and for that reason the idea of an independent committee of businessmen became more and more attractive. A proposal to appoint a committee of this sort had been floated in July, 1920 but rejected. By the summer of 1921, some such expedient seemed the only way to satisfy the public demand for economy stirred up by the Anti-Waste agitation. Anti-Waste had been the rhetorical banner behind which criticism of the coalition had rallied since 1919. With the founding of the Anti-Waste League in January, 1921 and its successful efforts to field candidates in by-elections, the movement became much more threatening in the eyes of the government. Anti-Waste victories in June at Hertford and Westminster convinced Lloyd George of the need "to throw a sop to Anti-Waste." He prevailed upon his old friend, Eric Geddes, to head a committee of businessmen to recommend cuts in expenditure. According to Geddes, he "reluctantly accepted the Prime Minister's strong desire to have a Committee" and agreed to chair.[56]

There were some qualms expressed within the government, by Churchill in particular, about the wisdom and propriety of giving over power to a group of "irresponsible outside businessmen." The appointment of such a committee would end up "lowering the dignity" of the government and "would amount to putting the Chancellorship of the Exchequer in commission." The Treasury were also somewhat ambivalent. The committee did bear a marked resemblance to what Warren Fisher had urged upon Lloyd George back in September, 1919, and by 1921 Treasury officials had come to realize that continued "cheeseparing" would produce insufficient savings. The Treasury had responded to the impasse, however, by issuing its own economy circular in May aimed "at securing a large reduction in the estimates for the year 1922-3" through cuts in departmental budgets of 20 per cent. It is not clear how successful this effort would have been on its own, but it indicates that the Treasury were not waiting upon an outside committee to propose cuts in expenditure. In addition, Treasury officials were not especially sympathetic to Anti-Waste. In July, in fact, Warren Fisher had written bitterly to Lloyd George complaining about the "contemptible" attacks directed by the press at the civil service. He was particularly upset that the criticisms had "been allowed to continue unexposed" and called upon the government to respond: "I would earnestly plead that some ministerial protest should be publicly uttered against the stream of billingsgate and imputation." In the context, the Treasury were unlikely to welcome a capitulation to the leaders of Anti-Waste.[57]

Still, from the moment the Committee was appointed, its work was closely co-ordinated with the Treasury. It was the Treasury that set the goal of £175 million in cuts at which the committee aimed and it was upon Treasury briefs that the committee relied in deciding how much to demand from each department. Geddes was in regular contact with the Chancellor and discussed with him the relative burden to be borne by the armed forces and the social services. When the committee reported, its rhetoric echoed the Treasury's and the targets of its criticism were usually long-standing objects of Treasury antipathy. In the end, the committee proposed £87 million in possible cuts. Together with the £75 million identified in the Treasury's earlier exercise, the total came remarkably close to the goal of £175 million. Only £ 52 million of the new cuts were implemented – only a third of the reductions in education and half of those aimed at the navy were actually accepted; and the plans to eliminate the Ministries of Labour and of Transport were ignored. Nevertheless, the report had a chilling effect on government. The "Geddes axe" effectively ended the era of reconstruction and foreclosed the possibility of further state expansion for some time. It also capped the drive to reimpose Treasury control.[58]

The Treasury were thus the true victors in the Geddes exercise. They would not fully enjoy their victory for another year, however. Almost as soon as he had appointed the Geddes Committee, Lloyd George had second thoughts. He retreated to Gairloch in Scotland in September, 1921 and while there wondered openly whether deflation had not gone too far. He was also visited by a group of Labour mayors from London, demanding government action to deal with unemployment. The result was a series of proposals for increased relief (£10 million), for export credits and facilities (£26 million) and for development loans (£25 million).[59] Even before Lloyd George could announce the details of his plan, the Governor of the Bank of England had sent word to the Cabinet that he was "strongly opposed" to it. It was quickly abandoned, but convinced the Treasury that Lloyd George was not wholeheartedly in their camp and that they could expect him to continue to tolerate "sins against the Treasury" and to give unwelcome proposals for expenditure a hearing in Cabinet. Indeed, "the question [of controlling the Cabinet agenda] became acute at the end of 1921, following on Gairloch" and apparently persisted after that. The Treasury sought to remedy the situation by taking on Maurice Hankey, the Cabinet Secretary, the next year, but they were not markedly successful.[60] Through 1922, therefore, the Treasury's actual control over government business, though enhanced, was still incomplete.

The full resumption of Treasury control was also curiously set back by the procedure adopted to put the Geddes Report into effect. In January, 1922 the Cabinet appointed sub-committees to review the report's recommendations and to decide on the final scope of reductions. The spending departments made vigorous representations and managed to fend off many of the proposed cuts. In the process the Treasury itself was bypassed and the final decisions were taken by ministers made fully aware of the likely political consequences. By the time the critical choices were made, moreover, the Anti-Waste movement was largely spent and the likely victims of expenditure cuts, teachers most notably, were beginning to mobilize. The effect was to blunt the edge of the axe, at least in terms of social services, and to provide a temporary protection from the ruthless workings of the logic of Treasury control.

The delay in the full imposition of orthodoxy and Treasury control was to prove short-lived, however. The Lloyd George coalition fell in October, 1922 and was replaced by a far more compliant Conservative government led by Bonar Law. It was a government led by men chastened by their association with that "dynamic force," Lloyd George, and his reformist activism, and the Conservatives" political need to re-establish themselves in the country ensured that they would listen very attentively to the pleas of business and the middle classes for cuts in spending and in taxes. By 1923, the Treasury's representative in the Cabinet Office could report that "the present Government is . . . on the whole rather more disposed to listen to the Treasury point of view . . . than its predecessor used to be." [61] Of course, the Treasury could never fully relax during the interwar years. The utterly safe government of Bonar Law would be replaced by the unpredictable, if ultimately rather tame, regime led by MacDonald and Snowden. Labour would be turned out by another safe government but, unfortunately for the Treasury and particularly for Warren Fisher, they were saddled with the irrepressible Churchill as Chancellor. What followed was hardly better, for even if Snowden was reliable, the onset of depression and the general unreliability of Labour forced the Treasury to work very hard after 1929 to prevent untoward items from getting onto the political agenda. And there was always Keynes, repeatedly challenging the Treasury's position with his insider's knowledge and his keen theoretical intelligence.

Still, the triumph of fiscal rectitude and Treasury control in the early 1920s made it possible for those who sought to restrict the social and economic role of the state to prevail. Not until the Second World War opened up the policy-making process yet again would the advocates of state expansion regain the initiative.

Chapter 6

The resilience of budgetary orthodoxy

The tax system in place between the wars was a product of over a quarter of a century of intense political conflict. From the tariff agitation just after the turn of the century to the publication of the Colwyn Report in 1927, questions about the form and the level of taxation had held centre stage in the drama of British politics. The specific contours of the tax system closely reflected the peculiar features of British society. It was overall a monument to fiscal responsibility, itself largely a product of the combined influence of the Treasury, City and the Bank of England. It was a system whose lineaments were highly visible and whose incidence spread the burden of taxation fairly widely among classes. This guaranteed an intense public scrutiny of tax policy and an equally sustained mobilization of interests, particularly middle- and upper-class interests, around tax policy-making. These were articulated primarily within the Conservative party and expressed in its policies, but had also an independent existence. They were ordinarily arrayed against increases and in favour of decreases in tax and were prolific in generating proposals to shift the burden onto some other interest. The effect was to make it hard to move tax policy in any direction other than towards a general reduction. That outcome, however, was extremely difficult to achieve in the face of a massive debt, a deepening depression and a mounting military threat. The tax system therefore proved very resilient throughout the late 1920s and 1930s. This resistance can be seen in the response of policy-makers towards three quite specific problems: the mounting difficulties over local taxation in the 1920s; the financial crisis of 1931; and the question of how to pay for rearmament. In each instance politicians and officials opted for the set of adjustments in taxation that did least to disturb the existing balance of interests embodied in the tax compromise of the 1920s.

LOCAL TAXATION AND 'DERATING'

The prewar tax revolution was stimulated in part by the growing crisis of local taxes. Local authorities were burdened with increasing responsibilities after 1888 but not given the resources with which to carry them out. The need to supplement the local rates with grants or "assigned revenues" from the centre was a critical factor forcing a permanent increase in national or "imperial" taxation. In 1880, government grants constituted only 5 per cent of local revenues; by 1920, they amounted to over 17 per cent; by 1940, they would add up to better than a quarter of what local governments got and spent. Despite this growing reliance on the centre, local rates continued to increase as well: from an average of less than £2 per head in 1914 to over £4 in 1921.[1]

Heavy local taxation produced recurrent outbursts of ratepayer resentment. The ratepayers' movement in London, for example, extended its agitation across the country in the early postwar years. Its new journal, the *Ratepayer*, began publication in April, 1921 and aimed its message at all those "whose object is economy in local government" and who wanted to participate in the "movement against High Rates and Socialism in local Government." There was considerable overlap between the organizations of ratepayers and local Conservative activists, but significant numbers of Liberals could also be brought in behind the banner of local economy. Various anti-socialist and Anti-Waste coalitions achieved considerable success in local elections in 1922–3. The coalitions against Labour proved unstable, however, and by the mid-1920s Labour was once again chalking up local victories. During 1927–8, moreover, the Liberals had settled upon a strategy of coming "back to national power via the town hall," and decided to fight the next round of local elections on their own, splitting the anti-socialist forces and allowing for further Labour triumphs. To the self-appointed spokesmen of the ratepayers, "the Labour–Socialist attempt to capture the local authorities" seemed, by the late 1920s, almost unstoppable. Their fears of socialist domination were compounded by the popular image of Labour profligacy and by the realities of the local rate burden. "Poplarism," and the supposed abuse of Poor Law administration that it came to symbolize, constituted a terrible bogey to ratepayers and to local Conservative activists and provoked a recurring demand for the reform of the Poor Law and for removing its administration from the control of the local boards of guardians.[2]

Ratepayers and Conservatives also demanded that local rates be lightened. It was increasingly clear that the responsibilities placed upon local authorities far outweighed their resources and that central government had to provide an even higher level of support. This concern was intensified by the uneven incidence of rates. Localities with high levels of unemployment and poverty were especially hard hit, for not only had they greater than average needs, but to meet those needs had to levy higher than average rates. The effect was to make the original inequities worse and in addition, it was argued, the imposition of higher rates discouraged businesses from locating in the more depressed areas. Winston Churchill, concerned to assist industry in some way ever since the return to gold in 1925, spoke eloquently of the problem:

What with the ever growing burden of the rates and the poisonous atmosphere created, industry flies from these districts or dies within them. Who would start a factory in West Ham? On the contrary everywhere we see industries shifting outside heavily rated areas . . . Frequently we see the new factory erected just outside the municipal boundaries to escape from being made a starveling milch cow. The whole impulse is for industry to quit the melancholy areas and leave behind them political agitation, State assistance and a forlorn mass of derelict humanity.

The Conservatives were thus eager to reduce local rates in order to satisfy their constituents and also to frustrate Labour's efforts at the local level. They needed, too, a sop to throw to businessmen aggrieved over local and national tax policy. The demands of business for relief from national taxation had met with little sympathy from officials or politicians throughout the 1920s. The report of the Colwyn Committee closed off the possibility of any substantial relief from income tax liabilities and argued that the most onerous burdens upon industry came from rates, not from income tax. That argument led directly to the demand for relief from payment of rates.[3]

The details of rating relief were worked out in a prolonged set of negotiations between Churchill and Chamberlain and their subordinates at the Exchequer and the Ministry of Health. Chamberlain had long aimed to reform the Poor Law by abolishing the boards of guardians, which had proved rather too susceptible to local pressure, and by transferring their responsibilities to larger local authorities. Between 1926 and 1928 he pushed through several measures – the Board of Guardians (Default) Act of 1926, the Audit (Local Authorities) Act of 1927 and the Local Authorities (Emergency Provisions) Act of 1928 – to control expenditure by the guardians while he prepared for a more thorough-going assault. Churchill was more concerned to produce a measure aimed at industrial revival. Relieving industry of the burden of local rates would appease business and allow the government to claim that it was doing something to stimulate industry. Churchill also calculated that, while tax reduction of some sort was a political necessity, other approaches such as tariffs might "divide the country along lines much less advantageous to the Conservative Party than the present cleavage between Socialism and anti-Socialism."[4]

The results of the bargaining and calculation were embodied in the 1928–9 budget and the Local Government Act of 1929. Industry was relieved of 75 per cent of its rate liabilities and agriculture, already relieved of 50 per cent of rates in 1896 and of 75 per cent in 1923, was completely "de-rated." Relief was also granted to the railways. The rates lost to local authorities, estimated at approximately £22 million per annum, were to be made up by central government grants financed by a tax of 4d per gallon on imported light oils. The grants would be distributed on a formula that took account of local needs and resources as measured by the unemployment rate, the number of children under five, road mileage in relation to population and the difference between local rateable values and the national standard. The administration of the Poor Law, both in terms of relief and of providing medical services, would be shifted onto county and county borough councils and the boards of guardians eliminated. Responsibility for town planning, highways and the collection of vital statistics would also devolve onto county councils.[5]

The consequences of derating and the accompanying shift in responsibility were more political than financial. The rates lost to local authorities were a significant portion of their revenue – perhaps 15 per cent – but they were made up for by grants from the centre and the transfer of liabilities did not slow the long-term growth of local government spending. The changes did reduce the flexibility and discretion of local authorities, however, for after 1929 virtually the only source of new finance was the central government. Raising the rates was close to impossible. During the 1930s roughly two-thirds of the revenue raised from rates came from households and the burden was distributed in a very regressive fashion. A survey done in 1937 found that workers typically paid about 5 per cent of their income in rates, the upper classes less than 3 per cent. The regressive character of the "domestic rate" ensured that even in areas controlled by Labour there would be scant scope for extravagance. In addition, as another study showed, "The loss of income from industrial derating has tended to be heaviest in the poorest districts because the factories were the largest ratepayers." These inequities would not easily be remedied, for many felt that "the objectives of autonomy and financial accountability were best served by a regressive tax system." The system in place after 1929 therefore imposed both fiscal and political limits on what local authorities could do in the way of social policy.[6]

The response of the central government to the problem of local taxes was thus particularly unenlightened. Local governments were given little or no room for innovation, while the precise nature of the relief granted to localities actually increased the burdens upon the national tax system and at probably the worst possible moment. Indeed, as early as the budget of 1930–1 the Labour Chancellor Snowden was forced to find an additional £15 million to pay for derating in the midst of rapidly declining revenues. Business and agriculture were presumably made a bit happier: as Lloyd George claimed, derating "would lead the Federation of British Industries, the mine-owners and the landowners into the promised land, leaving the vast majority in the desert." The basic shape of the national system of taxation was unaltered, but the exemption from local rates helped to reconcile industry and agriculture, two essential bases of Conservative support, to the tax levels imposed by that system. At the same time, Labour was largely denied the possibility of using its growing effectiveness in local elections as the basis for innovations in policy. The minor alteration made in local finances in 1929 thereby tightened still further the constraints which taxation had placed upon policy after the First World War and from which there would be no escape even during the depression of the 1930s.[7]

THE FINANCIAL CRISIS OF 1931

The inflexibility of Britain's system of government finance would be revealed even more dramatically in 1931. The social compromise embedded in the tax system of the late 1920s was delicate – a careful mix of progressive and regressive elements whose distributional consequences were finely adjusted to the balance of political power. Throughout the 1920s the tax structure had "become highly and increasingly progressive in the upper ranges, and at the same time definitely regressive over a gradually extending range of the lower incomes." Income tax and sur-tax in combination provided a large share of the revenue on a reasonably equitable basis. Politically, however, the acceptance of this level of direct taxation of income depended on the fact that the system privileged large sections of the Tory electorate. The lower-middle class was the least taxed section of the community, largely due to the generous provision of allowances, which had grown in value as prices declined after 1920 and whose nominal values had been increased under Churchill. The effect was to produce a "dip" in the curve of tax incidence for those earning between £200 and £800, with the greatest benefits accruing to those earning about £500. Numerically, taxpayers in these income ranges were a large majority of those liable to tax in the late 1920s. Further down the scale of income the bulk of the workers escaped direct taxation of incomes, but contributed a significant share of their wages in the form of indirect taxes and local rates. Snowden had lessened the burden of expenditure taxes in 1924 and Labour remained resistant to taxes on consumption thereafter, but the working class nevertheless paid their share to the state and got surprisingly little in return.[8]

The depression threatened to change this balance substantially. In the first place, the distributional impact of government expenditure became more progressive, for the growth in unemployment meant that the sums paid to those out of work would increase proportionally. The tax increases needed to finance this could conceivably have been levied in a more or less progressive fashion, but in fact the first instalment of new finance during the depression indicated that the burden would be placed largely upon the better off. The budget of 1930, the first submitted since Labour came to power in 1929, raised the standard rate by sixpence to 4s 6d in the pound. However, by raising allowances on those with incomes below £250, the government managed "to relieve about three-quarters of the whole number of income-tax payers of any increase, and to concentrate taxation on the small minority who already bore the brunt of direct taxation." Coupled with this was a set of changes in sur-tax designed to raise an additional £12 million a year and in estate duties calculated to net another £7 million.[9]

As the depression worsened, it became clear there would need to be further budget changes that would alter yet again the distribution of burdens and benefits. The financial and political crises of 1931 may be seen as a prolonged period of wrangling over how the adjustments would be carried out. The entire structure of taxes and expenditure – what Schumpeter had termed the "fiscal sociology" of the state – was called into question and the tax compromises of the early postwar years renegotiated. Just who would win and who would lose in this process was quite unclear in 1930; by the end of 1931 there was a clear set of losers and winners. In particular, it was very much in doubt until August, 1931 how much of the adjustment would involve cuts in expenditure and, by implication, sacrifices from those dependent upon the state, like the unemployed and those in public employment; and even after that it was unclear whether tax increases would fall upon those with higher incomes, as in 1930, or be spread further down the income scale. Those issues were resolved by the September, 1931 budget in a manner that made only relatively minor changes in the tax structure. The changes that were made, however, were uniformly regressive.

As the crisis unfolded, all the actors involved in shaping tax policy in the 1920s reappeared and played their accustomed roles. Business insisted characteristically that taxes not be increased and that the shortfall be made up by expenditure cuts and by a reduction, or suspension, of the sinking fund. City opinion was more orthodox and on its behalf the Bank of England claimed that half of the deficit must be made up by cuts. The bankers also used the crisis as an opportunity to revive their earlier proposals for higher taxation of the middle and lower-middle classes. The Treasury and the Inland Revenue also tendered advice very much in line with their previous positions: the Treasury were keen on expenditure cuts and on the importance of balancing the budget; the Inland Revenue was moved once again to speak up on behalf of the taxpayer and the integrity of the tax system and particularly concerned about the unfair burdens placed upon those of higher incomes. None of these positions was especially new or surprising. What was new and decisively different about 1931 were three things: first, the conjuncture of a budget deficit with an international financial crisis justified much more drastic remedies than any merely domestic difficulties would have required; second, the fact that it happened while Labour was in power meant that whatever actions were taken would be politically wrenching; and, finally, these unique circumstances prompted an unusually direct set of interventions by permanent officials and by the Bank of England, both in defining the crisis and in determining its outcome.[10]

Structuring the entire drama was a political discourse anchored on the commitment to balanced budgets, a commitment based in part upon economic theory and a sense of the fiscal prerequisites for economic stability but even more upon an intuition about politics and the state. Balanced budgets guaranteed the link between expenditure and taxation and hence restricted the natural profligacy of politicians. The distrust of democratic politics was articulated forcefully by the May Committee on National Expenditure: "At election times those desiring increased expenditure on particular objects are usually far better organized, far more active and vocal than those who favour the vague and uninspiring course of strict economy." Adherence to the principle of the balanced budget was a necessary counterweight. As Sir Basil Blackett put it in a classic statement from the early 1920s, "The political dangers of borrowing to cover ordinary expenditure are obvious. It is not Government expenditure which the House of Commons and the taxpayer dislike, but the consequent taxation. Once admit that expenditure can proceed without relative taxation and the floodgates are opened." [11]

Treasury officials knew that there was no simple translation of budget deficits into economic ruin and throughout the late 1920s and early 1930s engaged in very creative accounting to disguise actual deficits. But they would not give up the pretence of balancing the budget for fear of its political consequences. For them "it was political considerations that were paramount." It was, of course, not merely Treasury officials, bankers and Conservatives who supported balanced budgets. There was a strong commitment to fiscal orthodoxy in the Labour party as well. Labour's fiscal proposals differed from those of their opponents in the extent to which they were willing to effect redistribution through taxation, but they did not advocate budget deficits. Labour's antipathy to rentiers made them suspicious of government debt, and their enthusiasm for the capital levy was based partly upon the assumption that it would be used to reduce the debt and the burden of debt payments. The party's principal financial spokesman, Philip Snowden, displayed a particularly intense belief in fiscal orthodoxy: he favoured the gold standard, had a naively optimistic faith in free trade and was unwavering in his support for balanced budgets. As a young man he worked for the Inland Revenue and never lost the tax collector's mentality. He was also quite deferential toward bankers and Treasury officials. Otto Niemeyer at the Treasury had considerable influence over Snowden during the first Labour government and Snowden continued to be receptive to official advice. He was even more impressed by Montagu Norman, Governor of the Bank of England, who paid him a visit the day after he assumed office in January, 1924. Years later Snowden would write glowingly of the encounter, describing Norman as "the bodily expression of one of the kindliest natures and most sympathetic hearts it has been my privilege to know." For Norman it was a worthwhile visit, for it earned him Snowden's continued confidence. In 1925, for example, Norman used it to get Snowden to temper his criticism of the decision to return to gold. During the second Labour government, the sympathy that had grown up between Snowden and the bankers – Norman and his deputies, Harvey and Peacock – would prove an even more decisive influence upon policy. It is tempting to view Snowden as a Gladstonian relic whose status as Labour's financial expert was an historical anomaly, but unfortunately his perspectives on finance were shared by large sections of the party and by many in the trade unions.[12]

Highly orthodox advice was forthcoming from officials almost from the moment Labour took office. In November, 1929 Warren Fisher and Richard Hopkins began to warn of mounting deficits and the need for economy and possible tax increases. The budget of April, 1930 raised revenues by over £45 million, but even these massive increases proved insufficient. Throughout 1930 official concern over deficits mounted and in July the Treasury warned of still higher taxes and "further derangement of the finances." Attention turned increasingly to the cost of unemployment and a Royal Commission was convened near the end of December, 1930. For its benefit the Treasury produced yet another memo predicting that "continued state borrowing on the present scale without adequate provision for repayment . . . would quickly call into question the stability of the British financial system." By early 1931 there was a growing consensus, outside Labour at least, on the need for drastic action to bring the budget into balance. Whether that would take the form of higher taxes or expenditure cuts was as yet unclear, but political debate prior to the budget tilted the scales towards cuts. There was considerable support for tariffs: the Conservatives favoured protection and in March Keynes announced his conversion to the idea of a revenue tariff. But Snowden and his advisors remained adamantly opposed. Businessmen renewed their complaints about the burden of taxation and they were echoed by Baldwin and other Conservatives. The alternative was economy and pressure therefore grew for cuts in expenditure. After some brief partisan manoeuvring Parliament agreed in February to set up the Committee on National Expenditure, chaired by Sir George May of the Prudential Assurance Company. Just what economies, beyond cuts in unemployment, were envisaged is unclear. Snowden himself was rather dismissive of the committee and claimed he could write its report. But its appointment signalled an important turn away from tax increases and towards retrenchment. So, too, did the budget presented in April, which called for only another £8 million in additional revenues to be raised from an increase in petrol tax.[13]

The aversion to taxes on the part of businessmen and politicians was shared and reinforced by officials, who played a major role in ruling out a solution to the fiscal crisis either by borrowing or by taxation.[14] In testimony before the Royal Commission on Unemployment Insurance, for example, Hopkins had made clear the Treasury's opposition to further borrowing for the fund and portrayed its insolvency as a threat to the entire financial system. At a more detailed level the Inland Revenue and the Treasury raised repeated objections to various proposals for new taxes. The most likely source of further revenue, so long as Labour remained in power, would be increases in sur-tax and death duties, which would fall on the wealthier sections of the community. Even before Labour came to power the Inland Revenue had subjected the party's sur-tax proposal to withering attack, claiming not only that it was impractical but that it "sins in principle." When the financial crisis revived the plan, official reaction was sharper still. The budget of 1930 had already shifted the fiscal burden upwards; to do so again in 1931 would produce a substantially more redistributive system of government finance. Officials thus argued strongly against the proposal to increase sur-tax and death duties, claiming that taxes on the wealthy were already so high that any further increase would produce massive evasion which would not merely reduce the yield of the new impositions but threaten the integrity of the tax system. Thus; in March, 1931 P.J. Grigg forwarded the Board's revenue estimates to the Treasury together with a sharp warning clearly aimed at Snowden: "I am profoundly apprehensive of the possible results of further increases at this juncture of Sur-Tax and Death Duties and I do not want the Chancellor of the Exchequer to arrive at even provisional conclusions in favour of them without having heard all that we have to say on the impetus to increased avoidance which will undoubtedly follow such increases." Since Snowden was ill for a month in mid-March and opted in the April budget for very few changes, Grigg and fellow officials had plenty of time to demonstrate that proposals for further taxes on the wealthy were unworkable.[15]

The most politically appealing plan to emerge in 1931 was the proposal to place a special tax on the "rentier," which was strongly pushed by the Trades Union Congress. During the spring, employers and trade unionists had put forth rival proposals about the reform of unemployment insurance. The employers wanted relief from their contributions and benefit cuts of a third. The TUC believed the attack on benefit levels to be the opening gambit in a broader effort to reduce wages and therefore stood very firmly against cuts, arguing that benefits should be extended and the cost financed by an "unemployment levy" and higher taxes on unearned income. The plan to tax unearned incomes gradually evolved into a proposal to tax the "rentier." A scheme to effect this was seriously considered over the summer of 1931, and throughout the crisis remained the major fiscal alternative supported by the unions. The Inland Revenue and the Treasury responded very negatively, however. Who, they asked, was the rentier? Did the term include all those who held £100 in War Loan or "every one of the 12,000,000 depositors in Savings Banks?" Was the tax to be imposed on all investment income or just on securities bearing a fixed rate of interest? Already, officials argued, investment income was taxed at a higher rate than "earned income," and death duties also fell primarily upon investments. The case for taxing "rentier" incomes was based largely upon the fall in prices, especially since 1929, which meant that interest payments fixed before that date had greatly increased in value. But, countered the Inland Revenue, it was difficult to distinguish "rentiers" who had gained from the deflation from the mass of investors in all sorts of businesses who had lost during the depression. Even if it were possible to define the scope and incidence of a tax on "rentiers," officials argued, it would be very difficult to collect and would "give an immense impetus to legal avoidance," if not actual fraud. Its yield would be thereby reduced.[16]

The defence of the "rentier" led easily to a defence of the wealthy more generally and, somewhat less easily, to an attack upon the lower and middle classes. In August, 1931 the Statistics and Intelligence Branch of the Inland Revenue produced a "Note on Taxation borne by the Wealthy," which argued that "the increased taxation nowadays must have seriously diminished the saving capacity of this group" upon whom recovery must necessarily be based. "The burden on the rich is already so great," claimed Sir P. Thompson of the Inland Revenue, that further taxation would be a case of "killing the goose" and would have a "damping effect" on risk-taking. Most ominously, tax increases would produce taxpayer resistance: "even the honest would rebel against what he would call the inquisitorial tyranny of the Inland Revenue. It is almost certain that in the effort to enforce efficiently the collection of increased taxation we should lose that willing co-operation of the great majority of taxpayers on which the success of the tax machine rests, with disastrous results on the yield of revenue." [17]

The unwillingness of anyone in public life to advocate unbalancing the budget and the tireless efforts of officials to rule out taxes on the rich meant that the burdens would fall upon the poor and would take two forms: expenditure cuts and regressive taxation. Both were advocated by officials. At the Treasury, for example, Richard Hopkins had become convinced that the limits of direct taxation had been reached and so "can no longer be relied upon as before." Instead, further revenues should come from elsewhere. He had come to believe that "the taxation borne by the mass of the citizens is, for a period of grave emergency, comparatively light, and very substantial revenues could be obtained" by taxes on beer, tobacco and tea and, most important, "by reduction of the personal allowances granted in the Income Tax." Indirect taxes had in fact been lessened in the 1920s and the real value of allowances and deductions had increased. Based on this assumption, the Treasury put together recommendations intended "to bring into the Income Tax field people with lower incomes than those now chargeable, and to increase the relative charge on the lower and medium incomes." Officials also pushed hard for economy. Fisher, Hopkins and Grigg all argued that any increases in taxes would have to be accompanied by economies such that the entire package would be "received as a fair and just plan demanding equal sacrifices from all sections of the community." The notion of equal sacrifice was much talked about in 1931. In practice its meaning was construed as implying that the working classes needed to make sacrifices in the form of reduced unemployment benefit and that the middle classes should pay more taxes. No increase in direct taxes would be feasible, according to officials, if "it stood alone and were not accompanied by a diminution of expenditure and/or an increase of indirect taxation." [18]

The privileged advice of officials therefore pointed to a quite specific resolution of the financial crisis that would combine serious cuts in expenditure with tax increases that would not target the rich but rather spread out the increased burdens, both direct and indirect, over a wide section of the population. The outcome came very close to this formula, so it seems not unreasonable to suggest that the officials, especially at the Treasury, had a good deal to do with shaping it. But they did not act alone, and the counsel offered by the Treasury was echoed in tone and in detail by the press, by the May Committee, by the Parliamentary opposition and by the financial community. The role of the bankers was critical, however, since their opinions translated directly into "confidence" which made its impact felt upon the exchanges quickly and intensely. Their role was also the most controversial, for it was unusually visible and gave rise to charges that the fall of the Labour government was in effect a "bankers' ramp."

The Bank and the City had long advocated retrenchment in the pursuit of balanced budgets. They believed as well that a major source of Britain's economic difficulties was wages, kept artificially high by overly generous unemployment benefits. The Bank's economist Oliver Sprague, for example, spoke throughout the spring of 1931 of the need for prices to be brought down by 30 per cent to meet world competition and called implicitly for a reduction in wages and unemployment benefit.[19] So the banking community was fully in tune with the chorus of demands for economy and against increased taxation. What truly distinguished the bankers' intervention, however, was their role in the mounting financial crisis of the summer of 1931. To some extent they were merely the bearers of bad tidings from the world of international finance, conveying to the government the news that gold reserves were evaporating due to declining confidence in the pound. They were also, however, pivotally involved in the negotiations for foreign credits to shore up the pound and hence in conveying to the government the political preconditions which bankers in France and the US felt were necessary to secure those credits. It was entirely appropriate for the Bank to play this role of intermediary, but it seems that in so doing the Bank used its position to guarantee that the government would have to accept drastic economies.

Throughout the summer of 1931, for example, officials of the Bank seem to have watched the financial situation deteriorate without doing very much to stop it. Credits were arranged from the French and the Americans in late July, but as the crisis unfolded in early August neither the Bank nor the Treasury moved to take them up. Rather, as George Harrison of the Federal Reserve Bank of New York explained, the bankers chose to use the leverage of credits "to make the British government understand the seriousness of their position." In their consultation with the Americans, moreover, it appears that it was the British representatives who raised the most serious questions about the stability of the nation's finances and thereby conjured up the American insistence upon positive proof of the government's resolve to balance its books. Thus Montagu Norman met with J.P. Morgan and his London partners in late July and confided his own lack of confidence in the willingness of the government to balance the budget. Inevitably, Morgan took the cue and demanded to be reassured. It was just about this time that Norman himself was taken ill and undertook, for reasons of health, a cruise to Canada. Reached there by phone and asked his opinion of the government's programme to meet the emergency, he labelled it "inadequate" and went on to argue not only that "it is essential that we must force an adjustment now and not in a year or so from now.' but also that "it must be . . . drastic." Nor was Norman alone in using his influence to pressure the government. In Norman's absence Harvey and Peacock were equally resolute in their insistence upon economies as key to resolving the crisis and it was a collective decision on the part of the Bank of England that provoked the most intense phase of the crisis in August, 1931. On 6 August the Bank revised its estimate of the likely deficit upwards from the figure of £120 million, projected by the May Committee, to £170 million and informed the government that the situation was "extremely grave." "However black the Governor may have painted the situation in his discussions with you," Harvey wrote to Snowden, "his picture cannot have been more black than theirs today." [20]

It is difficult to say what might have happened had the Bank and the financial community been more supportive of the government and less convinced of the need for dramatic expenditure cuts. The instability of international finance during 1930–1 was deeply rooted and it is unlikely that Britain's commitment to gold could have been maintained indefinitely. Still, it would appear that the Bank had considerable discretion in deciding whether to interpret the financial difficulties of 1931 as a problem or as a fully fledged crisis of confidence, and it is certainly the case that in defining the moment as "critical" they helped to make it so. No doubt their belief in balanced budgets, the gold standard and the need for economy in government was genuine, but it is also likely that their judgment of the government's behaviour was partly based on politics. At the very least it can be argued that the bankers would probably have treated a Conservative regime with considerably more empathy and without the sense that they had to pressure it into acting responsibly. [21]

In fact, they proceeded to treat the government that replaced Labour much more generously. Before the fall of Labour, contacts between the bankers and the Cabinet had been handled largely through Snowden and MacDonald and the Chancellor had actually refused a request from the Cabinet Economy Committee to meet directly with the bankers. After the formation of the National government on 24 August, the relationship was transformed. The bankers negotiated credits from the French and Americans with relative ease and worked closely with the government to resolve the crisis. In a remarkable meeting held on 3 September 1931, the Cabinet met formally with Harvey and Peacock to plan strategy. In August the bankers had insisted single-mindedly that the run on sterling was due to want of confidence in the government; by September, they were much more willing to consider other factors, especially the unsettled financial situation in central Europe. In August the bankers had labelled the government's programme "inadequate"; in September Harvey conceded that "a programme giving total results similar to those which had been indicated by the late Government . . . would prove adequate." [22]

Even more startling was an exchange on the question of an early election. The bankers warned that "talk of the present Government remaining in office merely for a period of a few weeks had been rather disturbing." While worried that a general election could provide further upset, the bankers concluded that if, in the course of an election, "the country were aroused to a determination to rectify the financial position, it would probably make a considerable differ-ence." It was important, the bankers and the Cabinet agreed, to take "all possible measures to form a sound public opinion," and in that effort the bankers would do their share. MacDonald suggested specifically that "the Bank of England might help by seeing the chief editors of the principal newspapers and not merely the Financial Editors, whose articles were little read by the general public." Harvey and Peacock offered in response "to help in any way that might be possible." The meeting concluded with the Prime Minister thanking the bankers for their help and urging them to be prepared to respond to attacks upon their role in the recent crisis.[23]

A comparison of the measures taken by the National government with those proposed, and ruled out, under the Labour government also suggests a political dimension to the bankers' judgments. Prior to the fall of the Labour government it was considered anathema to propose going off gold, introducing tariffs or suspending the sinking fund. Within a very short time after the coming to power of the National government, each of these supposedly unthinkable proposals had been accepted and implemented. The continued difficulties of the currency led the National government, working in harmony with its own advisors at the Treasury and with the Bank of England, to jettison without great concern these three cornerstones of postwar economic policy. The one item of orthodoxy to which they continued to cling, of course, was the balanced budget, which was as much a political commitment as it was an economic policy. It was a rhetorical and, if people could be made to think it so, a constitutional mechanism for restraining government spending rather than a canon of economic theory.

The continued effort to balance the budget meant a determination to keep spending and taxation in a close relationship to one another. Labour had not in fact proposed to break that link; rather, they appeared ready to increase the burden of taxation in order not to see the connection severed. But in so doing they threatened to upset the distributional settlement embedded in the tax system. Only by increasing the taxes paid by the wealthy could the existing level of services and benefits be continued. The economic depression had created a zero-sum fiscal game in which some adjustment had to be made. There would be no real winners in this game, but there would be real losers. The September budget, together with the various economies imposed simulta-neously, made it very clear who had won and who had lost in the financial crisis. Unemployment benefits were cut by 10 per cent, as were the salaries of public servants. The standard rate of tax was increased, by sixpence to 5s in the pound; the sur-tax was increased by 10 per cent; and personal allowances and children's allowances were lowered substantially. Indirect taxes were also increased: taxes were put up on beer, tobacco, petrol and entertainment.

The government would claim that the budget was based on the principle of "equality of sacrifice," but the Inland Revenue knew better. In reviewing the tax changes brought about in September, 1931, officials noted that the lowering of allowances would make nearly two million persons with modest incomes newly liable to income tax, more than doubling the number of taxpayers. The effect was that a married man with three children with an income of £500 faced a 380 per cent increase in taxes between 1930 and 1932, while a man in a comparable family situation earning £50,000 experienced a rise of 11 per cent. Industry was also spared and actually given a 10 per cent increase in depreciation allowances. Other non-tax changes imposed in 1931 were equally regressive. Local government, for example, was prevented from borrowing for capital projects during the worst years of the depression and thus from engaging in efforts to put the unemployed to work. Still more outrageous was the decision, made by the Labour government and allowed to stand by the National government, to disqualify most married women from unemployment benefits.[24]

In sum, the effort to balance the budget placed the burden of adjustment on those in the middle or at the low end of the social structure and made a not terribly progressive tax structure even less progressive.[25] The threat posed by the slump and the policies of the Labour government to modify the system of taxes and benefits was in this way effectively thwarted. The existing shape of the tax system was largely preserved: most workers, though forced to accept lower rates of unemployment benefit and to pay slightly higher indirect taxes, remained exempt from income tax; the very wealthy had escaped from what was in fact the very real prospect of having to sustain the unemployed through the depression; industry, though still aggrieved, had also escaped with rather minimal increases; the great bulk of the taxpayers, basically the middle and lower-middle classes, had on the other hand to cope with much higher levels of taxation. As officials from the Treasury and the Inland Revenue argued, however, the decline in prices since 1920 had increased the real incomes of these groups. Viewed this way, the outcome of the tax changes of 1930–1 was a victory for the principle of stasis: a monument to the resilience of the tax system hammered out between 1906 and 1918 and refined after the war and a sign of the enormous difficulty which would attend any effort either to raise the aggregate tax burden or to shift its incidence in a more progressive direction.

TAXATION AND REARMAMENT

Neither the fiscal difficulties of the localities nor the much more dramatic crisis of 1931 sufficed to produce a significant shift in the shape or level of the tax system. The standard rate of income tax had been raised by a shilling to meet the costs of government in the depression, but that was a very unimaginative means by which to meet the emergency. The difficulties involved in changing the system of taxation and public finance would be demonstrated yet again in the late 1930s, as policy-makers confronted the challenge of rearmament. The package of changes introduced in 1931 could have made it easier to experiment with the budget later in the 1930s, but did not. Going off gold and abandoning free trade lifted two, critical constraints. For the first time since 1846, Britain was largely freed from the pressures of the international market, or at least afforded a considerable buffer against its more dramatic fluctuations. Tariffs, moreover, provided an increase in revenues – amounting to £73.4 million by 1935 – that could have served to relieve some of the burden on the taxpayer. The success of the war loan conversion operation of 1932 could also have provided an occasion for granting some relief to taxpayers, for it substantially reduced interest payments. Perhaps even more important, the draconian cuts and enhanced revenues imposed in 1931 produced a budget surplus by 1933–4. These results would seem to have allowed considerable scope for some relaxation of the stance adopted in 1931.[26]

In fact, there was no relaxation. Thus, when Keynes published a series of articles in *The Times* in March, 1933 calling for tax reductions as a stimulus to recovery, he was again rebuffed. Throughout the early 1930s, the National Government resisted calls for reflation and maintained a resolutely deflationary course. Indeed, the restoration of budgetary balance after 1931 was taken by officials as a vindication of the assumptions underlying that effort. As one Treasury official explained in April, 1933, "A balanced budget gives us solid advantages. Without underrating the hardships of the present situation – the tragedy of unemployment, the heavy burden of taxation, and the anxieties of those engaged in trade and industry – we at least have not in this country the fear that things are going to get worse. On the contrary things are getting better. The confidence in our future was in no small degree re-established by the existence of a balanced budget." The benefits allegedly derived from that renewed confidence included a prolonged period of low interest rates, but even more important were the psychological advantages. Keynes might well argue that tax reductions would give a psychological boost to industry and to investment, but the Treasury disagreed. "Undoubtedly," Frederick Phillips wrote on 21 March 1933, "a reduction in taxation produced a comfortable feeling for a few weeks or even a few months, but this is purely psychological and as it dies out it is replaced by fresh grumblings and by renewed insistence that a much bigger decrease in taxation must be effected before any real recovery takes place." The Treasury were not averse to doing what could be done to coax businessmen into investing, but they had little faith that businessmen would respond. In attempting to do so, moreover, there was a substantial risk that the confidence of investors more generally would be lost because of unbalanced budgets. To the demand for budgetary flexibility, then, Richard Hopkins was moved to reply: "The answer is that things throughout the world are so radically and utterly wrong that this expedient is quite incapable of correcting the maladjustment."[27]

Arguments of this sort did not permit innovation or relaxation, and through the early 1930s they justified a series of highly deflationary budgets. The government eschewed any radical departure and instead moved slowly to restore the cuts made in 1931 and to bring taxes back to the level prevailing at that time. In 1934, the standard rate was reduced by 6d and in 1935 allowances were raised, if by only half as much as they had previously been reduced. In 1934 unemployment benefit was put back to its 1931 level, although the means test and tighter overall administration remained; and in 1934 and 1935 the pay cuts suffered by public employees were also restored. With the budget of 1935, "the most pedestrian Budget in recent years" according to *The Economist*, the position of 1931 was almost recreated. The sufferings and turmoil of the depression had thus produced virtually no change in the nation's tax structure, except to make it marginally less progressive. Still worse, the impact of the budget on the economy was consistently deflationary, lowering growth and increasing unemployment from 1929 through 1935. The commitment to the balanced budget, which was also imposed upon local authorities, apparently precluded any more creative response to the depression and the economic woes it brought with it.[28]

Only the threat of war could move policy-makers away from that commitment. Even then, they were reluctant to depart from what was, after all, a political and moral commitment as well as an economic one. Still, the growing threat from Germany and Japan had to be met, and from 1935 the government was forced to embark upon a policy of rearmament. As early as 1933, there were those who advocated a measure of rearmament, among them Warren Fisher at the Treasury, but the threat was not widely perceived until 1935. It then became impossible to continue along the path of reducing taxes and expenditures; rather, it became necessary to find the means to fund rearmament. Policy-makers sought, however, to pay for rearmament with as little disturbance as possible to the basic shape of the tax structure. It was readily agreed that borrowing for defence was legitimate and did not in itself seriously abrogate the commitment to balanced budgets. Nevertheless, the Treasury felt that borrowing had to be accompanied by tax rises at least sufficient to cover the increase in interest payments that would ultimately be due on the loans.[29] Taxes should also be sufficient to maintain the defence establishment at the level it would have reached by the end of the rearmament period. Officials worried, too, about the impact of borrowing and increased spending upon the balance of payments and inflation. Nor were they oblivious to the political implications of borrowing for defence: if it was right to borrow for the emergency created by Hitler, why not for the emergency posed by unemployment? For all these reasons, the Treasury were slow to borrow for rearmament and not much more forward in putting up taxes. The standard rate was raised in small steps painfully taken – to 4s 9d in 1936, to 5s in 1937 and to 5s 6d in the pound in 1938. Borrowing was not undertaken at all until 1937 and not on a large scale until 1938. Throughout rearmament, moreover, Treasury officials sought to impose clear financial control and to force the services to make difficult choices about priorities.

Whether obstruction by the Treasury actually slowed rearmament is difficult to determine. There were real physical limits to how fast Britain could rearm and political constraints as well. Nevertheless, the Treasury's stance was controversial at the time and has continued to evoke controversy in retrospect. The Treasury justified its cautious policy by arguing that in a prolonged war success would depend as much on the strength of the economy, the "fourth arm of defence," as on its armed forces. That they defined in terms of "economic stability," measured not by employment and production but by the nation's "financial resources." "The maintenance of credit facilities and our general balance of trade," it was argued, "are of vital importance not merely from the point of view of our strength in peacetime, but equally for purposes of war." The Treasury therefore sought to turn the debate over defence into a series of tough choices. There would be no simple recourse to borrowing for defence: rather, policy-makers would have "to reconcile," as Sir Thomas Inskip put it, "the two desiderata, first, to be safe, secondly, to be solvent;" they would have to tax as well as borrow; and they would have to decide which programmes deserved priority. In retrospect, such a stance can be seen to have imparted a degree of realism to the rearmament process and brought about long-term benefits. At the time, it was strongly resented by the armed forces and their advocates and it would later be denounced for having forced the government into "appeasement". In fact, "appeasement" enjoyed wide support throughout the British political establishment, at least until the Anschluss; and the Treasury's reluctance to tamper with the fiscal system to provide for rearmament found favour within the City, among industrialists and in the ranks of the Conservative party.[30]

Moves to change the tax system, or to borrow without simultaneously increasing taxation, were on the other hand met with considerable resistance. In 1937, for example, the government began to move toward borrowing for defence but decided to demonstrate its fiscal rectitude by simultaneously imposing a tax, the National Defence Contribution, on profits generated during rearmament. Throughout 1936 and early 1937 City opinion had strongly opposed a defence loan and the new tax was thought necessary to ensure the success of the government's borrowing plans. In the event both the tax and the loan failed. Businessmen mobilized rapidly and massively against the new tax: "Astonished Tory industrialists," according to the *Manchester Guardian*, "considered duty had turned a hitherto safe and respectable Budget into a Socialist Budget, Socialism being to them of course not a political philosophy but pure brigandage." Industrialists were joined by bankers and together denounced the proposed levy as a "tax on recovery." Shocked by the strength of the opposition, the government pulled back and modified the tax, transforming it into a very mild 5 per cent profits tax. Not only did the tax fail, but so, too, did the loan. The National Defence Loan was announced in April, shortly after the budget, and it was quite undersubscribed – "a flop of the first magnitude," according to the *Banker* (May, 1939). The Bank of England was forced to take up £86.5 million of the total of £100 million in bonds issued by the government. This was considered dangerously inflationary and taken as a warning by officials not to depart from orthodox finance or tamper with the existing tax structure.[31]

Chastened by these events, the Treasury reinforced its efforts to get the defence departments to lower their demands. The Chancellor, Sir John Simon, called in March, 1938 for a straightforward increase in the standard rate because, as he put it, "we are not really yet on the basis of taxation which is necessary to support the load" imposed by rearmament. A tax increase remained the essential precondition for raising loans and "Further taxation imposed now might possibly drive into the heads of the spending Departments the idea that bigger and better ships and guns, lavishly established and impetuously demanded, are not an unmixed blessing." A "popular" budget, on the other hand, might encourage the unfortunate belief "that there is plenty of money left." Tax policy was thus used not merely to raise revenue but to send the right messages to potential creditors and to "the spending Departments." Tactically, those messages should be sent sooner rather than later, given the financial difficulties of 1937 and likelihood of an election in 1939 or early 1940.[32]

The commitment to orthodoxy maintained throughout the course of rearmament meant that, whether funds were raised by borrowing or taxation, they would not be used for purposes other than defence. Borrowing for defence was one thing; borrowing for social spending quite another. As Sir Richard Hopkins explained in 1937, "In financial quarters throughout the world . . . borrowing . . . which merely provides for men in idleness is regarded as one of the worst forms of borrowing, but borrowing for armaments . . . is regarded as unfortunate, no doubt, but still respectable." Taxation imposed with the aim of expanding social services was not much better. During rearmament, therefore, officials kept a wary and watchful eye on non-defence expenditure and some even wanted to see social expenditure cut. That was generally regarded as politically impossible, however, and in March, 1936 the Cabinet, having only recently restored the cuts of 1931, decided not to restrict the social services to finance defence. But there was to be no wholesale loosening of constraints, either. Thus by early 1939, when the rationing of funds for the defence departments had been relaxed and planes, tanks and guns accorded precedence over the "fourth arm of defence," the government held firm on social expenditure. Indeed, at the Treasury Hopkins asked rhetorically in April, 1939 "whether in the new conditions created by the international situation the country can afford to maintain social services and other civil expenditure at" current levels? As he saw it, "sooner or later the question is bound to arise of a general cut such as that experienced in 1931."[33]

On the very eve of the Second World War, then, the orthodoxy and conservatism that had produced 1931 was alive and well. Britain continued, as Warren Fisher was finally moved to complain, "to amble along in our old and well-tried and (for the small minority) very comfortable economic paths." Rearmament had been undertaken and pressed forward largely within the constraints of established principles of public finance. Officials at the Treasury were, of course, the most articulate and forceful defenders of those principles, but the stance of the Treasury was not simply a product of its peculiar, narrowly institutional, outlook. It was, rather, a product of the consensus among the powerful on the politics of taxation and the need to limit expenditure by keeping spending and taxes in close relationship to one another and preserving the basic shape and structure of taxation. If the link between taxes and spending was to be maintained, there had to be a proportionality between borrowing and taxation in the financing of defence, and in providing new revenues for that purpose the existing balance in the tax burdens borne by different social groups should be preserved. The financial limits imposed upon rearmament, therefore, derived in large part from the political imperative not to disturb the tax settlement worked out with so much debate and bitterness in the decade after 1918. Neither the mounting costs of local government, nor the crying needs of those hit by the depression, nor even the threat posed by Germany were sufficient to transform the structure of taxation. The tax system was apparently too deeply embedded in the institutions and practices of government, too much the product of hard bargaining between classes, interests and parties and too thoroughly implicated in the resulting distribution of burdens and benefits to be changed easily. The system was not inflexible – technically it was rather easy to move the standard rate up or down and to alter allowances and exemptions in response to short-term budget needs – but any more fundamental shift seems not to have been possible in peacetime. Hence, it would only be with the outbreak of war in 1939 that policy-makers would be moved to transform the tax system by rapidly increasing the total burden of taxation and dramatically altering its structure and incidence.[34]

Chapter 7

Labour and the state between the wars

The politics of retrenchment, which prevailed from 1919 through 1940, were deeply rooted. The economic climate made alternatives difficult even to imagine, and the institutional context of policy-making helped further to limit the political agenda. Still, the political system in place after 1918 was not a mere continuation of what had existed before 1914. The major opposition to Tory rule was now Labour, not the Liberals. Labour was the new actor on the political stage and its presence ensured that alternatives to retrenchment were never entirely off the agenda of high politics. Around Labour clustered proposals for expanding the state or using public funds to offset the dire consequences of the market. The fate of these proposals was inevitably tied to the fate of the party and the trade unions upon whose support it depended. It is thus essential to chart their linked political fortunes in order to understand the options that were not followed up before 1940.

The Labour party had adopted its new constitution, with its socialist commitment, by February, 1918 and its leaders used the next several months to prepare for the coming election. Under pressure from local activists, the party's June conference resolved to break the party truce, ensuring that an election would come sooner rather than later. During the election campaign that followed the armistice, Labour put forward its programme unabashedly and pressed its attack upon "war-time measures in restraint of civil and industrial liberty," especially upon conscription, and its advocacy of land nationalization, a major housing programme, the capital levy, the nationalization of the mines, railways, shipping, armaments and the electricity supply industries, and the so-called "national minimum" of pay and conditions. Their appeal was unable to overcome the emotions upon which Lloyd George based his campaign, but served to distinguish Labour's position and fix its newly independent image firmly in the minds of the electorate.[1]

Labour was not to contest a general election for another four years, however, and by that time the context had changed dramatically. The ending of the war served as the signal for an upsurge of industrial militancy inspired by the notion that "direct action" could achieve as much as, if not more than, electoral tactics. The militancy grew directly out of the enhanced power of workers in industry and the boom conditions that persisted after the war. It drew as well upon the example of workers in Russia and on the continent, where workshop-based politics seemed to hold the promise of a wider social transformation. And it was a response to the apparent failure of elections, particularly the election of 1918, to produce governments genuinely responsive to working-class interests. Industrial militancy was extremely threatening to the prospects and status of the Parliamentary Labour party. The party's steady progress in elections was eclipsed by the more spectacular battles being fought out in industry, and every victory achieved at the point of production called into question the party's strategic orientation. The radicalism of industrial unrest, moreover, was deeply disturbing to those moderate, middle-class voters whom the party was seeking to mollify, if not attract to its cause. In consequence, the leaders of the Parliamentary party spent considerable time and energy distancing themselves from the quasi-revolutionary rhetoric of industrial militants and seeking to discredit "direct action" tactics. Increasingly, Labour portrayed itself as the sane and respectable alternative to "revolution" and took on the mantle of moderation even if it did not yet possess a genuinely moderate, reformist programme. Union leaders adopted much the same posture but, given their intimate connections with the daily business of industrial conflict, with even more ambivalence and more regular recourse to the tactics and rhetoric of class confrontation.

No sooner had Labour and the unions begun to respond to the challenge of "direct action" than they were faced with the very different challenge of unemployment. The slump began late in 1920, continued for nearly two decades and imposed a whole new set of problems upon the labour movement. It did solve the problem of "direct action", for it proved extremely difficult for industrial militants to sustain strike activity when they were out of work. But the protracted depression pushed the questions prompted by prolonged unemployment – basically how to put people back to work and how, in the meantime, to care for the unemployed – to the top of the political agenda, where they would remain for almost the entire interwar period.[2]

Neither the party nor the unions had much of an answer to unemployment. Unemployment took a terrible toll on the unions and pushed them gradually towards less sectional, more collective solutions to the problem of providing work and welfare. Payments to the unemployed cost the unions £15.5 million in 1921, and losses on that scale simply could not be sustained for long. Prolonged unemployment meant in practice that most former union members soon lost their claim to benefits. From 1918 through the 1920s, moreover, state benefits for the unemployed steadily improved and from 1921 were supplemented by dependants' allowances. They became, therefore, more attractive than the lower, and by now less certain, benefits provided by the unions. With the granting of state pensions in 1908 and their extension on a contributory basis in 1925, state provision for old age likewise came to prevail over the meagre retirement benefits workers had been able to provide for themselves.[3]

The parallel evolution of national health insurance also caused working people to look more towards the state for social provision. The scheme was instituted in 1911, based on a state subsidy to "approved societies," and expanded its coverage from 13.3 million in 1922 to 20.3 million in 1938. Benefits remained grossly inadequate, however, and there were enormous gaps in coverage. The government's desire to control expenditure – symbolized by the £2.8 million cut imposed by the Economy Act of 1925 – prevented any remedy for these deficiencies, despite the strong recommendations of the Royal Commission on National Health in 1926. Reduced financial support from the state, lower contributions due to unemployment and a growing demand for services produced a serious crisis in the scheme's finances by the early 1930s, to which officials responded by mandating cuts in benefits, especially to married women. Officials also sought to avoid the responsibility for providing medical care for the unemployed and so required the approved societies to continue benefits for those out of work. The arrangement had obvious political benefits, for as Sir Walter Kinnear, the Controller, explained in 1937, "the Health Insurance scheme is highly decentralized and the 'buffer' Approved Societies divert much criticism from the Government." In the long run it also undermined support for the public–private mix embodied in the scheme and ensured the ultimate adoption of a more statist plan.[4]

In response to such trends, unions and their members began to look more favourably upon state solutions to social ills and upon the Labour party as the vehicle by which to influence the state. Labour, however, proved disappointingly weak and ineffective. The party did continue after the war and the onset of mass unemployment to introduce into Parliament a modified version of the "Right to Work Bill," now known as the Prevention of Unemployment Act, but they had little else to offer. They supported various proposals for public works, of course, and in 1925 added to their programme the demand for a National Employment and Development Board which would "look ahead and prepare schemes of national development to be put into operation in times of bad trade." They had little to say about how these various projects were to be funded, however. Labour rhetorically supported heavier and more progressive taxation, but by the mid-1920s its main innovation in financial policy, the capital levy, was being put forward as a means of paying off the war debt and allowing reductions in taxation. It was not to be used to finance recovery. The Labour party was, of course, more committed than its opponents to maintaining the unemployed at a reasonable standard of living and distinguished themselves while in office by liberalizing unemployment benefits. The party's downfall in 1931 actually came over the honourable principle of not cutting benefits for those out of work. Locally, too, the party became identified with "Poplarism," understood by its supporters to mean the humane handling of relief but for Tories and ratepayers a symbol of extravagance. On a national level, however, Labour could visualize an end to unemployment only on the basis of a revival of trade, which depended on the stability and openness of the international economy. A more activist strategy of national economic development, based on tariffs or on measures to boost domestic consumption, was not part of their mental equipment. Their proposals for dealing with unemployment ended up being too global for action by a British government and too narrow and localized to be effective. Labour was thus unable to fashion a coherent and credible policy throughout the interwar years.[5]

Preoccupied and greatly weakened by unemployment and unable to work out a proper response, the labour movement adopted an increasingly defensive posture from about 1921 onwards. To some, of course, the economic collapse was a sign of capitalism's lack of viability and the imminence of socialist transformation. As F.W. Jowett told the party conference in 1922, "Before the war our achievements in the way of Social Reform proved as helpful as we had any right to expect. But institutions are changed now . . . It is no use expecting to remove this massed collection of evil impositions by gradual ameliorative reform." "It is the new social order we want. Nothing else will prevent the degradation of Labour now." For most activists and leaders, however, the slump lowered expectations, and it is likely that the sense that little genuine progress was possible was one factor behind Labour's otherwise unintelligible decision to take power without a Parliamentary majority in 1924. As late as June, 1923 MacDonald had publicly ridiculed the idea of a minority Labour government: "No sane person," he explained, "would undertake to form a Government with a majority . . . [consisting of a mere] half a dozen, or which, perhaps, did not exist at all." Sidney Webb might speak ponderously of the time when Labour, "in due course comes to be entrusted with power" and of the need in such circumstances "to . . . rise to its responsibilities" and "to work and speak and act, under the sense of the liability, at any moment, to be charged with putting our plans and objects into operation," but no one seriously thought that Labour would come into power within a year with fewer MPs than the Tories and having polled scarcely more votes than the Liberals.[6]

It would appear, however, that Labour's minority status and its defensive mentality actually made it easier to assume office. Without a Parliamentary majority Labour could not be expected to implement much of its domestic programme and so could not easily be criticized for failing to make progress on these issues. Labour could, however, make minor improvements in the lot of the unemployed, begin hopefully to oversee the reconstruction of the world economy and use their period of office to prove they were indeed "fit to govern." MacDonald and Snowden seem to have been obsessed with demonstrating their reliability. MacDonald had long fretted over the popular prejudice that "Only gentlemen can govern; Labour Ministers would be no gentlemen; therefore Labour cannot govern," and was troubled as well by persistent charges about his lack of patriotism during the war. "When the opportunity came" to form a government in 1924, therefore, he "never had a moment's hesitation as to what we should do. To have shirked responsibility would have been cowardly, and this country does not like cowards. Altogether it would have shown the spirit of shivering fear rather than that of trustful gallantry, and the latter is the spirit of the Labour Party." [7] If Labour ministers could not be gentlemen, MacDonald apparently reasoned, they could at least be gallant and he for one was not going to be charged again with being a coward.

To MacDonald and those who shared his perspective, the opportunity to prove themselves "fit to govern" without having to deliver on programme was irresistible. The government would make some progress on pensions and Wheatley's Housing Act was a genuine advance, but little more was achieved or attempted domestically.[8] Freed from having to deliver at home, moreover, the government could focus on world affairs. This, too, constituted an irresistible temptation and MacDonald, long concerned with finding Labour men capable of filling the top jobs at the Foreign Office, the War Office and the Admiralty, was quickest to succumb.[9] He decided to be Foreign Secretary as well as Premier, thus keeping himself in the spotlight and the conduct of foreign policy out of less reliable hands. The concentration on foreign affairs gave the Labour Cabinet repeated opportunities to underline their national, rather than narrowly class, orientation and to proclaim internationalist and democratic sympathies without seriously antagonizing the vested interests threatened by their programme of domestic reform. It also allowed Labour to claim to be making progress on what the Cabinet, along with many others, assumed to be the main causes of the prolonged trade depression – the unstable international economy and the flawed peace settlement. Unfortunately for MacDonald, his grandest gesture led indirectly to his undoing. Labour's recognition of the Soviet Union was a welcome demonstration of international goodwill and of the rejection of the old diplomacy that might also lead to new markets for British products. But it was the relationship with Russia and the communists – over the Campbell prosecution for sedition and the Zinoviev letter – that brought defeat in October, 1924. Ironically, even in foreign affairs there were pitfalls.

Still, the experience of 1924 did not disabuse the Labour leadership of the taste for office, even if they accomplished little while holding it. Failure could be blamed on others and on factors outside the party's control – on their minority status, on the perfidy of their Parliamentary opponents, on the bourgeois press or even on the backwardness of the workers themselves. Hence, there was little support for Ernest Bevin's conference resolution stating that it was "inadvisable that the Labour Party should again accept office whilst having a minority of Members in the House of Commons." Nor was there much of an effort to think creatively about the problems of translating programme into policy. Instead, there developed a curious discourse combining two incongruent elements. On the one hand, party leaders adopted a quasi-apocalyptic rhetoric about the inability of capitalism to provide workers with a decent standard of living, or even a job, and about how only socialism could solve these problems. Regarding unemployment, for example, it was argued that "no permanent solution of the problem is possible apart from progressive advances toward the social ownership and control of the staple industries and the banking system." At the same time those in charge of Labour's policy sought wherever possible to distance themselves from its more controversial elements. The capital levy, in particular, was relegated to the status of a long-term goal rather than an immediately practicable policy. Plans for nationalization were similarly soft-pedalled, becoming more the dignified than the practical part of Labour's programme. The hoped-for effect of this curiously contradictory rhetoric was, presumably, to maintain the party's internal coherence while lowering expectations of what Labour in power would accomplish.[10]

The defensive posture of the labour movement in the 1920s was therefore reinforced by the party's first experience of office. The sense of what was possible was diminished still further by the General Strike of 1926. Once again, the defeat of the strike could easily be attributed to the workers" opponents rather than to any faults in its internal organization or even its tactics; and the solidarity displayed during the strike and the tenacity of the miners during the prolonged coal dispute were sources of pride and evidence of workers" collective strength. But the limits of that strength, and of what it could extract from a determined opponent and a recalcitrant state, were even more evident. Concluding that there was no choice but to make the best of the existing system, union leaders like Bevin and Citrine decided that they had to increase the power of the organized trade unions in order to influence both business and the state. As Citrine wrote in his autobiography, "The principal lesson I . . . learned [from the General Strike] was that the trade union movement must exert its influence in an ever-widening sphere and not be contained within the walls of trade union policy." [11] Their support for the famous Mond–Turner talks of 1928 followed logically, as did their 1929 decision to set up a TUC Economic Committee, designed to articulate a distinctly trade union vision of economic policy.

The shrinking sense of possibility also paralysed thinking about the implementation of reform. Without the prospect of Labour being able, in the near future, to institute serious changes, there was little incentive to confront realistically the difficult question of how to use the state to bring about structural reform. There was also no compelling reason to submerge sectional interests in the hopes of broader class advance; hence, the defeats of the 1920s prompted union leaders to adopt defensive stances towards the few state initiatives that remained on the political agenda. Labour's response to the Geddes Report was characteristic. The report, which Labour in general opposed, called for cuts in all sorts of services. But what the party and the unions got most exercised about was the proposal to merge the systems of unemployment insurance and national health, for this threatened the role of the unions in administering unemployment. Equally revealing was the response of Labour and the unions to the "endowment of motherhood" campaign. There was considerable support for family allowances within the Labour party and in some unions, but in the end the TUC came out against.

They feared that family allowances would be used to lower wages and proposed instead the provision of services in kind to families. In fact, some advocates did see family allowances as a cheap alternative to higher wages and anything that seemed to encourage the attack on wages was suspect to trade unionists. But the self-interest of male workers and their desire to maintain the fiction of "the family wage" were also clearly at work in their decision. The Labour party also lost the initiative to the Conservatives on pensions for widows and orphans. Having campaigned on the promise of state-funded pensions, they did little to advance the cause in their brief spell in office in 1924. The Conservatives, on returning to power, quickly passed a contributory scheme in the hopes of gaining credit for a major piece of reform while pre-empting a more expensive programme whose funding would have required an increase in progressive taxation or, still worse, a capital levy.[12]

DEPRESSION AND RETHINKING

Labour remained largely on the defensive throughout the interwar years, but its complacency towards the state was disturbed considerably by the events of 1929–31. The economic crisis of 1929 stimulated a new round of demands that government do something about unemployment and, with Labour in office once more, the problem of using the state to combat the depression fell directly upon Labour. Standing in the way of a state-sponsored solution to the economic crisis were innumerable obstacles. The first was Labour's lack of a reasoned programme for combating unemployment. Throughout the 1920s, Labour had used the stick of unemployment with which to beat the government, but had little positive to propose. The party's leadership believed that higher employment would follow from an upturn in world trade and so blamed the unsettled international situation for the prolongation of unemployment. As early as December, 1921, Labour and the TUC sponsored a "Special Emergency Conference on Unemployment and the International Situation," where it was argued that "our present industrial misfortunes are largely owing to the international policy which our Government has been pursuing, particularly as regards Russia and Central Europe.' Alongside this emphasis on trade co-existed proposals for public works. It was difficult to take them seriously, however, for there were no serious proposals about how to fund public works. Labour continually backed away from its commitment to increased, progressive taxation – in 1923, for example, the party actually promised to reduce income tax if elected – and therefore left virtually all of its plans hostage to the lack of funds. The only exception was the National Employment and Development Board, which was proposed in 1925 with a price tag amounting to £10 million annually, but it is difficult to believe the plan was ever taken seriously by the leadership.[13]

The party's failures were only partly failures of imagination. They represented deliberate choices in favour of orthodoxy and against the more creative, but unorthodox, positions on offer within the labour movement. The Independent Labour party, for example, was a continual font of new ideas throughout the 1920s. Under its auspices Oswald Mosley developed his thoughtful and provocative essay, *Revolution by Reason*, in which he outlined a "prematurely" Keynesian plan to revive output by credit expansion. Equally impressive was the ILP's official programme, embodied in *The Living Wage* (1926). Based largely on Hobson's underconsumptionist theories, *The Living Wage* advocated redistribution through taxes, family allowances and a minimum wage as the means to generate employment. The ILP sought support for its policies within the Labour party, but was rebuffed. Instead, Labour produced an even more moderate and uninspired programme upon which to fight the 1929 election. At least as constraining as the party's programme was the continued refusal to countenance budget deficits to reduce unemployment. Snowden told the 1928 conference that it would be easy enough for "an unprincipled Government in the absolute control of currency and credit" to reduce unemployment significantly, but it could only be done "at a terrible price which the country would have to pay sooner or later." By the time Labour took office in 1929, its leaders had effectively closed off major options in economic policy and despite their "unqualified pledge to deal immediately and practically with" unemployment, they were not equipped with a policy with which to do so.[14]

Nor would they be afforded the administrative flexibility with which to fashion a policy while in office. The intellectual inheritance of the Labour government may not have been rich, but the severity of the slump forced the government to think anew and to some extent opened up new opportunities. That these were not taken was at least partly the result of the hostility towards alternative policies displayed by officials, especially at the Treasury. The Treasury opposed expansionist policies on several grounds. For years they had argued against public works on theoretical grounds, claiming that increased investment by the state would simply replace private investment and produce no net increase in employment. To officials and their supporters among the economists, the case against public works remained solid, but the persistence of unemployment prompted insistent calls for intervention. As a result, the Treasury was called upon repeatedly to reformulate its views. A major restatement had been put forward immediately prior to the assumption of power by the second Labour government. The occasion was not the imminent prospect of a Labour victory, but rather a concern to discredit Lloyd George's expansionist plans. The Liberal "Yellow Book," *Britain's Industrial Future*, appeared in 1928; the more popular "Orange Book," *We Can Conquer Unemployment*, came out the following year. In response, the Treasury developed a detailed critique of Liberal plans for public works, a critique which served to marginalize later proposals of similar nature.[15]

Behind the Liberal proposals loomed the spectre of Keynes, and it was largely in response to Keynes' evolving views that the Treasury worked out the specifics of its own arguments. Keynes was closely involved in the development of the new Liberal proposals and his public criticisms of Treasury policies provoked a flurry of internal activity during 1928 aimed at refurbishing the orthodox case in more convincing language. The job of refuting Keynes fell to three Treasury officials: Richard Hopkins, who dismissed the great economist as both "a journalist and a currency heretic," Frederick Leith-Ross and R.G. Hawtrey. Leith-Ross and Hopkins repeated fairly standard charges against the assumption, implicit in Keynes, that there were funds available for investment but for some reason lying idle. Hawtrey's contribution was to proclaim that the only way public works could expand output was if they led to an expansion of credit and to suggest that, if credit expansion was what Keynes meant to advocate, there were more direct and efficacious ways of doing it. These emerging Treasury arguments had to be further refined in early 1929 when, in anticipation of the coming general election, the Home Secretary, Sir William Joynson-Hicks, proposed a programme of public works and the Minister of Labour, Arthur Steel-Maitland, asked for "a reasoned proof . . . that the financial policy by which we guide our steps is right" before rejecting such a programme. In this task Sir Frederick Phillips played the major role, restating even more forcefully the traditional "crowding-out" argument. Very quickly, however, Treasury attention was again directed to critics outside the government, for Lloyd George had come forth in March, 1929 with his pledge to cure unemployment. The response to Lloyd George took two forms: Churchill's refutation of the case for public works in his April budget speech together with his explicit endorsement of the traditional "Treasury view"; and the publication in May of the White Paper criticizing the Liberal proposals. By May, 1929, therefore, the case against an attack on unemployment by means of public works had been decisively rejected by the government, by officials and by the common sense of established opinion. Officials actually became more, rather than less, dogmatic as their argument took shape. As P.J. Grigg explained in a cover letter to Churchill accompanying his summary of "the orthodox unemployment argument," "For my part I am increasingly coming to the view that the argument is unimpeachable." [16]

Having so recently committed itself against public works and the expansion of credit, it was inevitable that the Treasury would continue to discourage proposals for more activist policies to combat the slump. Its influence would be asserted repeatedly over the next two years and would help to derail Labour's three major initiatives in economic policy. The Treasury worked hard, for instance, to control the agenda and the policy recommendations of the Economic Advisory Committee. Officials were equally dismissive of the unorthodox ideas that began to emanate from Oswald Mosley, the most active member of the government's Unemployment Committee. The third and most important venue for debating the causes and possible remedies for the slump was, however, the Macmillan Committee on Finance and Industry. The committee was set up in November, 1929 and reported in July, 1931, just in time for the collapse of the Labour government. Its hearings provided an opportunity for a full-scale critique of the direction of economic policy and of the institutions, especially the Treasury and the Bank of England, responsible for it. It proved a particularly appropriate showcase for Keynes, who used his position on the committee and his obvious brilliance to criticize prevailing orthodoxies and to educate the committee on his opposing views.[17]

The Macmillian Committee also provided the occasion for yet a further refinement of the Treasury's position on public works and reflation. The Treasury was very much on the defensive in the hearings. Keynes' exposition of his views was eloquent and compelling and seemed, early in the committee's deliberations, to be carrying all before it, and the Treasury was also deeply embarrassed by the incoherence of Montagu Norman's testimony on behalf of the Bank of England. They were pushed therefore to concede a number of theoretical points and to adduce new arguments against an activist policy. The Treasury's most effective spokesman was Hopkins, who adopted a pragmatic, open-minded stance quite at variance with his past and with his current private views. Having carefully studied Keynes' arguments before the committee, Hopkins and his colleagues softened their theoretical objections to public works but then proceeded to advance two practical objections that were likely to prove decisively negative in any particular case. First, a major programme of public works would be very difficult to put into place and administer. In Britain most public works were undertaken by local authorities and getting local authorities to undertake large-scale schemes would pose administrative difficulties that could only be solved by "a great extension of bureaucratic power' and central regulation that would strike most Englishmen as repugnant. Second, the financing of such a programme through deficits could adversely affect investor confidence, so that it might be accompanied by such a fall in confidence as to outweigh any direct economic effects. Before any programme of public works could be approved, the Treasury argued, it was necessary to guarantee that investors would not react unfavourably to its financing – something which no government could insure against and which would probably be elicited by the first rumour of administrative doubt about the worthiness of the project.[18]

The significance of the Treasury's response to the Macmillan Committee lay in its artful combination of theoretical and practical objections to intervention. This argument not only questioned the wisdom of particular policies but shifted onto their advocates the burden of demonstrating not only that their alternatives were desirable but also that they were feasible. This does not mean that the Treasury's concerns were merely "practical" but that they understood the difficulty of proposing schemes that were both attractive and administratively possible. And, of course, who knew better than the Treasury what the administrative machinery could and could not do effectively? The Treasury's insistence upon, in effect, the incapacity of the state was in many ways entirely appropriate. It fitted in with the basic thrust of Treasury policy since 1919 and with its minimalist conception of the proper role of the state in the economy. It represented as well an intuitive recognition of the fact that any serious proposal for new economic policies would have required substantial alterations in the machinery of government. In fact, virtually all of the proposals on offer in the 1920s and early 1930s called for policy innovations that could only be carried out by novel institutional arrangements. Labour's proposal for a Development Board, for example, would have meant the creation of an agency whose responsibilities would overlap the Treasury's and whose constitutional status would necessarily be a matter of contention. The ILP's plans likewise called for the nationalization of the Bank of England and the setting up of an "industrial commission" whose task it would be to supervise the reorganization of weak industries. Still more threatening to established ways of doing business were the plans put together by Oswald Mosley, who proposed that the Prime Minister become the chair of an executive committee, made up of the heads of the spending departments and the Chancellor, to direct the economic activities of the state and, by means of a development bank, intervene directly in the private sector. Even Ernest Bevin, typically very cautious about but also very sensitive to administrative matters, felt moved in February, 1931 to call for a reorganization of the state to deal with unemployment. Indeed, no serious proposal for dealing with the slump could avoid the question of whether, in its current form, the state had the ability to carry out new initiatives and, if not, what sort of changes would prove necessary. The problem for advocates of new policies was that every proposed new agency or reorganization of existing machinery threatened the interests of those currently atop the existing machine. By drawing attention to the details of administration, the Treasury further complicated the task of reformers.[19]

The set of theoretical and administrative objections cobbled together by the Treasury in 1930 served to block initiatives at least through 1935. The same arguments were used, for example, to criticize Keynes' articles in 1933 on the "means to prosperity," and were trotted out again in 1935 to combat Lloyd George's proposals for a "New Deal". By the mid-1930s, moreover, the government could claim to have presided over a revival of employment which might itself be jeopardized by "grandiose projects of public expenditure" that would disturb investor confidence. After 1935, revival sustained by rearmament lessened further the pressure on the state to alter its policies and the government continued to reiterate its opposition to public works and deficits up to the outbreak of war.[20]

There was to be no relief or revival for the lifetime of the second Labour Government, however. Impeded by its own lack of imagination and by the resistance of officials, especially at the Treasury, Labour could only vacillate between, as one writer has put it, "drift or deflation." It fell "when the pressure to abandon drift and adopt deflation became too strong." Some of the pressures brought upon the government were improper, verging on "unconstitutional," but not all. The mobilization of business sentiment against further taxation was no doubt proper, as were the machinations of the opposition parties, but the roles of the Treasury and of the Bank of England would be hard to defend. The monarch was also unusually active in bringing about his preferred resolution to the crisis of August, 1931. Within the government, moreover, the behaviour of MacDonald and especially Snowden was, if not criminally dishonest, at least dissembling and actively disloyal. Still, the overall record of the Labour government of 1929–31 suggests that some sort of unhappy ending was surely inevitable. The government had assumed office promising to deal with unemployment; it had in fact no realistic programme for dealing with it in 1929 and was blocked, by its own accumulated prejudices and gaps in its strategic thinking and by determined bureaucratic resistance, from developing a viable programme during the slump. The details of Labour's fall in 1931 may not have been predetermined, nor the behaviour of individual actors, but the general shape of the crisis was almost "overdetermined." [21]

TOWARDS THE SOCIAL-DEMOCRATIC STATE

The débâcle of August, 1931 stimulated a good deal of debate within the labour movement about the state and the policies of any future Labour government. Discussion that should have taken place in the 1920s – about how to make use of the state for reform and social transformation – began finally to occur, and out of it came a much clearer vision of Labour's policy and how it might be implemented. The road to a viable reformism was long and complicated, but by 1939 much of it had been successfully traversed.[22]

Progress toward reformism, if progress it be, was delayed for some time by the recriminations that followed the disaster of 1931. It was not unreasonable for activists in the party or in the unions to feel that they had been victimized by the establishment and to begin seriously to doubt the wisdom of Parliamentary politics. Among the leaders of the party it was Stafford Cripps and Harold Laski who most forcefully voiced such doubts. Labour's strategy to 1931 had assumed that its opponents would, as Laski put it, "concur in the erosion of their authority." The recent crisis called this assumption into question and forced Labour to consider an alternative scenario:

> The crisis made it clear that Labour may be betrayed by its own leaders; that finance-capital, on an international scale, will combine to threaten social security when its own power is challenged; that theories of constitutional form will be adjusted overnight to suit the interests of Conservatism. All this, inevitably, makes one pause before accepting the traditional hypothesis that the mere conquest of a majority is a sure road to a Socialist victory. It is a necessary path to follow; but the recent emergency makes one wonder whether the serious problems will not begin when its end is reached.

Cripps shared Laski's concerns and argued the need "for the development of a machinery of government which preserves the fundamental conceptions of democracy and freedom and yet at the same time enables the elected majority to carry through rapidly and without interference the drastic changes desired by the people." [23]

The new machinery of government would differ from the old in several critical respects. According to Cripps, a newly elected socialist government would immediately pass an "emergency powers bill" and would be prepared, if obstructed by the Lords, the monarchy or the courts, to override such opposition by whatever means necessary. The implementation of socialism would require, moreover, the enactment of an enormous legislative pro-gramme, which could only be dealt with by more regular recourse to executive power and by focusing the attention of Parliament on one major, omnibus piece of legislation each year. This would be the Planning and Finance Bill which would serve as a "general plan of the national life, economic and social." Parliament would debate and approve the Planning and Finance Bill, but little else; and would become more of a working body, organized into standing committees, assisting in the tasks being carried out by the reorganized administrative machine. That machine would be staffed by a revitalized civil service, consisting of those older officials committed to the "loyal functioning" of their departments and a presumably large number of "young and progres-sive civil servants who will set out with the intention of making a success of their job." Not surprisingly, the departmental structure within which the civil service operated would have to be changed as well, and the Treasury in particular would have to be absorbed into a new "department of finance, of which the Treasury may form a sub-department." Altogether, it would be a very different sort of state. [24]

Cripps' plan for reshaping the state machine was in fact only one of several such prescriptions on offer after 1931. Perhaps the most interesting was a proposal co-authored by Ernest Bevin and Colin Clark for the New Fabian Research Bureau. [25] Like Cripps, they were concerned with the efficiency of the Cabinet as well as of Parliament and proposed a smaller Cabinet that would concentrate in its hands a much greater degree of executive control. Most important, the Prime Minister's office would take over the broad direction of economic and social policy. Bevin and Clark were specifically interested in curbing "the present powers of the Treasury' which, they felt, had "grown up accidentally" and were "somewhat unconstitutional." They admitted frankly that a future "Labour Government is bound to be a 'spending' Government," and would need such a new arrangement in order successfully to "surmount the strong and inevitable bias of the Treasury against any considerable legislative commitments of the sort a Labour Government would wish to make.' The Bevin/Clark proposal also recommended a new Ministry of Overseas Affairs to co-ordinate foreign and colonial policy, a new Ministry of Justice to oversee the work of the Lord Chancellor, the routine administration of justice and the enforcement of industrial regulations previously monitored by the Home Office and the Ministry of Labour. Inevitably, the powers of the Exchequer would be considerably reduced and the Treasury would no longer have its own representatives placed as financial officers within the other departments. Instead, the Treasury would be mandated to form a National Investment Board to co-ordinate the provision of loans for public authorities and new state enterprises. The board would in turn be expected to provide capital for projects approved by a new Industrial Development Board, linked to a much-enlarged Board of Trade, renamed the Ministry of Industry and Commerce and empowered to intervene much more directly in the nation's economic development. There would also be created an expert National Economic Planning Board to carry out the "general plan" for the country, making sure that the various departments charged with economic policy would work effectively together. Three new, co-ordinating ministries would also be created: social services, which would integrate the administration of social programmes and make benefits and coverage more comprehensive; power and transport, which would oversee the nationalization of mining, railways and the gas industry and exercise public control of other utilities; and armaments, under which would be grouped the army, the Admiralty and the air force. Ironically, there would be no need in this system for a separate Ministry of Labour, which Bevin and Clark proposed to eliminate.

What distinguished the plan elaborated by Bevin and Clark was its combination of iconoclasm and pragmatism. It was not couched in revolutionary rhetoric, but it contained within it a set of very dramatic proposals. A state reshaped along these lines would have been capable of undertaking major initiatives in social and economic policy and would almost be forced by its inner structure and logic to do so. It would thus be at least as dynamic and threatening to established interests as the otherwise rather similar structure proposed by Cripps. The Bevin/Clark plan was also far more interesting than the plan worked out simultaneously by Attlee, who had himself been moved by the events of 1931 to speculate on "The Reorganization of Government."[26] Like Cripps, Bevin and Clark, he wanted a smaller, more efficient Cabinet and a new set of co-ordinating ministries. His vision of the role of the Prime Minister and his office was, characteristically and prophetically, more limited. The Prime Minister "should be a good Chairman" and for that "must have the architectonic sense," but would not necessarily require a much elaborated office to keep track of detailed policies. Attlee did feel, however, that the role of the Treasury, whose "present dealings . . . with the spending departments is most unsatisfactory," should be diminished. Under his scheme economic planning would be given new priority and institutionalized in a council of economic ministers chaired by the head of the Board of Trade. The vision informing Attlee's plan was that of the consummate committee chairman, concerned more for efficiency than for dynamism. Still, it represented a serious effort to think through the institutional implications of an interventionist policy and to rethink the relationship between Labour and the existing apparatus.

The criticism of the existing structure of the state, articulated most forcefully by Cripps and Laski, thus struck a responsive chord throughout the labour movement in the aftermath of 1931. Attlee's reaction was paradigmatic: by temperament much more moderate than Cripps or Laski, he nevertheless worked closely with Cripps during this period, shared his doubts about the readiness of capital peacefully to hand over its control of the economy and worked on his own plan for a new state machine. Left-wing positions in fact scored major programmatic victories at the 1932 party conference at Leicester, and their advocates succeeded in winning at least paper commitments to their implementation. In 1933, the party sharply criticized the "excessive authority" wielded in the past by the Chancellor of the Exchequer and committed itself to a set of guidelines on the relationship between the party and any future Labour government which severely restricted the politicians' autonomy. There was also broad support, reflected in the otherwise rather tame 1934 programme, for the idea that Labour had to act quickly and decisively when it again assumed office and be prepared to use emergency powers to counter the resistance it would inevitably face. Even Hugh Dalton accepted the need to "begin with a General Powers Act" that would enable Labour "to win the war against unemployment, poverty and economic anarchy. If we act boldly and in this spirit, we shall have our best chance of a quick victory over any organized forces of hostility or obstruction." [27]

Despite this apparently broad resonance, the left's views remained in the minority and provoked considerable opposition from within the labour movement and from outside. The willingness to contemplate dramatic constitutional changes was deeply disturbing to an establishment that had only recently installed a government committed to ensuring political stability. The left-wing criticism was also much too apocalyptic – "feverish" was how Dalton referred to it – and too diffuse to be truly effective. Cripps' casual reference to the possibility of a socialist dictatorship and his famous attack upon the crown in January, 1934 seemed almost calculated to give offence and to distract attention from his otherwise quite defensible positions. The attack by Cripps, Laski and the left was also much too broad. It was directed not against a well-defined set of opponents who could be isolated and defeated, but against all sorts of possible enemies – ranging from opponents within the Labour party to recalcitrant officials within the state, to the King, the Lords and the courts, to disloyal bankers and, in the extreme, to seditious military men. Appropriately, the broad-based character of the criticism conjured up an equally broad array of dissenters. [28]

The left-wing critique of the second Labour government and of the state itself was therefore dissipated relatively quickly and the left increasingly turned its attention to international questions – to the threat of fascism and to Spain – and to the need for a united front to protect democracy. The flaws in Britain's machinery of government, though serious, paled into insignificance when compared with the brutalities of the authoritarian regimes that ruled over ever-increasing portions of the European continent. Perhaps more important, the left within the party did not possess a credible vision of an alternative path to political power that differed significantly from that advocated by the centre. Cripps, Laski and the Socialist League – and even the ILP – had no more faith than did Henderson or Citrine in the efficacy of direct, industrial action and, in the context of mass unemployment, it would have been hard to fault that pessimistic judgment. Nor was there available to the left a viable strategy for social transformation that relied for its first steps upon achievements in local government. Labour was very active in local elections and administration between the wars and scored notable successes at that level. Indeed, after 1929 its main electoral victories were in the local elections of 1933 and 1934. It was especially effective in London, where Herbert Morrison was to be hailed as "the organizer of victory" in 1934 and again in 1937 and where Labour compiled a highly creditable record in office. After 1937 Labour's local advance stalled, however, and what had been achieved prior to that, even in London, could hardly be considered a triumph of the left. Outside London, the practical record of local government action during the slump served primarily to demonstrate its limitations. These were made still worse by the deliberate actions of the central state, which crippled local finance with the granting of rate relief to industry in 1929, which imposed severe cuts in 1931 and discouraged borrowing by local authorities throughout the early 1930s and which sought, in reforming the Poor Law administration, to remove even that function from effective local control. All of these factors made it impossible for the left, or the Labour party more broadly, to develop a strategy based upon the localities, despite the vitality of constituency parties and trades councils; and none of the party's strategists, left or right, was tempted to propose such an approach.[29]

The weakness of the challenge from the left allowed the centre to regain its confidence and reassert its control of the Labour party. Already in 1933, Herbert Morrison had succeeded despite opposition in getting the party conference to adopt his limited vision of worker participation in nationalized industries. In 1934, the party began to regroup around a new programme, For Socialism and Peace, a rough compromise between the centre and the left; and the gap in the leadership left by MacDonald and Snowden began to be filled by the careful and cautious guidance of the trade unions. The National Joint Council was revived after 1931 and the TUC representatives given more authority. In practice, this meant that control passed increasingly into the hands of Citrine and Bevin, highly capable but quintessentially moderate leaders of the unions. Their presence exerted a centripetal pull on party policy and helped to ensure that the programmatic victories of the left would be short-lived and unfulfilled.[30]

Somewhat surprisingly, the unions did not use their new status to impose a particular policy direction on Labour. On the contrary, the TUC's own efforts to think through a response to the slump remained underdeveloped. There had been promising beginnings: the wage consciousness of the unions had given them an intuitive understanding of the futility of wage reductions as a means of restoring prosperity and of the importance of internal demand for the maintenance of employment. The late 1920s collaboration between the TUC and the Federation of British Industries had also helped to generate a consciousness of the common interests of those involved in industry and a critique of the role of the City in the economy and of government policies designed to assist the City, such as the gold standard. Even after the collapse of the Mond–Turner talks this shared perspective remained and prepared the way for the coalition between Bevin, Reginald McKenna and Keynes that developed on the Macmillan Committee. It also created an openness to Keynesian formulations among trade unionists that did not exist in the higher counsels of the party. Despite the promise inherent in these early developments, the TUC did not contribute much to policy formulation in the 1930s. The unions fudged the issue of free trade versus protection, they were inconsistent in their advocacy of public works and their lack of support for the unemployed was shameful. Nor did they follow up on the thoughtful proposals for expansionist policies developed by socialists on the continent and well known to the TUC through the International Federation of Trade Unions.[31]

On the other hand, the new prominence of the unions within Labour did not prevent the party from developing its own plans. The main lesson learned by all sections of the labour movement from 1931 was the urgent necessity of implementing the party's programme as quickly as possible. That required that the details had to be worked out beforehand and to that end the party executive had set up a policy sub-committee in December, 1931. The party's official efforts happily coincided with the emergence of a new generation of socialist intellectuals in and around the universities. A particularly impressive group, including Hugh Gaitskell, Colin Clark, James Meade and Evan Durbin, gathered initially around G.D.H. Cole at Oxford and joined the New Fabian Research Bureau. Clark and Meade moved on to Cambridge and worked closely with Keynes; Durbin and Gaitskell went to the LSE, where Dalton also taught and Abba Lerner and Nicholas Kaldor were students. Gaitskell and Durbin organized a regular series of discussions in the early 1930s in London about Labour policy, while Gaitskell ran a seminar at University College with a socialist orientation. Dalton, for his part, was meeting with the XYZ Club of City journalists in hopes of introducing more detailed knowledge into Labour's thinking about finance and banking. This cluster of academics and writers proved remarkably effective in getting a hearing within the Labour party and functioned as the primary medium through which Keynesian ideas entered the party's thinking. Upon their reworking of Keynes would be erected the party's commitment to a policy of social-democratic reform. Within the party their chief sponsor was Dalton, but they were also supported by Attlee and at least tolerated by the leaders of the trade unions.[32]

The progress of reformism before the war was considerable. A great deal of preliminary work was done between 1931 and 1935 and some of it was embodied in *For Socialism and Peace*, adopted in 1934. The mixed results of the election of 1935 – Labour regained a large number of seats and its key leaders now re-entered Parliament, but the National government nevertheless triumphed decisively – encouraged the leadership to refine and further moderate its programme. Dalton became party chairman in 1936 and presided over the preparation of *Labour's Immediate Programme* in 1937. This document committed the party to "four vital measures of reconstruction," affecting finance, land, transport and energy; and to "four great benefits" – "abundant food, good wages, leisure and security." The programme down-played nationalization in favour of a policy to control the "commanding heights" of the economy and said little about constitutional reform. In general, it gave few hostages to fortune. It was by no means a thoroughly Keynesian document, for deficit financing remained a matter of contention even within the party, and it was not especially helpful on the issue of planning. Nevertheless, in its specificity and practicality it constituted a major advance for Labour as a party of reform.[33]

By the late 1930s, therefore, the Labour party was much better equipped for office than it had been in 1924 or 1929. It even possessed a confidential plan to deal with the "financial panic" and capital flight that, it was assumed, would follow a Labour victory at the polls. After roughly forty years of ambivalence towards the state, Labour had acquired a programme that could conceivably be implemented by the existing state or by a slightly reformed variant of it. Its policy commitments, even if they were all made into reality, would not have produced socialism, but would have created a more humane and egalitarian capitalism. No doubt there would have arisen obstacles to the achievement even of *Labour's Immediate Programme*, but at least by 1939 the party and the unions had a reasonable amount of experience upon which to draw for overcoming them. Labour's approach to the state and to its effective use as an instrument of reform had thus made considerable progress since the party was first formed as a simple instrument to protect the trade union interest. That progress had come at a price and it had naturally been marked by losses as well as gains. Not only were there disappointments – particularly during 1924 and 1929–31 – and setbacks at the hands of the voters – as in 1918, 1924, 1931 and countless local contests – but there were losses that effectively foreclosed what had once seemed promising paths to social transformation. In particular, the interwar years had forced the labour movement to abandon strategies that gave more scope to mobilization through industrial conflict, to workplace democracy and to local initiative in favour of a strategy in which industrial conflict was a liability, workplace representation a potential embarrassment and local politics a distinctly ancillary pursuit. What emerged was a strategy that privileged Parliament, the national political arena and the leaders of the national party and nationally organized unions. Its vision of social transformation was anaemic and incremental, uniquely suited to a working class whose grander aspirations had already been effectively quashed.[34]

Still, it was a strategy and a vision that promised to deliver needed structural reforms and that could at least begin to make effective use of the British state. It also imparted a new sense of self-confidence within the labour movement. When war broke out in 1939, therefore, the Labour party insisted upon a commitment to social reform as the precondition for effective war mobilization. "For the second time within a generation," the National Executive proclaimed, "the British people have been called to the profound and tragic sacrifices of war. These sacrifices are demanded, as in 1914–18, in the name of Democracy and Freedom; they can be justified only as these noble ends are made real and living things in the lives of ordinary men and women." [35] Labour reiterated its support for "that national minimum standard of living which is a vital test of civilization;" for economic planning based upon extensive nationalization and public works; for a vastly improved system of health care; for housing and greater educational opportunity; for the abolition of the House of Lords and a restructuring of the existing machinery of government; and for a massive increase in taxes on the wealthy, including death duties, income tax and sur-tax, an annual capital tax during the war and "a bold capital levy" at its end. Labour had not spoken with such authority since the years immediately following the Great War, and had never been able previously to specify the price of its co-operation in such detail. The clarity and firmness of its stance ensured that in the wartime bargaining over postwar reconstruction Labour's position would be strongly represented and that the terms of reconstruction would more closely approximate Labour's prewar programme than that of any other party or interest.

The war would, of course, delay the implementation of any such programme and Labour would not soon get the opportunity to put its plans into practice. The election expected in 1939 or 1940 would be put off until after the war and the wartime coalition that took power in 1940 would give Labour an important role, but would not place reform at the top of the political agenda while the war was in progress. The party's new realism was therefore never properly tested and the next Labour government would come into power in very different circumstances than those envisioned in 1939. That government would be led by men whose lengthy apprenticeship in the wartime coalition under Churchill not only proved their fitness to govern but also demonstrated the broader compatibility between Labour's vision and the national interest in time of war. During the war, moreover, the very nature of the state had been transformed. It would therefore be unnecessary for Labour to preface the implementation of its programme with a restructuring of the state even to the limited extent foreseen in the plans of the late 1930s. That made life much easier for the party's leaders, at least for a few years. Whether it served the party's interests in the long run and whether, in the years since 1945, a more thoroughly reformed state apparatus would have produced better results, is another question.

Chapter 8

The "people's war" and the transformation of the state

By 1939, the constraints upon the expansion of the state were much weakened. The gold standard had been replaced by tariffs and the automatic discipline of the exchange rate upon state activity thereby removed. The commitment to balanced budgets had also to be abrogated in the interests of national defence. The needs of rearmament had produced a recognition of the need to think about the economy in aggregate terms and to begin to inventory the nation's resources with an eye towards their most efficient allocation.[1] The demands for an extension of state action had also become greater and more widely dispersed than before. An important body of "middle opinion" had emerged in favour of planning and the Labour party, the nation's most consistent advocate of collectivist policies, had evolved a more feasible programme than ever before. The preconditions for a substantial extension of the state's role in economy and society were thus broadly in place.

This did not guarantee that the state would in fact expand, however. Labour was not much closer to achieving an electoral majority in 1939 than it had been in the mid-1930s. Within the state, the Treasury had by no means absorbed the message of Keynes and its relaxation of the balanced budget rule was understood as strictly temporary. It was "untouched" by the vogue for deficit finance and "still regarded a deficit with all the horror that was necessary to excite the utmost efforts to reduce it."[2] The Chamberlain government, moreover, was uninterested in reform and complacent about the state of the economy, which had recovered considerably from 1931–2. There was thus little reason to believe in 1939 that the new possibilities for expanding the state would be explored or the demands for more interventionist policies heeded. It is by no means clear what direction social and economic policy would have taken if war had not come in 1939.

But war did come, and in its wake the logic of British politics was revolutionized. What had previously been merely possible became now a matter of national survival. What had seemed beyond the capacity of the state now became feasible, indeed essential, objects of public policy. The agenda of high politics would be dominated, of course, by the requirements of war, but a wide variety of social and economic questions could be subsumed under that heading. The mobilization of society's resources for war dramatically shifted political rhetoric and opened up space for ideas and policies that had previously not been accorded a serious hearing. The changed political environment was especially conducive to the sorts of claims and arguments that Labour had been making for years and particularly inhospitable to the complex of ideas and policies identified with Conservatism. The Second World War, in short, not only called forth new policies to win the war but also stimulated a broader transformation of politics and policy.

The immediate impact was not so dramatic, for the leadership of the country remained in the hands of Chamberlain and those who had worked with him to avoid war and who were thus reluctant to accept the full consequences of its coming. They had "no real belief that the state of war had to be turned into a war of steel and blood." [3] Rather, they feared that further steps to mobilize for war would put too great a strain on the country's productive potential and so hesitated before taking more drastic measures. Taxation, for example, was increased but only modestly and reluctantly. The government submitted a supplementary budget in September, 1939 that provided for an immediate increase in the standard rate of income tax from 5s 6d to 7s and a further jump to 7s 6d in 1940. This was felt to be the outer limit of what was acceptable to the income taxpayer. Additional revenues, it was thought by the Treasury and the government, would have to come from the mass of consumers through a variety of indirect taxes on beer, tobacco, sugar and, to avoid the impression of taxing only the pleasures of the working man, also on wine and spirits. At the same time an excess profits duty of 60 per cent was imposed on all businesses and there was talk of preparing for a capital levy. In fact, such talk did not get very far either in 1939 or later. Overall, the tax structure initially put in place to fight the war was scarcely adequate and, despite the wartime rhetoric of "equality of sacrifice," managed to treat the well-to-do relatively lightly and the poor rather harshly.

The subsequent budget of April, 1940 was prepared during the period of "phoney war," and the complacency bred during that moment of unreality discouraged any radical departure from the principles embodied in previous budgets. Despite calls from Keynes, from Labour and from publications like *The Economist*, the resistance to higher taxes remained strong. [4] The April budget represented for that reason only a "feeble . . . step towards a policy appropriate to total war." It was still considered impossible to impose further increases in the standard rate or other taxes upon the rich. Instead, there was further reliance on indirect taxes, falling yet again on beer, spirits and tobacco and, in an unusual step, on postal charges. Most important was the institution of a new purchase tax intended both to raise revenue and to discourage home consumption. The tax was strongly criticized as administratively cumbersome and highly regressive. Other aspects of domestic policy reflected the same immobilism. The progress of rearmament continued but was not much increased and substantial unemployment continued into 1940. Pending reform proposals, few enough in any case, were put aside for the duration of the war;

and there was little official consideration of the true dimensions of the changes war would necessitate. Mobilization was hampered as well by a lack of political consensus. Labour, for example, strongly supported the war effort but refused to join a government led by Chamberlain. They felt that the men who had presided over "appeasement" were not to be trusted to run the government during the war.[5]

The collapse of France led in early May, 1940 to the fall of the Chamberlain government and its replacement by a coalition, led by Churchill, which instituted a series of dramatic changes in the prosecution of the war, in the methods of mobilizing and paying for it, in the organization of the state and in the political climate. Central to all of these changes was the new role accorded to Labour and the trade unions. The wartime coalition was on paper an alliance between the three major parties, but in practice it was dominated on the domestic side by Labour. In 1940 Churchill was "to all intents and purposes without a party affiliation" and had a relationship to the main body of Conservatives, loyal for so long to Chamberlain, that was ambivalent at best. He and his closest supporters were preoccupied, moreover, with matters of defence.[6] The Liberals were very much minor partners in the coalition, which left Labour capable of exerting great influence on issues of home policy. The novel status of the party of the working class was best symbolized by Ernest Bevin's appointment to the Ministry of Labour, from which position the trade union leader was to exercise effective control over the mobilization of society for the war effort.

The full implications of the political revolution of May, 1940 would become clear only over the course of the war. The change would not force a shift in the military prosecution of the war, except in so far as it helped to create the preconditions for effective mobilization. It would, however, affect virtually every aspect of domestic politics and policy: the new balance of political advantage established in 1940 would lead to the adoption of a more egalitarian financial policy with which to fund the war, to a reformulation of war aims that included an expansive vision of postwar reconstruction and to parallel changes in the conception of the state and in its institutional shape. None of these would guarantee the outcome of the 1945 election or the policies that would be implemented by the Labour government, but they would form the essential background to Labour's postwar achievements.

The transformation in financial policy began immediately. A supplementary budget was introduced by the coalition as early as July, 1940. The April budget had been prepared on the assumption that direct taxes were high enough and that the current priority was to boost indirect taxes in order to extract an equivalent contribution from the lower classes and to decrease demand and dampen inflation. The result had been higher excise taxes and the new purchase tax. The July budget was largely designed to deal with Labour's objections to the regressive character of purchase tax. It thus reversed the priorities of the spring budget and increased the standard rate of income tax from 7s 6d to 8s 6d and also the rate of sur-tax. Excess profits duty was simultaneously increased to 100 per cent.[7]

The new direction in financial policy did not, by itself, constitute as yet a proper "adjustment to the acceleration of the war effort." As one Tory MP wrote to Churchill in September, 1940, "The timidity of our budgets is . . . the weakest part of our war policy." Still worse, the Chancellor had "let slip the opportunity to impose adequate burdens in a moment of unparallelled patriotic fervour and enthusiasm." That perception would inform the preparation of the landmark budget of April, 1941 which did finally constitute an appropriate response to the exigencies of war. The 1941 budget was accompanied by the publication of the White Paper on National Income, in which for the first time Keynesian estimates of national income were used officially. The connection suggests that 1941 represented a critical moment in the process by which Keynesian analysis came to permeate official thinking. In the actual shaping of the budget's provision, however, the input of Keynes and Keynesian calculations was but one factor. The other major determinants were the overriding Treasury concern with inflation and the enhanced status of Labour and of the trade unions within the counsels of the state.[8]

The control of inflation was the guiding principle of the budget, which was touted as a "stabilization" budget. The budget had by this time "in fact ceased to serve its peacetime purpose of providing finance" with which to support policy, for taxes could cover only a fraction of the actual cost of the war. But taxes could have an effect on the use of scarce resources and would also have distributive effects with important political and economic consequences. The aim of the budget was to depress demand by a combination of tax policies that would be perceived as equitable by the public at large and by labour in particular. The amount by which to reduce consumption was decided in part by reference to Keynesian calculations of the "inflationary gap" and in part by tactical considerations of the amount of taxation that could reasonably be levied. Keynes had offered a first approximation of the sums needed to prosecute the war and of the amount by which consumption needed to be reduced in his articles on "How To Pay for the War" in November, 1939. He redid the numbers in September, 1940, settling on a projected gap of £400 million. The figures were further revised over the next six months and the estimated gap increased to £500 million. The provisions of the budget were designed to absorb about half of this figure; the other half was to come from increased voluntary savings.[9]

The purposes behind the budget were clearly indicated by the rationale for its most distinctive innovation: the scheme for deferred tax credits. Keynes had argued in 1939 that a system of tax credits would serve several purposes: it would reduce purchasing power and lessen inflation during the war; it would build up accounts in the names of individual workers, giving them a small stake in the nation's capital; and, finally, the release of these credits after the war could be so timed as to serve as countercyclical stabilizers. Working people,

Keynes felt, would be trebly served – first by not having to suffer losses of income through inflation, second by their accumulation of credits, and third by the prospect of more stable employment after the war. The workers' representatives were not impressed and criticized the scheme because it promised an immediate reduction of cash income at a moment when the stability of prices could not be guaranteed. They demanded at the very least much "higher taxation of the upper classes and the extension of rationing before" acceding "to any curtailment of their money incomes." As a result of working-class opposition, the scheme was dropped from consideration during the first year of the war.[10]

The scheme was revived upon Keynes' entry into the Treasury at the end of June, 1940, but would have to be coupled with policies controlling prices and imposing new taxes in order to be acceptable. Income tax would in fact be increased from 8s 6d to 10s in the pound, despite the initial opposition of Churchill. In February, 1941 the Prime Minister had professed himself "disturbed" at the talk of higher taxes and refused to believe "that an Income Tax of that rate would be compatible with National Thrift or enterprise," and proceeded to accuse his colleagues of a "spirit of deference not to sound financial canons but to harping and insatiable left-wing propaganda." The logic of coalition prevailed, however, and Churchill was forced to accept the new taxation. Of nearly equal importance to the increase in income tax was the adoption in the 1941 budget of a policy of stabilizing food prices by subsidies. The thinking behind this policy again reflected the power of labour in the wartime coalition. Officials had long doubted the effectiveness of broad-based wage and price controls to prevent inflation. They feared a breakdown that would stimulate widespread demands for wage increases to catch up with inflation, and were not at all sanguine about the government's ability to handle an upsurge of strikes of the sort that had occurred in the First World War. To avoid this, the government informally adopted a policy of controlling the cost of items essential to working-class consumption. The budget of 1941 formalized and extended this approach and committed the government to subsidize the cost of essential goods and thus keep the cost of living index at a level no more than 25–30 per cent higher than 1939. The provision of Treasury subsidies represented, as *The Times* of 8 April 1941 explained, the "most important single proposal" in the entire budget. It promised a policy of suppressing inflation without recourse to wage controls – a major symbolic and practical victory for the labour movement.[11]

The 1941 budget was a critical step that reflected in its mix of policies the new balance of interests governing domestic policy-making. It may not have signalled a full-scale triumph of Keynesian thinking. The goal of the Treasury remained, after all, the very traditional one of controlling inflation and the acceptance of Keynesian techniques of national accounting in no way implied the acceptance of Keynesian prescriptions for dealing with the problem of unemployment. As James Meade of the newly formed Economic Section explained in 1943, "The Treasury are interested in estimates of post-war income (when they are at last driven to become conscious of the problem at all) merely as contributing the basis for an estimate of post-war tax revenue and so on as an aid to post-war budgeting policy on the old-fashioned lines of a balanced budget plus £100 millions for Sinking Fund in good and bad years." Nor was it beyond the ken of the Treasury to utilize the techniques of national accounting to arrive at very conservative estimates of the nation's productive capacity from which to draw extremely orthodox implications for policy. Given the prominence during the war of manpower budgeting based within the Ministry of Labour and National Service in planning the war effort, moreover, the new openness to Keynesian techniques was not to be of immediate consequence in changing the way the government managed the economy. Nevertheless, the budget of 1941 did represent a *de facto* break with past methods of financing the activities of the state.[12]

It marked in particular the beginnings of a new era in the politics of taxation. Prior to 1940 fiscal constraints had played a major role in restricting the policy options of all governments, whatever their political complexion. The recurring need for new revenue had kept taxation at or near the top of the agenda of high politics for nearly the whole of the twentieth century and the routine politics of taxation had provided a terrain of political struggle on which opponents of the state and of innovative policies could regularly prevail by mobilizing taxpayers and ratepayers in favour of retrenchment and "economy." The budget of 1941 changed this in several ways. It broke precedent by proceeding on the implicit assumption that budget-making was not "an independent procedure" undertaken by accounting officers in the Treasury and the Revenue departments but rather a political process with "wider ramifications [on] economic and social policy." The 1941 budget thus furthered the process through which wartime policies became linked to questions about the shape of postwar society. More practically, the budget provided a sound basis upon which to plan for future state expansion. Wartime levels of taxation were extremely high and the consensual acquiescence with which they were met suggested that while there would be considerable room for tax reductions after the war, the pressure to do so might not be irresistible. The government's ability to finance the war by borrowing at 3 per cent also ensured that the burden of postwar debt would be far less onerous than had been the case after 1918. Whichever party came into office after the war would thus be able to reduce taxes moderately and still retain the fiscal capacity to carry out significant social and economic reforms. For Labour, this would offer a unique opportunity to implement the party's plans without having to call upon taxpayers for further sacrifices. Even during the war, the removal of the fiscal limits to state action served as a spur to thinking about what the state could do with its enhanced capacity after the war. Opponents of state expansion attempted, of course, to conjure up the spectre of angry taxpayers demanding major reductions after the war, but it was a far less credible threat than it had previously been. The financial solution of 1941 therefore lifted one of the structural barriers to state expansion, allowed the development of what Laski called "the dynamic of democracy," and thereby facilitated a major new episode in policy innovation during and after the war.[13]

THE POLITICS OF RECONSTRUCTION

Ironically, the intensity with which Churchill fought the war allowed others to focus on postwar. The "financial revolution" of 1941 also freed officials and politicians to look towards postwar, and the constant concern for wartime morale prompted a recurring interest in war aims and a demand to flesh out just what sort of future the nation was being asked to fight for. The result was a focus on reconstruction that resulted in a series of official policy statements on education, town planning, health, the social services and employment. Within the government, and on Churchill's part especially, there was considerable resistance to making commitments for reconstruction. Officials were also notably cautious. The pressure from public opinion, from Labour and from the momentum of war mobilization, however, forced the coalition to come up with at least the broad outlines of a reconstruction programme. The government would soon discover that the dynamic of policy formation and debate was not easily controlled, and the runaway discourse on reconstruction would increase popular expectations for reform and elicit broad-based demands for state action. The emphasis upon reconstruction altered as well the balance between parties, giving a decisive edge to Labour in the contest over which party would shape the postwar order.[14]

The debate on reconstruction began early in the war, even before the fall of Chamberlain. Labour held a series of conferences on the "Home Front" in November, 1939 and shortly afterwards the National Executive issued a major statement on "Labour's Home Policy," calling for immediate planning for "the new society." The "sacrifices of War," Labour claimed, "can be justified only" if the people know what sort of society they are fighting to achieve. It was necessary, therefore, to plan for "the national minimum;" for public ownership of "key industries and services;" for public control of the banks and investment and over the location of industry; for an annual capital tax and a capital levy; for a massive public works programme to prevent unemployment after the war; and for improved health and welfare services and better treatment for the unemployed. There was no visible response to these demands from the Chamberlain government, but Labour's prominent role in the coalition made it impossible to ignore such concerns after May, 1940. The new Cabinet quickly decided to develop a set of war aims that were not "purely negative" but, as Clement Attlee put it, "positive and revolutionary." Getting agreement on war aims proved difficult, however, and the committee appointed to draft a programme gave up on the job in December, 1940. In its stead Churchill contented himself with vague but grand pronouncements and appointed in

January, 1941 a Reconstruction Committee of the Cabinet under the direction of Arthur Greenwood to work on the problem at a more deliberate pace. Greenwood would do little during his two years as chair of the committee, and the committee itself met only four times. For the first two years of the new government's life, therefore, the public commitment to a "new order" remained extremely woolly and was backed up by few specific plans.[15]

Greenwood's major achievement was to appoint William Beveridge to a sub-committee to review the problems of social security. The publication of the Beveridge Report in December, 1942 marked the emergence of reconstruction at the top of the wartime political agenda. Beveridge's starting point was the need to bring order out of the patchwork of services that provided for the social security of British citizens. The problem could have been approached as merely an administrative question, but Beveridge was among those inspired by the demands of war to think expansively about the shape of the new order. He therefore adopted a broad approach to the question and chose to construct his recommendations on the social services on three assumptions that, while reasonable and effective as rhetoric, were highly controversial. The social services would do their job, Beveridge argued, only if coupled with family allowances, with universal health and rehabilitation services and with full employment. Only together could these policies and programmes successfully overcome the "five giants on the road of reconstruction": "Want . . .[,] Disease, Ignorance, Squalor and Idleness." [16]

The report was immensely popular. Beveridge orchestrated a public relations campaign on its behalf, for which he earned bitter resentment from officials and ministers, but clearly its popularity owed more to the message than to its packaging. It was not an especially glistening package but rather a mix of detailed recommendations and broad commitments. The report began unobtrusively by discussing the administrative confusion surrounding the social services and offered a surprisingly mild criticism of existing policy: "British provision for security, in adequacy of amount and in comprehensiveness, will stand comparison with that of any other country; few countries will stand comparison with Britain."(6) Existing practice thus stood in need primarily of "closer co-ordination," rather than radical extension.(6) The report went on, of course, to adopt as one of its guiding principles the need for "a national minimum" guaranteed by the state.(7) That would be possible only if the three famous assumptions about allowances, health care and the maintenance of employment were fulfilled.(8, 120) It was the combination of practical proposals for reforming social security with this much broader vision of the social policies needed to bring about "freedom from want" that gave the report its rhetorical power.(153–72) It was not a particularly profound document, it articulated no new philosophy of the state and no grand vision of the relationship between citizenship and welfare, but it was sufficient to capture and channel the popular desire for change and to reshape the wartime discourse on social policy.[17]

Particularly important was its impact upon the fortunes of Labour. The Beveridge plan was not socialist or even social-democratic in inspiration, and it may be doubted that anything like it could have come from either the unions or the Labour party. Labour's vision was more class-based and oriented more towards questions of distribution than was Beveridge's, and the unions and friendly societies had interests in the provision of various sorts of insurance that the Beveridge proposals were sure to infringe. It is likely in particular that the commitment to family allowances made by Beveridge would probably not have been so prominent or unambiguous in a plan of more purely Labour or trade union origins. Labour had been moving in the 1930s towards a reformist, social-democratic programme largely compatible with Beveridge, but it was embedded in an outlook of quite different hue. The party had also come around by the spring of 1942 to support for family allowances and had endorsed a set of proposals that clearly anticipated Beveridge. For his part, Beveridge worked so assiduously on obtaining TUC approval of the report that his behaviour prompted a spokesman for the employers to charge that he "has done little more than accept TUC conceptions." The perspectives of Labour, of Beveridge and of other "progressives" were clearly converging in 1941–2 on a common set of reform proposals.[18]

Whatever residual doubts Labour or the unions may have harboured about the philosophy articulated in the Beveridge Report or about its specific recommendations were overcome in the flurry of debate that greeted its publication. Labour came out quickly in favour, accepted most of the report's detailed proposals and began to press for its implementation.[19] The plan elicited considerable resistance from officials and from Conservatives in and out of the government, however. Whether to endorse the report turned into a highly partisan issue; and in the partisan contest that ensued the Conservatives were seen to be unwilling to embrace the report while Labour was perceived as being strongly in support. Opinion did not, of course, divide quite so neatly: a significant body of Conservatives responded favourably to the report; while Bevin, the most powerful Labour minister, initially criticized it; and other Labour ministers were compromised by their adherence to the position adopted by the Cabinet. Despite these qualifications, it was clear that Labour and the unions welcomed the Beveridge Report while the Conservatives did not. Labour thus became identified with and committed to a programme which may have arisen from a very different political quarter but which they soon made their own. The connection may have been in certain respects opportunistic, but it was no less effective for that.[20]

The Beveridge Report brought the debate about reconstruction to centre stage and intensified the efforts of politicians, officials and others to develop proposals in various policy domains. A host of official and private reports appeared on education, health, housing, town and country planning and kept the question of reconstruction at the top of the political agenda. They also contained proposals that would often form the basis of subsequent reforms and helped to create a consensus on the need for a thorough-going reconstruction of British society. On the other hand, there were enough specific disagreements to remind the public of the essential differences in outlook that separated the parties. Increasingly, Labour came to be viewed as the party that would make good on the promise of reconstruction, while the Conservatives were unable to escape the blame for the policies of the 1930s and the misery and failures with which they were so inextricably bound up. The Conservatives were particularly vulnerable on the question of unemployment, and it was over employment policy that the most important policy debates occurred after 1942. The fundamental spur to the discussion of employment was the stark contrast between the memory of the 1930s, with its persistent and mass unemployment, and the labour famine of the war. The experience of war seemed to prove that government could cure unemployment. But would the state in fact do so when the demands of war were no longer pressing? And if so, how? The issues were joined early on in the war. Labour demanded in 1939 that government commit itself to public works to prevent the re-emergence of unemployment after the war. In July, 1941, James Meade of the Economic Section began the official debate on the problem with a paper on "Internal Measures for the Prevention of General Unemployment." The paper laid out an essentially Keynesian argument: it began by distinguishing between frictional unemployment, structural unemployment concentrated in particular industries or regions, and general unemployment, and proceeded to suggest that "the solution of the problem of general unemployment is a necessary condition for the reduction of other types of unemployment." Preventing general unemployment was a question primarily of maintaining demand, which could be accomplished by monetary policy, by efforts to boost home consumption, by public works and by budgetary policy.[21]

The Keynesian proposals of Meade and the Economic Section met with predictable opposition from the Treasury. The Treasury's position was that the fundamental causes of unemployment in the 1930s were structural and that policy should aim at moving labour out of the old industries and regions into more prosperous employments. They argued further that the immediate postwar problem would be how to limit demand and control inflation, not how to stimulate demand in a slump. The Treasury was also unwilling to accede to a policy that committed the government to regular use of the budget to maintain aggregate demand. After the war, they argued, there would be an enormous debt to be repaid and in that context the prospect of budget deficits designed to stimulate employment would imply a permanent relaxation of the balanced budget principle. That was unthinkable: "It would be impossible in the Treasury's view to justify any policy which rested on the basis of the indefinite continuance of unbalanced budgets. The altered conditions of the modern world serve to increase rather than to diminish the importance of budgetary solvency." The Treasury's position was fully consistent with its views in the 1930s, and subsequent discussions would show how tenaciously those views were held.[22]

The positions articulated in 1941–2 would be repeated many times over the next two years and modified only slightly. Proponents of a more activist policy would propose specific mechanisms for controlling consumption and investment: consumer demand could be stimulated by variations in contributions to social insurance; investment in public works could likewise be varied counter-cyclically by forward planning by local authorities; private investment was more difficult to control, but could be influenced by the granting of tax credits for investment. Predictably, the Treasury and the Inland Revenue came up with objections to each of these proposals, although they felt compelled to accept the principle that efforts should be undertaken to maintain a steady level of demand and to stabilize public investment over the trade cycle.[23]

The debate among officials would most likely have dragged on inconclusively if it had not been for the impact of the Beveridge Report. Beveridge not only shifted the terms of the reconstruction discourse but, more specifically, he had premised his proposals for social security on the maintenance of employment. Attention therefore turned quickly in 1943 towards the question of employment policy. The fact that Beveridge himself moved on from the report on social security to the drafting of a parallel report on employment meant that the government would have to match his effort with a document of its own.[24] From early 1943 onward, therefore, it was clear that the Treasury would have to acquiesce in a policy incorporating major elements of the Keynesians" views. Their job henceforth would be to limit and contain these commitments; the result was the set of compromises which made up the White Paper of 1944.

The terms of the compromise gave some satisfaction to both sides. The White Paper adopted a basically Keynesian framework and committed government to "the maintenance of a high and stable level of employment after the war." On the other hand, it stressed the dependence of British prosperity upon the revival of international trade, the importance of increased industrial efficiency and the mobility of labour, and the dangers of inflation. The proposals put forward by the Economic Section for controlling demand and investment were included, but not without qualifications, and the section on budgetary policy was especially qualified and cautious. The White Paper conceded that it was not necessary to balance the budget on an annual basis but added that "None of the main proposals contained in this paper involves deliberate planning for a deficit in the National Budget in years of sub-normal trade activity." Treasury officials felt they had succeeded in limiting the specific commitments in the report to those "which will have no ill effect as regards budgetary stability and are unlikely to be embarrassing to future Governments." Their opponents had managed to extract a promise of future action, however vaguely defined, that would have been unthinkable before 1939 and that Keynes could with justice regard as "a revolution in official opinion." It can certainly be argued that "the White Paper willed the end of full employment but ducked most of the issues about means." That still represented an advance over earlier policies in which the proclamation of goals was held hostage to the demonstration that the means were fully adequate to their achievement.[25]

The nuances of the White Paper were largely lost on the general public and even ministers tended to exaggerate what had been agreed to. The desperate efforts by the Treasury and the Tories to limit the report's commitments were for that reason quite unsuccessful. The year 1944 saw the appearance of several public pronouncements on employment. The Labour party issued the first, *Full Employment and Financial Policy*, in April; the White Paper followed in May. The latter was rushed into print to beat Beveridge, whose *Full Employment in a Free Society* went to press in June and appeared in the fall. Later in the year came the TUC's *Interim Report on Post-War Reconstruction*. There were important differences in these reports, but the public debate on full employment did little to clarify them and instead served to escalate popular expectations while reinforcing the political message of the debate over the Beveridge Report about who would do the most to make it a reality. Labour was seen as the party genuinely committed to a policy of full employment, the Conservatives as reluctantly and hesitantly acquiescing. The perception was not wildly askew, and would be confirmed in small ways throughout the debate over reconstruction and in a large way during the election campaign of 1945.[26]

RECONSTRUCTION AND THE STATE

The debate over reconstruction was very public, even where officials took the initiative in formulating proposals and in framing the discussion. But there was simultaneously a debate over the machinery of government that was not so public and whose outcome was not much influenced by public opinion. It was widely understood that the policy commitments emerging from the debate on reconstruction would require some changes in the nature of the state. The relationship between innovations in policy and in administration was not consistently close, however, and politicians proposed novel policies without specifying the precise machinery needed to carry them out. The result was a debate on the machinery of government and a corresponding set of changes in administration, neither of which were truly adequate to the tasks being assigned to government in the plans for reconstruction.

The most telling example was probably that of employment policy. The White Paper was noncommittal over what changes in administration would be needed to carry out the state's responsibility for maintaining employment. To Beveridge, however, the issue had to be confronted. In preparing his more *dirigiste* plan, therefore, he sought advice from various quarters on what administrative machinery would be most appropriate. The Liberals called for an "economic general staff," as did Political and Economic Planning. Geoffrey Crowther of *The Economist* proposed a "supreme economic commander." To Beveridge, such proposals did not go far enough, for they left the Treasury largely intact. "But can we," Beveridge asked rhetorically, "build the new world upon the present Treasury foundations?" More to Beveridge's liking was a proposal from the Nuffield College Reconstruction Survey calling for a Minister of Planning and a National Investment Board.[27] Beveridge himself opted for the creation of a new Ministry of National Finance, responsible for ensuring that the "total outlay" of the state was sufficient to sustain employment. Beneath that would be a department of control "with no strictly ministerial function," analogous to the present Treasury but carrying out the distinctly subsidiary and "technical" task of ensuring value for money. The Ministry of National Finance would continue the wartime practice of "budgeting by man-power rather than money." It would carry out its mission with the aid of a National Investment Board and with detailed assistance from a new Ministry of National Development, dealing with town and country planning, housing and transport, and from a revamped labour ministry.[28]

Beveridge was unusually candid in his advocacy of new administrative machinery and was strongly criticized for it.[29] But he was not alone in believing in the need for serious alterations in the nature of government. Two crucial factors emboldened Beveridge and many others and allowed them to think new thoughts about the purposes of government and about how the state should be organized to achieve them. The first was the critique of the British political establishment that grew out of the revulsion over "appeasement" and the "phoney war." The same spirit that produced the fall of Chamberlain and the coalition government led to a sharp criticism of the old habits and institutions through which the policies of "appeasement" had been carried out. The established machinery of government produced, as Ivor Jennings put it, "excessive timidity" on the part of officials. Others put the matter more sharply: in a letter to Churchill in 1940 Lord Ampthill referred to the bureaucracy as a "5th column" impeding the war effort, and complaints of "Treasury obstruction" were widespread. Maurice Hankey, former Secretary to the Cabinet, claimed in 1943 that the "system" of administration before the war had to bear "some share of responsibility for the deplorable situation in which this country found itself in 1939 for the second time in twenty-five years and which brought us to the brink of disaster." Sir Bernard Gilbert, a staunch defender of the Treasury, was forced to acknowledge the force of the "wide attack on all the contributors to our unpreparedness . . . at the outbreak of the war." From 1940 onwards, therefore, there were persistent calls for a reform of the machinery of government, and in particular for changes in the Treasury and the Foreign Office. These two departments were thought to have been deeply implicated in past failures and thus most in need of restructuring.[30]

Novel thinking on the machinery of government was also stimulated by the practical transformation of the state during the war. The state over which Churchill presided after 1940 was a very different creature from the state as it had evolved up to 1939. Changes had occurred in the relationship between the state and the economy and in the very structure of the state. The changes were in theory temporary, but they raised pointedly the question of what shape the state should take after the war. How many of the innovations of the war should be continued, and what further alterations would produce a more efficient structure for postwar? It was almost inevitable that some aspects of the state's role and of its institutional configuration would not return to normal after the war, but which ones? It was essential to find out while the war was still on. The outcome of the pressures to rethink and reshape the administrative machine was a major debate on the nature of the postwar state. The debate took place mainly within the government, and primarily within the Anderson Committee on the Machinery of Government appointed in 1942.[31]

The starting point for Anderson and for all discussions of the structure of the state was the wartime regime of controls and intervention. That regime had been assembled gradually under Chamberlain and then more decisively under the coalition. In 1939 the Ministry of Labour was renamed the Ministry of Labour and National Service and given responsibility for co-ordinating manpower for civil and military purposes; Ministries of Food, Economic Warfare, Home Security, Shipping and Supply were also set up. After the change in government, further alterations were made in the allocation of tasks between departments. The Factory Inspectorate was shifted to the Ministry of Labour, giving the department (and Ernest Bevin) effective control over the conditions of work throughout industry. At Bevin's urging, a new Ministry of Works was established in 1940 to "plan and supervise all building and civil engineering work for the government." The Ministry of War Transport was created in 1941 out of the Ministries of Transport and Shipping, and in the next year the Ministry of Fuel and Power was set up to cope with the problem of coal supplies. The Board of Trade greatly expanded its functions during this same period and the Ministry of Production was established in 1942 to oversee the production programmes of various military and non-military departments and to co-ordinate the supply of raw materials. Later in the war a Minister of Reconstruction was appointed, and new Ministries of Town and Country Planning and of National Insurance established.[32]

These departmental changes were complemented by a strengthening of the centre of the administrative machine – primarily the Cabinet Secretariat and the Lord President's Committee. A Central Economic Information Service was begun in 1939 and divided in 1941 into the Central Statistical Office and the Economic Section, both within the Cabinet Secretariat.[33] The Economic Section was staffed by professional economists and would play a major role in facilitating the entry of Keynesian ideas into official thinking, especially on employment policy. Its location outside the Treasury allowed the section that measure of independence necessary for it to become a successful rival to the Treasury in the provision of economic advice to the government. Its advice could go directly to the Prime Minister, though ordinarily it went through the Lord President's Committee, which was established to co-ordinate the government's home policy and was chaired by Sir John Anderson until 1943 and by Clement Attlee after that. By "the beginning of 1942," it has been said, "this committee constituted almost a 'Home' Cabinet." [34]

The Lord President's Committee was typical of the style of administration practised during the war. Churchill preferred to work by committees that were organized by function and cut across traditional departmental boundaries. This not only brought the most crucial issues to the attention of senior ministers, but also allowed input from the different partners in the coalition and hence a forum for reconciling their differences. All of the most important work of the government was supervised through this system of interlocking committees of ministers. Beneath this level of ministerial committees, and designed to assist their work, was a series of more or less parallel committees of officials. At the very centre of all this activity was the War Cabinet, from which the Chancellor of the Exchequer, and by implication the Treasury, were excluded for much of the war. The pattern of responsibility that grew out of this arrangement was at first sight very confusing and filled with potential overlapping and conflicts of interest, but in practice it proved flexible and highly efficient. [35]

The much-expanded administrative machine oversaw the mobilization of virtually the entire economy for war. It operated a vast array of economic controls, usually referred to as "physical controls" because of their direct, often quantitative, character. The allocation of manpower, of scarce raw materials and even of financial assets was carefully rationed so as to minimize conflicts between domestic consumption and war production and competition between rival producers. Britain's dependence on American imports of food as well as strategic materials required close and detailed planning and a new level of co-ordination of foreign and domestic economic affairs. It was essential as well for the state to establish intimate links with the industries upon whose output the successful prosecution of the war depended. The major departments came to see themselves and to act as "production authorities," responsible for particular industries. The system was to be supervised by the Ministry of Production set up in 1942, but in practice it worked department by department and industry by industry. "Production authorities" came to act as sponsors for the industries and companies under their supervision, not only licensing firms and allocating supplies, but also speaking on their behalf within the government. The connections between these nodes of control at the centre and those whose activities were controlled were both extensive and pervasive. By the height of war mobilization in 1943 virtually the entire span of industry was covered, as were agriculture, mining and distribution. The system was "corporatist" in social and economic terms, bringing together industry, labour and the state in regular bargaining about production, but it was administratively structured by region, allowing for a degree of detailed intervention that would not have been possible from the centre. The Joint Production Committees set up at workplaces, particularly in engineering, even brought the principle into the very heart of industry. Overall, the system worked reasonably well enough to avoid many of the problems that had surrounded war production during the First World War.[36]

The wartime changes in the state provided both the starting point for discussions of the future shape of the state and also a model of how it might be organized. It was not a model that could be copied without modification; certain features would undoubtedly have to be adjusted to peacetime conditions. Still, it had many attractive features which might be continued. It was to prove especially appealing to Labour, and its ready availability in 1945 might well have prevented the emergence of a more thorough-going plan of administrative reform. The pattern of controls imposed during the war accomplished many of the tasks that Labour had identified previously as essential for an effective socialist government. Before the war, Evan Durbin argued, Labour had decided that control over "the creation and distribution of credit" was the key to socialist planning and had developed a set of detailed notions of how this was to be done. "During the war," he claimed, "every one of these 'ideas' had become a reality," with just a couple of exceptions.[37] The war had brought about the possibility of controlling the economy at the macro-economic level through the budget, and put into practical effect the comprehensive strategic direction of the economy through the manpower budget and a wide array of detailed physical controls. The question of just who at the centre was responsible for directing this machinery was not fully resolved during the war, but the use of ministerial committees and other mechanisms of interdepartmental co-ordination provided at least a forum for adjudicating disputes. This approach allowed the business of government to proceed without having to resolve thorny jurisdictional questions and without offending the major partners in the wartime coalition. It therefore served as a precedent and a model that were not easily jettisoned after the war.

A dramatic transformation of administration in 1945 was precluded as well by the inconclusive nature of the deliberations over the machinery of government that had gone on during the war. Those deliberations occurred mostly within the closed sessions of the Anderson Committee, and their results are worth examining in some detail. Like most other features of the wartime government, the committee was simultaneously a response to external pressure and a delicate compromise between the partners in the coalition. The pressure to reform the structure of government made some sort of inquiry essential. Labour, for its part, shared many of the criticisms made from outside and wanted in addition to restructure the administration with an eye towards postwar. Churchill was notably ambivalent. In 1940–1 he tolerated and even encouraged quite nasty criticisms of the civil service, but he was reluctant to undertake inquiries whose conclusions might imply a commitment to a more activist postwar state. The impetus to set up the Anderson Committee came from Stafford Cripps in June, 1942 and was strongly supported by Attlee, who was in the chair when the Cabinet agreed to its appointment in August. Shortly after this Edward Bridges, then Secretary to the Cabinet, wrote to Churchill about the possible membership of the committee, recommending against anyone who "might be influenced by the rather theoretical views of, e.g., Mr. Harold Laski and Mr. Kingsley Martin, Editor of 'The New Statesman'." Churchill was equally suspicious of theoreticians and expressed the hope that "these speculative inquiries will not be allowed to distract the attention of any of the Ministers from the urgent war tasks with which they are charged." Churchill delayed for some time and finally appointed Anderson, Cripps, Morrison, Kingsley Wood and John Simon in December, 1942. The committee's composition was a frank recognition of the importance of the issue to Labour, its form a distinct concession to officials who feared a public inquiry involving outsiders of "theoretical" bent. There was no Laski or Kingsley Martin on the committee, nor even a respectable critic like Ivor Jennings. Rather, the chair was held by the consummate insider John Anderson; the committee proceeded cautiously; its deliberations were covered in a "blanket of official silence" and it issued no public report.[38]

The Anderson Committee considered a wide range of issues – the reform of Parliamentary procedure, the role of non-governmental bodies in policymaking, the future of the regional administration, and questions of recruitment and training in the civil service. The most important question it confronted, however, was the shape of "the centre of the government machine" and the role of the Treasury within it. The committee received lots of proposals and ideas, but in the end took an extremely cautious line. Cripps, for example, was keen on the creation of "superintending ministries" and in particular a "superministry" for economic development; and he tried to extract from the committee an acknowledgment of such a need for "co-ordination." Keynes was also impressed with the possible "advantages of a grouping of the principal economic departments under a single super-Minister." From his wartime post at the Board of Trade, Hugh Dalton suggested that his department might play just such a role and in February, 1942 elicited Herbert Morrison's support for a scheme to place the Board of Trade "on a parity with the Treasury" and to submit every year "an industrial, as well as a financial, budget." Dalton and his young advisors, his "post-warriors," thus forwarded plans to the Anderson Committee proposing a greater role for the Board of Trade, and Dalton also reached an agreement with Ernest Bevin for a postwar division of responsibilities between their two departments that left the Treasury much diminished. Even before that Bevin had intervened on his own, urging in the spring of 1943 that the Ministry of Labour should take on the responsibility for employment policy and be accorded what one official described as a "dominant position in the economic field." The most "realistic" suggestions came from Attlee, who proposed "alterations in the government machinery" and "also changes in the methods of financial control." Attlee wanted the Treasury to be split along functional lines, with a permanent secretary in charge of financial matters and another permanent secretary working directly under the Prime Minister in charge of supervision of the civil service. He was interested as well in plans for wider recruitment, for the "interchange of personnel" between the Treasury and other departments and for the establishment of a staff college. Behind all of these plans, of course, was a desire on the part of Labour ministers and other reformers not to allow the Treasury to resume after the war the role it had played between the wars in blocking innovative social and economic policies.[39]

None of these proposals made much of an impact on the Anderson Committee, whose reports on the Treasury and on the "Centre of the Government Machine" were particularly disappointing to those who wanted a major restructuring of the state. The report on the Treasury, for example, defended the Treasury's role very strongly. The control of expenditure by the Treasury and the Chancellor was "a natural outcome of the development of our Parliamentary institutions" and thus entirely proper. So, too, was the Treasury's control of the Cabinet's agenda or, as the authors of the report judiciously described it, the "old-established practice by which proposals involving expenditure are only put before the Cabinet by Ministers after prior consultation with the Treasury, so that the Chancellor of the Exchequer is given an opportunity of examining their fiscal implications." Criticism of the exercise of these controls was "inevitable," but basically misplaced. Over the past two decades, the report argued, the Treasury had made great efforts "to remove the causes of criticism," and the regular use of the telephone had by now "broken down the distant hostility" between the Treasury and other departments. These efforts and technologies had helped to further the aim of creating a "unified civil service," which was also the purpose behind the appointment of the Permanent Secretary to the Treasury as the "Official Head of the Civil Service." In short, the report made virtually no concessions to the criticisms that had been levelled at the Treasury or at the administrative machinery in general.[40]

It was this quite defensive and unrepentant stance that prompted Lord Hankey's complaint in 1943. He was not alone, however, in regarding it as an insufficient response to the visible need for greater government involvement in social and economic issues. Later versions of the report therefore modified its tone and moved towards an acknowledgment of the future importance of economic policy. The subsequent report on "The Centre of the Government Machine," for example, represented at least a rhetorical concession to the new dimensions of policy-making. It assumed that the Treasury would be responsible for the co-ordination of economic policy and accepted the continued need for specialist economists within the government. Compared to the relatively grand proposals on offer in 1943, however, its recommendations were exceptionally modest. The report recognized that in postwar "there will need to be a co-ordination of measures of economic policy, much greater than has existed in the past," but beyond that envisioned merely a continuation of the practice of co-ordinating economic policy through a mechanism like the Lord President's Committee and of having the economists and planners, such as they were, attached to such a committee. It was a minimalist vision that deliberately excluded plans for a "grandiose economic general staff *à la Beveridge*" or even *à la Keynes*, *Cripps* or *Dalton*. Its vision was seriously constrained by official caution and self-interest and could barely be expanded to comprehend the full extent of wartime mobilization. It is no wonder that Labour ministers were unenthusiastic about the work of the Anderson Committee or that Attlee, reviewing its reports in late 1945, should describe them as constituting, in effect, "an examination by persons from within the machine." [41]

The uninspiring results of the Anderson Committee were replicated in the efforts to reform the machinery of government covering defence and foreign policy. Churchill himself, having assumed the position of Minister of Defence in 1940, oversaw the restructuring of the War Office over the next three years. His sense of reform was personal rather than structural, however, and the changes he introduced were largely superficial. The attempt to reform the Foreign Office was a more serious affair that engaged the attention not just of Anthony Eden, who carried it out, but also of the Labour ministers in the coalition and of the public at large. Critics of "appeasement" had focused most sharply on the Foreign Office, so obviously the preserve of a separate caste as to invite criticism of its social composition and its narrowness of vision. The foreign service, argued even Conservative critics, "is recruited from too small a circle . . . it tends to represent the interests of certain sections of the nation rather than those of the country as a whole . . . its members lead too sheltered a life . . . they have insufficient understanding of economic and social questions . . . the extent of their experience is too small . . . and . . . the range of their contacts is too limited." This basically class-based critique was followed up with particular zeal by Labour and Attlee, Bevin and Dalton all became involved in the debate over the reform of the foreign service. Bevin made the most interesting intervention, putting forward a surprisingly well-developed critique and counterproposal embodying a classically "Labourist" and "corporatist" vision. [42]

As Bevin saw it, the narrow social base of the foreign service meant that it was "out of touch with the growing forces of Labour, Trade Unionism and the socialist organizations in the world." Hence, it missed a "real chance" of mobilizing "the democratic forces in other countries" to resist "the growth of Nazism and fascism." Bevin's case rested heavily on the fact that the Foreign Office had been indifferent, if not actively hostile, to the International Labour Organization throughout the interwar years. He instanced in particular British obstruction of international efforts to regulate hours and conditions of work, and believed in general that by failing to take the ILO seriously, previous governments had failed to develop contacts with, and an understanding of, popular forces and attitudes in other countries. The Foreign Office chose instead to recruit from an exclusive social class and its staff preferred to move in similar circles when away from home. No wonder, Bevin argued, that the

Nazi characterization of British society as "plutocratic" was so subtly effective. Its projection abroad was in fact plutocratic. Bevin's critique was surprisingly thorough. It managed to connect the peculiar features of Britain's class structure with the patterns of recruitment and training of its elite foreign service, the style of work adopted by those in the service and the policies they pursued. His proposed remedies were less substantial: recruitment from a broader range of social classes; more training, especially in economic and social issues; more connection and interchange between the foreign service and the home civil service; the appointment in major foreign capitals of officers charged with keeping up with social conditions and movements – "labour attachés;" and a policy of international co-operation for development. Bevin's analysis and his recommendations reveal the strengths and limitations of the "Labourist" and "corporatist" outlook which he held in common with so many other Labour leaders. He was keenly aware of "the traditional attitude to Labour: that it was something separate and apart," and of the exclusion from the higher counsels of the state of men of his class and political allegiance. The failures of the old ruling class vindicated that sentiment and validated the claims of men like Bevin – and behind him a veritable army of solid trade union leaders – to be brought into the charmed circle of the political establishment. It was a perspective, however, which did not go much beyond minor changes in personnel and which left intact the basic structures governing the conduct of British foreign policy. It was the vision that Bevin would himself attempt to implement as Foreign Secretary after 1945 and whose limitations would become starkly visible during the onset of the Cold War.[43]

During the war even that limited vision was too radical to serve as a guide to the reform of the foreign service. The criticisms of the Foreign Office put forward in 1940 by Bevin, Dalton and others provided the impetus behind the reforms of 1943, but they were shaped by more reliable hands. Sir Malcolm Robertson produced a report in 1941, which was subsequently superseded by a proposal from Anthony Eden. Eden accepted the notion that the foreign, diplomatic and consular services should be merged, but rejected the proposal for a closer association with the home civil service. He accepted as well the need to "broaden the field of entry" into the service and, as a corollary to that, to increase the amount of training after entry. It was proposed in particular that a quarter of the new recruits after the war should enter not by the old method of examination but by interviews that would take into account other qualities and experience. Perhaps most important, Eden proposed an attractive "super-annuation" scheme to encourage early retirement for those deemed unfit for continued service and to provide "pensions sufficient to keep them out of poverty and to mark the fact that no disgrace is implied by their retirement." Eden was not keen on "labour attachés" or on the need for a new spirit of social reform, but recognized the need to carry out at least a modest purge of the old personnel.[44]

Eden's proposals were debated through the fall of 1942, with Conservative ministers generally hesitant and Labour ministers in favour of somewhat more thorough-going reform. Dalton, for example, wanted the Board of Trade to have more say over appointments and training. Officials were at least as cautious as Conservative ministers: Bridges, for example, worked very hard in December, 1942 to shape a committee to finalize Eden's proposals that would minimize criticism. After some manoeuvring, Attlee was made chair and supervised the last stages of the development of the new policy. The outcome was very much along the lines laid out by Eden, who thanked Attlee for his careful handling of the touchy subject. The plan was announced in the White Paper, *Proposals for the Reform of the Foreign Service*, published in January 1943.[45]

The wartime struggles over the machinery of government therefore produced far less dramatic changes than the rhetoric surrounding the crisis of 1940 or the needs of reconstruction might have suggested. The reasons are not hard to find. The process of deciding on administrative reforms was largely dominated by officials or by ministers whose experience in government made them relatively complacent about the existing structure. Officials were, for their part, under considerable pressure to adapt to the new demands put on the state during the war and to respond to the criticisms about the inadequacy of the initial response to the threat of war and to the war itself. The eclipse of the Treasury during the war and the need fundamentally to transcend the prior fiscal limitations upon policy significantly diminished the ability of officials to control the state apparatus and to restrict its sphere of activity. Still, they retained considerable influence over the implementation of policy and their advice on questions of administrative structure carried special weight. The limited character of the recommendations for permanent changes in the machinery of government thus marked in fairly precise terms the limitations of the fluidity and flexibility of administration produced by the war.

Politics was rather more fluid, however, and the shifts in public opinion, in popular expectations of what the state would do after the war and in political allegiance, were far more dramatic. The extent of those shifts was registered decisively in the election of 1945, when a sizeable majority of the voters accepted Labour's claim to be the party truly committed to reconstruction and to the use of the state to provide a better life for Britain's citizens. Labour's mandate was unusually clear: it was to carry out the commitments extracted from the coalition to institute policies which would guarantee a "national minimum" of social provision and to provide work for all who sought it. It was a mandate shaped by the politics of war and made feasible by the transformation of the state during the war. It was a set of commitments that Labour gladly accepted and undertook to fulfil by means basically compatible with its long-term preferences for planning, nationalization and central control of the economy.

Perhaps most important, it was a set of commitments which the Conservatives gave every reason to believe they would shirk. The debate over reconstruction revealed that Conservatives were far less committed to the proposals of the Beveridge Report and to full employment than was Labour, and the general election of 1945 reinforced that message. The Conservatives not only chose to attack Labour in the language of the 1920s, seeking to conjure up fears of bolshevism and of dictatorship, but also decided to campaign on the promise of restoring the free market. The Conservative manifesto of 1945 was largely an attack upon the expanded state. It promised a substantial and "early reduction of taxation;" called for a rejection of "docility to a State machine;" warned that "state ownership and control" would create a nation of "State serfs;" and tempered its support for full employment with a commitment to "individual liberty," "free enterprise" and the 'fullest opportunity for go and push." [46]

It was not an appeal calculated to reassure those uneasy over the Conservatives' commitments to Beveridge or to Keynesian employment policies. Clearly, it represented a wager on the capacity of Churchill's personal popularity to overcome scepticism towards Conservative policies. Those who made it overestimated the attraction of Churchill and, most important, seriously underestimated the scope of the popular rejection of Conservatism. The appeal, and the campaign based upon it, thus failed to restore the declining fortunes of Conservatism and in so doing ushered in a new era in public policy based upon a massively expanded role for the state. It was an outcome that had long been resisted by the "forces of order" and that the combined effects of the system of taxation, the peculiar structure of the British state and the enduring power of Conservatism had long prevented. The resistance to state expansion had been decisively broken, if only temporarily.

Chapter 9

Towards the "Liberal-Socialist" state, 1945–51

Surely the most remarkable thing about the postwar Labour governments was how much they accomplished. As Anthony King has argued, "The fit between what the Labour Party said it would do in 1945 and what the Labour Government actually achieved between 1945 and 1951 is astonishingly close." Backed by a solid majority in Parliament and served by an administrative machine retooled during the war, the Attlee government moved quickly and decisively to implement the promises of Beveridge and of the "social contract" for full employment and security implied in Beveridge and in the White Paper on Employment of 1944. It proceeded as well to fulfil the party's commitment to seize the "commanding heights" of the economy by a policy of selective nationalization. In a short time, therefore, the Labour government transformed the legal and institutional relationship between state and society in Britain.[1]

Labour's social reforms mirrored the proposals of the Beveridge Report quite faithfully. The Insurance Acts of 1946 created a unified system of pensions, sickness and unemployment benefits that marked a considerable advance on previous provision. Basic benefits were fixed at 26s a week for a single man, 42s a week for a couple and 49s 6d for a man, wife and child and were augmented by family allowances, enacted before the election of 1945 and coming into operation the following January. Victims of industrial accidents received 45s a week – a clear indication of the clout of the trade unions. All benefits were universal, and in theory financed by a flat-rate contribution. This preserved the form of the insurance principle, which remained popular, and avoided the means test, which remained deeply offensive to working people. The system was supplemented, however, by means-tested assistance provided under the National Assistance Act of 1948 and intended for the few whose needs would exceed the benefits universally available. In fact, quite large numbers of people, especially pensioners, required supplementary benefits, and their numbers were destined to grow. As of 1948, however, Labour had reason to believe it had successfully addressed the problem of poverty in a manner that broke decisively with the legacy of the Poor Law and the dreaded means test.[2]

Of equal importance to the reform of social security was the creation of the

National Health Service between 1946 and 1948. The Beveridge Report had not specified a shape for the health service, but merely assumed its establishment. During the war the Conservative Henry Willink had developed a scheme that was too radical for Conservatives and for the doctors, but too "watered-down" for Labour. The precise structure of the health service thus remained in 1945 a matter of some debate: there were questions over the role of local authorities and – a matter of more bitter controversy – over the role of the doctors. Aneurin Bevan, Minister of Health, confronted resentment from the local authorities – and their defender within the government, Herbert Morrison – and outright hostility from the medical profession. In the end he overrode local objections, nationalized the local and voluntary hospitals and set up a system of regional boards accountable to the centre. Bevan was forced to compromise with the doctors, who were given concessions on group practice and on private beds, assurances that the government would not attempt to create a full-time, salaried service and a more prominent role in running the system. These did not quiet the British Medical Association, which resisted to the end, but sufficed to guarantee co-operation when the system came into operation in July, 1948.[3]

Social security and health were the two areas of social policy where innovation required major institutional change and they constituted the fields of activity where Labour was most successful. In education and housing, on the other hand, Labour's initiatives produced less notable achievements. In education, for example, Labour largely contented itself with carrying out the provisions of the coalition's 1944 Education Act. That precluded any drastic revision of educational policy, any infringement on the role of private education or any movement towards comprehensive schooling. Labour did better on housing, but suffered from the contrast between promise and performance. Labour had proclaimed in 1945 that the seriousness with which the housing problem was addressed would offer "one of the greatest and one of the earliest tests of a Government's real determination." The nation's needs were estimated at over a million houses, and Labour resolved to work tirelessly "until every family in this island has a good standard of accommodation." In fact, Labour produced over a million new and permanent units by 1951, but it was a difficult job getting there. The housing programme was troubled by shortages of labour and building materials and by administrative inefficiencies. Specifically, the responsibility for housing was kept until 1951 within the Ministry of Health, which was preoccupied with the creation of the National Health Service. Thus very few houses were built in 1945–6 and the government, and Bevan in particular, came in for a good deal of criticism.[4]

Institutionally, Labour's other major achievement was its record of nationalization. The nationalization of industry was central to Labour's definition of socialism and had a special place in its programme. That place varied somewhat over time, according to the party's shifting sense of what was politically possible and desirable. Labour's Immediate Programme of 1937 specified a list of industries to be taken under public control and the party conference of 1944 added still more. By 1945, the party was pledged to nationalizing the Bank of England, but not the joint stock banks, as well as coal, gas, electricity, railways and road transport, canals and docks, aviation, cable and wireless communication, and iron and steel. The rationale behind this extensive programme was that private ownership had failed the nation. Socialization would replace inefficient private control with efficient state management and give the government control over the "commanding heights" of the economy and the broad direction of economic development.

The Attlee government moved decisively to transfer these industries to public ownership. The Bank of England was nationalized in 1946, as were coal, cable and wireless, and civil aviation. The taking over of coal and of the Bank was of major symbolic significance: the nationalization of coal marked the belated triumph of the miners over the owners and served as a vindication of the bitter struggles of earlier decades; the socialization of the Bank of England signalled Labour's resolve never to allow a repeat of 1931 and seemingly struck at the heart of capitalist power. These early efforts were greeted with general approbation: even the most retrograde Conservative found it difficult to defend the mineowners and the Bank found few public defenders. During the next year Labour pressed ahead with the nationalization of the railways, of long-distance road transport and of electricity, again with little opposition. There was trouble only over road transport, where Labour was forced to compromise and exclude from state control a large number of small, private operators. By 1948, the Conservatives had recovered their fighting spirit and there was considerable controversy over the nationalization of gas, while the prospect of a major battle convinced the government to defer the nationalization of iron and steel until 1948–9.[5]

The battle over iron and steel marked the decisive end of the period of easy and relatively non-controversial nationalization. Steel was a manufacturing industry, not a public service; hence its public control could not be defended as easily as the nationalization of transport or fuel and power. It was not a particularly prosperous or efficient industry, but neither was it especially depressed and backward. Its labour relations were reasonably harmonious as well. So the arguments for its socialization were not particularly compelling. Within the Cabinet, Morrison had never agreed with the need for the nationalization of steel and John Wilmot at the Ministry of Supply was also unenthusiastic. These reservations, underscored by more narrow political calculations, led the government to set up a Steel Control Board in 1947. To some this was seen as a preparation for nationalization; to others it was an alternative. After considerable debate, the government decided to press ahead with nationalization in the Parliamentary session of 1948–49. The proposed legislation, not surprisingly, left the basic structure of the industry intact. Despite this, the plan provoked bitter debate in Parliament and in the press and its passage exacted a heavy toll on the government's popularity. By the late 1940s, therefore, the most obvious candidates for nationalization were already owned by the state and the prospect of further socialization commanded less public sympathy. The party moved ahead in 1949, however, to develop a list of industries for future nationalization. Prominent among these were cement, about which it was difficult for anyone to get excited, and sugar refining, which proved very contentious. The proposal to nationalize sugar provoked the famous "Mr Cube" campaign launched by the sugar giant, Tate and Lyle. Between them, the controversies over sugar and steel put an effective end to the progress of nationalization.[6]

Taken together, Labour's innovations in social policy and its extensive nationalization added up to a substantial reshaping of the relationship between state and society, institutionalizing a new level of public responsibility for social provision and an enhanced role for the state in the economy. As T.H. Marshall would argue in 1949, they served to extend the meaning and the practical boundaries of citizenship from the sphere of civil and political rights to that of social rights. There were limits, of course, to the vision of citizenship embodied in Labour's reforms, limits that have become increasingly obvious in retrospect. It was a conception of citizenship that privileged the interests of men over women, of the centre over the periphery, of the organized over the unorganized, of leaders and officials over followers and the rank-and-file; and it was a very passive conception at that. Even in the 1940s, some of these limitations were evident. The nationalized industries were set up along the lines laid down by Herbert Morrison in his work on London Transport during the 1930s. Typically, this involved setting up a board to run the industry with little interference from the state and minimal input from the workers. The lack of industrial democracy within this model had provoked repeated debates during the 1930s, but Morrison's conception prevailed, due in part to Labour's desire to put in place a "neutral" administrative apparatus and in part to the reluctance of the unions to abandon their traditional, adversarial role within industry. Argument continued after the war, but no scheme emerged that could muster sufficient support to become a viable alternative to Morrison's. The structures that came into being in the 1940s were thus recognizably similar to what had existed before, and the simple change in ownership did little to transform industrial relations. Nor did nationalization lead to an increase in efficiency. The industries selected for socialization were among the most inefficient in the nation, and the generous terms on which the previous owners were bought out placed substantial debt burdens on the newly created public enterprises. Their performance inevitably disappointed those who believed nationalization would produce greater efficiency and appeared to provide confirmation for those who had opposed public ownership.[7]

To fault the Labour government for failing to turn a profit on industries such as coal was of course grossly unfair, as reasonable commentators understood. It is reasonable to ask, however, how far Labour's innovations in social policy and its programme of nationalization furthered its broader aims in social and economic policy. Thus, it is fair to point out that the benefit levels established in 1946, while a vast improvement on prewar, were overtaken by inflation as early as the late 1940s. It is legitimate, too, to weigh the benefits provided by public provision of social services against their cost in taxation, and to question in particular their distributive impact.[8] It is above all appropriate to ask whether the reforms undertaken by Labour in its first years of office were adequate to the primary task they had set themselves in 1945 – that of providing full employment. On this criterion, they did simultaneously better and worse. Labour did better in that demand proved very strong after the war and employment was, if anything, overly full. On the other hand, the Attlee government did not put into place mechanisms with the authority, knowledge and capacity to guide the nation's economic development. The failure to develop such a capacity was an enormous hole in Labour's otherwise impressive achievement, and it left the commitment to full employment without the institutional backing needed to make it a reality over the long term.

The roots of this failure go back to the war years and the battles over employment policy and the machinery of government. No serious alternative to a reassertion of Treasury control emerged from the wartime discussions of the administrative machine, but Labour clearly could not accept that outcome. Instead, they continued the wartime pattern of policy-making by committee, specifically by interdepartmental committees of ministers and of officials. This approach avoided placing power over the economy back into the hands of the Treasury; it provided a means of reconciling the conflicts between the powerful personalities within the new government – particularly Morrison and Bevin, but also Dalton and Cripps – without giving primacy to one over the other; and it fitted well with the regime of physical controls.[9]

It was an arrangement acceptable also to the Treasury and the civil service, at least temporarily. Edward Bridges, for example, aware that Labour distrusted the Treasury and doubted its commitment to employment policy, understood the need to demonstrate a willingness to make good on the promises of the 1944 White Paper. Bridges was at the time both Secretary to the Cabinet and Permanent Secretary of the Treasury and thus Oficial Head of the Civil Service. He embodied in his person the very ethos of Whitehall, but he had been much influenced by the experience of war and was committed to a more extensive role for the state after the war.[10] In taking upon himself the task of chairing the co-ordinating committee of officials responsible for planning, Bridges was in effect accepting the assumption by the Treasury of "substantially increased responsibility both in the preparation and continuous review of the general economic plan and in the day to day execution of it." He grasped as well that the Treasury would have good administrative reasons to be represented on virtually all "interdepartmental" committees and that its representatives would be primarily responsible for implementing the decisions arrived at through consultation with other departments. In the circumstances of 1945, it would seem, the best arrangement the Treasury could achieve was to secure a predominant role within such an "interdepartmental" committee system. Bridges and other top officials understood instinctively that the alternative to "interdepartmental" control was control lodged outside the Treasury and this they wished to avoid. They were also not at all eager to open up questions about the machinery of government to further review, for it was likely that an inquiry launched under Labour would be more deeply probing than the Anderson committee had been, and might even involve dreaded "outsiders" like Harold Laski or Kingsley Martin. Thus when a Labour backbencher, Geoffrey Cooper, proposed a new review of the "executive instrument," Bridges convened a meeting of permanent secretaries who came down strongly against the notion. Attlee acquiesced and, in effect, accepted the structure inherited from the war.[11]

Two committees were reponsible for policy in this system: broad issues came before the Ministerial Committee on Economic Planning, made up of Attlee, Herbert Morrison, Hugh Dalton, Stafford Cripps and George Isaacs (Minister of Labour); more specific questions were to be decided by the Lord President's Committee, chaired by Morrison. Under this arrangement power was genuinely dispersed between the Lord President's Office, the Board of Trade, the Ministry of Labour, the supply departments and the Treasury. At the official level a Steering Committee on Economic Development, chaired by Edward Bridges, supervised working parties on manpower, balance of payments, capital investment, statistics and economic development, and introduced a measure of co-ordination. In this they were aided by the Economic Section, which reported formally to the Lord President but whose advice went directly to the officials charged with preparing the annual *Economic Surveys* and was widely available to the Cabinet. The system closely resembled the regime that had mobilized the economy for war, and it would serve reasonably well to manage the transition to peace.[12]

Theoretically, this rather complicated machinery of control had at its disposal a variety of mechanisms for influencing the economy. The government could make use of the budget, presumably made more effective by the use of Keynesian techniques for estimating national income, of the physical controls inherited from the war and of the policy instruments discussed in Beveridge and in the 1944 White Paper: in particular, plans to vary countercyclically the level of national insurance contributions and the funding of public works. These novel devices, which were never really accepted by the Treasury, were designed to deal with a deficiency of demand and a resulting slump. Since that combination of circumstances never materialized during the life of the postwar Labour governments, they remained merely theoretical options, and the battles that would surely have ensued over implementation were never joined and their efficacy never decisively tested. What remained available to the government, therefore, were the relatively traditional mechanisms of monetary and budgetary policy and the wartime mechanism of physical controls. Debate centred, therefore, over the proper mix of these policy devices.[13]

The discourse over economic policy during the 1940s was in this way just as restricted as was the debate over the machinery of government. The major polarization occurred between those who favoured the continuation of physical controls and those who believed that budgetary and monetary controls would be sufficient. The alternatives were posed clearly by James Meade, the head of the Economic Section, who confided in his diary that within the Labour government there were two factions: there were "those (led by Cripps at the Board of Trade) who believe in the quantitative planning of the economy commodity by commodity" and whom Meade labelled "Gosplanites;" and there were "Liberal-Socialists" like himself who favoured a mixed economy with a greater reliance on market forces and, in terms of policy, on budgetary and monetary devices. The division of opinion had implications not only for the shape of Britain's domestic political economy but also for the workings of the international economy. A settlement with the United States would not be possible if the "Gosplanites" prevailed, whereas a more "Liberal-Socialist" outcome would allow for an arrangement with the United States over trade. The result would "be an alternative progressive socialist but liberal govern-ment to set against authoritarian Russia. The forces of the left in Europe will have a free as well as a totalitarian point of attraction." As outlined by Meade, the choice between "sensible global planning" and "senseless quantitative planning" was fairly obvious.[14] A regime of controls would be very hard to administer and quite unpopular over the long run, and the prospect of Britain deciding to sever the American connection and forfeit American aid was very remote. The adoption of the "Gosplanite" alternative was thus never very likely.[15]

A definitive triumph for the "Liberal-Socialist" approach nevertheless proved elusive, and would remain so until its proponents could demonstrate a mastery over Britain's economic problems. They were a long way from being able to do that in the 1940s, however, for they were as yet unable to make effective use of many of their preferred policy instruments. The policy of cheap money, for example, was very popular and so long as it remained in place there was no possibility of using monetary policy to regulate demand. Cheap money had prevailed since 1932 and was given credit for whatever recovery there had been in the 1930s; the war had also been fought with low interest rates, which had proved no serious impediment to government borrowing. Keynes, an advocate of cheap money since the late 1920s and largely responsible for the wartime policy, continued to favour cheap money after the war and actually looked forward to even lower rates. Keynes' followers were more ambivalent: Joan Robinson, for example, sought in 1943 to convince the Labour party to work towards a permanent low interest rate, "abandoning altogether the traditonal use of the rate of interest as a check to inflation." Meade, by contrast, thought it a mistake to foreclose any option that might be used as a lever over the economy. Dalton, Labour's financial expert and Chancellor, was more concerned with questions of distribution, the need- to control public expenditure, the cost of borrowing for local authorities and the rate at which the Labour government could borrow money for its nationalization programme. He therefore sided with Keynes and Robinson and pursued what has been termed a "cheaper money" policy through 1947. Even after Dalton was replaced at the Exchequer by Cripps and then Gaitskell, the case for raising interest rates was never sufficiently appealing to convince the Labour government to alter its disposition not to rely upon monetary instruments. Deprived of the use of monetary policy, the "Liberal-Socialists" were left primarily with the budget as a policy instrument. Backed up by the techniques of national income accounting, the budget had become a powerful device for managing demand, but there were problems in using it to steer the economy in detail. First, the Treasury's commitment to utilizing Keynesian methods for estimating demand and supply was by no means complete, at least until 1947. There were also technical questions about how rapidly the economy would respond to fiscal stimuli. In July, 1945, for example, the Inland Revenue argued that it was difficult to implement changes in the tax structure quickly enough to influence economic behaviour. Meade also found the problem "alarming. It means that changes in the income tax can never be used as a prompt means of control of the general inflation or deflation situation." In later discussions, the Treasury and the Inland Revenue would also question the fairness of giving tax breaks for certain kinds of investment and not for others, thus raising further objections to the use of the budget to control the economy.[16]

Political preferences and administrative difficulties thus came together to prevent the "Liberal-Socialist" model from being institutionalized. An outcome along the lines favoured by Meade was also delayed by the lack of resolution over questions of the machinery of government. Indeed, there was no correlation between the views of the "Liberal-Socialists" and the "Gosplanites" on matters of policy and their preferences on matters of administration. Meade, for example, considered Herbert Morrison a kindred soul on matters of policy, but as Lord President Morrison was deeply implicated in the regime of physical controls. Given the shared outlook between Meade and Morrison, the attachment of the Economic Section to the Lord President's Committee should have been acceptable to its members, but Meade and his successor Robert Hall always feared that their advice would be less effective the further removed it was from the Treasury. The leaders of the Economic Section also realized the importance of attaching themselves to powerful members of the Cabinet, hence their attraction to Cripps, particularly as Cripps himself became less identified with the "Gosplanite" approach. On the other hand, even after Cripps went to the Treasury in 1947, the "Liberal-Socialists" who populated the Economic Section were hesitant about a permanent attachment to the Treasury, for they feared being submerged within an institution whose commitment to employment policy and to Keynesian techniques remained tenuous.

Perhaps the most important circumstance preventing a resolution of the dilemmas surrounding the means and the machinery of economic policy-making, however, was the series of short-term crises that from 1947 threatened to overwhelm the government. Five related crises caused continual adjustments in policy and in the machinery for making policy, and repeatedly adjourned the debate over long-term questions. They also raised issues that none of the options on offer in the late 1940s were capable of dealing with – basically, questions about the rigidity and inefficiency of the economy, which would have required micro-economic interventions in the heroic era of macro-economic policy. Three of these hit in rapid succession in 1947: the fuel crisis in the winter of 1946–7, the mounting shortage of dollars, and the con-vertibility crisis of the summer of 1947. The fourth crisis centred around the devaluation of 1949 and the fifth was produced by rearmament in 1950. Labour's record in handling these successive difficulties was by no means a bad one, but the cumulative effect was to prevent the government from giving permanent embodiment to its new social and economic commitments within the institutional structures and practices of the state. Labour would therefore leave office in 1951 with key questions about policy and about the policy-making apparatus unresolved.

LABOUR'S RECURRING CRISES

Nothing reveals the extent of the constraints on Labour's options better than the set of crises which the government had to endure in 1947. The first to hit was the fuel shortage, whose effects were short term but very severe, and especially damaging politically. "Vesting day" in the coal industry came on 1 January 1947, and there was jubilation in the coalfields. Emmanuel Shinwell, Minister of Fuel and Power, spoke enthusiastically about the prospects for the mines and those who worked under the new ownership, and about the "Miners" Charter," which set forth the principles upon which the mines would subsequently be worked. Less than three weeks later Britain entered a cold spell that rapidly depleted existing stocks; by the second week of February the supply of electricity was affected and much of the transportation system had ground to a halt. Two million were temporarily thrown out of work. Shinwell's claims were seen to have been largely rhetoric and the government's commitment to planning revealed as seriously defective. The problems of the mines were undoubtedly historic and structural: the pits were old and outdated, the workforce was likewise old and worn-out and grossly underpaid. And no politician could have predicted the severity of the winter weather. Still, the government's prior planning and its response were noticeably inadequate. The fuel crisis began a process of re-evaluation within the Labour government that would lead to major changes in the machinery for planning. In March, 1947 Attlee announced the plan to create a Central Economic Planning Staff within the government and an Economic Planning Board composed of ministers, officials and representatives of business and the unions. The two institutions came into being in July, 1947, by which time the government was enmeshed in a more protracted set of difficulties that would necessitate yet further changes in the policy-making apparatus.[17]

The twin crises of the summer of 1947 were products of both long- and short-term factors. The long-term problem was a shortage of dollars with which to pay for imports. The shortage was obviously a product of the war, but also reflected the slow decline of Britain vis-a-vis the United States. That economic shift was reflected during 1945–7 in Britain's failure to export enough to earn sufficient dollars to cover the balance of payments. Throughout 1946 and the first half of 1947, therefore, Britain had been forced to use up a considerable portion of the £3750 million loan negotiated with the United States by Keynes in December, 1945. By the early spring, it was becoming clear that the loan would run out much sooner than 1951, as the original plan had anticipated. Still worse, one key condition for obtaining the loan was a promise to introduce convertibility on 15 July 1947. That date was fast approaching but the government was doing little about it. Dalton was unduly optimistic about Britain's ability to undertake convertibility, as were officials at the Treasury. In late July they were proved decisively wrong and there was a massive run on sterling. Convertibility had to be suspended again in late August, much to the chagrin of the Americans and the detriment of the government's reputation.[18]

The suspension of convertibility was followed by a series of policy changes. Dalton's "cheaper money" policy was abandoned and the government imposed an austere budget. The budget surplus announced in the spring had been achieved by policies adopted for traditional reasons and through the traditional budgetary calculus; the budget adopted in November, 1947 was more innovative in that it had been shaped with the explicit use of Keynesian techniques and consciously designed to control inflation by dampening demand, especially for imports. As Bridges put it to Dalton, "The purpose is, not the old-fashioned one of extra taxation to balance the Budget, but a reduction of the inflationary pressure." More specifically, the Treasury pushed Dalton towards increased taxes on tobacco and to lower food subsidies, both changes aimed at reducing consumption. The essentially Keynesian process by which the Treasury arrived at its budget recommendations no doubt constituted "a revolution in British practice," as Robert Hall would later claim, though it "passed almost unnoticed" at the time. And the proposals to which it gave rise were fiercely resisted by most of the Cabinet. The increased duty on tobacco was ultimately replaced by a rise of 1d a pint on beer and of a comparable amount on whisky; and food subsidies were frozen rather than cut. Higher rates of purchase and profits tax were accepted, however, and overall the package would soon begin to restore the nation's position.[19]

The crisis also produced a major set of changes in the personnel of the Cabinet and in the administrative structure. Dalton's position was much weakened by his handling of the problem of convertibility, and he was replaced at the Exchequer after a major indiscretion on the budget. Morrison had been ill during much of 1947, but was nevertheless held partly responsible for the failure of the existing machinery to anticipate the crises or deal effectively with them. His political stature was thus much diminished. Stafford Cripps, on the other hand, emerged as the strongest personality in the government, strong enough to attempt in September, 1947 a coup that would have replaced Attlee with Bevin as Prime Minister. Instead, Attlee manoeuvred Cripps into taking the new position of Minister of Economic Affairs, where he would exercise effective control over economic policy. When Dalton made his budget slip, Cripps succeeded him at the Treasury, carrying with him the primary responsibility for economic policy and much of the machinery for its implementation. The administrative changes produced by the crises of 1947 were rather less clearcut in their effects. On the surface it would appear that the creation of the Central Economic Planning Staff and the Economic Planning Board and their location within the Treasury would have produced a reassertion of the Treasury's traditional role. So, too, would Cripps' move to the Exchequer and his new-found prominence within the government. But it was not quite so simple. The Planning Staff, for example, had been conceived from the beginning as an interdepartmental body and considerable effort had been devoted in the summer of 1947 to keeping it independent. It was fought over by Morrison and by the Treasury, and neither prevailed. It was thus initially attached to the new Ministry of Economic Affairs run by Cripps, where it might have stayed had Cripps not become Chancellor. Even after that, the new machinery would not be dominated by the Treasury and would instead remain in important respects "interdepartmental." In the same spirit, a new Cabinet-level Economic Policy Committee with the Prime Minister in the chair, was set up in September, 1947 to meet the emergency.[20]

A thorough-going restoration of Treasury domination over economic policy was prevented by two further factors. First, there was a widespread feeling among ministers and the public that the Treasury had performed just as miserably in the crises of 1947 as had the rest of the administrative machine. The concentration of the apparatus for economic policy-making in the Treasury under Cripps was therefore counteracted by the determination of ministers collectively to supervise the direction of the economy and prevent another débâcle. Second, and perhaps most important, was the impact of the Marshall Plan. The crisis over convertibility was really a crisis over dollars and the balance of payments. The measures adopted in November, 1947 went some way towards moderating these long-term difficulties, but a genuine solution could only be brought about by another infusion of American aid. Secretary of State Marshall's speech on 5 June at Harvard had promised more serious help, but it would not come quickly or easily. The European countries would have to define their needs precisely, demonstrate to American policy-makers that they had realistic plans to meet future needs out of their own resources, and agree to work towards the sort of multilateral trading system favoured by the Americans. It still took until July, 1948 for Congress actually to vote Marshall Aid. Bevin as Foreign Secretary had responded quickly and enthusiastically to Marshall's proposal and took the lead in organizing European co-operation for Marshall Aid. Undoubtedly, the prospect of Marshall Aid exerted a strong pull upon British policy-makers from the moment it was proposed, and in critical respects guaranteed that Britain and the United States would come to an agreement on the shape of the postwar economic order and that its principle of organization would in the end be more "Liberal-Socialist" than "Gosplanite." Its more proximate effects were rather different, however. Obtaining Marshall Aid meant putting together a convincing recovery programme; keeping it flowing would require constant supervision over its use and hence over the economy as a whole. It would mean, among other things, a closer co-ordination of internal and external policy and an extension of the sort of interdepartmental organization for economic policy from domestic to international questions. The effect of the Marshall Plan was thus actually to accentuate the existing pattern of economic policy-making in Britain and to place yet another obstacle in the way of a restoration of Treasury control on the old model.[21]

Negotiations began in the fall of 1947 about what sort of organization would be needed to manage the balance of payments and the various components of the European Recovery Programme. In October, it was decided as a first step to set up an Overseas Negotiations Committee and an Exchange Requirements Committee to deal with the balance of payments and an Exports Committee to plan exports. Subsequently, a separate committee on European Economic Co-operation (the so-called London Committee) was established to supervise the detailed allocation of Marshall Aid. It was an explicitly and self-consciously "interdepartmental" system, and Attlee and his advisors would insist repeatedly on this sort of arrangement for the handling of Marshall Aid. Throughout the first half of 1948, therefore, the government was preoccupied with perfecting the machinery for co-operation with the Marshall Plan administration. British negotiators felt that the Americans were insufficiently "aware of the political difficulties" that would ensue from American efforts to infringe upon the sovereignty and autonomy of the states receiving aid and they sought to prevent that happening. By December, 1947, Cripps could reassure the Cabinet that, as he saw it, "We need not fear political conditions in the simple-minded sense, such as a ban on nationalization." In shaping the specific institutions that would administer Marshall Aid, the Cabinet sought further protections and tried in particular to ensure that no "opening should be given for excessive interference by US representatives in our management of our domestic affairs." The draft agreement worked out in the late spring did not fully meet this criterion, but was successfully renegotiated by June, 1948. The organization that emerged remained basically similar to that established in late 1947 and embodied the same principles. The net effect of the Marshall Plan upon the organization of British government was therefore to reinforce the reliance on interdepartmental machinery and prolong the wartime style of policy-making still further into peacetime. And it worked well enough in ensuring that the major priorities of the government were met. As Norman Brook explained in December 1948, "There is no doubt that Ministers have warmly welcomed the new system by which so much . . . work is now done through Committees whose papers and minutes are available to a fairly wide circle of Ministers." The Marshall Plan also provided the stimulus for the Labour government's most serious effort at planning. The Americans demanded in 1948 that recipients of Marshall Aid draw up plans to address their balance of payments problems and achieve "viability" by the time aid ceased in 1952 (it was actually terminated a year earlier). The "Long-Term Programme" submitted to the OEEC in October, 1948 was the outcome, a plan that was "tailored to fit OEEC requirements," but that built seriously upon and extended the work of the *Economic Surveys*. As a plan it was soon overtaken by events, but it served to reinforce the government's commitment to planning, to interdepartmental methods of co-ordination and, to some extent, to controls over key aspects of the economy.[22]

The confrontation with American objectives as reflected in the Marshall Plan also stimulated a clarification in Labour's understanding of Britain's role in the world economy. The Americans believed that a viable European economy should look like the United States: it should be a large, open and integrated market with few internal barriers. For the entire duration of the Marshall Plan, they sought to push the Europeans in that direction. The approach was supported within Britain by a substantial section of the business community: just after the convertibility crisis in August, 1947, for example, the Federation of British Industries urged the Planning Staff to accept the US proposals for the creation of a "larger economic grouping" involving closer links with Europe. The American proposals encountered stiff resistance from the government, however, who felt Britain had little to gain from European unity. The United Kingdom was still the centre of a powerful empire whose worldwide interests, commitments and resources precluded closer ties with the continent. The British and American positions also diverged on the causes of the dollar shortage. To Will Clayton, Under-Secretary of State for Economic Affairs, "the whole trouble" stemmed from the "failure of Europe to produce." British representatives disagreed strongly and argued that the dollar shortage was caused by a "world supply crisis" that prevented the European countries from relying upon "the traditional method in which Europe has paid the American continent" with earnings generated "by an export surplus with the rest of the world." In the postwar period, the developing countries were unable to supply their own needs for manufactured goods or commodities and had to turn to the United States for both. That meant more demand for US goods and for dollars, and consequently less trade with Europe. Only by restoring the balance in world trade could the dollar shortage be overcome. "It is therefore essential," concluded the Committee on European Economic Co-operation, "that there should be an adequate flow of dollars to the rest of the world so that the participating countries and western Germany may be able to earn dollars not only directly by their exports to the American continent but also indirectly by their exports to other countries." As "the bridge between the Western and Eastern Hemisphere," Britain considered itself uniquely vulnerable to these worldwide problems and uniquely positioned to help solve them. Doing so, however, required American recognition of Britain's special place in the world and their assistance in maintaining it.[23]

Britain would never get quite the treatment they wanted from the United States, but they got surprisingly close to it. British representatives successfully resisted pressures for closer European integration, for example, and succeeded at least in delaying American plans for a European Payments Union. They managed as well to get more than a fair share of Marshall Aid and they gave up little in return. After the suspension of convertibility in August, 1947, the sterling area "became a discriminatory economic bloc once more," but now it could also make use of American dollars. The Labour government also worked to exploit more efficiently what remained of the empire, seeking to build up trade and investment within the Commonwealth: the Overseas Resources Development Act of 1948 set up the Overseas Food Corporation with powers to borrow £55 million in order to make bulk purchases and the Colonial Development Corporation, which could tap into another £110 million for investment. The Labour government also took the initiative in the formulation of the "Colombo Plan" of 1950, which committed Britain and its Asian dominions to a long-term "development" plan.[24]

It would be difficult to argue that Britain's attempt to reclaim a world role was an effective response to the structural problems facing the economy. Bevin's hopes, for example, of organizing "the middle of the Planet" under British economic leadership and making America "dependent on us, and eating out of our hands, within four or five years," were simply fantasy.[25] Nevertheless, the government's decisions constituted a not unreasonable short-term response to the country's balance of payments difficulties, and to policymakers this was vastly preferable to a capitulation to American plans. The United States' position probably would have involved Britain in a serious deflation and compromised the government's commitment to full employment and its ability to fund the welfare state. Given that alternative, the adaptations in policy and in the machinery for economic planning produced in response to the sterling crisis and the Marshall Plan were both principled and effective. Britain emerged from the crises of 1947 with an institutional framework for economic management that was more integrated and coherent than what had gone before, with a set of policies reasonably well suited to its most pressing problems and with a vision of Britain's economic future that encompassed full employment at home, a rising level of international trade and the "development' of its former colonies.

What was most obviously lacking, of course, were policies aimed at making the economy more productive and efficient. The better planning and co-ordination established in 1947–8 did not put into the hands of policy-makers any new instruments with which to improve economic performance. There was still, for example, no plan to use the leverage over the economy gained by nationalization to improve productivity. On the contrary, the government gave considerable autonomy to those charged with running the "socialized industries" and resisted calls for more direct intervention. Nor did the government use the powers it possessed as an array of "production authorities" to induce change within industry. Its capacity for micro-economic intervention therefore remained underdeveloped and what had been developed previously was underutilized. The government did set up Development Boards for selected industries in 1947, but they were weak and ineffective. There was also an effort made to set up joint production councils or to utilize the few councils that remained in existence from the war to increase productivity, but the movement did not get far. Equally ineffective was the Anglo-American Council on Productivity, set up by Cripps in August, 1948 in response to the Marshall Plan. The tours and studies undertaken as part of this effort succeeded well enough in documenting Britain's lagging productivity, but doing something about it was another matter altogether.[26]

Underlying the government's inability to get inside the workings of industry to boost productivity was a more fundamental incapacity to influence the level and course of investment. In theory there were several means of doing this and an official committee, the Investment Working Party (later renamed the Investment Programmes Committee), was designed to oversee the implementation of policy. But none of the means at hand could be made to work and the officials responsible were forced to concede in 1949 that "Each of the separate instruments we have examined has turned out, on closer inspection, to be a good deal less effective than might have been expected."[27] Attempts to inventory the plans for investment in public works by local authorities and to create a reserve or "shelf" of projects, for example, were notably unsuccessful. Local authorities seldom planned ahead so rationally, those that did were not always willing to share their plans with central government and the Treasury remained suspicious of the exercise all along. The hope of using state control of investment in the nationalized industries proved no more realistic, for it ran up against the policy of granting de facto autonomy to the management of the public corporations and the requirement that they should "pay their way."

The prospects for exercising control over private investment were even more remote. During the 1930s Labour policy-makers had considered it essential that a future socialist government should have the means to control investment, and to that end discussed the nationalization of the Bank of England and of the joint stock banks. During the war, however, the government had appeared to exert effective control over investment without nationalization. This bred considerable complacency and led to a neglect of the difficulties of actually influencing the course of investment. When Labour nationalized the Bank of England in 1946, for example, nothing was done to ensure that it would follow a different set of policies towards industrial investment than it had before 1939. The Bank's board was dominated by virtually the same set of City bankers as before and its relationship with the Treasury remained basically unchanged. The government also decided not to set up a National Investment Board. Rather, Dalton and his advisors contented themselves with prolonging the existence of the wartime Capital Issues Committee. The committee was composed overwhelmingly of representatives of the City and saw little need for direct intervention; in 1949–50, its members had become so uninterested in exercising controls over capital that the committee itself began to advocate its own dissolution. Overall, control over investment remained beyond the reach of the interventionist state that Labour was trying so hard to create.[28]

Still, the failure to develop mechanisms for intervening more decisively in industry was not especially visible in the late 1940s. This was partly due to the fact that the most pressing problems were those requiring an essentially negative stance by the state, and this was what the postwar regime was best able to do. Even Bernard Gilbert, no friend of interventionist policy, conceded in March, 1945 that, "For some years it is likely that the policy will involve keeping the brake on with varying degrees of pressure, on both capital and consumer expenditure. I see no difficulty about that, it is in harmony with our past training and experience, and the constitution of the machinery of Government is well fitted for the exercise of negative controls.' Moreover, the Labour government did have in place in the late 1940s a set of policies that were reasonably well designed to address what were understood to have been the major obstacles to recovery before the war, and there was little basis at the time for arguing against their effectiveness. The government operated, for example, a firm and reasonably successful regional policy, using the powers of the Board of Trade and of the Ministry of Town and Country Planning to direct industry into older areas in need of employment. Policy-makers were also active on the question of monopolies and restrictive practices – a not unreasonable corrective to the official encouragement of concentration, consolidation and the liquidation of excess capacity that had been the policy of the 1930s. In retrospect, these efforts seem relatively feeble, particularly in view of the backwardness of British industry, but the performance of the economy during the late 1940s appeared to confirm the arguments of the Keynesian advocates of employment policy about the primacy of demand management in solving the country's economic problems. The Treasury, it will be remembered, insisted during the wartime debate on employment policy upon the importance of structural unemployment and the centrality of efforts to increase the flexibility of the labour market as a solution. The Keynesians, on the other hand, maintained that adjustments of this sort would be easier and more successful if coupled with a high level of aggregate demand. As of 1947–8, there was little reason to claim that the Treasury had been right and the Keynesians wrong.[29]

Indeed, the system of economic management gradually worked out by Labour during the late 1940s was quite effective in dealing with the main problems that confronted the government through 1951. Its strengths were demonstrated in particular in the government's successful handling of devaluation in 1949. The decision to devalue in September, 1949 was produced by a combination of factors. Policy-makers understood soon after the war that some adjustment in the relationship between sterling and the dollar was probably inevitable, but so long as currencies were not convertible the day of reckoning could be put off. The strengthening of Britain's position in 1948, due to the success of the emergency measures of 1947 and to the beginnings of Marshall Aid, led Robert Hall, head of the Economic Section, to propose devaluation in early 1949. He soon convinced Plowden, the chief planner, of the wisdom of a lower rate and began slowly to win over other officials. The Cabinet wavered, but was forced to take the proposal seriously later in the spring when rumours began circulating about an impending devaluation. The rumours were prompted to a considerable extent by the growing realization that American planners favoured a realignment of currencies. Ironically, the American position was itself a sign of the success with which Britain had pursued an independent line in the period after the granting of Marshall Aid. The American effort to push the Europeans towards closer integration had been largely thwarted by British efforts to forge closer economic ties with the sterling area. Specifically, the sterling area countries responded to a renewed dollar shortage, caused by the recession in the United States and a consequent drop in imports, by agreeing in July, 1949 to cut their own dollar imports by a quarter. It seemed to the Americans that Britain, and those countries linked with Britain economically, were increasingly moving towards the formation of a set of more enclosed economic blocs rather than towards the integrated and open world economy so favoured by the US.[30]

The US reacted by urging a realignment of currencies aimed at increasing trade in dollars, forcing Britain to confront the issue of the long-term relationship between sterling and the dollar and the long-term problem of the balance of payments. As they did so, two basic alternatives emerged. The orthodox policy, favoured by the City and by many within the Treasury, was "to aim at convertibility and multilateralism" and to accept with that the need for a classic deflation. The Governor of the Bank of England called for expenditure cuts and a halt to nationalization to restore confidence. Within the Treasury it was argued that the problem facing Britain was "an economic organization . . . in a singularly inflexible state . . . in which the lack of incentive for both managers and workers has been widely recognized." Devaluation, which many still regarded as "an alternative to unpleasant action," would do little or nothing to break up this "inflexible" system and restore incentives. That would require not devaluation but reductions in expenditure and in taxes, a decrease in the size of the "investment programme" and a tighter monetary policy. Labour ministers responded very negatively to talk that suggested a planned deflation and especially to calls for "economy," discerning in them terrible echoes of 1931. With the alternatives posed so starkly, they were led to favour devaluation as the means by which to adjust to the international situation while maintaining their commitment to full employment and the welfare state. The Keynesian planners within the government, including Hall and Plowden, agreed with the need to devalue but were convinced as well of the need to control public expenditure. Their compromise solution was to couple devaluation with a set of economy measures designed to ensure that the benefits of devaluation would not be dissipated in a round of wage and prices increases that would again make British exports less competitive.[31]

The relative influence of the various forces involved in making economic policy was clearly reflected in the debate over devaluation. The decision to devalue represented a reaffirmation of the government's commitments to full employment and to adequate funding for the social services. The rather weak set of accompanying cuts showed how little the orthodox concern for economy had penetrated the thinking of the Labour government. Against the preferences of Herbert Morrison, the most orthodox of ministers, and the official consensus – to which Bridges, Hall, Plowden and also, it seems, Gaitskell subscribed – on the need for economy, the government adopted a relatively insignificant package of economy measures in October, 1949. The choices that defined the terms of devaluation, moreover, were made very consciously. At a meeting of the Economic Policy Committee in late June, for example, ministers asked officials to leave the room and discussed quite candidly how they could not trust the advice they were being offered. As Cripps explained, "One of my difficulties is that my official advisors are all 'liberals' and I cannot rely on them to carry through a 'socialist' policy in these negotiations." Even the most sympathetic and co-operative officials, like Bridges, were apparently unable to resist the lure of orthodox solutions; nor were the planners like Hall and Plowden entirely immune to calls for expenditure cuts. Nevertheless, the machinery in place in 1949 allowed the preferences of the Labour ministers to prevail and for the government to execute one of the most purposive and effective moves in the long history of relatively ineffective economic policy-making. Dalton's private boast that 1949 saw "No flicker of surrender" suggested something of its boldness, as did the drastic character of the devaluation from \$4.03 to \$2.80.[32]

The effectiveness of devaluation could be seen in the easing of the balance of payments problem and the improvement of Britain's economic performance in 1949-50. Gold and dollar reserves increased by 70 per cent in the nine months following devaluation, and the current account remained in surplus for most of the period 1950-4. Britain gained a relatively permanent advantage in export markets, and actually made inroads into the American market. Output grew rapidly from 1948 through 1951, and almost all of the increase was in exports. Of course, devaluation did not address the long-term problems of productivity or resolve the dilemma of Britain's awkward position in the world economy. If anything, it encouraged complacency. Britain persisted, for example, in its anti-European stance and opted out of the process of integration begun by the Schuman Plan. Still, the success with which the British economy, and the policy-making apparatus which oversaw economic development, coped with the crises of the late 1940s justified at least some of this self-satisfaction. By 1950, the transition from war to peace had largely been accomplished and with little adverse effect on employment or living standards; output had surpassed prewar levels and exports were far ahead. Recovery was real and sustained. It was a record that could easily discourage the more fundamental changes in policy and in the nature of the state that would ultimately be required to make the planned economy work over the long term and to generate sufficient prosperity to maintain and expand the welfare state.[33]

LABOUR'S INCOMPLETE REVOLUTION

The successful management of the economy in the early postwar years therefore served to blunt further efforts to change policy or to alter the structure of policy-making. Robert Hall, head of the Economic Section after 1947, could write in September, 1950 that "The current situation is very good indeed." It was good enough, in fact, to allow policy-makers to cope with the strains imposed by rearmament in 1950-1 without major changes in policy. Rearmament also put to an effective end a series of important discussions undertaken during the final two years of Labour rule that might otherwise have led to more dramatic changes in the policy-making apparatus. These discussions addressed questions about the appropriate level and shape of taxation, the machinery of government and the future of direct controls. None of these discussions resulted in any serious innovations, but together they revealed the strengths and the weaknesses of the system put in place by Labour. In each area there were reasons to be satisfied with recent accomplishments, but also reasons to be concerned about the future and, more precisely, about the ability of current policies and administrative arrangements to deal effectively with the sorts of problems likely to arise in the future.[34]

On taxes, for example, Labour could congratulate itself on having sold the public on the need for high levels of tax with which to fund the welfare state and on the alterations it had made to the tax system since 1945. Labour had inherited a powerfully efficient system of raising revenues, and the need to keep the lid on inflation had convinced officials and the financial community of the wisdom of continued high rates. Of course, the ending of war made possible some reductions, but the reductions that came were of greatest benefit to the relatively less well-off. A significant number of working people had been brought within the reach of the tax collector during the war, especially after the introduction of the pay-as-you-earn (PAYE) system in 1943, but by raising exemption levels Labour removed many workers and their families from liability to tax. The budget of October, 1945 reduced taxes by almost £400 million. This was achieved through lowering the standard rate from 10s to 9s, increasing allowances to free nearly two million from having to pay tax, and also by reducing the excess profits tax (EPT) from 100 per cent to 60 per cent. Dalton's next budget, in April, 1946 further reduced the bite of income tax by increasing the relief granted to "earned income" and abolished EPT altogether. Death duties were raised in partial compensation and in pursuit of Dalton's long-standing desire to tax inherited wealth. The net effect of the first two Labour budgets was thus a reduction of taxation of about £500 million, most of it taken off the less well-to-do. The unfortunate year 1947 saw two budgets, both designed to reduce the "inflationary gap" and both contributing to a slightly regressive shift back towards indirect taxation. The government responded with changes in income tax, death duties and profits tax and with several measures aimed at reducing consumption: increased levies on drink and tobacco and a general rise in purchase tax.[35]

Cripps would continue Dalton's stern policies during 1948–50. In 1948 income tax was reduced by a further £100 million, most of the benefits again going to those with lower incomes, while indirect taxes were increased by about £55 million. An additional £50 million was raised by "a special once-for-all levy . . . largely payable out of capital" and assessed on the previous year's investment income. Overall, the budgetary stance of 1949 remained about the same as in 1948. By 1950 the pressure for lower taxes was much greater, but Cripps responded cautiously. He lowered income tax for those at the lower end of the scale and raised petrol tax to conserve dollars – the net effect being yet another "no-change" budget. As of 1950–1 the standard rate of income tax still stood at 9s in the pound and the share of national income taken by the central government, which had been a mere 19 per cent in 1938 and almost 38 per cent in 1946, remained a hefty 35 per cent. The distributional effects of the changes that took place between 1945 and 1951 had been markedly progressive, particularly for those changes introduced by Dalton. The tax structure in 1950–1 fell less heavily on the lower and middle incomes, more heavily on those at the higher levels; it was made more palatable all round by the near universal agreement on the need to use taxation to control inflation.[36]

Not surprisingly, the continued burden of taxation eventually provoked a reaction from business. Even during the war representatives of industry and of farmers had argued for the exclusion of certain expenses in the calculation of tax liabilities. Business support for investment and depreciation allowances persisted after the war. They met with a mixed response, however, for officials at the Treasury and especially at the Inland Revenue were sceptical of granting special treatment to any interest. Ministers were more open, as were the Economic Section and the Planning Staff. Keynes himself favoured using the 1944 budget to introduce, or at least to announce, a package of "reforms in the industrial sphere" designed to encourage exports after the war. The maintenance of high tax rates throughout the 1940s produced increased pressure from business to lower taxes to stimulate investment and by 1949–50, the idea that Britain had reached the limits of "taxable capacity" had been accepted within the Cabinet by Morrison and even by Cripps. Morrison complained in November, 1949 that "In education and other social services there is a tendency for expenditure to rise from year to year without full regard to the taxable capacity of the country;" while Cripps warned that the government "were reaching the limit on expenditure which could be raised by taxation." Simultaneously, those inside the government who wished to make more extensive use of the budget for economic management were coming to agree with the argument about the need to lower taxes in order to restore incentives. Even if they did not fully accept the arguments of businessmen about the effect of taxes on work, as Keynesians they could not help but believe that variations in tax rates could alter economic behaviour.[37]

There was, then, a convergence of opinion in the late 1940s on the need to review the system of taxation. The result was the decision in 1950 to appoint the Royal Commission on the Taxation of Profits and Incomes, which undertook a thorough-going review that would not be finished until 1955. Inevitably, the different groups pushing for the committee expected very different things from it: Conservatives, along with most businessmen, wanted to see a recommendation for lower taxes; among Labour supporters there was the hope that the committee would identify new sources of revenue; the Keynesians within the government hoped to find ways of harnessing the tax system more effectively to the task of economic management. This was particularly important in the late 1940s and early 1950s, for by then the planners could foresee the imminent abolition of physical controls and the need to replace them with the more sophisticated use of fiscal policy.[38]

Robert Hall put the case forcefully to Plowden and sought his help in shaping the terms of the tax inquiry. "Our own interests," Hall told Plowden, "are primarily in the field of the effect of taxation on productivity in the widest sense. This means: a. the incentive or disincentive effect of the system on enterprise and on labour; b. the indirect effects of taxation . . . [on] . . . the supply of saving and on capital." "The real trouble," he went on, "comes in the effect of taxation on enterprise and on the supply of capital." The problem confronting the Keynesians was that the government did not want changes that would lower tax yields and so wanted to restrain the committee from considering proposals to that effect. Hall's immediate objective was thus to get such proposals onto the agenda of the Royal Commission. He realized the political difficulties involved: "there is undoubtedly a conflict between the objective of social equality and that of industrial efficiency . . . At present, however, we cannot do very much because it is politically so difficult to lower the top levels of taxation. In the same way, it may be that considerable concessions could be made in the field of company taxation with no real effect on our overall Budget objectives, if we can only get over the political difficulties of doing anything at all for the capitalist." What was needed was, as another official put it, "a way of indicating to the Commission that they need not reject methods solely because they would be more appropriate to a lower level" of taxation. After some discussion involving Plowden, Hall, Bridges, Wilfrid Eady of the Treasury and officials at the Board of Trade, it was agreed that the terms of reference for the commission should include a mandate "to consider whether for the purposes of the national economy the present system is the best way of raising the required revenue," a wording that was thought broad enough to allow serious consideration of proposals that would reduce taxes on the well-to-do.[39]

In the five years that passed before the Royal Commission finished its work, the political context surrounding taxation changed dramatically. Indeed, the increased taxation imposed by Gaitskell to fund rearmament made the charge of the committee outdated even before it began to meet. Still, its appointment reflected clearly the new politics of taxation as they had evolved during the first Attlee government. The Conservatives were by then recovering their political confidence and were willing again to present themselves as the party of reduced taxation. Business and finance were happy enough to agree and to weigh in with calls for general reductions and pleas for special breaks. As of 1950, however, the pressure for all-round reductions was not terribly strong or especially broadly based. Labour's determination to keep taxation high enough to fund the welfare state enjoyed wide support, and there were many who wanted to see taxation increased, especially on business. The main problem to be solved, therefore, was the contradiction between maintaining taxes at a level sufficient to support the welfare state and varying taxation in ways that would influence the economy, particularly the supply of funds for investment. The solution was thought by many to lie in the granting of tax relief for profits reinvested by business. This was precisely what Hall and Plowden had in mind in crafting the charge of the Royal Commission, for only by achieving flexibility in the tax system could Keynesian techniques be made operative and the direction of the economy through fiscal policy made effective. They were, in effect, putting onto the Royal Commission the responsibility for solving problems about the methods of economic management that the previous decisions of the Labour government had left unresolved.[40]

The shape of the machinery that would supervise economic management was also not fully determined by 1950 and was itself the subject of further inquiry. The moving force here was Sir Edward Bridges, who set up a working group to study the government's "economic organization." Despite the decision in 1946 not to undertake an extensive review of the machinery of government, Bridges had remained interested in questions of administration and, prompted in part by calls in Parliament for greater "business efficiency," established a new Government Organisation Committee in late 1947. In 1948 he recruited Sir John Woods of the Board of Trade to head a subcommittee on "Treasury Organization" which would review the extent to which the Treasury had responded to the new responsibilities thrust upon it since the war, and especially since 1947. The central question was whether the Treasury was "now to be regarded as the leading department in economic policy generally." The committee had no difficulty in answering yes and proceeding on the assumption that the Treasury would continue to fulfil such a role. That implied the decisive rejection of "the idea of a separate Economic Affairs or Policy Department under either a separate Minister or the Cabinet Office." The Treasury's predominance would nevertheless continue to be checked by the system of interdepartmental committees and by the autonomy of the Planning Staff and the Marshall Plan organization.[41]

The relationship between the Central Economic Planning Staff and the Treasury had never been entirely clear. In the summer of 1947 Bridges had defended its independence but at the same time had refused to consider its recommendations as in any way binding upon the Treasury. With Cripps" move to the Treasury, the relation between the Planning Staff and the Treasury was transformed into an issue of internal departmental organization and the anomalous position of the Planning Staff led in 1948 to a proposal to submerge CEPS within the Supply Division of the Treasury. A similar ambiguity surrounded the organization set up to administer the Marshall Plan and led to a parallel proposal to subsume it under the Treasury's Overseas Finance Division. Both of these attempts to reassert Treasury hegemony encountered strong resistance and for the moment were rejected. The report of Woods" sub-committee in February, 1949 therefore recommended no major changes and, in effect, ratified the compromise among ministers, officials and policies embodied in the machinery of economic co-ordination as it had so far developed.[42]

The question of whether the existing machinery of government was adequate to the tasks it had to perform continued to worry ministers and officials, however, even after the relatively successful handling of devaluation. It was becoming obvious that many of the physical controls upon which government relied would be lifted sooner rather than later. It seems, too, that officials like Bridges and Norman Brook, his successor as Cabinet Secretary from 1947, wanted to stabilize the main features of the existing structure in anticipation of a possible return to power by the Conservatives. Whatever their reservations about the existing machinery, they were well aware of its considerable virtues. These considerations led Cripps and Bridges to set in motion yet another inquiry in 1950–1, this one undertaken by the so-called Economic Organization Working Group. The committee reviewed the main economic functions required of government and the methods and organization in place for making sure that each was actually performed. Its starting point was an agreement that the three main "objectives" of policy were to ensure full employment, manage the balance of payments and maintain and improve the standard of living. Attaining these objectives meant exercising control over the budget, the balance of payments and investment.[43]

The committee proceeded to break down these broad functions into more specific goals and to match up the tasks that had to be performed with the machinery and policies available to do them. The result was an impressive listing of jobs, policy devices and agencies responsible for bringing them together. The predominance of the Treasury over the broad range of government activities was clearly evident: "The Treasury," it was argued, "has a responsibility both greater in degree than and different in kind from that of any other department." The inquiry also recognized, however, that "interdepartmental" co-ordination was by now an essential feature of policy-making. There was also increased importance attached to the work of the Board of Trade, a recognition perhaps that only the Board had the linkages with industry that might allow for effective intervention at the level of the industry or even the firm. The same reasoning was presumably behind the special prominence given by the committee to the role of departments acting in their capacity as 'production authorities.' To one official, in fact, the emphasis on "the 'production authority' arrangement" was the distinct contribution of the report. It was assumed, for example, that the Ministry of Agriculture was broadly responsible for economic policy concerning agriculture. By a similar logic, the Ministry of Supply was assigned the supervision of the "engineering, iron and steel and non-ferrous metals industries;" the Ministry of Works was to look after building and building materials; and the Admiralty was to manage shipbuilding. In sum, suitable mechanisms appeared to be available to cope with the major, recurring aspects of economic management.[44]

The committee failed, however, to ask the hard questions about whether the policies and administrative machinery were really capable of carrying out the tasks assigned to them. The most noticeable gap concerned investment. By 1950–1, the inadequacy of government control of investment was crystal clear. Officials had come to realize that nearly three-fourths of investment in plant and machinery was in private hands and that the government's only control over it was "by the indirect and rather unreliable means of agreed export ratios for the output of the machine making industries." The government had rather better control over building, and through that over investment that required new construction, but overall its ability to shape investment was minimal. This perceived weakness in the planning mechanism was undoubtedly responsible for the renewed emphasis on the Board of Trade and on other departments in their role as "production authorities." There was very little discussion, however, of just how they would influence investment, and hence little follow-up to the report's emphasis upon the capacity of the government, as a co-ordinated set of "production authorities," to direct the course of industrial development. Nor, despite the complacent references to the centrality of the Treasury and its use of the budget to govern the level of demand, was there any sense of the limitations on the use of the budget which other contemporary documents and discussions revealed, and which the planners hoped to see tackled by the Royal Commission on Taxation. In sum, the inquiry ratified the system in place after 1949, but did virtually nothing to overcome its limits or confront its ambiguities.[45]

The uneasiness with which ministers and officials contemplated the future of economic planning was most in evidence when they dealt with the question of controls. Controls had served as the most effective policy device utilized by the government and were widely considered, as Gaitskell noted, "the distinguishing feature of British socialist planning." The system of controls was complex and included raw material controls, through which metal, timber, textiles, building materials and other producers" goods were allocated to different industries and firms; export licensing; import controls, affecting better than 90 per cent of imports throughout the 1940s; production controls, through which firms were granted licences to produce certain goods and which, in some instances, specified the kinds of goods businessmen could manufacture. The government in fact operated a set of sumptuary controls requiring, for example, that the furniture and textile industries produce a certain amount of "utility" goods to serve the mass of consumers. The control over building materials was augmented by a system of building licences that were required for any new construction. The allocation of scarce consumer goods was further controlled by rationing, which covered about a third of consumers" expenditure in 1948, including many items of food, clothing and fuel. The cost of consumer goods was kept in check by direct control of the prices of certain items manufactured and sold privately and, more often, by government purchase and subsidies, which allowed the state simply to set the price of key foodstuffs and other imports. In 1947, for example, 64 per cent of total imports were government puchases; and of this total over 60 per cent was food. The difference between the prices paid by the government and those offered to consumers was made up by subsidies from the Exchequer totalling almost £400 million by 1947.[46]

During the war, of course, all of these controls had been made more effective by the fact that they were coupled with controls over manpower. Manpower controls were lifted quickly after the war, however, while the rest of the system remained intact. There was a presumption that eventually most controls would be removed, but events conspired to put off decontrol. For example, the recurring dollar shortage led the government to strengthen the machinery for controlling imports and the intensified fear of inflation after 1947 led to the publication of the 1948 *Personal Incomes* White Paper, with plans for further tightening up price controls. Policy-makers also came increasingly to realize that physical controls were their most effective levers over the economy; and even quite "moderate" members of the Labour government, like Morrison and Gaitskell, were reluctant to abandon them.

Still, some relaxation was inevitable and Harold Wilson at the Board of Trade presided over a first "bonfire of controls" in November, 1948. Decontrol at this stage affected primarily non-essential consumer goods – including, among other things, toys, cutlery, pens and linoleum – but was extended as well to some raw materials. Bread, which was rationed in July, 1946, was derationed in 1948, as were potatoes and, for a brief period, sweets and chocolates. The process of relaxation continued after 1948, with many more raw materials left uncontrolled as of 1949, with the requirements for the production of "utility" grades of clothing and furniture gradually abandoned, and with food subsidies becoming concentrated on an increasingly narrow list of essential items.

As controls were abolished, policy-makers became more worried over how to exercise effective direction over the economy. Especially troubling was the problem of wages. With decontrol of prices and of rationing, there seemed a real danger that prices would rise and prompt a round of wage demands with highly inflationary consequences. Officials leaned towards an incomes policy, but the unions were opposed and pressured ministers to adopt more voluntary measures. The decision to opt for the latter was a clear testament to the enhanced collective power of the unions after the war. As Arthur Lewis explained in 1948, "It won't . . . matter who wins the next election. A Conservative Government will no more be able to act without the consent of the workers than will a Labour Government." The one measure to which the unions would not consent was state control of wages. With that option ruled out, Labour was forced to rely on other expedients to control inflation. These included a rigorous budgetary policy, which Dalton initiated in 1947 and Cripps continued through 1950; stabilization of the cost of living through food subsidies and controls over rent and other essentials; and voluntary limitation of wages.[47]

From 1948 through 1951, in fact, the success of the Labour government's economic policy rested on its ability to convince the unions to exercise wage restraint. The 1948 White Paper signalled the increasing importance attached by the government to wages policy and the beginnings of a serious effort to slow down the rise of wages.[48] It called for a voluntary freeze on wages and laid down guidelines to the effect that increases granted after February, 1948 would not figure in the calculation of costs upon which prices were fixed. A special meeting of the Trades Union Congress accepted the freeze, but with qualifications for those workers "below a reasonable standard of living" and for those seeking to maintain established differentials. In addition, the TUC called for sacrifices from employers. These demands led to the policy of voluntary dividend limitation, to which the FBI reluctantly agreed, and to the capital levy announced in the budget.

The policy adopted in February–March, 1948 slowed the pace of wage advances through the middle of 1949, but devaluation led to renewed concern. Intensive discussions were undertaken between the government and the TUC and resulted in the adoption of a one-year freeze, including a suspension of cost of living agreements. The only exemption was for the low paid; the only condition was that retail prices not be allowed to rise by more than 5 per cent. Restraint was continued through at least the first half of 1950, and with considerable effect. Wages had risen by almost 9 per cent per year during 1945–7, but by less than 3 per cent per year in the eighteen months from March, 1948; and by still less (around 1 per cent) in the year after devaluation. From early in 1948 until late in 1950, as a result, real wages probably fell slightly for most workers. By 1950, however, the unions" ability to deliver the good behaviour of their members was being very much called into question; and in June of that year the TUC proclaimed the need for greater flexibility in the setting of wages. Meanwhile, the government began to move towards the creation of a "Wages Advisory Council," to be made up of unionists, employers and representatives of the public and empowered to issue guidelines in general and for specific wage claims. When the plan was put to TUC leaders in February, 1951, they refused to go along and the scheme was peremptorily abandoned. After that, the government reverted to its earlier policy of moral exhortation and to efforts at reducing the pressure for wage increases by limiting the rise in the cost of living and in dividends.[49]

As with the debates over taxation, over the planning machinery, over investment control and other policy devices, the government's efforts to control wages had no clear outcome. The relative success of Labour's voluntarist and indirect approach encouraged ministers to feel that reliance upon the unions to police wages was reasonably effective. This would establish a precedent followed more than once in future years, in which Labour's best supporters would be called upon to sacrifice gains in income in return for the government's pursuit of economic and social policies supported by the unions. The danger of such a policy was that over the long term it served to discourage the search for more effective policy devices, while straining the relationship between Labour and its working-class base, particularly the skilled workers whose privileged position in the labour market would otherwise have secured for them substantial wage increases. More immediately, the obvious inability of the Labour governments of 1945–51 to develop a permanent mechanism for regulating wages made policy-makers even more nervous about the implications of decontrol. With so few other policy devices available to them, the prospective loss of physical controls betokened a genuine loss of state capacity in the sphere of economic policy. Thus, as the abandonment of controls proceeded in 1949–51, ministers held intensive discussions about just how far they should push liberalization, about what controls should be left in place and about what instruments might serve as effective substitutes.

The two most thoughtful contributions to the debate over controls came from Gaitskell and Harold Wilson during 1950. Gaitskell had found himself at odds with Cripps in late 1949 over the decision to liberalize European trade and was moved to draft a paper on "Economic Planning and Liberalization" in January, 1950.[50] In it he worried aloud about the consequences of abandoning physical controls. This had been done in other European countries, he claimed, and had led to greater unemployment "and/or," as he put it, "a much less equitable distribution of income." He feared that Britain would be pushed in this direction by "pressure from E.C.A. and from other O.E.E.C. countries which are no longer seriously attempting to plan their own economies." Gaitskell argued strongly that liberalization would not benefit the British economy and therefore urged his colleagues to recognize the need for continued controls.

Wilson's contribution to the debate about controls stemmed less from a concern with the effects of trade liberalization and more from a sense of how little government could actually do to intervene in the economy.[51] Like Gaitskell, Wilson did not want to be forced "to rely exclusively upon monetary and budgetary policy" to manage the economy, but he was even less sanguine than Gaitskell about the effectiveness of existing policy devices: "I am personally greatly apprehensive," Wilson wrote, "about our dependence on the decisions of private industry, over which we have no control, for the maintenance of full employment." Wilson was painfully aware of the difficulty of influencing the direction of investment, even when a combination of excess demand and rigid direct controls appeared to give the state maximum leverage over industrial decisions. As he forcefully argued, "if our control is so incomplete over excessive capital investment, how much weaker will our powers be to increase the volume of investment when we are threatened with unemployment." Wilson feared that the threat of a serious drop in demand might tempt the government into a "Maginot-like dependence on purely financial methods of preventing a depression." The government had in fact "no experience of the use of such techniques," and Wilson was highly doubtful "about their effectiveness in combating a real crise de confiance of the 1931 type, when private industry and finance are severely bearish about the future." He doubted, too, whether the nationalized industries could be induced at such a moment to increase their purchasing and output and thus to run the risk of serious commercial losses in the interests of maintaining aggregate demand. Wilson was equally sceptical about the possibility of using other existing policy devices to maintain full employment: control over the location of industry "does bite," as he put it, but it was essentially a negative control; direct controls were likewise powerul, but "blunt, rather than sharp and selective instruments."

This pessimistic assessment of the tools on hand to direct economic development led Wilson to make several controversial but highly innovative proposals. He argued that Labour should begin by accepting the "mixed economy" and granting that private industry would play an important role for decades to come, but from there he proceeded to specify the conditions under which private industry would be expected to operate. To that end Wilson proposed a package of policies that included the permanent power to control prices on selected goods so as to ensure the quality of the goods produced; a greater concern for consumer protection, to be symbolized through a "consumers" charter" and exercised in practice through "consumers" consultative committees" covering private industry; a more concerted use of the government's leverage as consumer through guaranteed markets and production guarantees linked to improved efficiency; increased competition between socialized industries and the private sector; further controls on restrictive practices, particularly in distribution (e.g., resale price maintenance agreements); the establishment by the state of a series of "Production Efficiency Services" which would survey the efficiency of private firms and whose recommendations would guide government decisions about state assistance to particular firms; and, possibly of greatest importance, the development of a system by which the state would designate in each industry certain "key firms" whose progress would be monitored, encouraged and, in extreme circumstances, taken under direct control. Wilson went so far as to suggest at one point that, in view of the importance of the chemical industry to future economic growth, it made more sense to nationalize Imperial Chemicals (ICI) than the steel industry.

Wilson's alternative was perhaps less coherent and compelling than his critique, but it was without doubt the most thoughtful proposal on offer in 1950–1. That did not guarantee it a favourable reception. The report was discussed at separate meetings of "junior" and "senior" ministers in May–June, 1950 and met with objections at both levels. Ministers felt that Wilson's policies were too *dirigiste* to be accepted by the public, and especially by industry. His proposals would probably have required new legislation and a rearrangement in the planning machinery. Altogether, it was too much to ask of a government uncertain of its popular mandate, increasingly preoccupied with its electoral prospects and as yet unconvinced that present policies were inadequate. Wilson's ambitious effort therefore left little impact either on policy or on the machinery of government.[52]

Neither did the roughly simultaneous discussions within the government over the "full employment standard" or the so-called "Full Employment Bill." Throughout the 1940s Britain had sought to build a commitment to full employment into the policies of the organizations set up to co-ordinate the international economy. During the war, for example, Keynes had argued with the Americans about the importance of employment policy and had resisted

American efforts to give priority to free trade over domestic employment. However hesitant officials may have been about Keynesian techniques for maintaining demand at home, British policy-makers were consistent advocates of Keynesian policies abroad. According to a key member of the Economic Section, pushing such policies on others

> was our role at Bretton Woods, the Philadelphia Conference of the ILO, the San Francisco Conference, at the various conferences leading up to the Havana Conference of the ITO [International Trade Organization], and at many meetings of the UN and of the OEEC. Broadly speaking, we have sought by various means to encourage the adoption by governments of high standards of achievement in the field of full employment, to foster the international exchange of information regarding the techniques of domestic policy, and to ensure that international action in the field of commercial and financial policy was so adapted as to mitigate the consequences of depression in one country on the balance of payments and on internal demand in other countries.[53]

Policy-makers were particularly concerned about the likely impact on the British economy of a depression in the United States, and worried actively about the lack of an American commitment to full employment.[54] The dependence of British prosperity upon the ups and downs of the American economy was made especially clear in 1949, when a brief downturn in the US caused a drop in exports to America and a balance of payments crisis. That experience reinforced British determination to extract from the Americans a commitment to full employment.

This was to be done through international organizations. In particular, British representatives encouraged the Economic and Social Council of the UN to request information from participating countries on their plans for avoiding a slump and, pursuant to that, on their standard for employment policy. There was some reluctance on the part of both officials and ministers to proclaim a specific target; and Beveridge's 1944 target of 3 per cent had long been considered too low. But the need to give a lead internationally and to provide a reference point for the Americans forced the government to consider committing itself to a low figure. Since the main danger confronting Britain was thought not to be a deficiency of internal demand but rather "a slump in the United States," "the lower we fix our figure the more pressure we put on them to match it and therefore to pull their weight against the trade depression, which might be tolerable to them but intolerable to us." The success of employment policy during the 1940s also made a low figure seem less threatening. The result was the official adoption of a 3 per cent target, announced to Parliament and submitted to the United Nations in March, 1951.[55]

Of course, the promulgation of an employment target did not guarantee a commitment to the adoption of any specific measures to combat unemployment. That issue remained unsolved, despite the attempt during 1950–1 to institutionalize a set of policy devices through the passage of a "Full Employment Bill." The physical controls upon which so much of Labour's efforts relied were due to expire with the lapsing of emergency legislation in December, 1950. That deadline imparted considerable urgency to the debate over controls; so, too, did the growing problem of inflation. The practical difficulty confronting the government was that a bill containing only negative controls would be an easy object of attack; it would also do nothing to overcome the deficiencies in the planning process of which ministers and officials were becoming aware. Gradually, therefore, the government came to a decision to put together a bill that would relate the continuation of controls to the commitment to full employment.

Serious discussion of what such a bill should look like began in the summer of 1950 and dragged on into 1951. Responsibility for drafting it was foolishly given to a committee of officials dominated by Sir Bernard Gilbert and Sir Wilfrid Eady, the two Treasury stalwarts whose postwar views most closely approximated the prewar orthodoxy. Gilbert objected to linking within the same bill a set of negative controls and the more positive proclamation of a full employment policy. He also objected to the inclusion within the bill of any new powers for exerting a more positive direction over the economy. In particular, proposals to maintain demand during a slump by government purchases and production, as Wilson had suggested, or by controlling private investment, were criticized on technical and constitutional grounds. The effect of giving sceptical officials the task of clarifying and codifying the government's objectives was thus to highlight the underlying contradictions between the government's commitment to full employment and its inability to devise policies adequate to the task. Ministers responded with yet another recasting of the proposed bill. They accepted the argument of officials that negative controls did not sit well in a bill rhetorically labelled a "full employment" bill, but concluded from that that the bill itself should be expanded to include more positive measures. The bill went through several drafts aimed at bringing positive and negative controls together under the banner of full employment, but agreement proved elusive. The Treasury reiterated its long-standing objection to variations in insurance contributions and the encouragement of public works by local authorities through the compilation of a "reserve of works" and special funding; officials also persisted in their opposition to plans for countercyclical purchasing and investing by central government or the nationalized industries; and specific commitments to use the budget to offset a depression were ruled out on constitutional grounds. Ministers were clearly frustrated by this catalogue of impossibilities and directed that a bill be drafted including, at the least, some commitment to subsidizing investment by local authorities and nationalized industries and to government purchase of capital goods. Even then, the commitments incorporated in the draft that finally emerged in February, 1951 were hedged about by qualifications and restrictions that suggested a deep resistance on the part of officials. Faced with such resistance and with a fundamentally unsatisfactory bill, the government decided not to proceed. Instead, they relied upon a continuation of emergency powers made palatable to Parliament by the Korean War and the need to rearm.[56]

The Korean War and the rearmament that accompanied it served, in fact, to adjourn the entire range of debates proceeding within the Labour government during 1950–1 and to prevent any permanent resolution of the outstanding issues concerning taxes, the machinery and techniques of planning, and the future role of direct controls. The decision to rearm represented a major turning point in the history of the Labour governments. During most of its first term of office, the Attlee government had presided over a steady decrease in military spending and by 1950, spending on defence was down to half of its 1944 level, despite Britain's vigorous participation in the Cold War. That level represented a substantial effort – amounting to 7 per cent of GNP – but it was a declining commitment and, given current rates of tax, not an impossible burden on the economy. Within the Labour government there had been considerable disagreement over defence: Dalton, backed up by Cripps and Bevan, regarded the continuing high level of defence spending as a liability; Attlee was inclined toward reductions and a pulling back from extensive foreign commitments, though not strongly so; Bevin, together with the "pompous, unconvincing and incompetent" Minister of Defence, A.V. Alexander – to use Dalton's description – was unwilling to countenance severe reductions in British military power.[57]

Even those like Bevin and Alexander were forced, however, to accept the need to economize on defence in order to have money left over for social services. Hence there had been no significant opposition to the government's decision in 1946 to set up a new Ministry of Defence, to be headed by Alexander, in the hope of enforcing retrenchment. It is perhaps doubtful whether the new structure did much to depress military spending, but it did not help it to increase. It brought the different services together in a single department and forced them to co-ordinate their requests and to submit to regular reviews of the overall needs of the forces considered together. The first such review was set in motion in 1948 under Lord Harwood and produced results quite unsatisfactory to the chiefs of staff. Harwood's study of the "Shape and Size of the Armed Forces" gave only mild support to the services" contention that they were underfunded and instead provided evidence used by Cripps in 1949 to limit military spending. By March, 1950 a Ministry of Defence official judged that "So far the Ministry of Defence has been one more hurdle for the Services to jump in the Estimates handicap." Despite Britain's "premature" commitment to the Cold War, the pleadings of the chiefs of staff and the carping criticism of Churchill and the Conservatives, therefore, the essential thrust of Labour policy to 1950 was towards a moderate but steady reduction in military spending.[58]

Korea changed all that, exacting from the government a commitment to massive rearmament. The United States had begun to pressure Britain to rearm in early June, 1950, just before the Korean conflict. Britain responded quickly, announcing in early August a programme projected to cost £3,400 million over three years and requesting aid from the United States worth £550 million. Throughout the late summer and early fall estimates of the amount needed for rearmament continued to increase. By the end of 1950, when the chiefs of staff had had their say, it had grown to £4,700 million. This would involve an increase in defence production by 1953-54 of four and a half times the level of 1950-1; it would require the diversion of roughly 650,000 workers; and it would most likely wipe out the current surplus on the external account. The government hoped to meet the burden of rearmament without recourse to borrowing and without sacrificing investment or exports. Sacrifices would therefore have to come from reduced domestic consumption, the effect of which would be a decline in living standards of no less than 5 per cent by 1953.[59]

The dramatic transformation in Labour's defence policy occasioned by the Korean conflict remains something of a mystery. At first, it looked as though the United States might foot the bill, but by the autumn of 1950 it was obvious that America's contribution would be minimal. Still, the government persisted in its plan to rearm and accepted the increasing totals of defence expenditure with surprising complacency. No doubt members of the government were genuinely concerned about the Russians and convinced ideologically that virtue was on their side in the developing Cold War. On the other hand, the speed with which the Attlee government fell in with American wishes contrasts sharply with the ability of British representatives to engage in hard bargaining with the United States over economic issues. This suggests that one reason behind Britain's turn to rearmament was a desire to enhance its bargaining stature vis-à-vis the United States and the other European powers. In a revealing memo jointly authored by Bevin and Gaitskell, for example, the two ministers claimed that the successes of the late 1940s – by which they meant not only the scale of Britain's economic recovery but also its role in the creation of NATO and the western alliance – had led by mid-1950 to a resurgence of British power throughout the world. As Bevin and Gaitskell put it, "We no longer had to rest content with the knowledge that we were a great power, but we were becoming able, for the first time since the war, to sustain our world-wide commitments.' The outbreak of the Korean War thus confronted policy-makers with a choice and an opportunity: Britain could pretend to be a great power and join up with the United States, perhaps extracting from the Americans the aid with which to do so, or resist the pressure for rearmament but in so doing lose power and prestige and run the risk of being put "back again in the European queue" and becoming, in American eyes, "just another necessitous European nation." Even as those words were being written, of course, the prospects of substantial American military aid were growing dim and the end of Marshall Aid was already in sight, but the logic of the argument was to proceed with rearmament anyway.[60]

Rearmament in this sense fitted in well with the inflated conception of Britain's postwar role which the Labour government had long nurtured. It also fitted rather well with the policy devices and the policy-making apparatus which the government had evolved since 1945. The sharp turn in defence policy represented by the Korean rearmament basically did not require drastic innovations in policy or in the machinery of government. Rearmament demanded higher taxes and Gaitskell, who had replaced Cripps in October, 1950, introduced a severe budget in April, 1951. The standard rate of income tax was increased from 9s to 9s 6d in the pound; additional sums were raised by higher purchase tax, particularly on cars, radios and electrical appliances, by taxes on profits and on petrol and entertainments. More controversial was the imposition of charges for false teeth and spectacles obtained through the National Health Service – a decision that prompted the resignation from the Cabinet of Nye Bevan, Harold Wilson and John Freeman. Such a stern budget was quite consistent with the policy pursued by Labour for the previous three years. Other measures were equally in keeping with Labour's prior record. In particular, a variety of direct controls were restored: prices were controlled, imports restricted, raw materials allocations reimposed, and some degree of "guidance" reasserted over the labour market. None of these policies was new or unprecedented; rather, they represented a reversion to the sorts of policy devices upon which the government had relied throughout the 1940s and with which ministers and officials obviously felt comfortable. Nor did rearmament require drastic changes in the way the government did its business. The need to exert detailed control over the economy led merely to a readjustment of the interdepartmental machinery through which economic policy had previously been co-ordinated. A new "Mutual Aid Committee" was established to take over from the old Marshall Plan organization and oversee the distribution of whatever aid was forthcoming from America, and representatives of the defence departments were added to the membership of various official committees on aspects of economic policy. The net effect was minimal and served to demonstrate once again that the policy-making machinery employed by Labour was more suited to the needs of war mobilization than to the administration of a planned economy during peacetime.[61]

The imperatives of rearmament thus provided an excuse for the Labour government to revert to the policies and policy devices of the past and to maintain the policy-making apparatus in the form it had attained by 1950–1. Rearmament thus allowed ministers and officials to postpone the difficult decisions that beckoned so insistently at the beginning of 1950. The pressure on Labour to reduce taxes effectively ceased with rearmament, and Conservative critics were largely silenced. The search for new ways to steer the economy also became less urgent, as physical controls returned to government the capacity for directly influencing production. The question of whether the existing structure of administration was adequate to the guidance of the economy was also postponed, for the need for continued interdepartmental co-ordination in the administration of the defence programme meant that the arrangements first developed during the war and further refined in 1947 were maintained for yet another few years. The debates that had preoccupied policy-makers during 1950-1 – over controls, over the proper long-term level of taxation, over the machinery for economic planning – were thus put aside in favour of a concentrated focus on rearmament. Labour would pay a very dear price for its neglect of these crucial issues, for it would mean that their resolution would be accomplished by the Conservatives, who would see to it that they would be resolved along lines that would make it harder for any future Labour government to implement its social or economic policies. Still, that was an outcome not easily foreseen in 1951 and not fully understood even when it happened.

Chapter 10

"Centring" the postwar settlement

THE CONSERVATIVES CONFRONT THE "POSTWAR SETTLEMENT"

The defeat of the Labour government in October 1951 brought to an end the most sustained effort to reshape the state in modern times. Labour left behind both an expanded set of public commitments to social and economic goals and a formidable array of agencies and policies with which to fulfil them. The commitments that Labour succeeded in grafting upon the state were not uniquely their own or entirely new in 1945. They consisted essentially of the promise that government would seek to provide work for all and a comprehensive system of welfare benefits as a matter of social right. Promises of this sort were implicit in Beveridge, in the rhetoric of reconstruction to which all parties contributed during the war and in the coalition's postwar planning. But it was the Labour victory in 1945 and the party's remarkable success in translating promise into legislation and, to a considerable extent, into economic performance that ensured that these commitments would become the cornerstone of public policy and of Britain's political culture for at least three decades after the war's end.

The policy devices and instruments that Labour evolved and bequeathed to subsequent governments, and through which the state's new-found responsibilities were to be discharged, were overall a less impressive achievement. Labour had worked hard at figuring out what mix of policies would be most effective at managing the economy, generating growth and improving the distribution of income and benefits, but it can hardly be said to have succeeded in finding that mix. Likewise, the politicians and officials who oversaw the expansion of government responsibilities during the 1940s sought at the same time to restructure the institutions of the state so as to ensure its capacity to deliver on its promises. But, again, they were not entirely successful: they failed to create a central mechanism for co-ordinating economic and social policy or to develop a set of practices that would ensure that what government decided at the centre would become reality throughout the land.

Labour's legacy was thus deeply contradictory, with aims and commitments vastly exceeding institutional capacity. This contradiction opened a critical space within which Conservatives could operate and enabled the Tories to limit the reach and effectiveness of the state without directly challenging the new, and still very popular, definition of citizenship and public responsibility. The precise scope of Conservative reaction would vary from one policy arena to another. On some issues the policies of the Labour government enjoyed such wide support that there was little room to hedge. By 1950–1, for example, the Health Service was extremely popular. Despite rising costs, therefore, the Conservatives could not renege on the promise of universal health care. Most of Labour's other welfare measures were also popular with voters and thus relatively immune from direct attack; and, with full employment, the burden on the social services was relatively modest. Full employment itself was the most basic point in what there was by way of a postwar consensus and the one element from which no politician could be seen to depart.[1]

The precise means by which Labour had run the economy were more easily criticized. Direct controls were particularly vulnerable. It was difficult to generate support for physical controls six years into the peace, even among Labour supporters, but Labour had not, over that period, found alternative methods by which to manage the details of the economy. With the onset of rearmament, moreover, the government had actually reversed the process of liberalization begun in 1948. So the Conservatives were given an issue with which to beat Labour during the general election and with which to contrast their own programme. Direct controls were probably more controversial than the other devices by which Labour managed the economy, but that did not mean that these were any more securely established. Labour's most effective method of economic management was undoubtedly the budget, kept in balance throughout the 1940s by a willingness to maintain very high rates of tax. The conduct of the Labour Chancellors – Dalton, Cripps and Gaitskell – had been a model of fiscal responsibility mixed with a visible concern for equity and income redistribution. From about 1947, however, businessmen had begun to complain loudly about the level of taxation and resentment over taxes was a major factor driving the middle classes back to the Tories in the elections of 1950 and 1951. The appointment of the Royal Commission on Taxation had served to put the issue off for a bit, and the need to pay for rearmament had allowed Labour to resist calls for lower taxes and actually to increase them. The Conservatives, moreover, were careful in 1951 not to give away future revenues by promising specific reductions in tax, but they did attack "socialist extravagance" and proclaim the need to reduce taxation.

Labour's record of economic management was also bound up with the successes and failures of nationalization. The party itself was divided over how much to push for further nationalization, and the ambivalence was reflected more broadly in the country. Conservative attacks on the existing nationalized industries were not especially telling, but their arguments against extending the policy were more effective. So, too, were criticisms of the management of the nationalized industries. The Labour government had chosen to follow the Morrisonian "public corporation" model in setting up the nationalized industries, creating governing boards with considerable autonomy and limiting the direct responsibilities of ministers.[2] This arrangement protected the government from being implicated in specific decisions and from being accused of using its power over nationalized industries for narrow political purposes. But it also prevented the government from making effective use of the power over economic policy which the sheer economic weight of the public sector might otherwise have afforded. Inevitably, the nationalized sector of the economy would take decisions about prices, investments, industrial location and choice of technique that would have considerable impact upon the economy as a whole. The public corporation model, however, offered no means by which to co-ordinate these impacts or to integrate these decisions within the broader direction of macro-economic policy. Nor did the public corporation model meaningfully change the character of industrial relations. Workers still worked in the old way, often for the same bosses and with roughly the same problems and grievances. Neither at the level of macro-economic policy nor at the mundane level of daily work did nationalization bring about major changes. Not surprisingly, it therefore had not, by 1951, produced a wave of enthusiasm for further nationalization or agreement on the virtues of the existing array of socialized industries.

The relative popularity of Labour's various policy initiatives, then, as well as the degree to which they had been embedded in the institutions of the state, would be critical factors in determining which of the changes brought into effect by Labour would be left intact by Conservatives and which would be modified. A third, and perhaps equally important, factor would be the set of constraints imposed on the incoming Conservative government by ideology and by the logic of electoral competition. Neither of these considerations produced a clear set of priorities with which to guide Conservative actions. The party's ideological stance in the early 1950s was particularly ambiguous. The defeat of 1945, as R.A. Butler has explained, "shook the Conservative Party out of its lethargy and impelled it to rethink its philosophy and reform its ranks." The reorganization of the party was reasonably straightforward: under Lord Woolton's leadership the Conservatives undertook a drive to recruit individual members and to improve fundraising, thus providing party funds directly to candidates and lessening its reliance on "the purchase of constituencies by gentlemen"; the work of the Conservative Research Department was upgraded and propaganda efforts enhanced by the setting up of the Conservative Political Centre; and a new youth organization, the Young Conservatives, was created.[3]

The reorientation of the party's outlook was more complicated and, in the end, far less thorough. During the war the "progressive" wing of the party was given a major boost by the formation of the Tory Reform Committee, to which over forty MPs gave public support. The Committee was deeply critical of the party's record in the 1930s and strongly influenced by the wartime spirit of social reform. They argued for a "national policy" that would include, as Quintin Hogg put it, "work for all" and "social democracy," and they were very much in favour of the Beveridge Report. The reformers were not, however, dominant within the party. A rival, but secret, organization was established in November, 1943 specifically to counter the support for Beveridge and the influence of the Tory Reform Committee. Approximately thirty MPs joined this so-called "Progress Trust" and its views were probably closer to that of the average party member than were those of the reformers.[4] Nor did the reformers have much influence on the conduct of the 1945 election, which was run as a nasty, anti-socialist campaign.

The reformers played a more prominent role in the reconstruction of the party after the war. Butler, who was sympathetic to the reformers, was made chair of the Research Department and proceeded to rebuild it by recruiting a highly able group of young researchers. Their efforts led to the production of *The Industrial Charter*, adopted by the party conference in 1947. The *Charter* blended support for the "Liberal tradition of free enterprise with the equally-traditional Tory concept of interventionism" in a highly effective fashion. Rhetorically, it stressed enterprise and individualism; practically, it leaned towards policies that assumed a more expanded role for the state. Full employment, the use of Keynesian techniques and a certain amount of public ownership were all accepted, along with a commitment "to humanize, not to nationalize" industry and to put in place a "Workers' Charter" in order to ensure the rights of workers and create a more harmonious system of industrial relations. *The Industrial Charter* seemed to betoken a new era in Conservative party history and a major alteration in the party's outlook.[5]

A genuine transformation proved elusive, however. The conference votes were heavily in favour of the programme, but Churchill was unenthusiastic. When Reginald Maudling drafted a paragraph for Churchill's speech summarizing the *Charter*, Churchill read it and complained that "I do not agree with a word of this." He proceeded to endorse the principles of the *Charter* in his speech, but it hardly reflected a firm commitment about the future direction of Conservative policy.[6] Nor did subsequent policy pronouncements follow the path towards the political centre laid out in 1947. To be an effective opposition, the Conservatives found it necessary to sharpen, rather than to minimize, the differences between themselves and Labour and, after 1947, they became more critical of the government and in so doing began to move back to the right. On the question of nationalization, for example, the party co-ordinated its resistance with the parallel campaigns mounted by business, particularly by the road haulage and iron and steel industries, and inevitably adopted the quite unreconstructed perspectives of private business. Similarly, Conservative attacks on direct controls and on tax policy echoed older themes of resistance to collectivism and to higher taxes.

The party's programmatic statements also moved to the right. *The*

Industrial Charter was followed up in 1948 by charters for agriculture, for Wales and Scotland, for the empire and for women, but the major effort to restate policy was the publication in 1949 of *The Right Road for Britain*. That road, it turned out, would involve a much greater reliance upon private enterprise and a correspondingly less central role for the state than had been envisioned by *The Industrial Charter*. *The Right Road* stressed the problem of rising costs as central to Britain's economic difficulties and placed much of the blame on the unions; it pointedly refused to promise not to cut social services; but it did pledge the party to lower taxation. The move to the right was even more visible in the party's election manifesto, *This is the Road*, which sharply attacked Labour for economic failure and for the government's commitment to high taxation for social services. Labour, the Tories claimed, had "spread the tale that social welfare is something to be had from the State free, gratis and for nothing." This excessive generosity had been financed by "a crushing burden of taxation," which constituted "a grave evil" in itself and reduced incentives, savings and investment. The Conservatives would somehow reverse these trends. They pledged also to "bring Nationalization to a full stop here and now," and to begin selective denationalization and the drastic reorganization of those industries, like coal and the railways, that would remain in government control. The specifics of the manifesto were linked together by a reiteration of traditional arguments about liberty, the constitution, patriotism, the virtues of thrift and hard work and the importance of "Christian ethics" and "love of home and family.[7] Rhetorically, the document reflected more accurately the mood of 1930s Conservatism than the centrist themes of 1947; and the practical commitments it offered were almost all negative.

The Conservatives' narrow defeat in 1950 provided an opportunity for yet further clarification of the party's outlook. Little of substance was changed during the eighteen months separating the two elections, but the tone of Churchill's 1951 manifesto "was certainly more libertarian than earlier statements."[8] The famous commitment to build 300,000 houses per year had been added to the party's platform in 1951, but otherwise the positions worked out by 1949–50 were reaffirmed. There was, in particular, no further movement towards the centrist consensus whose outlines were visible in 1947. The government elected in October, 1951 was therefore only partially reconciled to the changes wrought by six years of Labour rule. The "social-democratic," or "liberal-socialist," character of the postwar settlement was not at all assured, and the precise nature of the relationship between state and society remained very much to be determined.

The constraints imposed upon the Conservative government by the party's ideological inheritance were reinforced by electoral considerations. The pattern of electoral results during the late 1940s and into 1950–1 offered seemingly contradictory lessons to Conservative strategists. Despite the fact that the party had, by the late 1940s, obviously recovered its sense of political identity, largely rebuilt its organization and taken on a more up-to-date programme and rhetoric, its performance in by-elections remained weak. In particular, the Tories were unable to win back the votes of those sections of the working class whose support, it was widely believed, had been so important to their interwar successes. Instead, whatever recovery they managed to achieve during the late 1940s was based almost entirely on bringing back into the fold those sections of the middle classes that had deserted in 1945. The issues around which the party harassed the Labour government – nationalization, taxes, controls – strengthened still further the links between the Conservatives and the interests of business and the middle classes. Over the course of the Labour governments, therefore, the class basis of party alignment intensified and Conservatives were reminded of the electoral importance of their historic supporters. This suggested a strategic need, not to move towards the centre where one might woo the suspicious trade unionists, but rather to rally the faithful and hope that the increasing difficulties experienced by Labour in actually ruling the nation would disappoint just enough voters to afford Conservatives the margin of victory.

The elections of 1950 and 1951 demonstrated the wisdom of such a course. Labour outpolled the Conservatives by over half a million votes in February, 1950, but the party was returned with only a small majority in Parliament. In October, 1951 Labour increased its vote by nearly 700,000 and received almost a quarter of a million more votes than the Conservatives. Seats did not follow votes, however, and the Conservatives took power with a Parliamentary majority of twenty-six. Key to the Tory victory was the switch of over a million voters from the Liberals to the Conservatives. The margin of victory, then, owed virtually nothing to Conservative efforts to dent Labour support among its working-class followers. On the contrary, Labour received the support of about two-thirds of the working class and the Tories the votes of roughly two-thirds of the middle classes in what was probably the most class-based election of the century.[9]

Behind the Conservative triumph, therefore, was a re-creation of traditional class alignments. Churchill's failure in 1945 had been due in large part to the widespread revulsion against the Conservative policies of the 1930s and fear that the legacy would prevent the Tories from fulfilling the promises of reconstruction. Both the revulsion and the fear had affected significant sections of the middle and lower-middle classes and helped to create support for Labour across class lines. Six years of Labour government, however, had intensified class sentiments and allegiances. "Austerity," the *New Statesman* explained in November, 1947, "has awakened the middle classes and made them politically active." High taxes and continued controls kept the middle classes active and fuelled a much-discussed "middle-class revolt" in the late 1940s.[10] By the election of 1950, the bulk of the middle classes were arrayed once again behind the Conservatives and by 1951 middle-class support helped to push the Tories over the top.

The Conservatives thus owed their return to power in 1951 as much to petty-bourgeois *ressentiment* as to their own efforts to modernize the party's organization and outlook. Reading the electoral results did not, therefore, give Churchill and his Cabinet much of a sense of what policies to pursue. Certainly, the recovery of Conservative fortunes after 1947 provided a retrospective justification for the changes introduced by Woolton and Butler, but the specific arguments and allegiances that had produced victory did not suggest the need for any further move towards the political centre. On the other hand, Labour's continued strength demonstrated to Conservatives the precariousness of their position and the need for extreme caution when in office. The enduring support of the workers for Labour thus minimized the allure of a sharp turn to the right. So, too, did the obvious power of the unions. Indeed, it could be argued that the main difference between the political landscape of the 1930s and that of the 1950s lay in the position of the trade unions. Union membership had jumped from 4.8 million in 1935, the year of the last general election before the war, to 9.5 million in 1951. Whatever the Conservatives may have believed and felt in their hearts, they were forced to recognize the novel place within society and even in the counsels of the state attained by the trade unions, which had grown accustomed to being consulted and flattered, first by the wartime coalition and then by Labour. The Conservatives had little choice but to persist in the effort to incorporate the unions into the formation of policy or, at the least, to take their interests into account while weighing policy options. The massively increased power of the unions and the very narrow margin of their electoral victory thus made Conservatives extremely wary about a direct assault on the legacy of Labour.

Ideology and electoral calculation both, therefore, served to constrain the incoming Conservative government. The party's ideological inheritance, combining economic liberalism and "one-nation" paternalism, had been reworked during 1945–51 but not decisively transformed. Ideology pulled simultaneously towards the right and the centre. The message to be read from the election results was no clearer: the narrow balance between Labour and the Conservatives denied the Tories a mandate to dismantle the welfare state or to pull back from the new commitments that Labour had fastened upon the government, while the Conservatives' dependence on the middle classes reinforced their traditional antipathy to taxes, expenditure and controls. Combined, these factors ensured that the Conservative government of 1951–5 would surely tamper with the system left in place by Labour, probing its weak spots and subtly shifting its priorities, but that it would not fundamentally reshape the agenda of British politics and would move only incrementally to lower taxes and spending, to retract the boundaries of state control and social provision, and to free up the market.

THE CONSERVATIVES IN POWER

Not only did the Conservative government confront a contradictory set of electoral signals with a conflicted outlook; they also faced serious economic problems with personnel who were not at their peak. The massive rearmament programme initiated by Labour had begun to cause severe balance of payments difficulties and conjured up the spectre of a further devaluation. The men who were to deal with this crisis were largely those with whom Churchill had fought the war and with whom he was comfortable. They were not especially well suited to the tasks of peacetime economic management. Even more debilitating was the distrust that Churchill and his closest supporters felt towards the bureaucracy and the machinery of government which they had inherited from Labour. Cripps and Dalton may have fretted over the lingering attachment of officials to economic liberalism and their resistance to planning; but to the Conservatives in opposition it appeared that the civil servants had all become socialists and were not to be trusted. In part this attitude derived from Churchill's long-standing suspicion of the Treasury, in part from the fact that Labour had appeared to work so well with the existing apparatus. Ironically, therefore, the Conservatives came into power profoundly distrustful of the machine whose direction they assumed, and pledged to decrease its size and pretensions. As Lord Woolton put it, "In Opposition many of us concluded that the country was suffering under a weight of Government which was expensive both of money and of effort, and we looked forward to a freer society which relied less on either direction or support from government departments." [11]

That resolve translated into a fear that the existing apparatus could not be made to do what the Conservatives wanted it to do and into a desire to circumvent it. The effort to get around the inherited structure took two forms: one was Churchill's plan to appoint "overlords" or "co-ordinating ministers;" the second was the decision, or near-decision, to support the Bank of England's plan to make a radical break with economic planning and demand management by floating the pound through an operation known as "Robot." Neither initiative worked, but together they indicate the difficulty that the Conservatives had in settling in to their new roles as the governors of an at least mildly interventionist state.

The difficulty was anticipated by officials. Over the last two years of Labour rule, senior officials like Edward Bridges and Norman Brook had attempted to refine the structure of policy-making with an eye to a future Conservative government. The two did not fully agree – Bridges was more committed to the reforms of the 1940s and to the system of interdepartmental co-ordination, centred of course on the Treasury, that had evolved after 1947; while Brook was a more straightforward advocate of "Treasury control" and less enamoured of the vast network of committees through which the government had done its business under Labour. Bridges and Brook agreed, however, that the policy-making apparatus, especially the co-ordination of economic policy, worked reasonably well and needed only minor adjustment. They were opposed to major restructuring and resistant to any sustained debate about the machinery of government. Officials preferred to keep machinery of government questions off the agenda of ministers and sought to pre-empt Conservative initiatives in this field. They decided, for example, not to publish the report of the Economic Organization Inquiry set up by Bridges, although its work had been completed before the general election. The unpublished report may not have resolved, or even fully confronted, some of the outstanding questions about the levers by which economic policy would be made effective, but it did confirm the existing arrangements for determining policy and the then current division of labour between departments. It confirmed, in particular, the predominant role of the Treasury and the principle of interdepartmental co-ordination. The message of the report was not likely to please the new government, therefore, and so it was not delivered. Even eight months after the Conservatives had taken power, officials met to discuss what to do with the report and decided that it still "may be inexpedient to make it the subject of any formal enquiry." To take action on it would presumably have been still more "inexpedient." [12]

More practically, officials also sought to persuade Churchill of the wisdom of existing arrangements and to dissuade him from implementing his plan for a system of "co-ordinating ministers." In October, 1951 Norman Brook prepared a report for the in-coming Conservative premier advocating a small Cabinet but urging against the appointment of "overlords" or the removal of the responsibility for economic policy from the Treasury. [13] "Recent experience," Brook told Churchill, "has shown the advantages of bringing under a single Minister the supervision of both economic and fiscal policy, and both internal and external economic questions – and also the grave troubles which can arise if these supervisory duties are entrusted to a Minister outside the Treasury." And besides, "The conception of a super-Minister responsible for supervising the work of other Ministers of Cabinet rank is fraught with serious difficulties, both constitutional and practical."

Brook and Bridges worked feverishly in the first weeks of the new government to thwart Churchill's initiatives. The Prime Minister was not easily deterred by the doubts of his officials, however, even when expressed as forcefully as were Brook's. He proceeded, therefore, to recruit Lord Cherwell to the sinecure of Paymaster General to play the role of *eminence grise* within the Cabinet, Lord Woolton to co-ordinate the work of agriculture and fisheries and of the Ministry of Food, and Lord Leathers to supervise the workings of fuel and power and of transport. Obviously missing was an "overlord" for the economy. Originally, Churchill had planned to appoint Sir John Anderson to the position, but when he turned it down it went unfilled. In effect, the critical arena that seemed most in need of supervision was left unsupervised and the system for controlling the economy put in place by 1950–1 remained intact. Officials thus succeeded in protecting the most cherished centre of the government machine from being reshaped according to Churchill's peculiar design. Officials would be further vindicated when the "overlords" proved ineffective and found little to do, and the experiment was finally wound up with the Cabinet reshuffle of September, 1953.[14]

The failure of the plan for "overlords" did not greatly disappoint the senior members of Churchill's Cabinet such as Eden and Butler. They had never been keen on it and it was their power that would have been curtailed had any truly effective "co-ordinating ministers" been appointed. Butler in particular had resented Churchill's appointment of a "Treasury Ministerial Advisory Committee," intended as a sort of collective "overlord." [15] Churchill's Cabinet colleagues did tend, however, to share his dissatisfaction with the policies and policy-making machinery inherited from Labour. Particularly troubling were the looming problems of rising expenditure and the unfavourable balance of payments. Their fears were much heightened by the representations of officials. On polling day, in fact, Treasury officials had met to discuss a package of emergency measures to be pressed on the new government. Robert Hall of the Economic Section wondered privately whether it would be possible "to bully our new masters as fast as this," but the effort went ahead. Immediately upon taking office Butler was presented at the Treasury with a gloomy prognosis of the country's economic future. As one official later admitted, the Conservatives were provided with "some horrifying accounts of the economic situation and subjected to a fierce pressure from officials to take unpleasant decisions." [16]

Butler took the cue and informed his colleagues that, "We are in a balance of payments crisis, worse than 1949, and in many ways worse even than 1947." [17] The surplus of £350 million of the previous year had been replaced by "an external deficit . . . of £700 million a year' for a net "deterioration of more than £1,000 million per annum." Losses were likely to continue through 1952, creating an "insupportable position" in which "we stand to lose virtually the whole of our remaining reserves." This alarmist diagnosis was followed by an utterly traditional response: "The only chance of restoring the position before irreparable harm is done is to restore confidence." The new Chancellor proceeded to call for cuts in imports, including raw materials and food supplies, for monetary flexibility so as "to remove the rigidity in short term interest rates," for substantial cuts in public expenditure, and for investment cuts, especially in the building programme. The entire package was premised on the notion that the economy was "overloaded" and that government's "first objective must be to limit the load on the economy."

The sense of crisis conveyed in Butler's memo soon infected the entire Cabinet, whose response was to attempt to pin the blame on Labour. In November officials were asked to produce a wide-ranging report on "The State of the Nation" in order to demonstrate that, as Thomas Padmore of the Treasury put it, "When they got there the cupboard was bare." In putting together the report, however, officials reviewed the work of the Labour governments of 1945–51 and found, as Cherwell was forced to concede, that "the story was one of achievement – a picture of substantial recovery from 1945–50, succeeded by a period of difficulty due mainly to circumstances beyond our control. This," he concluded, "is not quite the picture which Ministers expected to get." Predictably, the document was never published. Even a damningly effective indictment of Labour would not have solved the new government's economic problems, but it was not clear in 1951–2 what would. Lacking a plan of their own and unwilling to rely upon the techniques developed by Labour, the Conservatives reached out for an alternative. That alternative was the plan that came to be known as "Robot." "Robot" was presented to the Cabinet by the Governor of the Bank of England; it took its name from the two Treasury officials, Leslie Rowan and Otto Clarke, and the banker, Sir George Bolton, who were among its main advocates. As early as November, the Bank had begun to lobby officials for drastic action against inflation and the balance of payments problem. On 27 November, for example, the Governor had seen Bridges and told him "We were going bankrupt rapidly" and that it was necessary to cut expenditure, particularly on food subsidies, to restore confidence. What was most striking about the incident, at least to Robert Hall, was the willingness of the entire upper level of the Treasury to go along. As Hall recorded in his diary, all of the officials who heard Bridges' report of the conversation quickly agreed and "chimed in with . . . fiendish glee to say yes that was the only thing to do." Plans were in fact set afoot to cut food subsidies, but the continued deterioration in the balance of payments prompted the Bank, and its allies in the Treasury, to develop a still more radical approach that might offer a permanent solution. The "Robot" proposal, as described by Alec Cairncross, entailed:

> (i) a floating exchange rate for sterling; (ii) full convertibility into gold, dollars or other currencies on a free market in foreign exchange for . . . "overseas" or "external" sterling; (iii) compulsory funding of 80 per cent of the sterling balances held by members of the sterling area and the funding or blocking of nearly all balances held by non-members outside the dollar area.

The intention was to create an automatic mechanism along the lines of the prewar gold standard to regulate the balance of payments and, by implication, to control the domestic economy.[18]

Behind "Robot" was a distaste for the practice of detailed intervention in the economy which had been repeatedly undertaken by Labour and which might have been necessary once again to handle the balance of payments crisis, coupled with profound doubts about its efficacy. This distaste and these doubts prompted a search for a panacea that would allow the state to escape once and for all from the necessity of such close economic management. These features of the plan proved tempting, at least initially, to a large body of officials and ministers. The Treasury supported it strongly; Norman Brook was in favour;

and among key ministers the only firm opponent was Lord Cherwell. The plan was intensely debated in the latter half of February, 1952 and for a time it appeared "that there was little hope of stopping its introduction." Butler was the most important convert and he fought hard for a decision that could be announced along with the budget in early March. He came very near to winning assent at a meeting held on 22 February, but it was decided to ask Eden, who was in Lisbon meeting with NATO ministers, about the foreign policy implications. By chance, Edwin Plowden, the chief planner, was travelling with Eden and he was given a long letter from his ally at the Economic Section, Robert Hall, who criticized the plan. Eden was quickly convinced to join Cherwell and the two economic advisors in opposing the proposal, partly because of its likely effects on relations with the United States and the Commonwealth but also for fear of its domestic repercussions. The Foreign Secretary warned Churchill on 23 February of the "suffering, and I fear, unemployment that must result" from its implementation. He was especially worried over the "political consequences," which "may be of the gravest character, not only for our party but for our country." Butler conceded that the proposals might lead to unemployment, but persisted in his advocacy. Churchill was apparently more politically sensitive and by the end of February the Cabinet decided for the moment not to adopt such "extreme measures." Neither the Bank nor the Treasury gave up on the plan, which would continue to dominate policy-making for another year, but beginning in March the balance of payments began a long-term improvement which undercut their arguments and effectively foreclosed the option of following such a drastic course of action.[19]

"Robot" would remain, therefore, merely an example of what might have been. Its central aim, the convertibility of sterling, would not be attained for some time: partial convertibility was restored in 1955, full convertibility in 1958. But "Robot" was only incidentally about convertibility. More basically, it was a plan to back off from the commitments to full employment and economic management assumed after the war. The wide support it generated among bureaucrats and politicians suggests how superficial was the conversion of policy-makers to these rhetorical commitments. The position of the Treasury was particularly interesting. Treasury officials had mounted only recently a strong defence of the institutional arrangements for making economic policy, presumably because the existing structure was centred on the Treasury. But they clearly had little confidence in the effectiveness of the devices by which their policy aims were to be implemented, for at the first opportunity they were ready to abandon the tasks of economic management in favour of a more or less automatic set of regulators. Among officials the only consistent dissenters, and hence the only strong defenders of the state's expanded role in the economy, were the Keynesians in the Economic Section, which remained formally outside the Treasury but in practice was increasingly integrated into its deliberations, and on the Planning Staff (CEPS), which continued to wield considerable influence so long as it was headed by Edwin Plowden. Their opinions, however, seem even in 1951-2 to have carried surprisingly little weight with senior officials, like Brook, Bridges, Bernard Gilbert, Otto Clarke or Leslie Rowan, all of whom favoured "Robot". The decision not to press forward with "Robot" may well be counted as a rare instance in which "the massed powers of bureaucratic darkness" were "routed by small forces of economic light," but the decisive consideration was political not economic.[20] Plowden and Robert Hall influenced the outcome primarily by getting the ear of Eden, who was swayed not by economic argument but by the fear that "Robot" might lose votes. The consensus on full employment was in this sense held together by the narrow, if none the less strong, thread of electoral calculation and the fear of the power of the trade unions. Its institutional and theoretical underpinnings, by contrast, were much weaker.

The argument behind "Robot" was that the balance of payments problem was not temporary – a result of rearmament and its impact on the terms of trade – but rather a more fundamental reflection of the "overloaded" character of the economy. Had that been true or fully accepted, it would have made sense for Butler to have introduced as an alternative to "Robot" a severely disinflationary budget on 11 March. In fact, the budget was comparatively "mild." Allowances for income tax and sur-tax were increased, thereby exempting taxpayers from liabilities of £230 million; food subsidies were cut by £160 million; petrol duties were increased slightly; and a new excess profits tax was announced, though it was not to take effect for another year. Simultaneously, bank rate was raised from 2½ to 4 per cent. The economic effects were said to be roughly neutral, and overall it was considered a "standstill" budget. The reception of the budget was favourable at the time, and economists have subsequently judged it appropriate as well. Already in the first quarter of 1952, it is now recognized, the economy was entering a recession and a severe budget would have had further negative effects on demand and employment. The mix arrived at in March, 1952 was thus moderately well suited to the needs of the economy. Whether it was arrived at for the right reason, and whether it was shaped with such a clear understanding of the state of the economy, is rather more doubtful.[21]

In formulating the budget of 1952, the Economic Section was at least dimly aware that demand was slack in some sectors of the economy and that a degree of relaxation was in order. The specific measures introduced in March, however, owed more to the essentially political predispositions of ministers and other Treasury officials. The plan to reduce food subsidies, "Operation Diogenes" as it was known to the Budget Committee, fulfilled the long-standing Treasury objective of reducing public expenditure – an objective pursued without much concern for its effect on wages and hence on inflation. The Conservative ministers were, of course, happy to see taxes reduced. The decision to make use of variations in interest rates was also popular with Conservatives, bankers and Treasury officials; even among the Keynesians there was little support for maintaining interest rates at permanently low levels. The package put together in March, 1952 reflected, therefore, the key political inputs into the policy-making process as much as, and probably more than, the macro-economic analyses of the planners.[22]

The budget of 1952 established a pattern for budgetary policy that would be followed by Conservative governments throughout the 1950s. The Tories made use of the calculations of the planners, but detailed innovations were made with political calculations very much to the fore. The Conservatives had been returned to power in 1951 on votes purchased with the promise of lower taxation and the removal of controls. Once in power they were determined not to lose that support; hence, as a member of the Economic Section later explained, "not to increase the weight of taxation seems to have become almost an independent aim, so that net tax changes tend to be only downwards." [23] The Tories were not foolish enough to give away too much revenue too soon, but instead adopted a policy of gradual, carefully timed and targeted reductions. This they were able to do largely because Labour had so successfully resisted demands for lower taxes and had passed on a very high level of taxation, and also because Labour had already begun to extract from taxpayers the cost of rearmament. By scaling back defence spending to a more realistic level, moreover, Conservatives could avoid serious cuts in social spending while granting modest tax relief.

The political imperative to cut taxes would continue to dominate Conservative budgetary policy after 1952, even if it was not Butler's top priority, and would result in a "steady process of lightening the burden of taxation." The tax remissions of 1952 were followed by still more concessions in 1953. In that year, "taxation was reduced more substantially than in any post-war budget." Business had been arguing for lower taxes for years and their arguments found echoes among bankers, officials and Conservative politicians. In late 1952 the financial press took up the theme and, within the government, Peter Thorneycroft at the Board of Trade began to assert that the taxation of profits prevented investment. By early 1953 a member of the Economic Section complained that "Everyone is crying out for a reduction of the intolerable burden of business taxation," and went on to predict that the "political pressure to reduce taxes on companies will succeed." Within the Section there was considerable disagreement over the validity of the businessmen's case, but Hall came down in the end in favour of "a cautious policy of expansion and tax remission." [24] Shortly before budget day, the Governor of the Bank of England weighed in with his advice to Butler and Bridges: "As you know," he wrote, "I have felt for a long time that the present level of taxation is intolerable in peace-time conditions and is doing great damage to our economy." He would not advocate anything that might unbalance the budget or endanger confidence, but looked favourably upon modest tax cuts.[25] In the budget that emerged "initial" allowances for business investment, discontinued in 1951, were restored; the standard rate of income tax was cut by sixpence; puchase tax was lowered by about 15 per cent; and the excess profits levy wound up.[26] The budget was obviously expansionary, but even clearer was its political intent. Business in particular and the middle classes in general were given substantial relief, while food subsidies were further cut.

The main obstacle to tax reductions throughout the 1950s was, of course, the level of public expenditure made necessary by the commitments taken on during 1945–51. The Conservatives did not risk an outright break with those commitments and instead sought ways to limit spending while maintaining them. The difficulties involved caused Butler and his officials to hesitate before acquiescing to specific reductions in tax, but in the end the pressure was irresistible.[27] Bridges told Butler in October, 1952, for example, that there was "absolutely no room to manoeuvre" within the budget and that expenditure had to be brought down. Butler was convinced and passed along the warning to Churchill, calling for "a determined onslaught on public expenditure." The Prime Minister in turn decided there should be "no increase in civil expenditure" in the coming year. Butler continued to fret, telling Bridges in November that "I get really anxious at times about expenditure." While recognizing that expenditure cuts were the first step towards tax cuts and thus "fundamental to our policy as a party," he felt that in view of the tightness of the budget "we can only look to reductions in taxation *pari passu* with reductions in expenditure." Others, like Thorneycroft, agreed that without more substantial economies "there was little prospect of any reduction in the burden of taxation on industry" and thus continued to press hard on both fronts. In practice, of course, taxes came down rather more steadily than expenditure.[28]

The political pressure to reduce taxes persisted even after the concessions of 1953, though orthodox opinion in the Treasury and in the City acted as something of a brake upon Conservative hopes for lower taxes. Butler was himself very susceptible to traditional arguments about budget deficits and intuitively agreed with those who felt the economy was "overloaded" and that government was attempting too much. In July, 1953 he informed the Cabinet that "The Budget prospects for next year are menacing." If reductions in expenditure could not be found, "it may prove impossible for me to maintain the move which I made in this year's Budget towards reducing the burden of taxation." Butler's concerns found support almost immediately in the press, where articles quickly appeared deploring the "Burden of Public Spending." The budget of 1954 was in fact formulated in an atmosphere of fiscal worry and macro-economic confusion, with Robert Hall and the Economic Section disturbed over the apparent weakness in demand but with others on the Budget Committee fearful that "'the psychological effect of any departure from the policy of a balanced Budget might well be disastrous." The result was a "carry on" Budget that did little more than to replace "initial allowances" with "investment allowances" serving much the same purpose.[29]

Fiscal and administrative caution had thus held back the process of lowering taxes in 1954, but by 1955 renewed pressure within the Cabinet combined with the prospect of a general election to sweep away doubts. The main ministerial proponent of lower taxes was Lord Woolton, who waged a sustained campaign against Butler's instinctive fiscal conservatism. Woolton had argued during the preparation of the budget of 1954 that "it should be a main object of Government policy to reduce the current level of taxation." The present high level, he maintained, was "curbing . . . initiative and . . . [the] willingness to take risks," and "denying industry the opportunity to accumulate reserves for new ventures." Woolton refused to be put off with vague declarations of intent or vapid incantations about the need for expenditure cuts. Instead, he proposed that the government set for itself the specific goal of getting the very highest rate down to 15s in the pound and went so far as to argue that if necessary the government should be willing to borrow to pay for defence stockpiling and for road building. Woolton's plan was attractive to many in the Cabinet, and Churchill himself had long been interested in borrowing to pay for rearmament. But borrowing was still very controversial, especially with the City and the Treasury. Cutting taxes only for the rich would also be politically difficult, as Lord Cherwell pointed out, and could only be done if taxes falling on the middle and lower classes were simultaneously reduced. Despite these practical and political difficulties surrounding Woolton's scheme, its attractiveness placed Butler very much on the defensive in Cabinet. He responded with his customary claim that "this country is, and has for many past years been, carrying too heavy a load of Government expenditure" and that the only solution was economy. Backed up by his officials, the Chancellor had prevailed in the short run, but he was pressed hard to find economies to allow a reduction of taxation in 1955.[30]

The search for expenditure cuts led to the appointment in the spring of 1954 of a committee charged with identifying economies totalling £100 million. It proved difficult to find non-essential items adding up to that figure, but fortunately the revenue projections for 1954 had been unduly pessimistic and the government was able to make some tax concessions in 1955 anyway. The size and shape of the concessions were largely determined by political calculations. The Economic Section estimated that minor concessions were possible, but they were worried that employment was very full and demand likely to remain high through 1955–6. Major reductions might threaten inflation, a rise in imports and a balance of payments crisis. As late as 5 April 1955, just two weeks before the budget, Robert Hall was still arguing that "a cautious policy would be to leave the general level of taxation unchanged." Butler shared these concerns and was reluctant to agree to large-scale reductions, but he was pushed towards more substantial cuts by Churchill, Macmillan and Eden, who took up the position long argued in Cabinet by Woolton and by Thorneycroft. They were supported, interestingly, by normally cautious Treasury officials like Bridges and Gilbert. Bridges, in fact, had argued at an early stage in the budget discussions that the coming fiscal year presented "a rare opportunity to reduce the standard rate of tax by sixpence" and declared, in the face of obvious disagreement from the economists, that there was "general agreement" to move in that direction.[31]

A powerful collection of interests therefore coalesced around the proposal for tax cuts in 1955. Conservatives had an obvious electoral interest in lower taxes; officials like Bridges and Gilbert appear to have sympathized and were more than willing to go along. The Keynesians in the Economic Section were resigned to an election budget and took comfort in the general health of the economy. The Bank of England, ordinarily keen to pile up surpluses, was also surprisingly supportive of tax cuts. Presumably, the bankers shared with high officials a desire to keep Labour out, and were also eager to encourage the government in its increased reliance on monetary policy and its move towards greater convertibility. Indeed, even in the spring it had been understood that the expansionary effects of the tax concessions were to be offset in part by higher interest rates, the reimposition of hire purchase restrictions and tighter credit.

It was thus virtually inevitable that the main feature of the budget of April, 1955 would be a reduction in the standard rate of income tax to 8s 6d. The immediate economic effect was to remit roughly £155 million in tax and to spur domestic demand; the political effects are more difficult to judge, but the Conservatives did win an increased majority in the election of May, 1955.[32] The Conservatives" political gains, whatever their origin, would persist through the decade. The economic consequences would turn quickly adverse, however. By the summer of 1955 the consumption boom had been translated into an increase in imports and a worsening of the balance of payments. It was obvious, moreover, that the effort to restrain the economy through a more restrictive monetary policy had not worked. Advances by banks had continued to grow, and the Bank of England refused to curtail loans to the private sector until public expenditure, specifically the investment plans of the nationalized industries, was cut back as well. Butler returned to office angry at the bankers but nevertheless unwilling to abandon the reliance on monetary measures. He was confirmed by recent events in his earlier faith in caution and restraint. It was essential, he told the Economic Policy Committee of the Cabinet, to "correct our present tendency to live beyond our means." The government were forced in response to impose "quantitative" controls on money and credit, to restrict hire purchase still further and to "prune" investment. When these measures failed to ease the payments crisis or reassure the financial markets, it was decided reluctantly to introduce an autumn budget. With the election over and the Conservatives securely back in power, a deflationary consensus rapidly emerged. Butler's position led logically to a policy of restraint and he was joined in his assessment by his various officials: the Economic Section came out for "a decisive measure of deflation;" and officials like Bridges reverted to their traditional stance and began to advocate stern measures to reduce inflation and restore foreign confidence. The October budget took back in tax almost as much as had been given away in April: £75 million by means of a 20 per cent increase in purchase tax and nearly £40 million through more rigorous taxation of profits. Between April and October, of course, the burden of taxation had been shifted from middle-class taxpayers to consumers, quite straightforwardly in the form of purchase tax and indirectly through taxes on business profits.[33]

The budgetary decisions of 1955 have often been viewed as aberrant, a set of lapses by Butler due largely to his personal problems and, on the part of the government more generally, to their understandable desire to be re-elected. But the pressure to reduce taxes, particularly on the middle classes whose votes the Conservatives held so dear, had been consistent throughout the history of the Conservative government and had been acted on before. Indeed, the record of budgetary policy from 1951 through 1955 suggests that two considerations, each identified with particular policy actors, were primary from beginning to end. The Conservatives as a party were keen to reduce the burden on the taxpayer and, to only a slightly lesser extent, on business. The most vocal proponents of this strategy were appropriately those, like Woolton, most sensitive to party political concerns. Officials – such as Bridges, Gilbert, Rowan and Brook – tended to be more worried over the level of expenditure and concerned to ensure budgetary balance. It was they who had engineered the panic over the balance of payments and expenditure when the new government took office and they who, despite their sympathy with the taxpayer, more than once put a brake on ministers" desire to lower taxes. Only in 1954–5, when the alternative was a severe budget and a possible Labour victory, did officials come out strongly for tax reductions.

The Chancellor himself does not appear to have bought into the supposed "Butskellite" consensus of the period. Instead, he leaned towards the position of the permanent officials in the Treasury. While he was willing to make use of data and policy recommendations presented to him by the more Keynesian officials on the Planning Staff or in the Economic Section, his instincts were more cautious and he regularly opted for the more restrictive policies advocated by the "mandarins." That left the Keynesians in an awkward position. The overriding importance attached to tax-cutting by Conservative ministers meant that, in an economic climate marked by the steady pressure of demand, the Keynesians had few supporters outside the Treasury. Plowden and Hall had helped to block "Robot" by teaming up with Cherwell and Eden, an unusual practice for officials and one not likely to recur very often. Within the Treasury itself, the advocates of the new approach to demand management were in a distinct minority and their status therefore steadily declined under the Conservatives.

The declining fortunes of the committed Keynesians were registered institutionally in the linked fates of the Central Economic Planning Staff and of the Economic Section. So long as Edwin Plowden remained as head of CEPS, the Planning Staff enjoyed considerable authority within the Treasury. Butler was personally fond of Plowden and found his advice clearer and more practical than that offered by the more academic Keynesians like Hall. Plowden's opposition to "Robot," however, and his willingness to go around Butler to enlist Eden on his side, put a chill on the relationship that would persist until Plowden went off to make bombs. When Plowden left in 1953 he was not replaced, the position of Chief Planner allowed to lapse. The Planning Staff was taken over by perhaps the least "Keynesian" of the permanent officials, Sir Bernard Gilbert, who was not only sceptical of Keynesian policies but also had led the resistance to the adoption of more "Keynesian" techniques in the presentation of the budget. The message was clear: as *The Times* noted on 30 June 1953, "After these changes the Treasury will be able to feel that economic planning has been well and truly absorbed." Inevitably, the Planning Staff quickly began "to lose faith in its role," and it was increasingly ignored. What was left of CEPS was soon folded into the Treasury's "National Resources Group" under Otto Clarke, one of the authors of the "Robot" plan and no partisan of Keynesian policies – and with whom Robert Hall was "not on speaking terms." [34]

From 1953, therefore, the advocacy of Keynesian techniques and policies fell to the Economic Section under Hall's direction. The Section had remained formally outside the Treasury until 1953, but co-operated closely with the Planning Staff and other officials. Hall himself was a regular member of the official Budget Committee and hence participated in the most important policy-making body outside the Cabinet. His input was seldom decisive, however, and with Plowden's departure in 1953 the section's voice lost an important echo. In that year, moreover, it was decided that the section should be moved permanently into the Treasury. With Plowden leaving, it became necessary to restructure once again the machinery for economic co-ordination. Hall was himself dissatisfied and at odds with key Treasury officials. He threatened to quit along with Plowden, but the promise of a substantial rise, the new title of "Economic Advisor" to the government and a knighthood persuaded him to stay on. The Economic Section, however, would have to be integrated into the Treasury and placed under Gilbert. The move clearly threatened the Section's autonomy, but most of the staff seemed to feel that it was "worth sacrificing a good deal of this to keep in touch" with those at the centre of policy-making. Independence was useful, Christopher Dow explained, but it was "No good being free to speak if no-one [is] there to listen." Hall confessed to having "considered the whole thing with anxiety," and wrote directly to his predecessors – Lionel Robbins and James Meade – to explain his acquiescence. He claimed that, since no minister other than the Chancellor ever consulted him, it was to the Chancellor that he should report. The argument was not especially convincing to either Robbins or Meade but, like Hall, they could not envision a realistic alternative. The Treasury had already, by 1953, "much more than regained [its] pre-war eminence," and it made little sense to resist. [35]

The move to the Treasury would mean that the commitment of the

Economic Section to planning would be further weakened, but as Dow conceded in 1954, "no-one . . . quite knows what planning is nowadays." [36] Planning was indeed seriously downplayed under the Conservatives, not simply because of the declining institutional status of the erstwhile planners, but also because there was no agreement on the policy devices through which planning would be implemented. The goal to which planning would be directed was broadly accepted to be full employment, but there was little sense of how that could be brought about by government. The commitment to full employment was highlighted by the debate over "Robot", which ultimately turned on the plan's potential impact on employment. That argument had reminded Conservatives of the danger of unemployment and the precarious-ness of their political position. As a result the government appointed a Cabinet committee under Lord Swinton to survey the effect of recent policy changes on employment and "formulate plans for checking any tendency towards wide-spread unemployment." [37] The committee found unemployment low overall and confined to certain specific localities, but recommended that officials continue to watch closely for any signs of serious unemployment. It was decided to set up a standing committee of officials to monitor the employment situation and to develop policy.

That committee, chaired by Plowden, rehearsed the debates of the late 1940s on the various means of meeting a drop in demand, and with depressingly similar and frustratingly inconclusive results. It was assumed once again that the most likely cause of unemployment would be a falling off of demand outside the United Kingdom, probably in the United States, and that the government would have to respond with policies to shore up both external and internal demand. Policy-makers could not agree on what to do in either arena, however. They split, for example, on whether to meet the international problem through devaluation or, as the Treasury insisted, by convertibility and a floating exchange rate along the lines of "Robot." Consensus was equally elusive on internal measures. "[L]ittle should be expected of monetary policy by itself," the planners argued, so it was necessary to look to other policy devices. Among these other options were the various proposals made in 1944 – for using variations in national insurance contributions, for repayment of tax credits accumulated during wartime, for "accelerated government purchases," and for preparing in advance lists of public works projects that could be put into operation in response to the onset of a slump – all of which were brought forward yet again. But, as in the late 1940s, none were found to be particularly feasible or likely to produce the desired results. Officials raised yet again their long-standing objections to compiling a "reserve of works," and even the Economic Section conceded that little could be done to influence investment, the main problem that any serious policy would have to address. What was left at the end of the discussion were two mechanisms by which to control the level of demand: the budget and hire purchase regulations. Of these the budget was much the most important, of course, and it was to the budget that the planners turned as the most effective means of controlling the economy.[38]

Ironically, though, the determination of the Keynesians within the government to rely on budgetary policy to prevent widespread unemployment did not ensure that Keynesian considerations would predominate in the actual framing of the budget. The likely effect of the budget on demand was by no means ignored in the making of fiscal policy, but it was of consistently less importance to ministers than the desire to cut taxes and it was a less urgent concern for Treasury officials than was the need to maintain a balanced budget. The practice of budgetary policy was therefore dominated by politics or, to put the matter more analytically, by two powerful political logics. The logic of tax-cutting, which derived from the Conservatives" relationship to their middle-class constituents and to business and from their ideological orientation, vied with the logic of fiscal responsibility, which appealed especially to officials and to the City and which gave priority to expenditure cuts over lower taxes. Those two logics produced a series of budgets granting steady, if minor, tax relief while restraining government spending. It was a pattern that bore a strong resemblance to the budgetary history of the interwar years. What differed were three critical factors: the rhetoric surrounding policy-making, within which full employment continued to occupy a prominent place; the levels of taxation and public spending inherited by the Tories, which were high enough to allow tax reductions without forcing the abandonment of the social programmes implemented by Labour; and "the 'friendliness' of external circumstance," specifically the rise in world trade, which helped to sustain economic growth whatever the policies adopted by the British government.[39]

By the mid-1950s, therefore, there had been re-created a politics of taxation reminiscent of the interwar pattern and geared to producing regular tax reductions, largely for the middle classes. The new politics of taxation was basically ratified by the reports of the Royal Commission on Taxation, which appeared between 1953 and 1955. The final report, in particular, contained a sophisticated discussion on the definition of income and a thoughtful consideration of proposals for the taxation of capital gains. Appended to the report was an even more interesting dissent crafted by Nicholas Kaldor and arguing for shifting the basis of taxation from income to expenditure. In the end, however, the Royal Commission rejected the arguments for capital gains and for an expenditure tax, opting instead for minor adjustments in the system. It was an outcome that broadly endorsed the existing structure of taxation and, in effect, reinforced the pattern of tax politics then being followed by the Conservatives.[40]

"ECONOMY," DEFENCE AND THE WELFARE STATE

The differing emphases given by Conservative ministers and officials to tax cuts versus expenditure cuts did not typically put them at odds during 1951–5. Conservatives, in fact, agreed wholeheartedly that spending should be controlled and, in any event, cutting expenditure was the surest route to tax reductions; conversely, officials like Brook, Bridges and the even more orthodox men of the Treasury – Gilbert, Clarke, Rowan, Eady, and the like – were fundamentally sympathetic to the plight of the taxpayer and saw their own efforts to trim expenditure as in the latter's interest. In practice, therefore, the differences between Conservatives and officials were overcome and, in fact, effectively combined into a fairly coherent and sustained pressure to reduce taxation and expenditure.[41] The two emphases were basically compatible, and it was undoubtedly this convergence of opinion behind the effort to lower both taxes and spending that lay behind the growing *rapprochement* between the Conservative government and the civil service. The Conservatives had returned to office in 1951 profoundly suspicious of the men running the state machine, Churchill for one complaining that his personal staff were all "drenched with socialism." These suspicions dissipated very quickly, however, as Conservatives discovered that the permanent officials largely shared their antipathy to high taxes, the growth of public expenditure and the maintenance of economic controls. By 1955, officials were happy to collaborate with the Tories in putting together a budget aimed at winning the next election, and the government elected in 1955 was willing to accept the rather uninspired and uncritical *Report* of the Royal Commission on the Civil Service, chaired by Sir Raymond Priestley.[42]

The increasing compatibility between the views of officials and those of their Conservative masters was evident in the zealous quest for economies in the social services and even in defence. On defence, for example, a consensus quickly emerged that the rearmament programme undertaken by Labour was much too grand. Early in November, 1951 officials reported that the production targets in the rearmament plan could not be met due to shortages of labour and raw materials; by December, Churchill was convinced of the need for drastic reductions. The service chiefs objected, but not at first in very strenuous terms. They agreed to participate in a review of "Defence Policy and Global Strategy" which concluded that Labour's build-up was excessive. Even more significant than the recognition of the material constraints on rearmament was the acceptance by the Ministry of Defence and the services that nuclear weapons had fundamentally transformed strategy. The review called for a strategy of deterrence based upon atomic bombs and conceded that Britain might have to decrease its overseas commitments and conventional forces.[43]

With its tilt towards nuclear rather than conventional forces and strategy and its frank recognition of the material constraints within which policy must necessarily operate, the discussion clearly adumbrated the subsequent evolution of defence policy. Within the government, however, there was considerable contention over the limits that would actually be placed on military spending. The resistance by the services to proposed cuts began to stiffen in the latter part of 1952 and the chiefs fought hard against reductions, claiming ominously that "such a complete departure . . . cannot be accepted without a marked change in . . . policy," and insisting that "the fighting power of the Services could not be maintained at this level" of funding. But ministers and officials were in agreement that defence spending had to be cut and refused to relent. "Defence," argued one Treasury official, "is absorbing the best part of half the national revenue; and that with taxation at a penal level for 'peace-time'." Getting military spending down was understood to be essential to the objective, shared by Conservatives and their bureaucratic advisors alike, of lowering taxes. Ministers thus strongly backed up the efforts of officials to impose more rigorous control by the Treasury on the defence departments. The services complained bitterly, but were met with unaccustomed firmness and a certain amount of disdain. Humphreys-Davies of the Treasury, for example, responded forcefully to complaints from the War Office: "I, for one, am not going to pledge the Treasury to abandon their criticism of, for instance, the scale of ordering for the new jeep which (at about five times the normal cost of a light load carrier) will go as fast backwards as forwards, can be driven indefinitely under water and can simultaneously withstand arctic cold and equatorial heat." The War Secretary took his complaint to a still higher level, apparently hoping for sympathy from Butler or at least from Bridges, but none was forthcoming. Bridges instead defended the stance of the Treasury and wrote to Humphreys-Davies with the reassuring message that, "Your minute has been much praised." [44]

The pressure of officials and Conservative politicians succeeded in holding down, even reducing slightly, military spending. Expenditure on defence fell marginally in cash terms from 1952 to 1955 and, as a share of the national income and of total expenditure, dropped rather more significantly. In real terms defence spending per head was nearly 10 per cent less in 1955 than in 1952. This achievement was only possible because of the enormous spending increases set in motion by Labour, and, by international standards, military spending in Britain remained at a high level. Close to 10 per cent of GNP went to the military in 1955, and it would continue at approximately that level throughout the decade.[45] Still, it did not go higher; and the modest savings made by the Conservatives were available for tax reductions or, to a lesser extent, for spending on social services, from the mid-1950s onwards.

The stabilization of defence expenditure was intimately connected to the government's resolution to rely largely upon atomic bombs for its security. The decision was not lightly taken. Labour had proceeded steadily, and without American help, with the development of Britain's nuclear capability and the first bomb "with a Union Jack on it" – to use Bevin's famous phrase – was exploded in October, 1952. Upon coming to office Churchill had thought that he could re-establish co-operation in nuclear weapons research and production with the United States and that he could arrange for Britain "to be allocated a reasonable share of what they have made so largely on our initiative and substantial scientific contribution." That proved impossible, and the government undertook to manufacture its own bombs and to continue research on the development of the hydrogen bomb. The Tories thus edged a step closer to committing the country to a military strategy based primarily on nuclear weapons.[46]

Several further steps were taken in 1954–5. In 1954 NATO, and through NATO Britain, began receiving tactical nuclear weapons from the Americans to compensate for the alleged gap between the conventional forces of the east and the west. Work continued on the hydrogen bomb, whose progress was entrusted to the new Atomic Energy Authority headed by Edwin Plowden. Between April and July, 1954 the Cabinet conducted a lengthy debate over whether to proceed with the production of hydrogen bombs and over the role of nuclear weapons in defence strategy. There was little hesitation among ministers, who decided "that in order to preserve our position as a leading military power and to maintain our influence in world affairs it was necessary that we should possess a stock of the most up-to-date thermo-nuclear weapons." Britain would not explode a hydrogen bomb until 1957, but its intention to do so was registered in the White Paper on Defence of February, 1955, which signalled the government's thorough-going commitment to a strategy of nuclear deterrence and, in practical terms, to building up the weapons and air power with which to make that strategy credible. It was a decision fraught with long-term consequences both military and political; in the short run, however, it was a choice from which few dissented. Attlee, deeply implicated in the original decision to build a British bomb, endorsed the White Paper; and only a minority within the Labour party were opposed. To Conservatives the issue was scarely worth debating, for it was assumed that Britain would do what was necessary to remain a great power. In those days before Suez, such illusions were extremely widespread. The choice to go nuclear had one further consequence to recommend it: it appeared cheaper and easier in the short run to build nuclear bombs than to maintain and arm conventional forces. That view might well prove inaccurate in the long run, but in 1954–5 it served to reconcile Conservatives and officials to the decision to produce nuclear weapons and, to some small extent, aided their efforts to economize on defence expenditure.[47]

The Churchill government were just as eager to pursue economies in spending on the social services, and they enjoyed the backing of officials on this issue as well. Even before Labour had left office, Norman Brook had complained that there was no mechanism in place to review and control social expenditure. Brook found it "remarkable that the present Government have never reflected upon the great increase in public expenditure . . . which has come about during the past five years," and proposed as a remedy that twice a year Cabinet should be presented with "'forecasts of the trend of future expenditure." Presumably, such forecasts would produce alarm and prompt efforts to trim expenditure. The Labour government, though scarcely profligate, was unwilling to give such priority to reducing expenditure. The return of the Conservatives to office provided an opportunity to do so, and officials were eager to utilize the occasion of a change of government to attempt to bring expenditure, especially on the social services, under control.[48]

In practice, it would turn out to be very difficult to effect genuine reductions. Part of the problem lay in the inconsistency of ministers. While in opposition the Conservatives had contented themselves with vague denunciations of waste and extravagance. This view no doubt comforted the party's supporters, but it allowed its leaders to avoid the much harder job of developing a social policy distinctly their own. On the contrary, Churchill routinely claimed credit for having initiated the policies subsequently implemented by the Attlee government. After he was returned to office in 1951, Churchill was not eager to be seen trying to dismantle the welfare state. Still, his victory was based to a considerable extent on middle-class anger over taxes, controls and spending. Indeed, as Richard Titmuss pointed out in 1955, there had been after 1948 a significant shift of opinion away from support for the welfare state and towards the view that " 'The Welfare State' was 'established' too quickly and on too broad a scale." Given the election results of 1950–1, that shift presumably did not much affect the working class, who rallied strongly behind the record of the Labour governments. But the climate of resentment at the welfare state did have an impact on the middle and upper classes: it was obviously what lay behind the claim of the *Sunday Times* in early 1952 that "the Welfare State, thanks to the mismanagement of our finances and the lack of clear thought among its Socialist exponents, has got into a muddle;" it encouraged the doctors to persist in their criticisms of the Health Service, allowing the *British Medical Journal* to assert in 1950 that "The National Health Service is heading for the bankruptcy court . . . and we are facing bankruptcy because of the Utopian finances of the Welfare State;" and it was a view widely shared by the Conservative rank-and-file.[49]

What prevented the translation of these anti-welfare beliefs into a policy of wholesale expenditure cuts was a set of rather awkward and indisputable facts. Primary among these was the precarious political balance of 1951, which made the Conservatives wary of anything other than an indirect assault on social programmes. Of no doubt equal importance in forestalling any reduction in expenditure was the expansion of the demand for social services. Just to meet the welfare commitments made by Labour required increasing levels of expenditure. The pent-up demand for health care was much greater than previously imagined, and years of comparative neglect made care hard to deliver without substantial expenditure. Tories deluded themselves into thinking that substantial savings could be had from more efficient manage-ment of existing resources, but even its own committee of inquiry was led to conclude that the National Health Service was well run and highly effective. The Guillebaud Report found, in fact, that "The rising cost of the Service in real terms during the years 1948–54 was kept within narrow bounds . . . Any charge that there has been widespread extravagance in the Service, whether in respect of the spending of money or the use of manpower, is not borne out by our evidence." If anything, it was found that too little had been spent on the nation's health, especially on hospitals, and it would prove impossible for the Tories significantly to reduce expenditure on health care.[50]

Nor were economies to be found in education, for a rising population of school-age children caused spending on schools to increase considerably. Total expenditure on education grew by nearly one-half from 1950 to 1955, a rate well ahead of inflation. Much of that went to pay the salaries of the 25,000 extra teachers needed in classrooms or to build new schools or remodel older buildings for use as schools. But the effort was quite inadequate and better than half of all classes remained overcrowded in 1955. The major problem was financial. The Minister of Education, Florence Horsbrugh, was forced to cut 5 per cent from the education budget immediately upon taking office and was unable subsequently to make headway against the Treasury's steadfast resistance to higher expenditure on education.[51] Equally crippling were the financial difficulties of local government. A substantial share of education expenditure was undertaken by local authorities, and nearly half of that had to be raised from rates. There was near universal agreement among policy-makers that the structure of local government needed to be reformed and its financial basis strengthened, and any serious effort to upgrade educational provision would have required such an improvement in local fiscal and administrative infrastructure for its success. But the Conservatives were unwilling to undertake the task for fear of disturbing ratepayers. The party continued after the war to derive consistent backing from organizations of ratepayers and to profit from middle- and lower-middle-class opposition to the efforts of Labour-controlled local authorities to increase spending on social services, and they were unwilling to jeopardize that support.

In theory, the reform of local finance could have taken several forms – an increase in domestic rates achieved either through higher poundage or more up-to-date assessments; the "re-rating" of commercial or industrial property, which had benefitted from "de-rating" in 1929; or the imposition of local sales or income taxes. The Treasury were strongly against giving local authorities any new taxing powers, and Conservatives were fearful of antagonizing industry or shopkeepers by eliminating their exemptions. That left policy-makers with one real option, which was to revalue real property and to raise rates accordingly. Updating and rationalizing property valuations, and impos-ing somewhat higher rates, had much to commend it as policy. Rates had not been raised in step with other taxes during the 1940s and hence constituted a relatively lighter burden in the early 1950s than they had before the war. Even before the war, rates had been a distinctly regressive imposition and they had become still more unfair due to the lack of a general revaluation of property. The reassessment scheduled for 1933 had been dropped for reasons of cost, that planned for 1938 remained incomplete due to the coming of war. New valuations were supposed to have been done in 1953, but the Conservatives put off the process to 1956 and thus postponed even further the reform of local government finance. The proximate effect was to leave local authorities saddled with the responsibility for education and, to a considerable extent, for housing as well, but to deny them access to the money with which to do the job. The indirect effect was to force an increasing share of the burden of education expenditure to be provided by the Exchequer; and that left its overall level subject to the constant downward pressure of Treasury officials. The result was a system unable to respond to the growing demand for education but equally unable to offer up the sort of savings desired by Conservatives.[52]

Reductions in social service expenditure were further ruled out by the election promises made by the Tories in 1950–1. These were not excessive, but had to be redeemed in some fashion. The Conservatives had pledged to build 300,000 houses a year, to meet "crying needs" in education and health and to aid pensioners hurt by inflation. They might hope to do all this on the cheap, but it was not possible. The combination of political constraints and a growing demand for social services thus precluded any overall reduction in the amounts spent by government on the social services. The most that could be achieved was to hold spending on social services more or less constant. Between 1952 and 1955 expenditure on social services increased by only about 15 per cent, roughly the same as the rate of inflation; and actually declined as a share of national income. What that meant in practical terms was that many of the "crying needs" noted earlier by Conservatives and repeatedly by Labour, simply were not met. Specific promises were kept, however. By the end of 1953, Macmillan as Minister of Housing and Local Government had put in place a programme that produced 300,000 houses per year. Earlier on, in 1952, the Conservatives had found £60 million with which to raise family allowances, retirement pensions, unemployment and sickness benefits. Pensions were raised again in 1954, though not without a row over who would pay for them. The rates at which national assistance was paid were also increased modestly in 1952 and 1954. Modesty was, in fact, the main characteristic of all these increments, for they did little more than keep up with the increase in the cost of living. The only funds allocated to the social services that could be labelled generous were those devoted to doctors. The government agreed in 1952 to raise the pay of doctors by £40 million over four years.[53]

Aside from these specific, and rather limited, increases the pressure to keep spending down was sustained and successful. Any desires individual Cabinet members may have harboured for increasing expenditure on particular needs were overriden by a collective resolve to reduce taxes. It was this pressure to lower taxes, made more insistent by the knowledge that a general election was not far off, that had led the Cabinet in the spring of 1954 to appoint a Committee on Civil Expenditure designed to ensure economies that could be translated quickly into tax concessions. Genuine economies were hard to find, but the exercise had helped to prepare the way for the tax concessions of 1955, which were to prove so important in the Conservatives" subsequent election victory.[54] In sum, the Conservatives largely acquiesced in the maintenance of the social programmes put in place during the late 1940s, but spent hardly a shilling more than was required by the exigencies of politics and the growing demand for services.

INDUSTRY AND LABOUR

The same contradictory pressures and impulses affected Conservative policy towards industry and labour. Ideologically and rhetorically, the Conservatives were committed to the free market, and while in opposition they had attacked nationalization and detailed controls vociferously and also pledged to defend consumers. In office, it was possible to move steadily away from controls, to halt the progress of nationalization and, more gradually, to privatize sections of the nationalized industries. Defending the consumer turned out to be more difficult, for it conflicted with the Conservatives" political dependence upon support from the business community, which was not much interested in unrestricted competition.

Conservative policy towards the unions was even more ambivalent. The Tories had been forced during the war to recognize that the unions constituted a *de facto* estate of the realm and to deal with them accordingly. The unions" postwar strength precluded any abandonment of that approach and guaranteed that the sort of "corporatist" consultation that had grown up during the 1940s would be maintained. The power of the unions to disrupt the delicately balanced economy also ensured that the Conservatives would not revert to their interwar stance on industrial relations. Churchill in particular was eager to shed the anti-labour image he had acquired during the General Strike of 1926, and it was this desire that lay behind his advice to Walter Monckton, Minister of Labour. As Monckton recalled, "Winston's riding orders to me were that the Labour Party had foretold industrial troubles if the Conservatives were elected, and he looked to me to do my best to preserve industrial peace." [55] These rather tactical considerations conflicted, however, with the Conservatives" more basic beliefs about the economy and the role unions ought to play in it. Most Conservatives believed that the unions were too strong, and that their new-found clout was bad for the economy. As they saw it, the most serious economic problems confronting Britain were inflation and the weakness of exports and they held the unions responsible for both. Indeed, their focus on the distorted market for labour as the source of the nation's difficulties probably prevented the Conservatives from pursuing other mechanisms for controlling inflation and increasing productivity. The result was a policy that could, with considerable overstatement, be labelled as "industrial appeasement," but that was carried out within a framework of increasing hostility to the claims and pretensions of the unions. It was an approach that could not work and that could not last.

What could work and last beyond its initial application was the Conservatives" broad-based effort to remove controls from the economy. The balance of payments crisis provoked by rearmament had forced the government to continue controls for a couple of years, but by 1953-4 it was possible to dismantle most of them. Between February, 1953 and July, 1954, the rationing of sweets, eggs, sugar, margarine, butter, cheese, and meat and bacon was ended. Import restrictions were also eased considerably: government purchases, which amounted to nearly 40 per cent of imports in 1951, were reduced to a mere 6 per cent in 1955; private traders were allowed to import an increasing range of foodstuffs and raw materials, largely from the dollar area; raw materials allocations were also more or less eliminated by 1954; and European imports were liberalized to such an extent that 85 per cent came in without restriction by the end of 1955. Building licensing was also removed during 1954-5 and the government's power to determine the location of new construction was likewise exercised more liberally.[56] Two other levers over the direction and amount of investment – the "production authority" system and the Capital Issues Committee – were also largely abandoned. The relationships between ministries and the industries with which they dealt became less *dirigiste* and more corporatist. On this issue the government adopted the viewpoint of the business community, as articulated most clearly by the Federation of British Industries, which urged that "production departments and the Production Authority system should be downgraded but not abolished, so as to allow industries to resume self-government, free from dependence on the state, without losing the advantages of access to advice and protection from the state." [57] The Capital Issues Committee, though it continued to supervise new issues, was similarly allowed to relax its stance, and by 1955 only 4 per cent of applications for new issues were refused or modified.[58] Overall, the Conservatives managed to eliminate direct controls over most of the economy during their first term of office.

They succeeded as well in restricting the scope, and to some extent the effectiveness, of nationalization. The Conservatives had promised to return iron and steel and road haulage to private ownership and to make what remained of the public sector more competitive and efficient. The former was relatively easy to accomplish and, although some of the party's supporters wanted them to move even faster, the government succeeded in denationalizing both industries in 1953. It was rather more difficult to dispose of the assets held by these industries at prices acceptable to the government. The restoration of genuine competition also proved elusive, again particularly in iron and steel. Still, denationalization was carried through reasonably effectively. Restructuring the industries that remained in the hands of the state would prove much more difficult. Most Conservatives believed that the nationalized industries were characterized by " 'over-centralization', 'bureaucracy', 'waste' and 'general inefficiency'," and many academic commentators shared this negative image. In fact, productivity had increased substantially in the first years of nationalization and administrative staffs had remained modest.

Labour was indeed proud enough of the achievements of the nationalized industries to promise, in its 1953 programme, to extend public ownership beyond industries like coal, transport and "utilities" into more dynamic and profitable industries such as chemicals and engineering. The Conservative government, by contrast, were determined to find evidence of inefficiency and set in motion official inquiries to evaluate the performance of several of the nationalized industries. The results were inconsistent: the Ridley Committee reported on fuel and power in 1952 and largely endorsed the existing arrangements; the Fleck Report on the Coal Board, published in 1955, recommended greater centralization; while in 1956 the Herbert Committee on electricity came out for a move towards decentralization. Even without an inquiry, the government proceeded in 1953 to reorganize transport, coupling the privatization of road haulage with railway reorganization: the Railway Executive was abolished and the regions allowed more autonomy and greater flexibility in the setting of prices.[59]

The benefits of these restructuring efforts were not immediately apparent. While the industries and the government remained preoccupied with reorganization, little long-term planning of investment was undertaken. Indeed, while there was little agreement, inside or outside the government, over the relative merits of centralized versus decentralized control or over the extent to which ministers should get involved in the day-to-day management of the industries or over pricing policy, there was a definite consensus among ministers, civil servants and the business community over the need to limit public spending on the nationalized industries. For that reason investment in the public sector was regularly sacrificed to other objectives. The balance of payments difficulties of 1951–2 led to sharp cuts in plans for investment in the nationalized industries at a time when new technologies and enhanced capacity could have made a considerable difference. By 1954–5, the need for investment had become still more pressing and plans for substantial increases were put in place. The "Modernization Plan" for the railways, though cobbled together without proper study in 1955, nevertheless promised to reverse two decades of disinvestment with an infusion of £1,240 million; electricity and gas produced new development programmes in 1954; and there were plans for increased investment in nuclear power and in roads. The balance of payments crisis that developed after the election of 1955 forced the government once again to make substantial cuts in these programmes and only coal, whose investment plans were already underway, escaped the axe. The effect was a further delay in making the necessary investments and further demoralization among the industries' staffs and advocates. By 1955–6, therefore, much of the early promise displayed by the enlarged public sector had been dissipated. No wonder that the subsequent reports of the Select Committee on the Nationalized Industries, set up in 1955 and strengthened in 1956, would serve primarily to document failures, mistakes and missed opportunities.[60]

If Conservative plans to create a more efficient and competitive set of nationalized industries resulted in a muddle, their efforts to increase competition in private industry were no more successful. When they denationalized iron and steel, they left the industry under the direction of the Iron and Steel Board and did little to increase competition. The Conservative commitment to the market did not, moreover, result in strong action against monopolies. The government had inherited from Labour a Monopolies and Restrictive Practices Commission, operating under the Board of Trade, and they continued its functioning and even strengthened it administratively in 1953. But the Conservatives acquiesced to pressure from business that the commission proceed on a case-by-case basis, thus ensuring very slow progress and decisions that did not constitute precedents or result in general guidelines. Thorneycroft, as President of the Board of Trade, was ideologically predisposed towards free markets and competition, but he was frustrated by the position of the business community and turned his attention elsewhere. Ministers also chose to look the other way over resale price maintenance, which Labour had threatened to abolish but which persisted under the Tories.[61]

What did increasingly capture the attention of ministers and officials was the increase of wages. The actual course of wages after 1945 was relatively undramatic: money wages moved up slowly from 1946 through 1951, but rather more slowly than prices, leading to a very slight decline in real wages. With the rearmament boom of 1950–2, wholesale prices jumped by over 20 per cent and began to work their effects throughout the economy during the first years of Conservative rule. The Tories were unable to extract from the unions the level of restraint that Labour had elicited and so money wages were pushed up in response, increasing by over 20 per cent between 1951 and 1955. By 1955, real wages had finally begun to recover and had attained a level roughly 7 per cent above that of 1950–1.[62] The process was more alarming than the results revealed by the data, however, for both the Labour and Conservative governments had made the suppression of inflation a top priority. Indeed, they had developed a virtual fixation on inflation and its alleged origins in the pressure of wages and attributed most of Britain's problems – from the difficulty of expanding exports to the excessive demand for imports – to rising prices. Even before the Korean War boom and the acceleration of price increases, policy-makers had become preoccupied with inflation and wages and even Labour had felt compelled to adopt a quasi-voluntary incomes policy.

The Conservatives were even more worried over inflation than Labour had been and were encouraged in their fears by business and the City. Throughout the early 1950s, for example, representatives of the Bank of England kept warning officials and ministers about the dangers of inflation and of the need to control it. To them, the belief that the economy was overheated and that inflation was the main threat to its smooth functioning, had become an article of faith that could not be dented by the mere presentation of contrary facts. Thus, the Economic Section had argued in preparation of the 1953 budget that, according to the data available, the economy was in a mild slump and in need of some budget stimulus. The policy prescription – a tax cut for business in the form of investment allowances – was accepted, but the evidence and the reasoning rejected. Thus Robert Hall described the strange process by which the budget speech was written:

> E.B. [Edward Bridges] took the third draft of the Budget speech this afternoon. I have written a good deal of it and it is a relief to have got as far as this. The first draft is always repetitive and rather formless but all the subsequent ones are a great deal easier. I have now been told about four times by E.B. *not* to argue in documents for the public that the changes in employment and production are credible evidence of disinflation. I cannot get used to this especially as the Chancellor is so sensitive to the accusation of the Bank Chairmen that we are still in a state of inflation.[63]

Presumably, it was the very commitment of the bankers to a diagnosis of inflation that prevented Butler from voicing an opposite view.

Finding the proper techniques for controlling inflation was particularly difficult, for the Conservatives were resolute about abolishing the direct controls by which Labour had kept inflationary pressure in check. Nor were the Tories keen to get involved in the details of production and distribution. Increasingly, therefore, ministers and officials identified wages as both the source of inflation and the point at which it could best be stopped. At least there was a visible bargaining process between organized groups that could perhaps be influenced. The problem was that the Tories were afraid to interfere with "free collective bargaining." Conservatives feared the enhanced power of the unions and preferred to stay out of industrial relations. Their policy was not unlike that adopted by Stanley Baldwin after the General Strike: the state would encourage the responsible organization of both sides of industry and allow the parties a considerable measure of self-government. After 1945, however, the balance of advantage within industry had shifted to the unions, and full employment thereafter reinforced that shift of power, so the neo-Baldwinian approach proved unequal to the task of moderating wages. But no alternative presented itself. Prior to the general election of 1951, for example, the Conservatives had pledged to introduce a "Workers" Charter" which would contain an "Industrial Code" to guide the actions of employers and unions and which was intended to usher in a new era in industrial relations. There was no plan to make the charter or the code binding, but even this benign proposal smacked too much of state intervention and was dropped by the party once in office.[64]

In the absence of any more serious mechanism by which to intervene in the setting of wages, policy proceeded on two, rather distinct, tracks. On the one hand, the Ministry of Labour became involved in informal efforts at mediation or, if these failed, through more formal arbitration or the appointment of a court of inquiry. Disputes in the electrical industries, in engineering, in the mines, on the railways and the docks and in the newspaper industry were all dealt with in this manner. The most controversial instance came with the government's handling of the railway disputes during 1953–5. Churchill at one point argued that "a strike now might ruin our Election prospects," and the government proceeded subsequently to urge the Transport Commission to give way.[65] Many Conservatives, and some officials, fretted over such interventions, but the alternative was never very clear or attractive.[66] The second dimension of government policy towards wages involved the recurring pattern of exhortation aimed at convincing workers to moderate their demands and employers to resist them. Labour had initiated the practice and was able to carry the message directly into the counsels of the TUC. The Tories stood outside, but delivered much the same message. Full employment, they claimed, imposed on both sides of industry the duty to be reasonable and to keep wage and price increases within the bounds set by rising productivity. This argument was made in budget speeches, at meetings of the National Joint Advisory Council, chaired by the Minister of Labour, and in numerous other settings. But it seemed increasingly to fall on deaf ears and appeared to be regularly ignored by unions and employers.

Pressure therefore grew for a more authoritative statement of policy on wages. Shortly before leaving office, Labour had considered issuing a White Paper on full employment, economic controls and wages but chose to defer the matter until after the election. Butler was also tempted by the notion and had several drafts produced before he, too, decided not to proceed. The rekindling of inflation in 1955 led to renewed interest, but the impending election deterred the government from publishing a document that might be taken as a backing off from the commitment to full employment. With the election safely out of the way, the government finally worked up the courage to proclaim more forcefully the need to hold down wages and in March, 1956 published a White Paper on *The Economic Implications of Full Employment*. The paper was an obvious compromise that pleased no one. Labour understood that its appearance signalled, if not the abandonment of the goal of full employment, at least a recognition that other objectives had now been accorded equal importance. Business, by contrast, was disappointed at what they saw as the timidity of the document. It proposed no mechanism by which to enforce restraint, and seemed to suggest that unions and employers were equally responsible for the increase in wages. Among the rank-and-file of Conservatives, moreover, it did nothing to lessen the growing antipathy toward the unions and the by now almost axiomatic belief that strong unions and high wages were at the root of Britain's economic problems.[67]

THE SHIFTING TERMS OF THE POSTWAR SETTLEMENT

The gap between aspiration and accomplishment that so characterized Conservative policy towards wages and the unions was especially transparent.

Similar contradictions, though less visible in the mid-1950s, beset the practice of government in virtually every other sphere of social and economic policy during the years of Conservative rule. The state remained committed to full employment and to maintaining the value of the social services, but even at the level of rhetoric those objectives had to compete with the rather divergent goals of tax reduction, economy and price stability that dominated the thinking of Conservatives and the outlook of officials. At the level of policy, moreover, the Conservatives may have persisted in the belief that they were seeking to manage the economy in the interests of full employment and growth, but they voluntarily abolished the most powerful instruments for actually directing economic activity. Officials were by and large happy to go along, with only a very few convinced Keynesians expressing reservations.

By 1955–6, therefore, the fundamental tenets of the "postwar settlement" had already been seriously compromised. The social programmes that comprised the welfare state had been firmly established, but the will to fund them was being steadily eroded. The Conservatives had not only re-established themselves as serious contenders for power, indeed the natural party of government, but had reasserted their historic identification with the taxpayer. That connection seemed to preclude any increase in taxes for social programmes and ensured that there would be a constant downward pressure on taxation. The basic outlines of the welfare state would remain secure for some years to come, but the government was neither willing nor able to adapt its fiscal and administrative capabilities to changing needs.

The gap between what the state and the politicians professed and what they could deliver was even greater in economic policy. Of the various devices by which Labour and its Keynesian allies had sought to influence economic activity in the early postwar years, very few remained in the repertoire of policy-makers by the mid-1950s. The direct controls that distributed scarce manpower and raw materials and maintained price stability were all gone or soon to disappear. The government was left to make do largely with the budget, a very blunt instrument whose formation was dominated more by the politics of taxation than by the logic of demand management. Policy-makers increasingly turned to monetary policy – both by means of interest rates and, through its control over the terms of hire purchase, by regulating consumer credit – to supplement the workings of the budget. The effects of both budgetary and monetary policy were, however, too broad and undiscriminating to be effective. Unfortunately, no other devices for influencing investment or production commanded any significant support among officials or Conservative ministers. Labour in opposition continued to call for further nationalization and for more concerted efforts to prevent unemployment, but it was under Labour that the drift away from control and back to the market had begun. And it was Labour that had failed during its six years in office to institutionalize within the state either the practice of planning or the mechanisms by which the government's objectives could be carried out.

The long-term consequences of the failure fully to anchor the commitments to full employment and to adequate welfare in the fiscal and administrative structures of the state would be devastating, but they would be some time in coming. For a quarter of a century after the onset of the Marshall Plan in 1947 the British economy would prosper, along with most of the rest of the western world. Its steady growth would produce sufficient revenue to sustain the key programmes of the welfare state and to provide close to full employment. Only in the 1970s would the economic climate change so thoroughly as to cause an unravelling of the different strands of the postwar political settlement and expose the surprisingly thin institutional foundations for both economic management and enlightened social policies. The collapse of what had previously appeared to be quite secure aspects of British political life – indeed for many the defining features of its political system – would then come swiftly and with dire consequences.

Chapter 11

Epilogue: Decline to Thatcher

The essential premise of the "postwar settlement" was the commitment to full employment. It would not be challenged directly for many years, and not formally abandoned until after the election of Margaret Thatcher. But the confident, comfortable assumption that it was within the capacity of government to ensure full employment was questioned much sooner. Even in the mid-1950s policy-makers worried about whether it was possible to combine full employment, price stability and a healthy balance of payments. Treasury officials fretted over the steady increase in spending, businessmen worried about the apparently inexorable rise in wages and economists became concerned with Britain's lagging growth.[1] Implicitly, the critics all understood that the existing institutional structure and repertoire of policy devices were not up to the tasks which the parties had set for government. But there was little agreement on precisely what was wrong and still less on what to do about it. In consequence, from the late 1950s British politics were dominated by a series of urgent, but inconsistent, arguments about the nation's underlying economic problems and about what changes in policy and in the shape of government were needed to remedy them. Both parties joined in the debate and competed to offer solutions. None of the proposed solutions worked very effectively, however, and the succession of diagnoses, policy prescriptions and institutional changes gradually undermined faith in the parties, the politicians and the state itself. As Britain's economic performance deteriorated, the sense of cumulative failure mounted and the very goals of full employment and adequate welfare provision ultimately came to be doubted.

Confidence in the existing arrangements for policy-making began to be dented as early as 1955–7. The government was beset by a lingering balance of payments problem which the normal and preferred remedies failed effectively to address. Churchill had by this time been succeeded as Prime Minister by Eden and Harold Macmillan had gone to the Treasury. Macmillan and his Economic Secretary, Sir Edward Boyle, were in fact sceptical of the dogmatic liberalism prevailing at the Treasury and sought to curb "the primitive faith in the efficacy of market mechanisms free and unrestrained" that had emerged more fully in Butler's last months as Chancellor. But they did not get far, for the deflationary policies adopted in late 1955 and early 1956 had yet to make much impact on the economy and officials unanimously called for further cuts. The result was a rather orthodox "combination of an expansionist speech and a restrictionist Budget" which helped to make 1956 "a year of stagnation." Perhaps more significantly, Macmillan's brief stint at the Treasury also witnessed the failure of the Treasury's effort to rein in expenditure on the social services. Dismayed at the ineffectiveness of previous economy drives, the Treasury proposed in late 1955 a major inquiry into how spending on social programmes might be curtailed. Officials wanted to freeze the share of national income going to the social services and aimed specifically at identifying cuts in projected spending of no less than £137 million. After six months of wrangling, they could specify a mere £16.6 million and the exercise itself had provided advocates of social spending with an opportunity to defend particular programmes and to formulate a defence against the Treasury, whose arguments did not stand up to close scrutiny. By early 1957, officials had indirectly conceded that social spending was not growing disproportionately; and even before that, ministers had begun to turn their attention to the prospect of securing economies in defence.[2]

Within a year of the Conservatives' triumphant return to power, the government's faith in its ability to control the economy while setting it free had already begun to weaken, as had its comfortable belief that a firm resolve to reduce expenditure could produce easy economies. Further shocks lay ahead. By 1955, businessmen had become openly critical of the Conservatives' policy of "industrial appeasement" and the alleged coddling of the trade unions. They had come to feel in particular that the government's failure to stand up to the unions in the public sector made it impossible for private employers to resist unreasonable demands. Employers took heart when Iain Macleod replaced Walter Monckton as Minister of Labour, and secured an implicit agreement that the government would back them up in a confrontation with the unions. Needing little encouragement, the Engineering Employers' Federation refused the unions" claim for an increase of 10 per cent, submitted in October, 1956. A strike was set for March, 1957 but by then the government was confronted simultaneously with labour troubles in engineering, on the railways, among miners and at power stations. With Macmillan arguing that "the umpire is better than the duel," the government settled with the railway unions and told the engineering employers to back off and accept the appointment of a court of inquiry. Employers felt betrayed, while ministers and officials had to acknowledge that facing down the unions required more than simply the desire to do so.[3]

What had intervened, of course, between the state's encouragement of employer resistance and its failure ultimately to back it up was Suez and the change of government prompted by the débâcle. The government had not only bungled the operation, but ministers had been caught lying about it; and its *dénouement* revealed Britain's weakness and raised the spectre of a broader retreat from empire. A major reason for calling off the adventure, moreover, was the fear of what it would do to the pound – another painful reminder of the tenuous basis upon which the nation's credit and prosperity rested. The direct effects were modest and short-lived, but the political consequences would linger in the form of an increased willingness to criticize Britain's rulers and a further weakening of the self-confidence of the "establishment." Nor was the government allowed to forget the economic lessons of Suez, for by the second half of 1957 speculation against the pound was again causing serious difficulty.

Macmillan's replacement at the Treasury was Peter Thorneycroft, who was assisted by a pair of bright, young advisors – Enoch Powell and Nigel Birch. The three fell in line with the Treasury's preferences for lower taxes and reductions in expenditure and found themselves in sympathy with those who believed, as the *Financial Times* put it on 20 July 1957, that "the government has . . . given up the fight against inflation." Shortly afterwards, Thorneycroft warned Macmillan: "We have survived a debate on inflation. But we both know that our troubles on the economic front are likely to grow worse – not better, particularly as the next Election draws closer." The Chancellor's solution was a more resolute attack on expenditure; at his prompting, the Prime Minister issued a directive in August informing departments that estimates for 1958–9 should be no higher than those for 1957–8. Thorneycroft also prepared a series of restrictive measures to be imposed in the autumn. While these were still taking shape, there was a major run on the pound, caused by a combination of the belief that spending was out of control and rumours about a possible devaluation. Thorneycroft imposed cash limits to public investment, tightened credit for private industry and raised bank rate to 7 per cent. These "September measures," as they came to be known, were couched in a monetarist rhetoric whose anti-inflationary message evoked considerable support in the City and among businessmen, however uncertain ministers and even Treasury officials were about their ultimate wisdom.[4]

The "September measures" formed only part of a more sustained effort to wring inflation out of the economy. The effort became even more contentious as the estimates for 1958–9 began to come in. By December, Thorneycroft was appalled to learn that the spending plans for the next year "show the largest increase ever recorded in peace-time . . . £175 million higher than the total Estimates" for 1957–8. In response, he demanded economies of £150 million and proposed cuts in family allowances and increased NHS charges. The Cabinet refused to go along, Macmillan himself claiming that what was at issue was a mere 1 per cent of the outlay of the Exchequer and that "an increase of this order, largely attributable to factors over which the Government had no control, could not fairly be represented as indicating any weakening in the Government's resolve to resist inflation and to support sterling by all possible means."[5] Unable either to prevail or to compromise, Thorneycroft resigned together with Powell and Birch.

The "little, local difficulties" produced by the resignation of the three

Treasury ministers were really much more than that. They symbolized the failure of the package of policy instruments, evolved by officials and ministers over a considerable period and wielded not long before with relative complacency, to deal effectively with the nation's mounting economic problems, symbolized by recurring balance of payments difficulties. The so-called "climacteric of 1955–7" was capped, therefore, by a highly visible signal that policy-makers were unable to agree on the fundamentals of how to manage the economy and administer the welfare state. The response was a wide-ranging re-evaluation of economic and social policy and of the institutions of policy-making. The rethinking did not much affect voters at first or change political alignments. The Conservatives managed, with the aid of a consumer boom and another round of tax reductions, to win a third term in 1959.[6] But there were rumblings to be heard nevertheless, especially on the right. The three Treasury ministers immediately became a focal point of opposition within the Tory party, and their dissent from the practice of economic management was soon echoed by the newly founded Institute of Economic Affairs, by the Conservative lawyers whose pamphlet, "A Giant's Strength," was sharply critical of the unions, and by a significant section of the business community.[7] These discontents did not merge, however, with the much-discussed "middle-class revolt" over inflation, taxes and union power of the late 1950s; instead, the long period of Conservative rule continued.

Conservative hegemony was accompanied, however, by a reorientation in the language and agenda of high politics. The most notable innovation was the prominence within political rhetoric of the concept of growth. Growth may have been implicit in the policy discourse of the 1940s and early 1950s, but stabilization was the more proximate and explicit concern. The emphasis on growth represented, therefore, a logical next step in the development of policy. The urgency of taking this step was demonstrated forcefully by the policy failures of 1955–7 and reinforced by mounting evidence of lagging productivity. Growth seemed also to promise a means of transcending the dilemmas of policy-making and for that reason resonated broadly among the political classes. Economists began to come round to growth in 1954–5; in 1958, Andrew Shonfield's book on *British Economic Policy since the War* served as a more popular manifesto. The virtues of growth were extolled repeatedly thereafter and the term quickly found a prominent place in the discourse on economic policy.[8]

The emerging consensus on growth would produce within a short time a dramatic reversal of Conservative rhetoric and a new, or renewed, emphasis on "planning" by leaders of both parties. The consensus obscured as much as it illuminated, however, and lurking behind the apparent agreement on aims were two distinct, if overlapping, visions of what it was that stood in the way of growth and of what therefore had to be done to achieve it. One view held the main obstacle to growth to be inflation, whose deleterious effects were registered by recurring balance of payments crises and whose cause was typically seen as excessive wage pressure. The second saw the difficulties in more institutional terms and coupled critiques of institutions – of the civil service, of the machinery of government and the Treasury in particular, of the Bank of England and City, of stodgy businessmen and of the backwardness of the British "establishment" – with a variety of reforms to revamp old structures or breathe new life into them. Neither vision paid much attention to specific industries and their problems or to how government might intervene at the "micro" level to increase productivity. The focus remained on the economy as a whole, on central government and on national institutions and social structures. The failure to recognize and resolve the divergent perspectives on the obstacles to growth and the inability of policy-makers to push beyond the arguments about inflation versus the structural problems at the top to detailed plans at the level of firms, regions or economic sectors would ensure that little of substance would emerge from all the talk about growth. That did not, however, prevent the discussion of growth from dominating political rhetoric for at least a decade.

"Growthmanship" became a pervasive discourse, in fact, because its very vagueness made it possible to pursue established agendas and interests within its terms. The focus on inflation, for example, was almost ideological in its intensity and was in its essence directed against the organized working class. It was thus curiously consistent both with the traditional antipathy towards unions and with more novel "Keynesian" formulations about policy. The effort to control inflation had been central to the entire "Keynesian revolution," which won partial acceptance from the Treasury largely because it promised a more effective means of stabilizing prices than any alternative. Nor was the willingness to place the blame for inflation or the burden for halting it on the workers particularly novel in the late 1950s. It had been done before, and done most effectively by Labour in the late 1940s. What was new in the period after 1955 was the emergence of a more coherent set of arguments that located the source of Britain's "stop–go" economy in the impact of inflation on the balance of payments. Given that connection, growth required a decisive battle against inflation: as Lionel Robbins put it somewhat earlier, "Stop the inflation, stop it at all costs: that is the paramount need of the moment in the economic sphere." Inflation, moreover, was seen by the late 1950s as more deeply rooted in the economy and in the sustained high level of employment of the postwar era than had earlier been thought. The classic statement of the anti-labour formula, the so-called "Phillips curve," appeared in November, 1958.[9]

Very few were willing as yet to follow the argument to its logical conclusion and challenge the commitment to full employment. Instead, they focused on discovering the means by which to get workers to moderate their demands. The fear of rising wages prompted Robert Hall to admit that for the moment "Economic policy is . . . directed towards minimizing the annual wage round." It was increasingly recognized, however, that budgetary policy by itself would do little to restrain wages. The experience of greater reliance on monetary controls during 1955–7 had also proved disappointing, and the response of the unions and the employers to the platitudes of the 1956 White Paper on the *Economic Implications of Full Employment* had been equally discouraging. In 1956, moreover, the TUC General Council had formally refused a plea from the government to institute a wage freeze and the annual conference reaffirmed the "right of labour . . . to use its bargaining strength to protect workers from the dislocations of an unplanned economy." The failure of the employers" offensive of 1956–7 seemed at the same time to rule out a direct industrial confrontation. The only solution was an incomes policy. The decision to impose an incomes policy was not taken lightly or quickly, for it conflicted with the traditions of industrial relations to which officials and the leaders of both parties subscribed. The tentative first step was actually counter-productive: in July, 1957 the government appointed the Council on Prices, Productivity and Incomes – known also as the Cohen Council or the "Three Wise Men" – with the responsibility for advising government and the public on wages and prices. The council reported in February, 1958, siding with Thorneycroft in his recent battles over expenditure and interest rates, criticizing the record of economic management since the war and questioning the commitment to full employment. It was a contentious report that probably served to delay the imposition of an incomes policy, but even in 1958 such a policy was clearly coming.[10]

Advocates of a more institutional approach to the problem of generating growth did not disagree about the importance of controlling inflation. What they found objectionable was the way the battle against inflation took precedence over other objectives and how a preoccupation with inflation led almost automatically to policies concerned to bolster foreign confidence and support the balance of payments and the exchange rate. Such policies, it was argued, had the effect of "breaking the will to invest" and thus slowed down the modernization of British industry, retarded the growth of productivity and of exports and thus ensured that balance of payments problems would recur. This flawed pattern of policy-making was rooted, critics claimed, not simply in the preferences and mistakes of policy-makers but in the institutional structure within which they operated. That structure encompassed the public and the private sector, industry and the City; and the entire complex of institutions came to be criticized together. The most sustained and famous critique was Thomas Balogh's essay of 1959: "The Apotheosis of the Dilettante." Balogh directed his strictures at the civil service, which as early as 1918 had become "a vast, completely centralized service facing its ever-growing responsibilities with increasing insistence on a lack of expert knowledge." The creation of such an "unsuitable bureaucratic organization" was "the result of the victory of the Treasury' within the counsels of the state. The Treasury was firmly committed to the cult of the amateur and preferred those with a "reputation for solid commonsense" to those with genuine expertise. To Balogh this outdated and inadequate organization of the civil service was "the principal explanation of the drift towards *laissez-faire*" of the 1950s; restructuring the civil service and the Treasury was the essential precondition for implementing a more interventionist policy designed to promote growth.[11]

Balogh's essay appeared in a symposium on *The Establishment*, together with criticisms of the class structure, the educational system, the City of London and even the BBC.[12] The volume marked the emergence of a new genre of political writing that located the source of Britain's economic and political decline in its archaic ruling class and the institutions through which they governed. It offered a critique that would be echoed widely and that would inspire a series of efforts to undertake structural reform, especially during the mid-1960s. So long as the Conservatives remained in power, however, the impact was minimal. The government pre-emptively initiated two major inquiries into the policy-making process, the Radcliffe and Plowden Committees, but neither dealt with fundamental issues. Both exercises were undertaken by highly reliable members of "the Great and the Good" and reached quite judicious conclusions. Even so, their appointment was at least oblique testimony to the growing perception of the inadequacy of the existing institutional framework for policy-making.[13]

The failure of monetary measures to check inflation – a failure guaranteed in practice by the unwillingness of the Bank of England to make them effective – had been made clear in 1955 and led officials to press for a review of the "working of the monetary system." Robert Boothby and Nicholas Davenport, representing an all-party industry group in Parliament, proposed an inquiry prior to the 1956 budget. They were put off with an internal committee whose report reached no firm conclusions. Continued discontent with monetary policy and resentment at the Bank's apparent lack of co-operation with the aims of economic policy made a more formal inquiry inevitable. To ensure its reliability, the Bank itself proposed the creation of what would come to be the Radcliffe Committee on the Working of the Monetary System, appointed in April, 1957. Before the committee could report, Thorneycroft's "September measures" had been taken in yet another, and highly controversial, attempt to use the control of money to check inflation. The committee would take evidence from the government's and the Bank's most articulate critics, like Balogh and Nicholas Kaldor, and its deliberations would provide the occasion for a major debate about growth. Its report in 1959 was in no way revolutionary, but it did recommend tighter political control over the setting of interest rates, which both the Treasury and the Bank of England resisted. In addition, its scepticism about the effectiveness of monetary devices served to rule out for a considerable period reliance upon monetary policy as a viable option for policy-makers.[14]

The Plowden Committee was equally the work of "insiders," though it too served to some extent to discredit the routine administrative practices of the late 1950s. In July, 1958 the Select Committee on Estimates proposed an independent inquiry into Treasury control of expenditure. The Treasury wanted "no formal committee . . . no evidence in public or the seeking of evidence from the public" but rather "an internal enquiry by the government itself." They asked Plowden to undertake the task and he reported in 1961, recommending the establishment of a new system for controlling public expenditure, PESC, which would involve comprehensive reviews of spending across all departments for five years in advance. The aim was to make the Cabinet take "collective responsibility" for the level of expenditure and to ensure that all "individual decisions involving future expenditure should be taken against the background of such a survey and in relation to prospective resources." The obvious hope was that this more rational system would lower spending and allow for a more effective exercise of Treasury control. Plowden's proposal was accepted and the new system would dominate public spending decisions until, faced with 26 per cent inflation, the Labour Chancellor Denis Healey introduced a policy of "cash limits" in July, 1975. Ironically, "PESC, which began as a design for control, ended as a symbol of uncontrollability." [15]

Neither the Radcliffe nor the Plowden Committees undertook the sort of "root and branch" investigations that might have followed from the sharp criticisms then being levelled at the bureaucracy or the "Establishment." Nor did their recommendations lead to more than minor shifts in policy or rearrangements of the policy-making apparatus. More serious efforts in this direction would have to wait upon Labour's return to power under Harold Wilson. Even before that, however, the fascination with growth had produced a vogue for planning. But planning as instituted under the Conservatives suffered from a series of ambiguities inherent in the discourse on growth that preceded it. The competing visions obscured by the common rhetoric of growth – the one focusing on checking inflation, the other on structural and institutional transformation – were not, of course, completely incompatible. But they were different and did lead to different emphases in the direction of policy. British policy-makers failed, or refused, to make a choice and instead adopted a set of policies that appeared to deal with the concerns central to each vision while in fact not coping adequately with either.

The turn to planning, embodied institutionally in the National Economic Development Council, provides a perfect illustration. Throughout the 1950s planning had remained highly unpopular with businessmen, officials and Conservatives. But the prevailing climate of worry over the economy gradually turned policy-makers' attention to France and the apparent success there of "indicative planning." The initiative actually came from a small group of industrialists who began meeting over dinner in early 1960 and who managed to win over their colleagues within the Federation of British Industries during a conference held at Brighton in November, 1960. The businessmen were resentful over the government's recent changes in interest rates and hire purchase restrictions, designed to curb the boom that had brought the Conservatives their latest election victory, and wanted the government to abandon "stop–go" and instead commit itself to maintaining a steady course in economic policy. In particular, they called for "a more conscious attempt to assess plans and demands in particular industries for five or even ten years ahead" in order to get government, together with business and labour, "to agree on an assessment of expectations and intentions which could be set before the country for the next five years." The new Chancellor, Selwyn Lloyd, was impressed and urged the proposal on Macmillan, who also agreed. It took longer for the Treasury to come round, for they were not eager to undertake detailed intervention in the economy or to witness the setting up of a rival in the making of economic policy. They acquiesced, however, because they came to feel that the establishment of a new institutional framework independent of the Treasury was the only way to get the unions to sit down with employers and the state to discuss wages. Planning therefore was accepted as the route to a more effective wages policy.[16]

What appeared, therefore, as an institutional innovation aimed at overcoming bureaucratic conservatism was in reality intended as a device by which bureaucrats and politicians could get their way with the unions. In practice, it would not be so simple, for the TUC understood precisely what was at stake and they were angered as well by the crisis measures of July, 1961 – a rise in bank rate to 7 per cent, expenditure cuts and the "pay pause," followed in August by an IMF loan of £714 million – all of which they opposed. The unions demanded that the new body be free to set its own agenda, that the TUC have complete control over who was to represent the workers and that the council not be used to "trap" the unions into a formal incomes policy. After some tough bargaining, Neddy was established in early 1962. By 1963, however, Neddy was issuing reports urging wage restraint and discussing ways of making it stick.[17] Planning had come to Britain, not under the auspices of Labour and as part of an effort to intervene in the economy, but with the sponsorship of Conservatives and officials seeking a forum for working out an incomes policy.

The conversion to planning is therefore less surprising than it might at first seem. Its confused origins, however, helped to ensure that its practice would be marked by confusion and incoherence. Neddy, aided by its policy-making office (NEDO) and flanked by the Economic Development Committees (little Neddies) established in twenty-one different sectors and parallel in structure to the central council, remained ineffective. It was "not well-integrated into the policy-making process," for the Treasury naturally retained control over taxes and spending, and Neddy lacked the power and resources to make its prescriptions authoritative. The council's "principal contribution . . . to the British economy was to provide a forum for the negotiation of incomes policies," while the little Neddies degenerated into "institutions which industry used to lobby the government for special subsidies or protection, rather than instigators of fundamental microeconomic change."[18]

Nevertheless, the shift in the climate of policy-making occasioned by the transition from "the expansionist economic liberalism of Mr Butler's time at the Exchequer towards the interventionist policies of indicative planning and incomes policy which dominated both Conservative and Labour Governments in the 1960s" was quite dramatic.[19] The impetus behind the transformation was the reorientation and critique that had been stimulated by the prolonged crisis of economic management beginning during 1955–7. The consequence would be a new pattern of policy-making characterized by repeated efforts to devise a workable incomes policy and by a series of administrative reforms. The pattern would last well into the 1970s, as first Harold Wilson, then Edward Heath and then Wilson and Callaghan would lead governments seeking, but failing to discover, a way out of the impasse inherited from the settlement of the mid-1950s. The effort became increasingly frantic and decreasingly successful and, as it proceeded, the cumulative failures of policy undermined support for the government's social and economic interventions more broadly and for the goals its interventions were aimed to secure.

The failures of the 1960s and 1970s have been chronicled at length in other contexts. Here a brief summary must suffice. The Labour government of 1964–70 came into office firmly committed to both of the visions subsumed under the metaphor of growth. As Alec Cairncross, the chief economic advisor put it, the new government "believed strongly that restructuring would strengthen the economy" and "that it could get the agreement of the unions to more moderate wage settlements." Wilson was most attracted to notions of structural reform, but nevertheless unwilling to tolerate inflation. Thus Labour moved both to restructure the apparatus of policy-making and to control incomes. Upon taking office, five new departments were created: the Department of Economic Affairs, the Ministries of Technology (Mintech), of Overseas Development, and of Land and Natural Resources, and the Welsh Office. The most visible was the Department of Economic Affairs, which was to serve as a counterweight to "the mighty Treasury departmental power" and to produce a National Plan. Great things were expected of the department, led by George Brown and staffed by an extremely talented mix of "insiders" and "irregulars". Very little came of it. The relationship between the DEA and the Treasury was never clarified, and the new department never wrested control of the key instruments of policy from the Treasury. Theoretically, the Treasury was to work on short-term issues and on finance; Economic Affairs was to take the long view and concern itself with more structural factors affecting growth. But the division of labour, embodied in a famous "concordat," was not workable. As Macleod mockingly observed in November, 1965, "we have a minister of long-term 'go' and a minister of short-term 'stop'.' The new department had one major achievement to its credit: the National Plan of 1965, upon which Wilson fought the 1966 election. But the plan was, in effect, stillborn and from 1966 the initiative in economic policy had passed decisively to the Treasury. By 1969 the DEA was eliminated.[20]

Wilson's other institutional changes fared slightly better, but in no way lived up to their promise and only the Welsh Office outlived the government unchanged. The most effective work was done by Mintech which, together with the Industrial Reconstruction Corporation established in 1966, had available substantial funds with which to streamline industry and aid research and development. The two agencies oversaw fifty mergers involving over one hundred and fifty companies, renationalized and reorganized the steel industry, set up the Shipbuilding Industry Board, assisted the foundation of International Computers and sponsored research in the machine tool industry. Still, these more selective interventions were limited in scope, hampered by a tendency to favour concentration at the expense of change at the "micro" level and in any case overwhelmed by the more restrictive character of the government's overall economic strategy, particularly after 1968.[21]

The government's most direct assault on bureaucratic conservatism, the Fulton Committee, was scarcely more effective. The committee was set up in 1966 to inquire into the "structure, recruitment and management, including training" of the civil service and chaired by an old friend of Harold Wilson's who shared his critical attitude towards the amateurism and inefficiency of full-time officials. The inquiry was extremely wide-ranging and much-discussed, but from the start it was restricted to looking at the personnel of the civil service and not at the broader, but closely related, question of the 'machinery of government." Its *Report* in June, 1968 contained a long list of recommendations, of which three were of major importance: the creation of a Civil Service College, the setting up of a new Civil Service Department to take over "establishments" work from the Treasury, and the unification of the classes and gradings of the civil service. The first two were not especially controversial and were quickly adopted. The third had more far-reaching implications and elicited from officials, especially from Sir William Armstrong (then Permanent Secretary to the Treasury), a protracted effort to delay its implementation and dilute its impact. A much modified scheme was introduced under the Heath government.[22]

As Labour's hopes of generating growth through structural reform and planning began to fade, the government turned to what it could do best, and that was to impose an incomes policy on its supporters. Labour inherited an "overheated" economy in 1964, for the Tories had resisted deflation in the run-up to the election. Immediately upon taking office, therefore, it had to deal with mounting inflation and a balance of payments deficit that was said, with some exaggeration, to be approaching £800 million. There was some sentiment for devaluation, and in retrospect most commentators feel it would have been of great benefit to the incoming regime. But the Labour leadership's residual conservatism, coupled with its desire not to be labelled as the party of devaluation and its deference to the United States, prevailed and delayed devaluation until November, 1967. James Callaghan, the new Chancellor, had met with the Chairman of the Federal Reserve Bank in New York in May, 1963 and promised not to devalue, and later reiterated the pledge to the Secretary of the Treasury, Henry Fowler. The Americans were keen to resist devaluation, seeing it as the first step in a process that would lead to an attack on the dollar. They therefore assisted the Wilson government in its efforts to avoid devaluation, agreeing secretly in 1965 to prop up the pound if Britain neither devalued nor reduced its military commitments "east of Suez." The decision not to devalue was taken three days after Labour assumed office, when Wilson, Callaghan and George Brown met with officials who, but for one, concurred with the Treasury argument that devaluation would be a "confession of failure." [23]

With devaluation ruled out, at least temporarily, the Labour government was unable to resolve the contradictions implicit in its vision of growth between policies aimed at planning and structural reform and those designed to control inflation by moderating wages. Though they sought to pursue both, the logic of the battle against inflation soon came to predominate. Initially, the government's efforts to hold down wages enjoyed the support of the unions, whose leaders were willing to co-operate to bring about "the planned growth of incomes." The unions and the employers agreed on a "Joint Statement on Prices, Productivity and Incomes" in late 1964 and the National Board for Prices and Incomes (NBPI) was established in February, 1965. A pay norm of 3–3.5 per cent was agreed and promulgated officially in a White Paper, published in April, 1965 which also laid down criteria for the granting of increases that exceeded the norm and for determining prices. Prominent among the reasons for exceeding the pay norm was productivity; from that time forward productivity bargaining, real or imagined, became a major feature of industrial relations. The new board was scarcely more effective than Macmillan's National Incomes Commission, which it replaced, and it had to be supplemented in November, 1965 by the Incomes Policy Commission set up to operate an "early warning system" that would monitor and vet all wage claims. The effort to control wages continued to operate on a voluntary basis until July, 1966 when a six-month, statutory freeze was imposed along with a package of severely deflationary financial measures. The freeze brought down the rate of increase of wages, but it operated very bluntly and produced enormous resentment among the unions. It was followed by a further six months of "severe restraint," by which time the TUC was so alienated from the government that it was moved to condemn its efforts to control wages as no better than "Tory deflationary policies." [24]

Labour's attempts to run an incomes policy had sufficed to drive a wedge between the government and the unions, but it did not stave off devaluation. From April to November, 1967 the pound was under constant pressure. In November the government devalued and promised the IMF that, to make devaluation work, it would adopt an even more sharply deflationary stance. The new Chancellor, Roy Jenkins, cut £500 million from the budget and introduced substantial increases in taxation in 1968. Incomes policy was to be continued by applying the narrow criteria established in 1967 to all claims for increases and by keeping settlements below a maximum of 3.5 per cent. The measures succeeded in correcting the balance of payments, but any pretensions the government had of running a policy of growth were abandoned. By the fall of 1968 both the Labour party and the TUC had come out decisively against the new policies and the split between government and its erstwhile supporters had become even wider. It was to grow wider still when the government, by now convinced that what was needed was a fundamental reform of industrial relations that would weaken the unions" position in the labour market, published *In Place of Strife* in January, 1969. The reaction from the unions was extremely hostile and the proposals were withdrawn in return for a "solemn and binding" agreement from the TUC to clamp down upon unofficial strikes. By this point the government's successive efforts to control wages had exhausted themselves and wages began to rise even faster than before. By mid-1970, they were growing at a rate of 14 per cent. Not only had incomes policy failed, but in making the control of wages its primary objective the Wilson government had abandoned its efforts at planning and at restructuring the bureaucracy and the economy, and had permanently weakened the ties between the Labour party and its supporters among the skilled, unionized workers. It was not a happy legacy.

The Conservatives who came to power in 1970 were not eager to retrace the path of the Labour government of 1964–70. Edward Heath, in particular, sought a decisive break and had used his time as leader of the opposition to work out an alternative approach. At its core was a greater reliance on the market, a preference articulated forcefully at a series of meetings prior to the election of 1970 – the most famous of which took place at Selsdon Park in January, 1970 and gave rise to the term "Selsdon Man." The Conservatives wanted to pull back from the sort of corporatist bargaining between unions, employers and the state which seemed to have failed in the 1960s. In its stead the government wished to recreate a more flexible labour market in order to hold down wages. To do so, however, would require a higher level of unemployment and the curbing of trade union power through what would become the Industrial Relations Act of 1971. Neither policy would be popular, and neither would stick.

Heath was eager as well to deal with questions concerning the machinery of government: he wanted to bring businessmen into government on a large scale, to find ways of reducing the workload of Cabinet by merging departments and "hiving-off" routine administative work, and to institute more effective and systematic policy analysis. As with most such plans, implementation was partial and had less of an impact than had been hoped. The most notable innovation was the setting up of a "think tank," the Central Policy Review Staff, led during Heath's premiership by Lord Rothschild. Under Rothschild and Heath, the CPRS undertook a large number of studies of major issues, but it was systematically prevented from delving into foreign and defence policy, the budget (and hence large sections of domestic policy) and the "machinery of government" which William Armstrong, by this time Head of the Civil Service and of the Civil Service Department, had come to regard "as his private turf." Inevitably, the new office focused on specific projects but did not review the government's policy as a whole. Similarly, the Heath administration's new procedure for reviewing programmes and budgets, Programme Analysis and Review (PAR), operated in too piece-meal a fashion to be effective. The Conservative government's administrative initiatives therefore came, much like Labour's under Harold Wilson, to very little.[25]

The failure to secure administrative reform was, of course, the least of the government's problems. Its most spectacular failures were in its economic and industrial relations policies. Convinced in 1970 that the price stability necessary for sustained growth could best be achieved through the market, the government had to concede in November, 1972 that the market had not worked. Particularly ineffective was the Conservatives" substitute for a formal incomes policy – an approach labelled "de-escalation," which was to work by reducing successive wage settlements in the public sector by 1 per cent. It was never very effective, but was completely destroyed by the miners" strike of 1972, settled with a 20 per cent increase. Equally troubling to the government was the steady rise in unemployment. To counter that threat the government adopted an expansionary budget in March, 1972, but began to worry even more about inflation. Fears of inflation were further increased by uncertainty over the value of the pound, which had recently been allowed to "float" along with the dollar. The government's dilemma was to find a way to deal simultaneously with unemployment and inflation. Their solution was to attempt to run the economy at a high rate of growth – 5 per cent was the target – while imposing a firm incomes policy. It was hoped at first that wage restraint could be achieved voluntarily. To secure the co-operation of the unions the government turned again to the NEDC, which from July, 1972 became the site of hard bargaining between representatives of the Confederation of British Industry (CBI), the Trades Unions Congress (TUC) and the state. Negotiations broke down over the unions" demands for price controls and the abandonment of the Industrial Relations Act. On 6 November Heath announced a statutory "freeze."

Modelled largely on Richard Nixon's policy in the US, the "freeze" was to last for three months, after which it was replaced by a policy aimed at holding increases to about 8 per cent and managed by two new agencies armed with considerable authority: the Pay Board and the Price Commission. The policy succeeded in moderating the growth of wage rates, if not earnings, but throughout 1973 inflation continued to increase as the impact of rising oil prices began to be felt. Until November, 1973 moreover, the government continued to maintain its expansionary fiscal policy. By then, prices were rapidly rising and a third phase of incomes policy, designed to limit the rise in earnings to about 11 per cent, was instituted. This phase was distinctive in that it contained a provision for the granting of "threshold payments" of up to 40 pence per week for every 1 per cent rise of prices beyond 7 per cent. The purpose was to prevent workers from incorporating expected price increases into their wage demands, but the effect was to index wages to inflation and thus to increase both. The third phase of Conservative incomes policy was to be the last, for it was quickly challenged by the miners who began their overtime ban on 12 November. By February, the country was confronted with a three-day week, a full-scale strike in the mines and a general election called by Heath to reinforce the government's hand in dealing with the miners. The Conservatives lost, the miners were given 30 per cent and Harold Wilson was returned as head of a minority Labour government.[26]

In the two elections held in 1974 neither Labour nor the Conservatives could win a decisive mandate. Instead, the voters in effect rendered a negative verdict on a decade of policy failure. That failure had been rooted in the ambiguities and contradictions of the politics of growth, to which both parties had been, and still remained, committed. The emphasis on growth had, of course, developed out of the failure of earlier policy devices to sustain the commitments embedded in the postwar settlement. But the consensus on growth had not extended to an agreement on how to engineer it, and so policy vacillated between a focus on structural reforms designed to make government or industry more efficient and a concentration upon policies to curb inflation by controlling the growth of wages. The dilemma confronting policy-makers may well have been insoluble given the narrow range of options and policy devices within which they had to operate. It would, in any event, not be solved and would lead by the 1980s to the abandonment of the commitment to full employment that had been so central to postwar political culture and to attacks upon the very contours of the welfare state. But before even that sad outcome could emerge, Labour would be forced to grapple once more with Britain's mounting economic problems.[27]

Labour's time in opposition had been largely taken up with the effort to repair the damage done to the party's relationship with the workers and the unions during 1964–70. A superficial reconciliation was achieved through the vehicle of the "Social Contract." The precise terms of the agreement were left vague prior to 1974, but the general idea was to trade increases in money wages for various social benefits and "public goods." Among the latter would be price controls, subsidies for food, housing and rent and a more redistributive package of taxes and benefits. While the "Social Contract" was being bargained out, the Labour party also proceeded to adopt a far more radical programme of state intervention in the economy. The Heath government had already begun to move towards greater intervention with the creation of a strong Department of Trade and Industry and the passage of the Industry Act of 1972. Labour planned to go much further and promised to nationalize the nation's top twenty-five firms, establish a National Enterprise Board to undertake direct public investment in industry, force businesses to sign planning agreements, implement workers' control and issue directives to the private sector. Together, these enhanced powers would allow a Labour government successfully to operate a new economic strategy. By 1973, the party had coalesced behind what Michael Foot called "the finest Socialist Programme I have seen in my lifetime." [28]

The reconstruction of Labour's policies and its links with the unions undoubtedly helped it back into power in 1974, but it raised expectations that the party had no means of meeting. Its economic strategy in particular was premised on assumptions about the ability of the state to engineer growth that had never been demonstrated and that in the 1970s were hardly credible. The British economy, and not just its financial sector, had long been oriented to world markets and after the decisions taken under Heath to float the pound and to enter the Common Market the country was becoming even more integrated into the international economy. Labour's interventionist plans took little note of this and would have had a chance of working only if Britain had been prepared to move away from Europe and to rely more exclusively upon its own resources. Whether to follow such a difficult course was implicitly what was being decided in the debate and referendum over the EEC in 1974–5. When that argument ended with a solid vote for Europe, the prospect of the Labour government carrying out its industrial policies was effectively foreclosed. The verdict rendered by the voters in May, 1975 was to be driven home even more forcefully by the financial crises of 1976, which compelled the government to seek assistance from the IMF and to accept its conditions for managing the nation's finances. The "alternative economic strategy," worked out in impressive detail during 1975–6 and endorsed by the Labour Party conference in September, 1976 therefore never had a chance. [29]

Disillusionment with the Labour government's performance was thus almost inevitable. It would come slowly, but in the end would be nearly total. It was easy enough to settle with the miners and to replace the Tories" Industrial Relations Act with bills guaranteeing union rights and "employment protection." It was more difficult to take positive action. This was reflected in the new government's lack of major plans to restructure the machinery of government. Wilson did split up the Department of Trade and Industry, sending Tony Benn to Industry and Peter Shore to Trade, and created a new Department of Prices and Consumer Protection to be run by Shirley Williams, but personnel considerations seem to have provided the main reason for the changes. His other innovations were quite low-key. Harold Lever was appointed Chancellor of the Duchy of Lancaster with the job of reviewing economic questions and policies; and the Downing Street Policy Unit was set up under Bernard Donoughue. The Policy Review Staff (CPRS) was kept on as well, leaving ministers with plenty of advice but no more real options than before. Labour also presided over yet another review of the civil service, the English Committee, whose 1977 report produced no major changes. [30]

The 1974–9 Labour government placed its faith not in reforms in the machinery of government, but in the package of policies it proposed to use to influence the economy. Its industrial policy was to prove especially difficult to implement, however. Immediately upon taking office, the Cabinet began arguing about its plan to intervene drastically in industry and its aims had already been watered down by July, 1974, when the White Paper on *The Regeneration of British Industry* appeared. A new Industry Act was duly passed in 1975 and the National Enterprise Board brought into being later in the year, but by this time Tony Benn had been moved from Industry to Energy and with him went the ministerial resolve to make it effective. The necessary *dirigiste* aspects of the board were absent from the start; in response to pressure from the CBI, the guidelines under which it was to operate were narrowed and made more commercial and managerial; and in practice it came increasingly to resemble the Industrial Reconstruction Corporation, giving out public funds to "lame ducks" and getting very little in return. When a new and rethought "industrial strategy" was announced in November, 1975, the emphasis was on voluntary planning through tripartite bargaining. The reversion to "corporatist" bargaining also led to a renewed emphasis on the NEDC, which undertook a series of joint studies on how to make various industries more competitive. By July, 1976 thirty-nine "working parties" had reported; by late 1977, the government had allocated funds to assist in the restructuring of several industries. But the results were meagre and the NEB's identification with the policy of bailing out faltering private sector firms served to discredit both the Board and the policies it was to implement.[31]

What did most to discredit the government, of course, was the failure of its broader economic policy. The Labour government was confronted in mid-1974 with an inflation rate of 16 per cent and a mounting balance of payments deficit. Little was done to slow down the economy until after the election of October, 1974 by which time wage claims were being raised to catch up with prices. In the second half of 1974, settlements averaged about 27 per cent – 10 per cent higher than inflation. TUC leaders soon began to concede the need for a more aggressive policy to control incomes, while the Chancellor, Denis Healey, responded with a severe budget in April, 1975 – the first postwar budget to deflate in the face of rising unemployment. By May, Jack Jones of the Transport and General Workers' Union was moved to call for a flat-rate pay increase for the coming round of wage bargaining. With sterling collapsing around them, Healey and the unions met over the summer of 1975 and agreed on a £6 limit with very few exceptions. The new policy worked and inflation was cut nearly in half over the next six months. The government sought to extend the policy and to reduce the rate of wage increases still further, proposing for 1976–7 a guideline of 3 per cent to be supplemented by tax cuts. Spurred on by yet another financial crisis, the TUC eventually agreed in May, 1976 on a set of norms averaging about 4.5 per cent.[32]

There was mounting resentment among the unions over the government's efforts to restrain wages in the face of the sustained growth in prices, leading to warnings that incomes policy could not be sustained beyond the summer of 1977. But a return to free collective bargaining was prevented by the financial crises of 1976. The crisis of the spring of 1976 had been met by borrowing from foreign banks, backed up by a set of tax increases in the form of an additional 2 per cent in employers' national insurance contributions and expenditure cuts amounting to £1 billion. It was followed by yet another attack on sterling early in the fall. Callaghan, who had replaced Wilson as Prime Minister in April, proceeded to negotiate a loan from the IMF. The IMF demanded further, massive cuts in expenditure together with lower direct taxes. From the end of 1976, the government found it impossible to deliver on the "social" benefits implied in the "Social Contract." That made it even harder for workers and their union leaders to accept wage restraint. But the government pressed ahead and in July, 1977 imposed a limit of 10 per cent for 1977–8. The unions found ways around the policy and secured increases of that much or more. By the following year both sides were more resolute: the government tried to hold the line at 5 per cent and the TUC formally rejected the proposal. The government's new standard was first breached at Ford in November, 1978, when workers settled for 17 per cent after a strike of nine weeks. Workers in the public sector, whose pay had been more effectively restrained over the previous several years, followed suit with a series of strikes during what became known as the "winter of discontent." The government was soon forced to admit that its 5 per cent guideline was unworkable and in February put out a joint statement with the TUC on *The Economy, the Government and Trade Union Responsibility*. This so-called "Concordat" was supposed to mark the beginnings of a new, more realistic stage of incomes policy, but the public were not impressed. In the election of May, 1979, Labour's vote slipped further and the Tories, led by Mrs Thatcher, won a clear Parliamentary majority.

The Conservatives would go on to claim that their victory represented more than a rejection of Labour's recent efforts or a reaction to temporary economic difficulties. To them it represented as well a repudiation of the entire pattern of postwar politics and of the commitments to full employment and the welfare state. Their claim gained credence from the fact that the Labour government of 1974–9, and before that the Conservative government of 1970–4, could be said to have failed systemically. They failed not only in their efforts to reinvigorate government and engineer growth but failed more conspicuously to control prices and provide jobs. Inflation and unemployment were both much worse after a decade, indeed nearly two decades, of concerted and even frantic efforts to improve Britain's economic perfomance. The ability of government to manage the economy successfully was thus inevitably called into question. So, too, was the set of political commitments that justified government intervention and, more precisely, the level of spending and taxes that had been imposed to fulfil them. The Conservatives were thus able to construe their victory as a mandate to restructure the relationship between state and society, pushing back the boundaries and reducing the capacity of the state while expanding the scope for the market.

It was a contentious reading of their election mandate, but it was made at least plausible by the fact that the failure of economic policy seemed to coincide with a perceived failure to control taxes and spending. The data were in fact more ambiguous, but the trends were nevertheless troubling to Conservatives and to many ordinary taxpayers. Since the late 1950s there had been a steady upward pressure on both taxation and expenditure. In the early 1950s, Conservatives had succeeded in moderating the growth of spending and begun a process of steadily reducing taxes, especially at election time. They continued to give away revenues as long as possible: the 1959 budget lowered income tax by ninepence, reducing revenues by £360 million, and gave voters another £71 million by repayment of postwar credits. By 1960, the share of taxation in the national product dropped to 28.4 per cent, a postwar low. In 1961, Conservatives went on to raise the threshold for sur-tax from £2,000 to £5,000 in a move carefully calculated to reward their middle-class constituents. After that it became harder to sustain a policy of tax reductions and while the Tories avoided any increase in direct taxation, they were forced, despite an impending election, to impose modest increases on drink and tobacco in April, 1964. Spending also began to increase more steadily from the late 1950s. The Conservatives were able to limit public expenditures to approximately 35 per cent of national income until 1960, but government spending rose to over 40 per cent by 1963.[33]

The upward inflection of taxes and spending continued after Labour returned to power in 1964. Total revenues roughly doubled between 1964 and 1970 while prices increased by one third; and the share of national income taken in taxation jumped from 33 per cent to 44 per cent. Inflation proved a powerful engine for increasing revenues, for not only did it automatically push taxation up along with prices but, in a process that has been termed "fiscal drag," it actually increased the liability of ordinary workers to income tax, lifted many lower-middle-class incomes into higher rates of tax and thus took a bigger share of most incomes. Throughout the 1950s most workers had remained outside the net of income tax, but by 1970 it was estimated that the average worker paid 20 per cent in taxes and national insurance contributions. Taxes were also increased under Labour by the imposition of several new taxes: capital gains tax, corporation tax and selective employment tax. Capital gains tax had been on Labour's agenda since the early 1950s, and the rise in speculative profits produced by the late 1950s stock market boom had led even Conservatives to concede the need to tax at least "short-term" gains. In 1965 Labour imposed a comprehensive tax of roughly 30 per cent on capital gains in order, as Callaghan explained, to "bring to an end the state of affairs in which hard work and great energy are fully taxed while the fruits of speculation and passive ownership escape untaxed." Corporation tax was also a long-term Labour objective, though it was meant primarily as a replacement for profits tax. Selective employment tax was a more curious, and much debated, innovation. It was a per capita add-on to the employer's national insurance contribution, which would be repaid with a premium to manufacturing and without a premium to agriculture, transport and mining. That left construction, distribution and services bearing the full weight of the tax. It was a device aimed at discouraging employment in the service sector and at stimulating manufacturing and exports. Of these three new impositions, capital gains and corporation taxes raised little new revenue while eliciting considerable antagonism from the business community. SET, though even more controversial, produced almost 4 per cent of central government revenues by 1970. Overall, however, the major factors affecting taxation were inflation and the inertial weight of existing impositions.[34]

Inflation and inertia would continue to increase taxes throughout the 1970s, but even more important would be their impact on the incidence and structure of taxation. "We will reduce taxation," the Conservatives pledged in 1970, and the new government did immediately lower the standard rate of income tax by sixpence. But over the next several years tax receipts continued to grow, actually doubling between 1970 and 1975. Revenues had not increased much faster than inflation and the ratio of taxes to national income decreased slightly from 44 per cent in 1970 back down to around 40 per cent by the late 1970s. By then, however, the relative contribution of different taxes had changed a good deal. The share of revenues produced by direct taxes had grown from 57 per cent in 1970 to over 70 per cent in 1975 and stayed high thereafter, while the share of indirect taxes had shrunk correspondingly. The Conservatives had sought to reverse the trend towards direct taxes by replacing purchase tax and SET with value added tax (VAT) in 1973, but the rates were insufficient for the purpose. The result was that the sort of taxes Conservatives liked the least had increased the most. But it was not only the Tories and their middle-class supporters who were now arrayed against high direct taxes. Inflation continued to bring more workers within the income tax net and resentment began to spread, especially among the better-paid, skilled workers. By 1976, the Labour government had begun to recognize the transformed relationship between workers and the tax system, and it was two Labour MPs who gave their names to the Rooker–Wise amendment that from 1977 forced the Chancellor to report on the connection between changes proposed in the budget and changes due to inflation with the aim of ensuring some measure of indexation. The government itself sought in its discussions with the unions to exchange tax reductions for wage restraint. By cutting rates Labour actually did manage to keep down the share of national income going to taxes, despite the doubling of actual receipts. The government also introduced a new capital transfer tax in 1974 to replace estate duty, though in practice it produced less revenue, and proceeded with plans for a wealth tax, but the proposal was effectively dropped in 1976. Labour's record on taxation was therefore in fact quite mixed. Still, when the Conservatives returned to office they would inherit a system heavily weighted towards direct taxation, with a standard rate of 33 per cent and a top rate of 83 per cent.[35]

The changing structure of national taxation probably did as much to discredit the tax system as did the level of taxes. Business was angered by repeated efforts, even if they failed in practice, to tax profits and wealth and by high overall rates. The middle and lower-middle classes experienced substantial increases in effective rates, and so, too, did workers who also had to pay rising national insurance contributions.[36] By the late 1970s, there were few who would voice support for the fairness of the tax system. Resentment was further increased, especially among the middle and lower-middle classes, by the evolution of local rates. In 1960 local government spending stood at about 12 per cent of national income, precisely its level two decades before. By 1975 it had grown by half again. The money was spent on an increasingly narrow range of services – primarily education and housing – whose provision was almost by definition redistributive. This expenditure was financed by revenues which were also becoming to some extent more progressive. Grants from central government, whose tax structure was based increasingly on direct taxes, amounted to approximately 36 per cent of local revenues in 1960 but over 45 per cent in 1975 and more than 52 per cent in 1980. The share produced from local rates decreased and, at least as important, their incidence shifted. With the "re-rating" of industry in 1958, the revaluations of 1963 and 1973 and the "super-rating" of commercial and industrial property in 1967, the burden was shifted onto property and away from households. Among households, moreover, the system of rate rebates introduced in 1966 provided exemptions for roughly the poorest 30 per cent. The net effect of these complex changes defies precise calculation, but obviously they had worked to make the finance of local government more progressive and more burdensome to business and to middle- and upper-class ratepayers. Ken Livingstone could thus argue in the early 1980s that the "rating system is the best method of redistributing wealth that the labour movement has ever had its hands on." Successive reforms in the structure of local government – the creation of the Greater London Council in 1964 to replace the old, Labour-dominated London County Council and the establishment after 1972 of metropolitan counties large enough, it was hoped, to dilute Labour's strength in the inner cities – were designed largely to prevent Labour from getting its hands on this device, but the party was notably more effective at winning and keeping local office than in holding onto power through Parliament.[37]

While revenues grew from the early 1960s, expenditures grew even faster. Public spending increased from about a third of national income during 1955–7 to 38.5 per cent during 1967–9 and 43.5 per cent for 1977–9. Most of the increase came in the social services, which made up 36 per cent of spending in 1951, 42 per cent in 1961 and over 53 per cent by 1978, by which point social service spending stood at 28 per cent of national income. At first the social services grew at the expense of defence, whose share of spending dropped from 24 per cent in 1951 to 13 per cent in 1971. Eventually, however, increased spending had to be financed by higher taxes, largely the pattern during the

1960s, or by borrowing, which characterized the 1970s and produced a steady rise in the so-called "Public Sector Borrowing Requirement" (PSBR). The long-term growth of public expenditure became increasingly controversial and promoted considerable debate about its causes as well as repeated efforts to bring it under control. The debate about expenditure was intensified, however, by a developing critique of the "quality" of the services provided by the welfare state. Ironically, a good deal of this dissatisfaction was first voiced by the left, who early on began to criticize the inadequacies of the welfare state. Richard Titmuss, for example, was writing in the 1950s about the ways in which the structure of collective provision allowed for the growth of private power and inequality; later on, critics began to point out how much the middle classes benefited from public programmes. During the late 1960s and 1970s, critics also became concerned with the arrogance of bureaucratic and professional power and the tendency of the welfare state to increase both. These critiques from the left found curious echoes on the right, who in the late 1970s and 1980s creatively combined traditional arguments about dependency with more novel criticisms of the practical failures and the growing expense of the welfare state.[38]

It was the cost of the welfare state, however, that would ultimately erode public support for social provision.[39] Policy became focused for that reason on finding ways to control spending. But control proved elusive, for the sources of growth lay in factors normally outside the purview of government. There have been, in fact, relatively few significant innovations in social policy since the 1950s. Institutionally, the main initiatives were the creation of the Department of Health and Social Security in 1968 and the 1970 decision, following the report of the Seebohm Committee, to require local authorities to set up social service departments. The DHSS has not proved a success, but neither has its existence by itself led to increased expenditure.[40] The encouragement of greater involvement by local government in social services did lead to the appointment of more social workers, but with a modest effect on spending. In terms of programmes and benefits, pensions were improved considerably in 1959 and graduated contributions and benefits introduced in 1961, redundancy payments were begun in 1965 and earnings-related supplements for unemployment and sickness instituted in 1966. Conservative improvements in pensions had been adopted primarily to forestall a more thorough-going scheme adopted by the Labour party in 1957. During the 1960s it became obvious even to Conservatives and to private insurers that the minimum pensions provided by the state were becoming increasingly inadequate and that a more generous earnings-related system was needed. A revised Labour plan (SERPS) was finally announced in 1969 and embodied in legislation in 1975, coming into operation in 1978. There were also changes in the form taken by certain programmes: supplementary benefit, for example, replaced national assistance in 1966 and child benefit replaced family allowances in 1977. The sums involved in the changes were modest, however. More serious initiatives were undertaken in education. Real spending on education tripled between 1950 and 1980; there was a major expansion of higher education, especially after the Robbins Report of 1963; and secondary education was transformed by the move to comprehensives begun in 1965. Housing policy varied over the years and spending fluctuated considerably, but the share of public spending devoted to housing stood at precisely the same level in 1978 as it had in 1951. Regional policy was more costly and arguably the most successful part of the state's effort to engineer growth, but its contribution to the long-term growth in public expenditure was not especially significant. Major innovations were therefore far less frequent than the often intense discourse over social policy might have suggested. The Labour party's two periods in office were particularly notable for the rhetorical attention given to questions of poverty and equality. Labour's stance as the party of reform, moreover, did allow a number of important issues to get onto the political agenda – like equal pay, race relations and the broader "rediscovery" of poverty symbolized by the founding in 1965 of the Child Poverty Action Group – and the Labour government provided an opportunity for the liberalization of the laws on homosexuality, abortion and divorce. Still, the opening up of political discourse did not regularly translate into public programmes and so was not directly reflected in the rise in public expenditure.[41]

What then caused the growth of spending? A critical factor was demographic change. The need for collective provision is obviously greatest for the very young and the very old. "The peculiar position that Britain has been in for much of the period since the Second World War," according to one authority, "is that *both* the size of the *elderly* population and the *younger* population has grown." The right to claim benefits has also spread across the "at risk" population. Some growth can be attributed as well to the "relative price effect" by which the cost of social services increases more than the cost of other goods and services. Put slightly differently, it has been very hard to increase productivity in the delivery of services. Most of the growth in social expenditure, however, has been due to increased benefit levels. At times this has occurred through linking benefits to prices or to earnings, at times through more generous provision. Sickness and unemployment benefits were tied to earnings as of 1966; national insurance contributions and pension benefits were linked to prices and earnings from 1974. This ensured that these benefits rose along with, or even faster than, inflation. But other benefits were also raised accordingly: the relative value of unemployment benefits, pensions, supplementary benefit and child support all roughly doubled from the early 1950s through 1980. The increase in value, moreover, was extremely steady and occurred under both parties, at least until 1979.[42]

The lack of a connection between the party in power and the growth of social service spending points to a more general absence of political control over expenditure. What seems to have happened from the late 1950s to the late 1970s is that the traditional constraints on state activity ceased to work, allowing demographic pressure, changing definitions of need and the short-term preferences of politicians to push up expenditure. Budgetary constraints were loosened very broadly by the triumph of Keynesian thinking, which reduced the fear of deficits, and more specifically by inflation. Inflation drove revenues inexorably upwards, even while successive Chancellors claimed to be offering voters tax reductions. The politics of taxation became therefore less iron-clad in its workings. The Conservative party was particularly affected, for by 1955–6 the Conservatives had come to terms with the broad outlines of the postwar welfare state and by roughly 1958 opted for growth over economy. The party maintained its rhetorical attachment to reducing taxes, of course, but lacked the persistent incentive and, after 1964, the opportunity to deliver on its promises. During the 1960s the party's attitude towards tax policy was distinctly moderate and instrumental, and the banner of resistance to taxation had to be taken up by fringe groups like the Institute of Economic Affairs.[43] Eventually, the anti-tax sentiments aroused by a decade and a half of inflation and the apparently uncontrolled growth in taxation would flow back into Conservative channels and help to revive the party's fortunes after 1975. Prior to that, the new and less constraining politics of taxation would allow spending to increase.

The other traditional constraint on spending, the bureaucratic power of the Treasury, was also less effective after 1958. The Treasury had been restored to its position at the centre of the government machine by the early 1950s, but it had not recovered its ability to control spending. It made valiant efforts to do so – launching repeated reviews of public spending during the 1950s – but the mechanism ultimately put in place to limit the growth of expenditure, PESC, proved inadequate to the task. The theory behind the system was that spending could be reduced by forward planning, but because the planning was linked to existing programmes and to the changing demand for services, it led in practice to steady expansion. The Treasury's ability to restrict government growth was further hampered by criticisms, reorganizations and the setting up of rival agencies. The establishment first of Neddy, then of the Department of Economic Affairs, the appointment of the Fulton Committee followed by the creation of the Civil Service Department, all served to put the Treasury on the defensive throughout the 1960s. Pressed to defend itself, the Treasury did very well and ultimately prevailed over its bureaucratic rivals and political critics. But it was not in a position strong enough to oversee the effective control of public spending.

Nor was the Treasury restored to power with the advent of the Conservatives in 1970. Heath's innovations at the centre of government – the establishment of CPRS and of the policy of Programme Analysis and Review (PAR) – were regarded as further infringements on the authority of the Treasury, and the government's subsequent defeat at the hands of the miners was deeply demoralizing to officials. Wilson's creation of the Downing Street Policy Unit provided ministers with yet another source of policy advice, and hence a greater ability to overrule the Treasury, and the English Committee provided one more occasion for a public bashing of the Treasury and the civil service. The Treasury only began to regain its influence in 1975-6, when PESC was abandoned in favour of "cash limits" and a reformed Cabinet procedure designed to make it more difficult for ministers or officials from spending departments to prevail over the Treasury. The Treasury's position was reinforced by the IMF's pressure for reductions in expenditure and in taxation. Still, even after 1976 the Prime Minister refused to concede to the Treasury the primary role for shaping the government's economic strategy or its spending decisions. Callaghan involved the entire Cabinet in his bargaining with the IMF and afterwards relied upon an unofficial group known as the "Economic Seminar" to discuss economic policy. The Economic Seminar consisted of Callaghan, Healey, Harold Lever, a representative of the Bank of England and a small number of officials. The Treasury were not left out, but were scarcely dominant. Prior to the election of Mrs Thatcher, therefore, the restoration of the traditional constraints upon the expansion of the state was incomplete. From 1976, taxes and expenditure had begun to be brought under control, James Callaghan had already in 1976 told the Labour party that the terms of the postwar settlement had changed, and even before the triumph of monetarism Labour had begun setting strict targets for monetary growth. Only after 1979, however, would the process of government growth be set in reverse.[44]

Stopping and reversing the expansion of the state was the main task that the Conservatives set for themselves during the 1980s. The seriousness with which Mrs Thatcher and her fellow ministers approached the issue of the state was often missed, for there were so many peculiar characteristics of the "Thatcher revolution" that captured public and scholarly attention.[45] But what is most distinctive historically about the Conservatives under Thatcher was their obsession with the state and with the institutional bases of power and policy. They displayed a particularly intense desire to limit the size and restructure the shape of the state itself, to reduce the extent to which government was held responsible for the economic and social welfare of its citizens, to diminish the capacity of the state to undertake or to avoid that responsibility and to eliminate those state institutions and policies that had provided support for Labour. In this they showed keen insight into recent politics and an intuitive understanding of the process by which the very structure of the state shapes politics: creating expectations and opportunities for placing demands upon government, opening or limiting the arena for political mobilization, offering or withdrawing the political recognition of interests that is so essential to their existence and successful mobilization.

The concern of 1980s Conservatism with political institutions, especially the institutions of the state, did not go unnoticed, but it was not accorded sufficient emphasis by those seeking to understand "Thatcherism." Two facts in particular served to obscure the centrality of structural reform in the

Conservative project. The most awkward fact was the Conservatives" inability to reduce taxes and expenditure for a considerable period. The government's first budget did lower income tax, but sharply increased VAT and added substantially to the overall tax burden. The rise in unemployment in the early 1980s, coupled with the need to meet commitments made by previous governments, also meant that expenditure would not quickly be reduced. The record of the Thatcher government on taxes and expenditure, therefore, did not for some time reflect accurately its determination to shrink the boundaries of the state. It was only in the late 1980s that expenditure totals began to reveal the long-term impact of restraint and it was really only in the run-up to the 1987 election that the Conservatives" commitment to reducing taxes was convincingly reaffirmed with the cutting of income tax to 25p. Also helping to mask the Conservatives" antipathy to the interventionist state was their desire, and willingness, to augment the state's repressive capabilities. The only group of public employees whose numbers grew and whose pay and conditions improved under Thatcher was the police. The concern with leaks and secrecy, the promise of a restoration of "law and order," the tough talk of placing a "barrier of steel" across the permissive path leading to "social disintegration and decay," the disdain for civil rights displayed in the government's treatment of the Irish, and the readiness to deploy thousands of police for months on end to crush the miners did not suggest a party or a leadership reluctant to make use of the state's powers of control. Nor did the centralizing effects of so many of Thatcher's policies betoken a concern to avoid the concentration of power at the centre.[46]

Neither the delay in getting spending and taxes under control nor the Conservatives" fondness for the "despotic powers" wielded by the state should be allowed, however, to mask the Tories" desire to reverse the secular growth of government since the late 1950s, to restore and even strengthen the traditional budgetary, political and bureaucratic constraints upon state activity, and to alter the framework of policy-making by diminishing the state's "infrastructural powers."[47] That desire inspired a wide range of initiatives – too wide to survey or even to inventory. The following partial list of initiatives undertaken between 1979 and 1990 – each of them aimed at recasting the institutional underpinnings and the routine workings of the political system – should suffice, however, to indicate the central thrust of Conservative policy.

Perhaps the most striking feature of the behaviour of the Thatcher governments was their amazing and steadfast refusal actively to stimulate the economy. The Conservatives" early monetarism may well have been discarded, but their willingness to tolerate mass unemployment was constant. The Thatcher regime was, in fact, bent on convincing the public that the state could do very little to create jobs and that it bore no responsibility even to try. It sought both to insulate the state from economic failure and to redefine economic success so that it might coexist with massive unemployment.[48] Success on that narrowed basis was, of course, much more easily achieved, and

Thatcher's re-election campaign in 1987 was premised upon the claim to have produced significant economic growth. But the modest growth of the period after 1982 did nothing to reverse the decimation of Britain's manufacturing base, to eliminate the by now structural unemployment of a large section of the population or to repair the devastation of the older industrial areas brought about by sustained economic decline.

Equally characteristic of Conservative rule in the 1980s was a series of repeated and sharp attacks on civil servants and public sector workers generally.[49] Even before coming to power, Mrs Thatcher and her supporters evinced an open antipathy towards those who ran or staffed the allegedly bloated state machine. Upon taking office, the government was forced to acquiesce in the terms of the Clegg award and thus to give substantial wage increases to the civil service. From then on, however, the government turned sharply against any further increases to public sector workers; and they showed themselves willing to take on civil servants in strikes long before they found the fortitude to confront the miners. The principle of setting civil servants" pay by comparison with those outside government service was therefore soon abandoned, provoking the bitter dispute of 1981, and, in the same year, the Civil Service Department was abolished because it was perceived as being too sympathetic to the claims and interests of public sector workers.

Simultaneously, the government sought to put in place at the higher reaches of the bureaucracy a team of officials more fully committed to carrying out Tory policies. The outcome was a wave of retirements that allowed Mrs Thatcher to appoint an unusually large number of Permanent Secretaries and to begin to remake the top of the civil service in the image of 1980s Conservatism. No less than forty-three Permanent Secretaries and 138 Deputy Secretaries left and were replaced between 1979 and 1985. The government also undertook a series of inquiries and initiatives designed to make the bureaucracy smaller and more efficient. These included the reduction in the number of civil servants from 732,000 to approximately 600,000 between 1979 and 1987; the attempt by Lord Rayner to introduce business methods into government; the Financial Management Initiative (FMI) of 1982; and the extremely radical proposals for the decentralization and privatization of government itself contained in Sir Robin Ibbs" 1987 report, *The Next Steps*. Taming, demoralizing and shrinking the state apparatus was thus a top priority in the Conservative programme throughout the 1980s. Whatever its long-term effect might be, in the short run it produced a definite restoration of old-fashioned "Treasury control" throughout the bureaucracy, but with an added political edge.[50]

The government's policies of "privatization" represented a third, and especially critical, step in the attempted restructuring of state–society relations. "Privatization" operated at several levels. At its most mundane, "privatization" was a strategy for saving money by sub-contracting out various government services. More important politically were efforts to sell off council housing to former tenants, for this was intended to weaken the historic allegiance of many working people to Labour and to attach them to the Conservatives. More significant institutionally than either of these strategies, however, was the policy of selling off the most valuable properties held by the state – from British Telecom to Rover to the gas and water authorities. The stated goals behind these sales were to further the creation of a property-owning democracy by encouraging wider share ownership and to induce greater efficiency through increased competition. Among the unstated goals were undoubtedly the prospect of providing some quick profits to Tory (or would-be Tory) investors and, probably most important, restricting the scope and effectiveness of future government intervention in the economy. Public ownership in the aerospace and telecommunications fields, together with the state's role as an oil producer and exporter, could have provided the British government with powerful levers for influencing the shape of industrial development, but the Thatcher administration pre-emptively gave away any such potential.[51]

The attack upon the autonomy and financing of local government constituted perhaps the most daring attempt by the Conservative governments of the 1980s to reshape the institutional bases of politics. Though legal sovereignty has always resided at the centre, local democracy was until recently no mere fiction in British politics. Local government, however, was more likely in the 1970s and 1980s to be dominated by Labour, especially in urban areas. Indeed, throughout the period of Conservative hegemony what political strength Labour retained was based largely on its role in local government. This did not please Conservatives or endear them to local democracy; and instead provoked a series of measures designed to curtail the prerogatives of local governments in setting rates and in determining the level of services offered. The attack on local government achieved its greatest triumph with the abolition in 1986 of the Greater London Council, Labour's most notorious site of local power. Subsequent proposals to restructure education, eliminating in particular London's education authority (ILEA), proved more controversial. The most notable failure, however, was over the poll tax. The plan to replace local rates with a poll tax, the euphemistically termed "community charge," provoked large-scale opposition in the spring of 1990, led to huge Conservative losses in local elections and was largely responsible for Mrs Thatcher's downfall.

These policies towards economic management, the civil service, privatization and local government represent only a selection from a large number of initiatives aimed at dismantling or restructuring the state, but they should suffice to convey the importance the effort held within the broader programme of "Thatcherism." It suggests, too, that these attacks upon the state represented more than an effort to save money. In theoretical terms, it would seem that they were intended to help resolve that dilemma which regularly confronts proponents of the market in democratic politics. As the political philosopher Brian Barry has argued, "the workings of the market are not in fact conducive to the well-being of the majority;" hence "any government concerned with re-election finds itself intervening, whatever its official doctrine, to cushion people from the effects of unconstrained market forces." In consequence, politicians like Thatcher, "whose primary commitment is to the market," tend to "look on the democratic state . . . with antipathy. The political problem facing that person," Barry goes on, "is how to get democratic approval for tying the hands of elected government in perpetuity." [52] The political benefit to be gained from such efforts is that, if the structure and capacity of the state are diminished and the political culture that controls the agenda of politics narrowed, it becomes possible to prevent the implementation, possibly even the discussion, of interventionist policies even when pro-market forces are not in power.

What distinguished the Thatcher regime from previous Conservative governments, then, was its exceptionally clear understanding of this dilemma and its determination to resolve it. For a brief while, in fact, the Tories appeared willing to court electoral defeat to accomplish it. Historically, then, the truly interesting question is what lay behind the emergence of a style of Conservatism marked by such an intense concern with the structures of politics and, more precisely, by such an unrelieved antipathy towards the interventionist state. The argument suggested here is that the critical factor must be the dramatic transformation that occurred in the pattern of state expansion over the course of the twentieth century. The behaviour and beliefs of Conservatives during the late 1970s and 1980s can be understood as a not totally unreasoned response to a genuine change in the workings of British politics, a change that made the expansion of the state a normal, rather than an exceptional, political outcome. The transformation can be glimpsed most clearly in the contrast between the politics of government growth before and after the Second World War and located with some precision in the late 1950s. Before 1939, Conservatives could rely on the routine functioning of politics to limit the sphere of state activity and to restrict the state's revenues. That situation produced a complacency towards the state among British Conservatives which lasted until quite recently and which was reflected in their qualified acceptance of commitments to the provision of social services and the maintenance of employment forced on the state during the 1940s and in the corporatist practices of Conservatives from Butler to Heath. Some time after 1955, the routine functioning of politics began to change, and the inertial forces of politics combined to produce a steady expansion of the state's role in the economy and society. This *de facto* shift in the "rules of the game" ultimately called into question both the reigning style of Conservatism and the legitimacy of the rules themselves. Thatcherism, in this perspective, can be understood as a manifestation of resurgent Tory liberalism with very deep roots, but with an urgent contemporary programme of redefining the rules of politics yet again in order to break the new pattern of secular state expansion and to return to a situation in which state growth was the exception and limited public responsibility the norm. It was an ambitious project of dubious merit and one whose outcome will not be clear for a very long time.

Notes

1 INTRODUCTION: THE POLITICS OF STATE EXPANSION IN TWENTIETH-CENTURY BRITAIN

1 Jan Pen, "Expanding Budgets in a Stagnating Economy: The Experience of the 1970s," in Charles S. Maier, ed., *The Changing Boundaries of the Political: Essays on the Evolving Balance between the State and Society, Public and Private in Europe* (Cambridge: Cambridge University Press, 1987), 323–61.

2 The best summaries of social and economic policy build extensively on this monographic research. See Pat Thane, *The Foundations of the Welfare State* (London: Longman, 1983); Bentley B. Gilbert, *The Evolution of National Insurance in Britain* (London: Michael Joseph, 1966), and *British Social Policy, 1914–1939* (London: Batsford, 1970); Derek Fraser, *The Evolution of the British Welfare State* (London: Macmillan, 1973); and Hugh Heclo, *Modern Social Politics in Britain and Sweden* (New Haven: Yale University Press, 1974); as well as the essays by Thane, "Government and Society in England and Wales, 1750–1914," and by José Harris, "Society and the State in Twentieth-Century Britain," in F.M.L. Thompson, ed., *The Cambridge Social History of Britain*, Vol. III: *Social Agencies and Institutions* (Cambridge: Cambridge University Press, 1990), 1–61 and 63–117. On economic policy, see Jim Tomlinson, *Public Policy and the Economy since 1900* (Oxford: Clarendon, 1990); and Alan Booth, *British Economic Policy, 1931–1949* (London: Harvester Wheatsheaf, 1989). For attempts to review economic and social policy together, see George Peden, *British Economic and Social Policy: Lloyd George to Margaret Thatcher* (Oxford: Philip Allan, 1985); and S.G. Checkland, *British Public Policy, 1776–1939* (Cambridge: Cambridge University Press, 1983).

3 The data summarized in this and the following paragraph come primarily from Alan Peacock and Jack Wiseman, *The Growth of Public Expenditure in the United Kingdom* (Princeton: Princeton University Press, 1961).

4 W.H. Greenleaf, *The British Political Tradition*, I: *The Rise of Collectivism* (London: Methuen, 1983); and Moses Abramovitz and Vera Eliasberg, *The Growth in Public Employment in Great Britain* (Princeton: Princeton University Press, 1957).

5 W. McNeill, *The Pursuit of Power* (Chicago: University of Chicago Press, 1982); D. French, *British Economic and Strategic Planning, 1905–15* (London: Allen & Unwin, 1982); P. Kennedy, "Strategy versus Finance in Twentieth-Century Britain," *International History Review*, III (1981), 44–61; J.T. Sumida, *In Defence of Naval Supremacy: Financial Limitation, Technological Innovation and British Naval Policy, 1899–1914* (London: Unwin Hyman, 1989); and Aaron Friedberg, *The Weary Titan: Britain and the Experience of Relative Decline, 1895–1905* (Princeton: Princeton University Press, 1988).

6 See P. Dunleavy, "Bureaucrats, Budgets and the Growth of the State," *British Journal of Political Science*, XV (1985), 299–328 for a useful critique.

7 Peacock and Wiseman, *The Growth of Public Expenditure in the United Kingdom*; S. Krasner, "Approaches to the State: Alternative Conceptualizations and Historical Dynamics," *Comparative Politics*, XVI (1984), 223–46; and J. Dryzek and R. Goodin, "Risk-Sharing and Social Justice: The Motivational Foundations of the Post-War Welfare State," *British Journal of Political Science*, XVI (1986), 1–34.

8 On this point more generally, see Charles Tilly, *Coercion, Capital and European States, A.D. 990–1990* (Oxford: Basil Blackwell, 1990).

9 Michael Shalev, "The Social Democratic Model and Beyond: Two 'Generations' of Comparative Research on the Welfare State," *Comparative Social Research*, VI (1983), 315–51; R. Klein, "Public Expenditure in an Inflationary World," in L. Lindberg and C. Maier, *The Politics of Inflation and Economic Stagnation*, (Washington, DC: Brookings Institution, 1985), 196–223; P.D. Larkey *et al.*, "Theorizing about the Growth of Government," *Journal of Public Policy*, I (1981), 157–220; T.H. Marshall, *Citizenship and Social Class* (Cambridge: Cambridge University Press, 1950) and M. Freeden, "The Stranger at the Feast: Ideology and Public Policy in Twentieth-Century Britain," *Twentieth Century British History*, I, 1 (1990), 9–34.

10 The neglect of taxation by scholars has recently begun to be remedied. See, for example, Carolyn Webber and Aaron Wildavsky, *A History of Taxation and Expenditure in the Western World* (New York: Simon & Schuster, 1986); Margaret Levi, *Of Rule and Revenue* (Berkeley: University of California Press, 1988); James Alt, "The Evolution of Tax Structures," *Public Choice*, 41 (1983), 181–222; D. Tarchys, "Tributes, Taxes, Tariffs and Trade: The Changing Sources of Government Revenue," *British Journal of Political Science*, XVIII, 1 (1988), 1–20; and John Brewer, *The Sinews of Power: War, Money and the English State, 1688–1783* (New York: Knopf, 1989).

11 G. Sutherland, *Studies in the Growth of Nineteenth Century Government* (London: Routledge, 1972).

12 On state capacity, see P. Evans, D. Rueschemeyer and T. Skocpol, eds, *Bringing the State Back In* (Cambridge: Cambridge University Press, 1985).

13 Brewer, *Sinews of Power*, chapters 4 and 7.

14 The phrase "tax state" comes from Joseph Schumpeter, "The Crisis of the Tax State," (1919), reprinted in Alan Peacock *et al.*, eds, *International Economic Papers* (New York: Macmillan, 1954). On progressivity, see F. Shehab, *Progressive Taxation* (Oxford: Clarendon, 1953).

15 G. Ingham, *Capitalism Divided? The City and Industry in British Social Development* (New York: Schocken, 1984); Frank Longstreth, "The City, Industry and the State," in C. Crouch, ed., *State and Economy in Contemporary Capitalism* (London: Croom Helm, 1979), and "State Economic Planning in a Capitalist Society: The Political Sociology of Economic Policy in Britain, 1940–1979," Ph.D Thesis, London School of Economics, 1983; P. Thane and J. Harris, "British and European Bankers: "an aristocratic bourgeoisie"?" in Thane, G. Crossick and R. Floud, eds, *The Power of the Past: Essays for Eric Hobsbawm* (Cambridge: Cambridge University Press, 1984), 215–34; S.G. Checkland, "The Mind of the City, 1870–1914," *Oxford Economic Papers*, n.s. IX (1957), 261–78; Y. Cassis, "Bankers in English Society in the late Nineteenth Century," *Economic History Review*, XXXVIII (1985), 210–29; M. de Cecco, *Money and Empire: The International Gold Standard* (Oxford: Basil Blackwell, 1974); D. Nicholls, "Fractions of Capital: The Aristocracy,

the City and Industry in the Development of Modern British Capitalism," *Social History*, XIII, 1 (1988), 71–83; and R. Pahl, "New Rich, Old Rich, Stinking Rich," *Social History*, XV, 2 (May, 1990), 229–39.

16 W.D. Rubinstein, "Wealth, Elites and the Class Structure of Modern Britain," *Past and Present*, 76 (1977).

17 Nigel Harris, *Competition and the Corporate Society: British Conservatives, the State and Industry, 1945–1964* (London: Methuen, 1972); and W.H. Greenleaf, *The British Political Tradition*, II: *The Ideological Heritage*.

18 K.O. Morgan, *Consensus and Disunity: The Lloyd George Coalition Government, 1918–1922* (Oxford: Oxford University Press, 1979); M. Pugh, *The Tories and the People, 1880–1935* (Oxford: Basil Blackwell, 1985); and J.A. Ramsden, *The Age of Balfour and Baldwin* (London: Longman, 1978).

19 C. Bellamy, *Administering Central-Local Relations, 1871–1919: The Local Government Board in its Fiscal and Cultural Context* (Manchester: Manchester University Press, 1988); Avner Offer, *Property and Politics, 1870–1914* (Cambridge: Cambridge University Press, 1981); K. Young, *Local Politics and the Rise of Party: The London Municipal Society and the Conservative Intervention in Local Elections, 1894–1963* (Leicester: Leicester University Press, 1975).

20 Harold Macmillan to Michael Fraser, 17 October 1957, cited in Alistair Horne, *Harold Macmillan* Vol. II: *1957–1986* (New York: Viking, 1989), 62.

21 Henry Roseveare, *The Treasury: The Evolution of a British Institution* (New York: Columbia University Press, 1969); R. Chapman and J. Greenaway, *The Dynamics of Administrative Reform* (London: Croom Helm, 1980).

22 P. Fraser, "The Impact of the War of 1914–18 on the British Political System," in M. Foot, ed., *War and Society* (New York: Barnes & Noble, 1973), 123–39; John Turner, "British Politics and the Great War," in Turner, ed., *Britain and the First World War* (London: Unwin Hyman, 1988), 117–38; and Kathleen Burk, ed., *War and the State* (London: Allen & Unwin, 1982).

23 See A. Calder, *The People's War* (London: Jonathan Cape, 1969); 'Cato," *Guilty Men* (New York: F.A. Stokes, 1940); G.D.H. Cole, "Reconstruction in the Civil and Municipal Services," *Public Administration*, XX (1942); Sixteenth Report from the Select Committee on National Expenditure, Session 1941–2: Organization and Control of the Civil Service, *Parliamentary Papers* (1941–42) III; and R. Lowe & R. Roberts, "Sir Horace Wilson, 1900–1935: The Making of a Mandarin," *Historical Journal*, XXX, 3, (1987), 641–66; and J.P. Mallalieu, *Passed to You, Please: Britain's Red-Tape Machine at War* (London: Gollancz, 1942), Introduction by Harold Laski.

24 PEP (Political and Economic Planning) (1941), "The Machinery of Government," *Planning*, 173, 15 July 1941.

25 Paul Addison, "The Road from 1945," in Peter Hennessy and Anthony Seldon, eds, *Ruling Performance: British Governments from Attlee to Thatcher* (Oxford: Basil Blackwell, 1987), 5–6; Ben Pimlott, "The Myth of Consensus," in L.M. Smith, ed., *The Making of Britain: Echoes of Greatness* (London: Macmillan, 1988); D. Kavanagh and P. Morris, *Consensus Politics from Attlee to Thatcher* (Oxford: Basil Blackwell, 1989), Kenneth Morgan, *The People's Peace: British History, 1945–1989* (Oxford: Oxford University Press, 1990) 3–28; and Rodney Lowe, "The Second World War, Consensus, and the Foundations of the Welfare State," *Twentieth Century British History*, I 2 (1990), 152–82.

26 Booth, *British Economic Policy*; Jim Tomlinson, *Employment Policy: The Crucial Years, 1939–1955* (Oxford: Clarendon, 1987); Donald Winch, "Keynes, Keynesianism and State Intervention," in Peter Hall, ed., *The Political Power of Economic Ideas: Keynesianism across Nations* (Princeton: Princeton University Press, 1989),

107–27; and K. Schott, "The Rise of Keynesian Economics in Britain, 1940–1964," *Economy and Society*, XI (1982), 292–316.

27   R.C.O. Matthews, "Why Has Britain Had Full Employment since the War?" *Economic Journal*, LXXVIII (1968), 555–69.

28   As Karl Deutsch has argued, "the welfare state tends to expand the scope of government – that is, the ensemble of its tasks – relatively quickly by an order of magnitude, while increasing the capabilities of government much more slowly, if at all." See K. Deutsch, "The Crisis of the State," *Government and Opposition*, XVI, 3 (1981), 340.

29   Peter Hall, *Governing the Economy* (New York: Oxford University Press, 1986); Keith Middlemas, *Power, Competition and the State*, Vol. II: *Threats to the Postwar Settlement: Britain, 1960–1974* (London: Macmillan, 1990).

30   Samuel H. Beer, *Britain against Itself: The Political Contradictions of Collectivism* (New York: Norton, 1982).

2   THE VICTORIAN INHERITANCE

1   Neal Blewett, "The Franchise in the United Kingdom 1885–1918," *Past and Present*, 32, 27–56.

2   Joseph Chamberlain, "State Socialism and the Moderate Liberals," 28 April 1885, in C.W. Boyd, ed., *Mr. Chamberlain's Speeches*, Vol. I (London: Constable, 1914), 164.

3   By stressing the strength and legitimacy of the British state in the middle of the nineteenth century, we do not mean to suggest that the British state was particularly weak in earlier periods. In fact, recent work suggests that the British state was much stronger than traditional stereotypes and contrasts would imply. See, among others, John Brewer, *The Sinews of Power: War, Money and the English State, 1688–1783* (New York: Knopf, 1989); Michael Mann, *The Sources of Social Power*, Vol. I (Cambridge: Cambridge University Press, 1886), esp. chapter 14; Peter Mathias and Patrick O'Brien, "Taxation in Britain and France, 1715–1810," *Journal of European Economic History*, V (1976), 601–50; O'Brien, "The Political Economy of British Taxation, 1660–1815," *Economic History Review*, XLI, 1 (February, 1988), 1–32.

4   Pat Thane, "Government and Society in England and Wales, 1750–1914," in F.M.L. Thompson, ed., *The Cambridge Social History of Britain*, Vol. III: *Social Agencies and Institutions* (Cambridge: Cambridge University Press, 1990), 1–61; and S.G. Checkland, *British Public Policy, 1776–1939* (Cambridge: Cambridge University Press, 1983), 61–81.

5   Checkland, *British Public Policy*, 80.

6   G.K. Ingham, *Capitalism Divided? The City and Industry in British Social Development* (New York: Schocken, 1984), 102–16, 128–31.

7   Mathias and O'Brien, "Taxation in Britain and France," 611; O'Brien, "The Political Economy of British Taxation," 1–32; and Brewer, *Sinews of Power*.

8   Mann, *Sources of Social Power*, 483–95.

9   Income under £60 was exempt, while income between £60 and £200 was taxed at reduced rates. See B.E.V. Sabine, *A History of Income Tax* (London: Allen & Unwin, 1966), 29.

10   H.C.G. Matthew, "Introduction," *The Gladstone Diaries*, Vol. V: *1855–1860* (Oxford: Clarendon, 1978), xxxv.

11   Norman Gash, *Sir Robert Peel* (London: Longman, 1972), 304. The quote from Ashburton comes from Gash, 302.

12   Matthew, "Disraeli, Gladstone, and the Politics of Mid-Victorian Budgets," *Historical Journal*, XXII, 3 (1979), 615–43 esp. 630; Gladstone's speech to the House of Commons, 20 April 1855, cited in Matthew, *Gladstone Diaries*, xxxvii; Matthew, *Gladstone, 1809–1874* (Oxford: Clarendon, 1986), 127; B. Baysinger and R.

Tollison, "Chaining Leviathan: The Case of Gladstonian Finance," *History of Political Economy*, XII (1980), 206–13.

13 Meta Zimmeck, "Gladstone Holds His Own: The Origins of Income Tax Relief for Life Insurance Policies," *Bulletin of the Institute of Historical Research*, LVIII, 138 (November, 1985), 167–88.

14 Entry for 14 February 1857, *Gladstone Diaries*, 197; Sabine, *History of Income Tax*, 112.

15 Boyd Hilton, *Corn, Cash and Commerce: The Economic Policies of the Tory Governments, 1815-1830* (Oxford: Oxford University Press, 1977); Peter Mandler, "The Making of the New Poor Law Redivivus," *Past and Present*, 117 (November, 1987), 131–57; M.E. Rose, *The English Poor Law, 1780-1930* (Newton Abbot: David & Charles, 1971); M.A. Crowther, *The Workhouse System, 1834-1929* (Athens, GA: University of Georgia Press, 1981); and Peter Dunkley, *The Crisis of the Old Poor Law in England* (New York: Garland, 1982).

16 Gladstone to Lord John Russell, January, 1854, cited in Henry Roseveare, *The Treasury: The Evolution of a British Institution* (New York: Columbia University Press, 1969), 170; Peter Gowan, "The Origins of the Administrative Elite," *New Left Review*, 162 (March-April, 1987), 434; Noel Annan, "The Intellectual Aristocracy," in J.H. Plumb, ed., *Studies in Social History* (London: Longmans, Green, 1955), 241–87; and G. R. Searle, *The Quest for National Efficiency* (Oxford: Basil Blackwell, 1971), 22–3. On the minimal changes since 1900, see K. Theakston and G. Fry, "Britain's Administrative Elite: Permanent Secretaries, 1900-1986," *Public Administration*, LXVII (1989), 129–47.

17 José Harris, "The Transition to High Politics in English Social Policy," in M. Bentley and J. Stevenson, eds, *High and Low Politics in Modern Britain* (Oxford: Clarendon, 1983), 59.

18 Charles Tilly, "Britain Creates the Social Movement," in J. Cronin and J. Schneer, eds, *Social Conflict and the Political Order in Modern Britain* (New Brunswick: Rutgers University Press, 1982), 21–51; Brian Brown, "Industrial Capitalism, Conflict and Working Class Contention in Lancashire, 1842," in Charles and Louise Tilly, eds, *Class Conflict and Collective Action* (Beverly Hills: Sage, 1981); Gareth Stedman Jones, "Rethinking Chartism," in *Languages of Class* (Cambridge: Cambridge University Press, 1983), 90–178; John Saville, *The British State and the Chartist Movement* (Cambridge: Cambridge University Press, 1987); Richard Price, *Labour in British Society* (London: Croom Helm, 1986), 71–93; Neville Kirk, *The Growth of Working Class Reformism in Mid-Victorian England* (Urbana: University of Illinois Press, 1985); and Eugenio Biagini, "British Trade Unions and Popular Political Economy, 1860-1880," *Historical Journal*, XXX, 4 (1987), 811–40.

19 Price, *Labour in British Society*, 83–4.

20 Joan Scott, "On Language, Gender and Working-Class History," *International Labor and Working Class History*, 31 (Spring, 1987), 1–13; and Carol Pateman, "The Patriarchal Welfare State," in Amy Gutmann, ed., *Democracy and the Welfare State* (Princeton: Princeton University Press, 1988). On the state's economic interest in enforcing certain definitions of the family and of women's place in it, see M.A. Crowther, "Family Responsibility and State Responsibility in Britain before the Welfare State," *Historical Journal*, XXV (1989), 131–45.

21 Paul Johnson, *Saving and Spending: The Working-Class Economy in Britain, 1870-1939* (Oxford: Clarendon, 1985).

22 Price, *Labour in British Society*, chapter 4.

23 J. Cronin, "Strikes and the Struggle for Union Organization: Britain and Europe," in W. J. Mommsen and H.-G. Husung, eds, *The Development of Trade Unions in Great Britain and Germany, 1880-1914* (London: Allen & Unwin, 1985), 55–77; E.

H. Hunt, *British Labour History, 1815-1914* (London: Heinemann, 1981), 304–15.

24 See Price, *Labour in British Society*, chapter 6 on the resulting openness of political debate within the labour movement down to 1914.

25 W.L. Burn, *The Age of Equipoise* (New York: Norton, 1965), 289.

26 See Peter Weiler, *The New Liberalism: Liberal Social Theory in Great Britain, 1889-1914* (New York: Garland, 1982); Stefan Collini, *Liberalism and Sociology: L.T. Hobhouse and Political Argument in England, 1880-1915* (Cambridge: Cambridge University Press, 1979); Michael Freeden, *The New Liberalism: An Ideology of Social Reform* (Oxford: Oxford University Press, 1978); P.F. Clarke, *Liberals and Social Democrats* (Cambridge: Cambridge University Press, 1978); Greenleaf, *British Political Tradition*, Vol. II (London: Methuen, 1983), 124–41; and David Sutton, "Liberalism, State Collectivism and the Social Relations of Citizenship," in Mary Langan and Bill Schwarz, eds, *Crises in the British State, 1880-1930* (London: Hutchinson, 1985), 63–79.

27 José Harris, "Society and the state in twentieth-century Britain," in Thompson, *Cambridge Social History of Britain*, III, 69.

28 Ingham, *Capitalism Divided?*, chapters 5–6.

29 P.J. Cain and A.G. Hopkins, "Gentlemanly Capitalism and British Expansion Overseas, II: New Imperialism, 1850-1945," *Economic History Review*, XL (1987), 1–26. Cf. also M. J. Daunton, "'Gentlemanly Capitalism' and British Industry, 1820–1914," *Past and Present*, 122 (February, 1989), 119–158.

30 Moses Abramovitz and Vera Eliasberg, *The Growth of Public Employment in Great Britain* (Princeton: Princeton University Press, 1957), 8–18; Lance Davis and Robert Huttenback, *Mammon and the Pursuit of Empire: The Political Economy of British Imperialism, 1860-1912* (Cambridge: Cambridge University Press, 1986), 7–24, 145–65; Ann Burton, "Treasury Control and Colonial Policy in the Late Nineteenth Century," *Public Administration*, XLVI (1966), 169–92; P. O'Brien, "The Costs and Benefits of British Imperialism, 1846-1914," *Past and Present*, 120 (August, 1988), 163–200; and Peacock and Wiseman, *Growth of Public Expenditure*, 37, 47.

31 Matthew, "Disraeli, Gladstone, and Budgets," 615–43; Olive Anderson, *A Liberal State At War: English Politics and Economics during the Crimean War* (New York: St Martin's, 1967), 190–216; PRO, T172/954, memo by J.S. Bradbury on "The Financing of Naval and Military Operations, 1793-1886," 12 February 1900.

32 Salisbury, quoted in Robert Taylor, *Lord Salisbury* (London: Allen Lane, 1975), 16; *The Radical Programme* (London: Chapman & Hall, 1885), 220; David Brooks, ed., *The Destruction of Lord Rosebery: From the Diary of Sir Edward Hamilton, 1894-1895* (London: Historians' Press, 1986), 13–42; and F. Shehab, *Progressive Taxation* (Oxford: Clarendon, 1953), 189–209.

33 Harcourt and Asquith quoted in H.V. Emy, "The Impact of Financial Policy on English Politics before 1914," *Historical Journal*, XV, 1 (1972), 109, 119; J.W. Mason, "Political Economy and the Response to Socialism in Britain, 1870-1914," *Historical Journal*, XXIII (1980), 565–587; and Sabine, *History of Income Tax*.

34 A.R. McBriar, *An Edwardian Mixed Doubles: The Bosanquets versus the Webbs* (Oxford: Clarendon, 1987), 48–50; Michael Barker, *Gladstone and Radicalism* (Brighton: Harvester, 1975), esp. 154–164; Peter Gourevitch, *Politics in Hard Times* (Ithaca: Cornell University Press, 1986), chapter 3; Donald Read, *England, 1868-1914: The Age of Urban Democracy* (London: Longman, 1979), 309–339, 355; H.J. Hanham, *Elections and Party Management* (London: Longman, 1959); John Vincent and A. B. Cooke, *The Governing Passion: Cabinet Government and Party Politics in Britain, 1885-1886* (Brighton: Harvester, 1974), 3–23. Cf. also M. Ostrogorski's classic study, *Democracy and the*

Organization of Political Parties, Vol. I, *England* (1902, reprinted Chicago: Quadrangle, 1964).

35 John Davis, *Reforming London: The London Government Problem,1855-1900* (Oxford: Clarendon, 1988); Christine Bellamy, *Administering Central-Local Relations, 1871-1919: The Local Government Board in its Fiscal and Cultural Context* (Manchester: Manchester University Press, 1988); Douglas Ashford, *The Emergence of the Welfare States* (Oxford: Basil Blackwell, 1986), 121-32; N. McCord, "Ratepayers and Social Policy," in P. Thane, ed., *The Origins of British Social Policy* (London: Croom Helm, 1978), 21-35; Avner Offer, *Property and Politics, 1870-1914* (Cambridge: Cambridge University Press, 1981); K. Young, *Local Politics and the Rise of Party: The London Municipal Society and the Conservative Intervention in Local Elections, 1894-1963* (Leicester: Leicester University Press, 1975); and Susan Pennybacker, "'The millennium by return of post': Reconsidering London Progressivism," in David Feldman and Gareth Stedman Jones, eds, *Metropolis - London: Histories and Representations since 1800* (London: Routledge, 1989), 129-62.

36 Ivy Pinchbeck and Margaret Hewitt, *Children in English Society*, Vol. II (London: Routledge & Kegan Paul, 1973), 492-95.

37 Jill Pelew, "Law and Order: Expertise and the Victorian Home Office," in Roy MacLeod, ed., *Government and Expertise: Specialists, Administrators and Professionals, 1860-1919* (Cambridge: Cambridge University Press, 1988), 59-72; and, more generally, Pellew, *The Home Office, 1848-1914: From Clerks to Bureaucrats* (London: Heinemann, 1982); Checkland, *British Public Policy*, 136-37; Peter Bartrip, "Expertise and the Dangerous Trades, 1875-1900," in MacLeod, *Government and Expertise*, 89-109; and Mary Drake McFeely, *Lady Inspectors: The Campaign for a Better Workplace* (Oxford: Basil Blackwell, 1988).

38 Report of the Committee to consider the Position and Duties of the Board of Trade and the Local Government Board (the Jersey Committee), Cd. 2121, *British Parliamentary Papers*, lxxviii (1904); Roy MacLeod, *Treasury Control and Social Administration*, Occasional Papers on Social Administration, 23 (London: G. Bell, 1968), 43-7; Roger Davidson, *Whitehall and the Labour Problem in Late Victorian and Edwardian Britain* (London: Croom Helm, 1985); Rodney Lowe, "The Ministry of Labour, 1916-1924: A Graveyard of Social Reform?" *Public Administration*, LII (1974), 415-438; Davidson and Lowe, "Bureaucracy and Innovation in British Welfare Policy," in W. J. Mommsen, ed., *The Emergence of the Welfare State in Britain and Germany, 1850-1950* (London: Croom Helm, 1981), 263-295; John Turner, " 'Experts' and Interests: David Lloyd George and the Dilemmas of the Expanding State, 1906-1919," in MacLeod, *Government and Expertise*, 206-8; Hubert Llewellyn Smith, *The Board of Trade* (London: Putnam's, 1928); Vivien Hart, "Gendered in All But Name: The Minimum Wage in Britain," paper presented to the Social Science History Association, Minneapolis, Minnesota, October, 1990.

39 Bellamy, *Administering Central-Local Relations*, 235.

40 Bellamy, *Administering Central-Local Relations*, 12-15, 248-250, and more generally, chapter 4; Kathleen Woodroofe, "The Royal Commission on the Poor Laws, 1905-1909," *International Review of Social History*, XXII (1977), 137-64.

41 G.A.N. Lowndes, *The Silent Social Revolution* (Oxford: Oxford University Press, 1969), 64-74; Brian Simon, *Education and the Labour Movement, 1870-1920* (London: Lawrence & Wishart, 1965), 278-289; John Lawson and Harold Silver, *A Social History of Education in England* (London: Methuen, 1973), 370; and Andrew McDonald, "The Geddes Committee and the Formulation of Public Expenditure Policy, 1921-1922," *Historical Journal*, XXXII, 2 (1989), 643-74.

42 Gillian Sutherland, "Introduction," in *Studies in the Growth of Nineteenth-Century Government* (London: Routledge & Kegan Paul, 1972), 8.
43 Lord Bridges, *The Treasury* (London: Allen & Unwin, 1964), 23–7; Roseveare, *Treasury*, 138–42; Goschen to Reginald Welby, 1887, cited in Maurice Wright, "'Treasury Control, 1854–1914," in Sutherland, ed., *Studies in the Growth of Government*, 223. See also Sir Horace Hamilton, "Treasury Control in the Eighties," *Public Administration*, XXXIII (Spring, 1955).
44 Wright, "Treasury Control," 195–205; Richard Chapman and J.R. Greenaway, *The Dynamics of Administrative Reform* (London: Croom Helm, 1980), 58.
45 Wright, "Treasury Control," 200–3.
46 Lord Salisbury to Hicks-Beach, October, 1899, cited in Roseveare, *Treasury*, 184; *Hansard*, 78 (30 January 1900). See, more generally, Roseveare, *Treasury*, 183–6; and Peter Marsh, *The Discipline of Popular Government: Lord Salisbury's Domestic Statecraft, 1881–1902* (Brighton: Harvester, 1978), 290–301.
47 See T172/956 on "The Reorganization of the Treasury, 1903–4;" and also the 1905 discussion on Treasury control in T160/373/F2879/1.
48 W.S. Hamer, *The British Army: Civil–Military Relations, 1885–1905* (Oxford: Clarendon, 1970), 246–52.

3 LABOUR AND THE DEMAND FOR STATE EXPANSION: 1890–1918

1 See Michael Shalev, "The Social Democratic Model and Beyond: Two Generations of Comparative Research on the Welfare State," *Comparative Social Research*, VI (1983), 315–51; John Stephens, *The Transition from Capitalism to Socialism* (London: Macmillan, 1979); and Gøsta Esping-Anderson, *Politics Against Markets* (Princeton: Princeton University Press, 1985). For critiques, see Peter Baldwin, *The Politics of Social Solidarity* (Cambridge: Cambridge University Press, 1990); and Fred Pampel and John Williamson, *Age, Class, Politics and the Welfare State* (Cambridge: Cambridge University Press, 1989).
2 Henry Pelling, "The Working Class and the Welfare State," in *Popular Politics and Society in Victorian Britain* (London: Macmillan, 1968) represents the beginning of the debate. There is at present no end in sight, but see below for more recent contributions.
3 Gareth Stedman Jones, *Outcast London* (Oxford: Oxford University Press, 1971); A.M. McBriar, *An Edwardian Mixed Doubles: The Bosanquets versus the Webbs* (Oxford: Clarendon, 1987); Report of the Select Committee on National Provident Insurance, *Parliamentary Papers* (1887), XI; Charles Booth, "Enumeration and Classification of Paupers, and State Pensions for the Aged," *Journal of the Royal Statistical Society*, LIV (December, 1891), 600–43; Bentley B. Gilbert, *The Evolution of National Insurance in Great Britain* (London: Michael Joseph, 1966), 180; Pat Thane, "Contributory versus Non-Contributory Old Age Pensions, 1878–1908," in Thane, ed., *The Origins of British Social Policy* (London: Croom Helm, 1978).
4 This view of Booth's plan was first articulated by Canon Blackley, by now a partisan of Chamberlain's approach, and repeated by J. Lister Stead of the Foresters. See Gilbert, *Evolution of National Insurance*, 185–6.
5 See the Report of the Royal Commission on the Aged Poor, C. 7684, *Parliamentary Papers* (1895); and the Report . . . of the Committee on Old Age Pensions, C. 8911, *Parliamentary Papers* (1898).
6 Gilbert, *Evolution of National Insurance*, 187–8, 210, 218; Pelling, "The Working Class and the Origins of the Welfare State," 10; Pat Thane, "The Working Class and State 'Welfare' in Britain, 1880–1914," *Historical Journal*, XXVII (1984), 888; and "The Labour Party and State 'Welfare'," in K. D. Brown, ed., *The First Labour Party, 1906–1914* (London: Croom Helm, 1985), 184–5; José Harris, *Unemploy-*

ment and Politics. A Study in English Social Policy, 1886-1914 (Oxford: Clarendon, 1972), 269-71. See also Thane's Ph.D thesis: Patricia Williams, "The Development of Old Age Pensions Policy in Great Britain, 1878-1925," Ph.D thesis, University of London, 1970.

7 Kenneth D. Brown, *Labour and Unemployment, 1900-1914* (Newton Abbot: David & Charles, 1971), 144-5, 148-59; Harris, *Unemployment and Politics*, 317-18.

8 Gilbert, *Evolution of National Insurance*, 299-300.

9 S. Reynolds *et al.*, *Seems So! A Working Class View of Politics* (London, 1911), quoted in Thane, "The Working Class and State Welfare," 894; Anna Davin, "Imperialism and Motherhood," *History Workshop*, 5 (Spring, 1978), 9-65; Fiona Williams, *Social Policy: A Critical Introduction: Issues of Race, Gender and Class* (Cambridge: Polity, 1989), 156-7; and D. Dwork, *War Is Good for Babies and Other Young Children: The History of the Infant and Child Welfare Movement in England, 1898-1918* (London: Tavistock, 1987); and Sonya Michel and Seth Koven, "Womanly Duties: Maternalist Politics and the Origin of Welfare States in France, Germany, Great Britain and the United States, 1880-1920," *American Historical Review*, VC, 4 (1990), 1076-1108.

10 Pat Thane, "Labour and Local Politics: Democracy and Social Reform, 1880-1914," in A. Reid and E. Biagini, eds., *Currents of Radicalism* (Cambridge: Cambridge University Press, forthcoming).

11 J. Ramsay MacDonald, *Socialism and Society* (London, 1907), 161; M.G. Sheppard and J.L. Halstead, "Labour's Municipal Election Performance in Provincial England and Wales, 1901-1913," *Bulletin of the Society for the Study of Labour History*, No. 39 (Autumn, 1979), 39-62; Kenneth Young, *Local Politics and the Rise of Party* (Leicester: Leicester University Press, 1975), 35-55, 93-7; John Davis, "Radical clubs and London politics, 1870-1900," in David Feldman and Gareth Stedman Jones, eds., *Metropolis - London: Histories and Representations since 1800* (London: Routledge, 1989), 103-28; and Susan Pennybacker, " 'The Millenium by return of post": Reconsidering London Progressivism, 1889-1907," in *Metropolis - London*, 129-62.

12 Kenneth Wald, "Advance by Retreat? The Formation of British Labour's Electoral Strategy," *Journal of British Studies*, XXVII (July, 1988), 283-314; MacDonald, *Socialism and Society*, 123, cited in Thane, "Labour and Local Politics".

13 MacDonald, 29 May 1911, quoted in Thane, "The Labour Party and State 'Welfare'," 186; *Foresters' Miscellany* (November, 1895).

14 MacDonald, *Socialism and Society*, 166-7; Brown, *Labour and Unemployment*, 47-62, 84-97; Harris, *Unemployment and Politics*, 235-44.

15 Joan Scott, "On Language, Gender and Working-Class History," *International Labor and Working Class History*, 31 (Spring, 1987), reprinted in *Gender and the Politics of History* (New York: Columbia University Press, 1988); Sonya Rose, "Gender Antagonism and Class Conflict: Exclusionary Strategies of Male Trade Unionists in Nineteenth-Century Britain," *Social History*, XIII, 2 (May, 1988), 191-208; Wally Seccombe, "Patriarchy Stabilized: The Construction of the Male Breadwinner Norm in Nineteenth-Century Britain," *Social History*, 11, 1 (January, 1986), 53-76; Patricia Hollis, *Ladies Elect: Women in English Local Government, 1865-1914* (Oxford: Clarendon, 1987); Brian Harrison, "Class and Gender in Modern British Labour History," *Past and Present*, 124 (August, 1989), 128, 131-2; Sandra S. Holton, *Feminism and Democracy: Women's Suffrage and Reform Politics in Britain, 1900-1918* (Cambridge: Cambridge University Press, 1986); and Christine Collette, *For Labour and for Women: The Women's Labour League 1906-1918* (Manchester: Manchester University Press, 1989).

16 Gilbert, *Evolution of National Insurance*, 314. On the general question of how the political context shapes the demands put upon the state, see James E. Cronin, "The

British State and the Structure of Political Opportunity," *Journal of British Studies*, XXVII, 3 (1988), 199–231.

17 J. Cronin, "The Crisis of State and Society in Britain, 1917–1922," in L. Haimson and C. Tilly, eds, *Strikes, Wars and Revolutions in International Perspective* (Cambridge: Cambridge University Press, 1989), 457–73.

18 Lloyd George, quoted in Iain McLean, *The Legend of Red Clydeside* (Edinburgh: John Donald, 1983), 24; R.J.Q. Adams, *Arms and the Wizard* (London: Cassell, 1978); Trevor Wilson, *The Myriad Faces of War: Britain and the Great War, 1914–1918* (Cambridge: Polity, 1986), 207–14, 396–401; Ramsay MacDonald, *A Policy for the Labour Party* (London: Leonard Parsons, 1920), 87.

19 James Hinton, *The First Shop Stewards' Movement* (London: Allen & Unwin, 1973); Gerry Rubin, *War, Law and Labour: The Munitions Acts, State Regulation and the Unions, 1915–1921* (Oxford: Clarendon,1987); and Alastair Reid, "Dilution, Trade Unionism and the State in Britain during the First World War," in S. Tolliday and J. Zeitlin, eds, *Shop Floor Bargaining and the State* (Cambridge: Cambridge University Press, 1985), 46–74.

20 Commission of Enquiry into Industrial Unrest, Summary of the Reports, Cmd. 8696, *Parliamentary Papers* (1917–18), XV.

21 Julia Bush, *Behind the Lines: East London Labour, 1914–1919* (London: Merlin, 1984); G. Bain and R. Price, *Profiles of Union Growth* (Oxford: Basil Blackwell, 1980), 37–8; and J.M. Winter, *The Great War and the British People* (Cambridge, MA: Harvard University Press, 1986).

22 See Samuel Beer, *British Politics in the Collectivist Age* (New York: Knopf, 1965).

23 Fred Leventhal, *Arthur Henderson* (Manchester: Manchester University Press, 1989), 73–8; Royden Harrison, "The War Emergency Workers" National Committee, 1914-1920," in A. Briggs and J. Saville, eds, *Essays in Labour History, 1886–1923* (London: Macmillan, 1971), 211–259; J. M. Winter, *Socialism and the Challenge of War* (London: Routledge & Kegan Paul, 1974), 191–4; and Joel Wolfe, *Workers, Participation, and Democracy: Internal Politics in the British Union Movement* (London: Greenwood Press, 1985), 131–48.

24 Ross McKibbin, *The Evolution of the Labour Party, 1910–1924* (Oxford: Oxford University Press, 1974), 91–106; Kenneth Wald, "Advance by Retreat? The Formation of British Labour's Electoral Strategy," *Journal of British Studies*, XXVII, 3 (July, 1988), 283–314; and Bernard Waites, *A Class Society at War: England 1914–1918* (Leamington Spa: Berg, 1987), 71–4 and chapter six.

25 Noel Whiteside, "Concession, Coercion or Co-operation? State Policy and Industrial Unrest in Britain, 1916–20," *Annali* (forthcoming, 1991). In some ways the ambivalence toward state welfare actually intensified. The attempt to extend unemployment insurance to workers engaged in war work but not covered by the 1911 Act was deeply resented and made largely inoperative. Resistance to the Act stemmed partly from its specific provisions, which did not suit some of the trades involved, partly from the fact that the unions had not been consulted and partly from the fact that inclusion meant, in effect, a new tax and hence a deduction from wages at a moment when prices were rapidly increasing. See Whiteside, "Welfare Legislation and the Unions during the First World War," *Historical Journal*, XXIII, 4 (1980), 857–74.

26 Paul Johnson, *Land Fit for Heroes: The Planning of British Reconstruction, 1916–1919* (Chicago: University of Chicago Press, 1968); Rodney Lowe, *Adjusting to Democracy: The Role of the Ministry of Labour in British Politics, 1916–1939* (Oxford: Clarendon, 1986).

27 MacDonald, *A Policy for the Labour Party*, chapters VI–VIII. Labour's main efforts to alter social relations would, according to MacDonald, be carried out by a beefed-

up Ministry of Labour and a more activist Board of Trade (139–45). His view of the Treasury was especially naive: he felt the details of the budget could easily be left in the hands of officials and that a Labour Chancellor needed only, as Gladstone had supposedly done, to lay down "sound theory" to guide the bureaucratic deliberations. Treasury control, moreover, should be strengthened and not weakened in a Labour government (145–59).

28 Ministry of Reconstruction, Report of the Machinery of Government Committee, Cd. 9230, *Parliamentary Papers* (1918), XII. In addition to Mrs Webb, J.H. Thomas sat on the committee representing the Labour point of view. There is no evidence of his contribution, however.

29 In many ways, they actually encouraged the Anti-Waste mentality. MacDonald, for example, argued in 1920 that the control of expenditure might well give a Labour Chancellor real difficulties and that "he may have cause to regret that his immediate predecessors have departed from the sound maxim that the Chancellor of the Exchequer is a financial watchdog of other Departments. His first business to-day would be to cut down Whitehall expenditure and to lop off many of the tentacles which it has thrust out over the country." See MacDonald, *A Policy for the Labour Party*, 156.

4   WAR AND THE CREATION OF THE MODERN TAX STATE

1 Michael Freeden, *The New Liberalism* (Oxford: Clarendon, 1978); H.V. Emy, *Liberals, Radicals and Social Politics, 1892–1914* (Cambridge: Cambridge University Press); Stefan Collini, *Liberalism and Sociology* (Cambridge: Cambridge University Press, 1979), 101–7, 115–20, 132–37; Peter Weiler, "The New Liberalism of L.T. Hobhouse," *Victorian Studies*, XVI, 2 (1972), 154–5; H.C.G. Matthew, *The Liberal Imperialists* (Oxford: Oxford University Press, 1973), 264; Herbert Samuel, *Liberalism, An Attempt to State the Principles and Proposals of Contemporary Liberalism in England* (London: Grant Richards, 1902); Haldane in the House of Commons, 21 April 1902, quoted in Matthew, *Liberal Imperialists*, 255.

2 Robert Taylor, *Lord Salisbury* (London: Allen Lane, 1975), 157, 145–65; Peter Marsh, *The Discipline of Popular Government* (Brighton: Harvester, 1978).

3 D.A. Hamer, *The British Army: Civil-Military Relations* (Oxford: Clarendon, 1970), Part VI; G. R. Searle, *The Quest for National Efficiency* (Oxford: Basil Blackwell, 1971), 34–53.

4 A. Peacock and J. Wiseman, *The Growth of Public Expenditure in the United Kingdom*, 201–2; E. P. Hennock, "Finance and Politics in Urban Local Government in England, 1835–1900," *Historical Journal*, VI, 2 (1963), 212–25; Norman McCord, "Ratepayers and Social Policy," in P. Thane, ed., *The Origins of British Social Policy* (London: Croom Helm, 1978), 21–35; John Prest, *Liberty and Locality: Parliament, Permissive Legislation and Ratepayers" Democracies in the Nineteenth Century* (Oxford: Oxford University Press, 1990); Ursula Hicks, *British Public Finances, 1880–1952* (Oxford: Oxford University Press, 1954), 107–12; Avner Offer, *Property and Politics, 1870–1914* (Cambridge: Cambridge University Press, 1981) 283ff; and Bruce Murray, *The People's Budget 1909/10: Lloyd George and Liberal Politics* (Oxford: Clarendon, 1980), 38–44.

5 See, for example, M. J. Daunton, "'Gentlemanly Capitalism' and British Industry, 1820–1914," *Past and Present*, 122 (February, 1989), 119–58, on the contradictory interests and pressures among businessmen.

6 Alan Sykes, *Tariff Reform in British Politics, 1903–1913* (Oxford: Clarendon, 1979), 62–77; Offer, *Property and Politics*, 216–7, 311–2. For the elaboration of socialist tax policy before 1914 one has mainly to look at the Fabians. See, for example, J.F. Oakeshott, "A Democratic Budget," *Fabian Tract*, No. 39 (London: Fabian Society, 1892); Robert Jones, "Our Taxes As They Are and As They Ought

To Be," *Fabian Tract*, No. 152 (London: Fabian Society, 1910); and Sidney Webb, "What about the Rates? or Municipal Finance and Municipal Autonomy," *Fabian Tract*, No. 172 (London: Fabian Society, 1913); and also Philip Snowden, *The Socialist's Budget* (London: George Allen, 1907).

7 P.J. Cain and A.G. Hopkins, "Gentlemanly Capitalism and British Expansion Overseas, II: New Imperialism, 1850–1945," *Economic History Review*, XL, 1 (1987), 1–26; Avner Offer, "Empire and Social Reform: British Overseas Investment and Domestic Politics, 1908–1914," *Historical Journal*, XXVI, 1 (1983), 119–38; Herbert Samuel, *Liberalism*, 189–92; and "The Taxation of the Various Classes of the People, "*Statistical Society of London Journal*, LXXXII (1920). A lower estimate of the contribution of the working classes was made by Bernard Mallett, "Incidence of Imperial Taxation . . . on Income Tax and Non-Income Tax Paying Classes Respectively," January, 1904, PRO, IR74/83. The issue continued to be debated into the interwar years. See T160/283/F.11914.

8 See Sir Robert Giffen's articles in *The Times*, 7, 9 and 10 January 1902.

9 Murray, *The People's Budget*, 38.

10 Thomas Usborne, 8 February 1897, cited in Roy Douglas, *Land, People and Politics* (London: Allison and Busby, 1976), 12; Offer, *Property and Politics*, 201–17; Trevelyan, cited in Murray, *The People's Budget*, 43–4.

11 J.L. Hammond, ed., *Towards a Social Policy, or Suggestions for Constructive Reform* (London: Speaker Publishing, 1905), 123–4.

12 Leo Chiozza Money, *Riches and Poverty* (London: Methuen, 1905), 282.

13 Murray, *The People's Budget*, 310–14.

14 Carolyn Webber and Aaron Wildavsky, *A History of Taxation and Expenditure in the Western World* (New York: Simon & Schuster, 1986), 544.

15 PRO, T171/33, "Budget Statement, 1913, Yield of New or Increased Duties, 1912–13."

16 Jim Tomlinson, *Public Policy and the Economy since 1900* (Oxford: Clarendon, 1990), 19–21, 35–7; E. Green, "Radical Conservatism: The Electoral Genesis of Tariff Reform," *Historical Journal*, XXVIII (1985), 667–92; Frans Coetzee, *For Party or Country: Nationalism and the Dilemmas of Popular Conservatism in Edwardian England* (Oxford: Oxford University Press, 1990).

17 Offer, *Property and Politics*, 167–70.

18 Ken Young, *Local Politics and the Rise of Party: The London Municipal Society and the Conservative Intervention in Local Elections, 1894–1963* (Leicester: Leicester University Press, 1975), chapters 2–3; Paul Thompson, *Socialists, Liberals and Labour: The Struggle for London, 1885–1914* (London: Routledge & Kegan Paul, 1967); and Offer, *Property and Politics*, 297–308.

19 On the business support for tariffs, see A.J. Marrison, "Businessmen, Industries and Tariff Reform in Britain, 1903–1930," *Business History*, XXV (1983), 148–78.

20 Sykes, *Tariff Reform in British Politics*, 192–209, 258–84, 293–4.

21 The contribution of Chamberlain and tariff reform to the making of the modern Conservative party is discussed in Andrew Gamble, *The Conservative Nation* (London: Routledge & Kegan Paul, 1974), 19–23.

22 The connection between the Treasury's ability to handle public debt, its role within the state and its efforts to maintain the confidence of the financial community is subtly argued in Geoffrey Ingham, *Capitalism Divided? The City and Industry in British Social Development* (New York: Schocken, 1984), 128–34.

23 H.W. Primrose, "Graduation of Income Tax. As to 'Practicality' Thereof," 22 June 1903. PRO, T168/96.

24 On the Dilke Committee, see F. Shehab, *Progressive Taxation* (Oxford: Clarendon,

1953) 223–45; on the yield of Lloyd George's budgets, see Murray, *The People's Budget*, 292–302.

25 Hamilton Memo on Debt, 14 January 1905, PRO, T168/94.

26 As Offer argues, "Taxation and borrowing are the two arms of domestic policy. In failing to sustain Consols, the government effectively tied one arm behind its back and surrendered the resource of borrowing." See Offer, "Empire and Social Reform," 133.

27 Jebb to F. Ware, 30 July 1912, quoted in Murray, *The People's Budget*, 294.

28 The proportion of total revenue raised from direct taxes increased from 49.4 per cent in 1900–1 to 57.5 per cent in 1913–14 and 60.1 per cent in 1914–15, according to Bernard Mallet and C. Oswald George, *British Budgets, 1913-14 to 1920-21* (London: Macmillan, 1929), Table XX.

29 Ernest Bogart, *Direct and Indirect Costs of the War* (New York: Oxford University Press, 1919), 40.

30 Sidney Pollard, *The Development of the British Economy, 1914-1967* (New York: St Martin's, 1969), 62–6; Mallet and George, *British Budgets, 1913-1921*, 320–328, 395–400, Table XX.

31 Mary Short, "The Politics of Personal Taxation: Budget-Making in Britain, 1917–31," Ph.D Thesis, University of Cambridge, 1985, 37 and chapter two more generally; Royden Harrison, "The War Emergency Workers' National Committee, 1914–1920," in Asa Briggs and John Saville, eds, *Essays in Labour History, 1886-1923* (London: Macmillan, 1971), 245–7; Sidney Webb, *How To Pay for the War: Being Ideas Offered to the Chancellor of the Exchequer by the Fabian Research Department* (London: Fabian Society and Allen & Unwin, 1916).

32 Philip Snowden, *Labour and National Finance* (London: Leonard Parsons, 1920), 40–1, lists a series of "Labour principles of taxation" with which most "New Liberals" could easily have agreed. See also Harrison, "War Emergency Workers" National Committee," 254; and R.C. Whiting, "The Labour Party, Capitalism, and the National Debt, 1918–1924," in P.J. Waller, ed. *Politics and Social Change in Modern Britain* (Brighton: Harvester, 1987), 140–60.

33 "Conscription of Wealth – Trade Union Congress Resolution, Birmingham, 1916," in Snowden, *Labour and National Finance*, 160; and Webb, *How To Pay for the War*, 221–71.

34 F.W. Pethick Lawrence, *A Levy on Capital* (London: Allen & Unwin, 1918), 75, 84. While Webb had proposed a postwar tax rate of 10s in addition to the capital levy, Pethick Lawrence estimated the likely rate without a capital levy at 7s 6d and, with a 38 per cent capital levy, a rate of 3s 6d.

35 Unsigned notes on "Conscription of Wealth," in PROT170/143; Pethick Lawrence, *A Levy on Capital*, 62–6, 74.

5 THE STATE IN WAR AND RECONSTRUCTION

1 See David French, "The Rise and Fall of 'Business as Usual'," in Kathleen Burk, ed., *War and the State: The Transformation of British Government, 1914-1919* (London: Allen & Unwin, 1982), 7–31.

2 R. Boothby *et al.*, *Industry and the State* (London: Macmillan, 1927), 35.

3 Martin Pugh, *The Making of Modern British Politics, 1867-1939* (New York: St Martin's, 1982), 161–76; Trevor Wilson, *The Myriad Faces of War: Britain and the Great War, 1914-1918* (Cambridge: Polity, 1986), 192–214, 408–23; Cameron Hazlehurst, *Politicians at War* (London: Cape, 1971); John Turner, "British Politics and the Great War," in Turner, ed., *Britain and the First World War* (London: Unwin Hyman, 1988), 117–38; John Stubbs, "The Impact of the Great War on the Conservative Party," in G. Peele and C. Cook, eds, *The Politics of Reappraisal,*

1918–1939 (London: Macmillan, 1975), 14–38; Keith Middlemas, *Politics in Industrial Society* (London: Andre Deutsch, 1979), chapters 4–5; Beatrice Webb's Diaries, 10 August 1914, quoted in A.M. McBriar, *An Edwardian Mixed Doubles: The Bosanquets and the Webbs* (Oxford: Clarendon, 1987), 351.

4 Paul B. Johnson, *Land Fit for Heroes* (Chicago: University of Chicago Press, 1968); Rodney Lowe, "The Ministry of Labour, 1916–1919: A Still, Small Voice," in Burk, *War and the State*, 108–34.

5 Jonathan Boswell and Bruce Johns, "Patriots or Profiteers: British Businessmen and the First World War," *Journal of European Economic History* XI (1982), 423–45.

6 Middlemas, *Politics in Industrial Society*, 113–14.

7 Morant to J.L. Garvin, 7 January 1916, quoted in Wilson, *Myriad Faces of War*, 415. The complaint about union influence comes from businessmen in East Anglia, cited in Middlemas, *Politics in Industrial Society*, 111.

8 Roy Hay, "Employers and Social Policy in Britain: The Evolution of Welfare Legislation, 1905–1914," *Social History*, 4 (January, 1977), 435–55; John Turner, 'The Politics of 'Organised Business' in the First World War," in Turner, ed., *Businessmen and Politics: Studies of Business Activity in British Politics, 1900–1945* (London: Heinemann, 1984), 33–49.

9 Final Report of the Committee Appointed to Enquire into the Organization and Staffing of Government Offices (Bradbury Committee), Cmd. 62, *Parliamentary Papers* (1919), XI, 4, 6; R.J.Q. Adams, *Arms and the Wizard: Lloyd George and the Ministry of Munitions* (London: Cassell, 1978); Burk, "The Treasury," 96–100, and Chris Wrigley, "The Ministry of Munitions: An Innovatory Department," in Burk, *War and the State*, 32–56.

10 Peter Fraser, "The Impact of the War of 1914–18 on the British Political System," in M.R.D. Foot, ed., *War and Society* (New York: Barnes & Noble, 1973), 132–4; John Turner, "Cabinets, Committees and Secretariats: The Higher Direction of War," in Burk, *War and the State*, 57–83; and Turner, *Lloyd George's Secretariat* (Cambridge: Cambridge University Press, 1980).

11 W.H. Beveridge to A.S. Beveridge, 14 January 1917, quoted in José Harris, "Bureaucrats and Businessmen in British Food Control, 1916–1919," in Burk, *War and the State*, 148.

12 See the First and Second Reports of the Select Committee on National Expenditure, *Parliamentary Papers*, (1917–18), III; and also the committee's Second Interim Report, which was a short note criticizing the "unsatisfactory conditions" found in the Ministry of Pensions and urging the immediate appointment of an establishments officer to bring it into line. (See the Second Report, Cd. 9219, *Parliamentary Papers* [1918], VII.) The evaluations of various departments are contained in the Third and Fourth Reports of the committee, Cd. 9220, *Parliamentary Papers* (1918), VII, and Cmd. 61, *Parliamentary Papers* (1919), XI. Of the new departments, only the Ministry of Shipping met with the committee's approval. Their comments on the Ministries of Reconstruction and of Labour suggest considerable antipathy, but as both were involved in internal review and reorganization at the time of the committee's own investigations, it was difficult to find specific practices to criticize. For the committee's recommendations, see its Final Report, 21 February 1919, Cmd. 62, *Parliamentary Papers* (1919), XI, 6. It is perhaps worth noting that Warren Fisher, soon to be appointed Permanent Secretary to the Treasury and "Official Head of the Civil Service" was also a member of the committee.

13 Ministry of Reconstruction, Report of the Machinery of Government Committee, Cmd. 9230, *Parliamentary Papers* (1918), XII.

14 War Cabinet, Report for the Year 1917, Cd. 9005, *Parliamentary Papers* (1918), XIV, 130, 148. On the dimensions of growth, see Moses Abramovitz and Vera

Eliasberg, *The Growth of Public Employment in Great Britain* (Princeton: Princeton University Press, 1957), 39–43; and D.N. Chester and F.M.G. Willson, *The Organization of British Central Government, 1914–1964* (London: Allen & Unwin, 1968), 24–6, 59, 276, 439–40.

15 War Cabinet, Report for the Year 1917, xv, xix.

16 R. S. Sayers, *The Bank of England, 1891–1944*, I (Cambridge: Cambridge University Press, 1976), 236–7; Leslie Hannah, *The Rise of the Corporate Economy* (London: Methuen, 1976); Sidney Pollard, "The Nationalisation of the Banks: The Chequered History of a Socialist Proposal," in David Martin and David Rubinstein, eds, *Ideology and the Labour Movement: Essays Presented to John Saville* (London: Croom Helm, 1979), 167–90; John Scott and Catherine Griff, *Directors of Industry: The British Corporate Network, 1904–76* (Cambridge: Polity, 1984), 50–2; and Steven Tolliday, *Business, Banking and Politics: The Case of British Steel, 1918–1939* (Cambridge, MA: Harvard University Press, 1987), 189–210.

17 Sayers, *The Bank of England*, I, 99–109; Burk, "The Treasury," 94. Burk quotes another banker, Grenfell, to the effect that Cunliffe's strange behaviour was due to bad teeth "which had poisoned his system." The remark about his insanity was made by Montagu Norman, who took over as Governor of the Bank in April, 1920 and whose own behaviour under stress, especially in 1931, would subsequently become a matter of considerable concern.

18 Nona Newman, "The Role of the Treasury in the Formation of British Economic Policy, 1918–1925," Ph.D Thesis, University of Durham, 1972; First Interim Report of the Committee on Currency and Foreign Exchanges after the War, Cd. 9182, *Parliamentary Papers* (1918), VII, 3, 6; Donald Moggridge, *British Monetary Policy, 1924–1931: The Norman Conquest of $4.86* (Cambridge: Cambridge University Press, 1972), 18; Alan Booth, "Corporatism, Capitalism and Depression in Twentieth-Century Britain," *British Journal of Sociology*, XXXIII (1982), 200–23; and Arthur McIvor, " 'A Crusade for Capitalism': The Economic League, 1919–1939," *Journal of Contemporary History*, XXIII (1988), 631–55.

19 José Harris, "Society and the State in Twentieth-Century Britain," in F.M.L. Thompson, ed., *The Cambridge Social History of Britain*, Vol. III: *Social Agencies and Institutions* (Cambridge: Cambridge University Press, 1990), 76.

20 Kennedy Jones, MP, quoted in B. Waites, *A Class Society at War: England, 1914–1918* (Leamington Spa: Berg, 1987), 53.

21 Chris Wrigley, "The British State and the Challenges of Labour, 1917–1920," International Colloquium on "Labour Movements and Revolutionary Potential in Europe at the End of World War I," Graz, Austria, June, 1989; Kenneth Morgan, *Consensus and Disunity: The Lloyd George Coalition Government, 1918–1922* (Oxford: Clarendon, 1979), 243–6, 298–300.

22 For a general discussion, see J. Cronin, "Coping with Labour, 1918–1926," in Cronin and J. Schneer, eds., *Social Conflict and the Political Order in Modern Britain* (New Brunswick, N.J.: Rutgers University Press, 1982), 113–45; and Christopher Nottingham, "Recasting Bourgeois Britain? The British State in the Years which followed the First World War," *International Review of Social History*, XXXI, Pt 3 (1986), 227–47.

23 Maurice Cowling, *The Impact of Labour* (Cambridge: Cambridge University Press, 1971).

24 See Michael Bentley, "The Liberal Response to Socialism, 1918–1929," in Kenneth Brown, ed., *Essays in Anti-Labour History: Responses to the Rise of Labour in Britain* (London: Macmillan, 1974), 42–73; and *Liberalism Divided: A Study in British Political Thought, 1914–1939* (Oxford: Clarendon, 1986).

25 R. G. Hawtrey, *The Exchequer and the Control of Expenditure* (London: Oxford University Press, 1921), 64.

26 B. Mallet and C.O. George, *British Budgets. Third Series, 1921–22 to 1932–33* (London: Macmillan, 1933), 457–65, 575; Sidney Pollard, *The Development of the British Economy 1914–1967*, (New York: St Martins, 1969) 65–6; Alan Peacock and Jack Wiseman, *The Growth of Public Expenditure in the United Kingdom* (Princeton: Princeton University Press, 1961), 52–61, 164–9, 184–7.

27 On the significance of the "normal year" for postwar financial planning, see Mary E. Short, "The Politics of Personal Taxation: Budget-Making in Britain, 1917–31," Ph.D Thesis, University of Cambridge, 1985, 5–14; and the report of 6 February 1920 by John Anderson of the BIR to Austen Chamberlain giving data simultaneously "for 1920–21, and for a "normal year," of the taxes collected by the Board," in PROCAB27/101, Cabinet Committee on Taxation. On the warning of impending bankruptcy, see Otto Niemeyer, "The Financial Position and Future Prospects of this Country," 18 July 1919, in T171/155.

28 Richard Hopkins to Churchill, 26 November 1924, in T171/239, cited in Short, "Politics of Personal Taxation," 227; memo by G.R. Hamilton and P. Thompson of the BIR to Chancellor, 18 January 1922, in T171/204. See also the Report of the Royal Commission on the Income Tax, Cmd. 615, 1920; B.E.V. Sabine, *A History of Income Tax* (London: Allen & Unwin, 1966), 157–62; and for the deliberations surrounding the appointment of the Royal Commission, T172/985, Inquiry into Income Tax. On "fitting the burden to the back," see P. Thompson and R. Hopkins to the Chancellor of the Exchequer, 20 February 1922 in T172/1264.

29 Sir Basil Blackett, "Budgeting for a Deficit," 24 March 1922, T171/202.

30 Norman to Chancellor of the Exchequer, 17 April 1920. Accompanying this was another memo of 12 April 1920, signed by Norman and by representatives of Baring Brothers, the Accepting House Committee, Prudential Assurance, the Bank of Liverpool, Lloyds Bank, Barclays, the Stock Exchange Committee, the London Chamber of Commerce, the Westminster Bank and others outlining the need for such temporary increases in tax in order to bring about debt reduction. The memos are contained in T172/1105.

31 See Leslie Scott to Horne, 11 March 1922, and the flier dated 10 March 1922 and signed by James P. Rudolf of the Liverpool Chamber of Commerce and Max Muspratt of the FBI, in T172/1232.

32 See, for example, the report of the joint delegation of the Association of British Chambers of Commerce and the Federation of British Industries to the Board of Inland Revenue on 16 March 1921, in IR113/7; the report on the deputation of businessmen to protest double taxation on 5 April 1918 in T172/837; the reports of the meetings between the Chancellor and the National Union of Manufacturers on 19 May 1920 and 1 December 1921 in T172/1187 and T172/1204; the reference to FBI representations on income tax in February, 1922 in T172/1264; the record of the meeting between Snowden and the so-called League to Enforce Economy on 5 December 1924 in T172/1366; and the reports of meetings of the Chancellor with the ABCC on 14 March 1922 and 10 March 1925; with the Income Tax Payers" Society on 12 March 1925; with the National Chamber of Trade on 1 April 1925; with the Industrial Group of the House of Commons later in that month; with the National Citizens" Union on 10 March 1925; and with the FBI on 12 March 1925, in T172/1409. The ABCC returned to visit Churchill once more in November, 1925 to make sure he knew of their opposition to further taxation (see T172/1516). Again in 1926 the ABCC met the Chancellor in April and November; the FBI did so in March; and the Income Tax Payers" Society in the same month, according to

reports in T172/1410. The reports in T172/1411 on "Taxation Generally, 1927–29" suggest that such lobbying continued throughout the 1920s.

33 Deputation of the National Union of Manufacturers to the Chancellor of the Exchequer, 19 May 1920, in T172/1187; Memo of 17 December 1920 on Excess Profits Duty prepared for the Cabinet Committee on Taxation, 1919–20, in CAB27/101.

34 T172/1516 contains evidence both of Churchill's skill and of official views on the relative importance of the ABCC and the FBI.

35 H.J. de Courcy Moore, speaking at the Fishmongers" Hall in the City of London, 28 September 1921, cited in "Industry and the Weight of Taxation," Memo by the Board of Inland Revenue, January, 1922, in T171/203. Earlier drafts of this memo appear in IR64/48.

36 McKenna, quoted in Short, "The Politics of Personal Taxation," 157–9. Such claims did not go uncontested, of course. J. A. Hobson, for example, offered a rival concept of the "taxable surplus" in his *Taxation in the New State* (New York: Harcourt, Brace & Howe, 1920), 12-44. A more "scientific" treatment was contained in Josiah Stamp, *Wealth and Taxable Capacity* (London: P.S. King, 1922), esp. 109–11, which built on arguments and methods developed in *British Incomes and Property* (London: P.S. King, 1916), 355–75, and applied to the case of Ireland. It is nearly impossible to imagine a discussion of "taxable capacity" which was truly scientific, for the very phrase encompasses a subjective dimension and seems to require an overly sympathetic hearing of what might be a quite self-interested case. As Ursula Hicks has argued, "it is extremely difficult to give any precise meaning to the concept of the limit of taxable capacity, except in the sense that powerful classes in the community may be unwilling to have particular taxes raised beyond a certain point and consequently withdraw factors of production under their control." See Hicks, *The Finance of British Government, 1920-1936* (Oxford: Clarendon, 1938, 1970), 232. Taxable capacity, in short, is an essentially political and contested notion, not an economic or scientific concept. It would seem not unreasonable, then, to conclude with Hugh Dalton that "In the interests of clear thinking, it would be well that the phrase 'taxable capacity' should be banished from all serious discussions of public finance." See Dalton, *Principles of Public Finance*, 8th edn. (London: Routledge, 1934), 169, and more generally, 159–69. Still, the perception that British taxpayers were overburdened was widespread in the early 1920s. See, for example, Elie Halévy's reference to "The English Taxpayer, overburdened by taxation to a degree the French Taxpayer can scarcely imagine" in "The State of the Social Question in England," (1922), in *The Era of Tyrannies* (Garden City, NY: Anchor, 1965), 198.

37 Cabinet Committee on Taxation, 17 December 1920, in CAB27/101; Philip Snowden, *Labour and National Finance* (London: Leonard Parsons, 1920), 84–7, 95.

38 "Industry and the Weight of Taxation," 9–11, 13, in T171/203; and R.G. Hawtrey, "The Burden of Taxation," 3 April 1922, in T208/44.

39 See T171/204, "Budget 1922 Taxation Proposals II," and T172/1757, "Unadopted Proposals for New Taxes, 1918–28." The substitution of indirect for direct taxes was also considered in the memo on "Industry and the Weight of Taxation," in T171/203, but rejected because of its possible impact on prices and thus on labour relations.

40 The reference to industry's "self-interest" comes from "Industry and the Weight of Taxation," 10, in T171/203. The dispute between Horne and his officials is visible in this file and in T171/202 and T171/205, and is discussed in Short, "Politics of Personal Taxation," chapter 4. The resistance to tax breaks for industry can be seen in various files, but see in particular IR74/210, in which Warren Fisher and Nott-

Bower from the Inland Revenue argue against the "state subvention" of particular industries during the First World War, and also T172/1763, which contains the official reaction to a proposal from Professor A.C. Pigou to relieve employers of their liability for unemployment insurance payments. More precisely "targeted" incentives were viewed even less favourably, and would continue to be so viewed even after 1945.

41 See, in general, the Report of the Committee on National Debt and Taxation (Colwyn Committee), Cmd. 2800, *Parliamentary Papers* (1927), XI. On the negative attitude toward tax incentives, see Roger Middleton, *Towards the Managed Economy: Keynes, the Treasury and the Fiscal Policy Debate of the 1930s* (London: Methuen, 1985), 71–7. The testimony by Coates and Bradbury is reprinted as part of the report and is also found in IR64/56, "Evidence to the Committee on National Debt and Taxation, December, 1925." Coates' views are also discussed in Duncan Black, *The Incidence of Income Taxes* (London: Macmillan, 1939), 19–29. Business reactions were exemplified by the FBI, which complained vigorously to Churchill on 9 March 1927, reported in T172/1570.

42 See W.H. Hurst to Lloyd George, 19 December 1917, in T171/150; Nott-Bower and Warren Fisher to Chancellor of the Exchequer, 14 December 1917, in T171/150; report of the meeting of 14 November 1917 between representatives of the TUC, the Labour party, the WEWNC, and the Miners" Federation and Bonar Law and Treasury officials, in T172/503; *New Statesman*, 17 November 1917; report of the TUC delegation to the Chancellor in 1920, in T172/1166; and the memo on "Industry and the Weight of Taxation."

43 Report of the Select Committee on the Proposed Taxation of War-time Increase of Wealth, *Parliamentary Papers* (1920), VII; and J.S. Nicholson, *War Finance* (London: P.S. King, 1918), 492.

44 BIR Memorandum on the "Proposed Capital Levy in France," 15 March 1919, in T171/167; Sir Alexander Johnston, *The Inland Revenue* (London: Allen & Unwin, 1965), 52–9; Warren Fisher and H.P. Hamilton to Chancellor of the Exchequer, 15 March 1919, on the "Proposed Capital Levy in France," T171/167.

45 Nott-Bower and Fisher to Chancellor of the Exchequer, 6 November 1917, in T171/167; Nott-Bower to Hamilton, 22 September 1917; Memo on "Methods of Increasing Direct Taxation," 24 September 1917; summary of meeting of official committee, 12 March 1918; in T171/150; BIR Memo of November, 1919 on the practicality of taxing war wealth, in CAB27/101; Short, "Politics of Personal Taxation," 57, 68–9; Report on the Taxation of War-time Wealth, and also the memoranda submitted by the Board of Inland Revenue on the suggested Taxation of War-Time Increases of Wealth, Cmd. 594, *Parliamentary Papers* (1920), XXVII.

46 Short, "Politics of Personal Taxation," pp. 47–50, 75; A.C. Pigou, *A Capital Levy and a Levy on War Wealth* (London: Oxford University Press, 1920); J.C. Stamp, "The Capital Levy: Theoretical and Academic Aspects," in IR74/153, Pts 1–4, Capital Levy, Theoretical Aspects, 1917–1920.

47 Hopkins IR75/108, and Bradbury Memorandum on the "Conscription of Wealth," January, 1918, in T170/143, both quoted in Short, "Politics of Personal Taxation," 43, 59.

48 On the attitude of the Conservative party, see Sir George Younger's letter to Balfour of January, 1918 arguing against even "the slightest support of any such suicidal policy" as the capital levy, quoted in John Stubbs, "The Impact of the Great War on the Conservative Party," in G. Peele and C. Cook, eds, *The Politics of Reappraisal, 1918–1939* (London: Macmillan, 1975), 34. On the Bank's position, see Montagu Norman to Chancellor of the Exchequer, 17 April 1920 and the memorandum

signed by Norman and various representatives of Baring Brothers, the Accepting Houses Committee, the Prudential Assurance, the Bank of Liverpool, Lloyds and Barclays, the Stock Exchange Committee, the London Chamber of Commerce and others proposing a three-year increase in income tax and surtax explicitly earmarked for debt reduction, in T172/1105. The positions of Bonar Law and Stamp are discussed in Short, "Politics of Personal Taxation," 77–83.

49 On Baldwin's strange decision, see Keith Middlemas and John Barnes, *Baldwin: A Biography* (London: Macmillan, 1969), 212–49.

50 Report of the Committee on the National Debt and Taxation, Cmd. 2800, *British Parliamentary Papers* (1927), XI.

51 The figures are from Mallet and George, *British Budgets, 1921-33*, 561–66, 577.

52 Otto Niemeyer, "The Financial Position and Future Prospects of the Country," 18 July 1919, in T171/155; Burk, "The Treasury," 101; Short, "The Politics of Personal Taxation", 5–9; Morgan, *Consensus and Disunity*, 84–91; Bentley B. Gilbert, *British Social Policy, 1914-1939* (London: Batsford, 1970), 54–74.

53 On the origins of the plan to re-organize the Treasury, see Burk, "The Treasury," 97–8, 107, who attributes it to Bradbury. On its workings, see Frederick Leith-Ross, *Money Talks* (London: Hutchinson, 1968), 53. Cabinet agreed to the new procedures on 6 January 1920 and they were embodied in a Treasury Circular of 12 January 1920. For Treasury efforts to reaffirm the policy, see T160/639/F.6064, "Proposals for Expenditure. Procedures prior to submission to Cabinet."

54 The fullest discussion of Fisher's career is E.J. O'Halpin, "Sir Warren Fisher, Head of the Civil Service, 1919–1939," Ph.D Thesis, University of Cambridge, 1982. On his plans for reform, see Fisher to Lloyd George, 3 September 1919, in T172/1228.

55 Susan Howson, *Domestic Monetary Management in Britain, 1919-1938* (Cambridge: Cambridge University Press, 1975), 10; Morgan, *Consensus and Disunity*, 88–98; R.H. Tawney, "The Abolition of Economic Controls, 1918–1921," *Economic History Review*, XIII (1943), 1–30; Susan Armitage, *The Politics of Decontrol in Industry* (London: LSE, 1969); Noelle Whiteside, "Private Agencies for Public Purposes: Some New Perspectives on Policy Making in Health Insurance between the Wars," *Journal of Social Policy*, XII (1983), 165–94; Stephen Stacey, "The Ministry of Health, 1919–1929: Ideas and Practice in a Government Department," Ph.D Thesis, University of Cambridge, 1984; Anne Crowther, *British Social Policy, 1914-1939* (London: Macmillan, 1988), 32–3; and Chester and Willson, *Organization of British Central Government*, 72–7, 86–8.

56 H.A.L. Fisher, quoted in Morgan, *Consensus and Disunity*, 105; Geddes to Horne, 9 August 1921, in T172/1228. Geddes' role in politics has been the subject of considerable attention: see Peter Cline, "Eric Geddes and the 'Experiment' with Businessmen in Government," in Brown, *Essays in Anti-Labour History*, 74–104; and Keith Grieves, *Sir Eric Geddes: Business and Government in War and Peace* (Manchester: Manchester University Press, 1989).

57 Andrew McDonald, "The Geddes Committee and the Formulation of Public Expenditure Policy, 1921–1922," *Historical Journal*, XXXII, 2 (1989), 651–54; Cabinet Minutes, 15 August 1921, 68 (21) in T172/1228; Reduction of Public Expenditure, Copy of Treasury Circular, dated 13 May 1921, Cmd. 1309, *Parliamentary Papers* (1921), XIX; Warren Fisher to Lloyd George, Robert Horne and Austen Chamberlain, 20 July 1921, in T172/1215.

58 McDonald, "The Geddes Committee," 661–4; Geddes to Horne, 22 January 1922, in T172/1228; First, Second and Third Reports of the Committee on National Expenditure, Cmd. 1581, Cmd. 1582 and Cmd. 1589, *Parliamentary Papers* (1922), IX.

59 Morgan, *Consensus and Disunity*, 285–7; Gilbert, *British Social Policy*, 47–8. The

substance of the proposals had been hinted at early in October by Hilton Young, Financial Secretary to the Treasury, but Lloyd George's announcement occurred on 19 October. Norman's opposition was conveyed through Horne to the Cabinet on 17 October.

60 G.C. Peden, "The Treasury as Central Department of Government, 1919-1939," *Public Administration*, LXI (1983), 373; Stephen Roskill, *Hankey: Man of Secrets*, 3 volumes (London: Collins, 1970-1974), Vol. II, 304-20.

61 See the letter from the Cabinet Office to P.J. Grigg, 2 March 1923, in T160/639/F.6064.

6 THE RESILIENCE OF BUDGETARY ORTHODOXY

1 W.H. Greenleaf, *The British Political Tradition*, Vol. III: *A Much Governed Nation*, Pt I (London: Methuen, 1987), 72; Ursula K. Hicks, *The Finance of British Government, 1920-1936* (Oxford: Clarendon, 1970), 150. Rates averaged £1 18s 11d per head in 1914, £4 0s 11d in 1921.

2 See Ken Young, *Local Politics and the Rise of Party: The London Municipal Society and the Conservative Intervention in Local Elections, 1894-1963* (Leicester: Leicester University Press, 1975), 130-7, 145 in general and for the citations from the *Ratepayer* of April, 1921 and September-Octber, 1927.

3 On Churchill's ambivalence over the return to gold, see Robert W.D. Boyce, *British Capitalism at the Crossroads: A Study in Politics, Economics and International Relations* (Cambridge: Cambridge University Press, 1987), 73-7. His remarks of 1928 are quoted in Richard Jackman, "Local Government Finance," in Martin Loughlin, M. David Gelfand and Ken Young, eds, *Half a Century of Municipal Decline, 1935-1985* (London: Allen & Unwin, 1985), 154. On Colwyn's attitude towards local taxes, see B. Mallet and C.O. George, *British Budgets, 1921-22 to 1932-33* (London: Macmillan, 1933).

225 4 David Dilks, *Neville Chamberlain*, Vol. I: *Pioneering and Reform, 1869-1929* (Cambridge: Cambridge University Press, 1984), 534-57; Bentley Gilbert, *British Social Policy, 1914-1939* (Ithaca, NY: Cornell University Press, 1970), 221-24; and Churchill, speaking in Cabinet on 20 January 1928, quoted in Gilbert, 227.

5 On the financial implications of the new system, see Mallet and George, *British Budgets, 1921-2 to 1932-3*, 222-3, 479-83; K.B. Smellie, *A History of Local Government* (London: Allen & Unwin, 1946), 157-9; Hicks, *Finance of British Government*, 151-2.

6 A. Peacock and J. Wiseman, *The Growth of Public Expenditure in the United Kingdom* (Princeton: Princeton University Press, 1961), Table A-20; J.R. Hicks and U.K. Hicks, *The Incidence of Local Rates in Great Britain* (London: National Institute of Economic and Social Research, Occasional Paper 8, 1945), 24-5, quoted in Jackman, "Local Government Finance," 155; Hicks, *Finance of British Government*, 165.

7 Robert Skidelsky, *Politicians and the Slump* (London: Macmillan, 1967), 157; Lloyd George, quoted in *The Times*, 9 July 1928. On Labour's local successes see John S. Rowett, "The Labour Party and Local Government: Theory and Practice in the Inter-War Years," D.Phil. Thesis, Oxford University, 1979.

8 Hicks, *Finance of British Government*, 265-77; G. Findlay Shirras and L. Rostas, *The Burden of British Taxation* (Cambridge: Cambridge University Press, 1942), and Ross McKibbin, "Class and Conventional Wisdom: The Conservative Party and the 'Public' in Inter-war Britain," in *Ideologies of Class* (Oxford: Clarendon, 1990), 270.

9 Mallet and George, *British Budgets, 1921-33*, 286-7.

10 On the position of the Federation of British Industries, see Robert Skidelsky, *Politicians and the Slump*, 157, 297. The Bank's stance was well known, but was

conveyed authoritatively to the Cabinet on 21 August 1931. See CAB23/67, Cabinet 43 (31) for the appropriate minutes. More generally, see P. Williamson, "A 'Bankers Ramp'"? Financiers and the British Political Crisis of August 1931," *English Historical Review*, IC (October, 1984), 770–806; and Williamson, "Financiers, the Gold Standard and British Politics, 1925–1931," in John Turner, ed., *Businessmen and Politics: Studies of Business Activity in British Politics, 1900–1945* (London: Heinemann, 1984), 105–29.

11 Report of the Committee on National Expenditure, XVI, Cmd. 3920 (1931), 13; Blackett, "Budgeting for a Deficit," 24 March 1922, in T171/202. The memo served as the Treasury's definitive statement on deficits and as late as 1935 Hopkins was still commending it to fellow officials.

12 Roger Middleton, *Towards the Managed Economy: Keynes, the Treasury and the Fiscal Policy Debate of the 1930s* (London: Methuen, 1985), 87, and more generally 80–90; Mary Short, "The Politics of Personal Taxation: Budget-Making in Britain, 1917–1931," Ph.D Thesis, University of Cambridge, 1985, 263–9. Snowden's quote comes from *An Autobiography*, Vol. II (London: Nicolson & Watson, 1934), 615, cited in Boyce, *British Capitalism at the Crossroads*, 51, which also contains an account of Snowden's dealings with Norman in 1925, p. 77.

13 Hopkins and Fisher to Snowden, 19 November 1929 in Short, "Politics of Personal Taxation," 274; Middleton, *Towards the Managed Economy*, 98; "National Development and State Borrowing," July, 1930, reprinted in Skidelsky, *Politicians and the Slump*, 409–13; Treasury Memorandum, 29 January 1931 and Hopkins' testimony to the Royal Commission on Unemployment Insurance, Report, Cmd. 3872, and Minutes of Evidence (1931), 381–91, para. 3294 esp., cited in Skidelsky, 288, 298, 308–10; Stuart Ball, *Baldwin and the Conservative Party: The Crisis of 1929–1931* (New Haven: Yale University Press, 1988), 153–4; and Mallet and George, *British Budgets, 1921–22 to 1932–33*, 423–9.

Officials not only weighed in on the side of cuts but actually opposed measures that might lessen the pressure for expenditure cuts. Thus in March, 1931 C.R. Gregg of the Inland Revenue argued against a proposal to lower employers' national insurance contribution on the grounds that it would weaken support among employers for cutting the dole. Such relief, as Gregg saw it, "would prejudice also the prospect of that much needed reform of unemployment insurance that would restrict its costs and remove its abuses, for employers as a class would no longer have any interest in reform." See Gregg's memo in T172/1763.

14 Throughout the 1931 crisis, according to Roger Middleton, the Revenue departments "ensured that the form of fiscal adjustment proposed would proceed along conventional lines and that less orthodox solutions would be easily dismissed." See Middleton, *Towards the Managed Economy*, 59–60.

15 See T172/1757, "Unadopted Proposals for New Taxes, 1918–1928," which lists several proposals that were reviewed again in 1930–1 but again found wanting by officials; P.J. Grigg to Chancellor, 19 January 1931, in IR113/42, ruling out various special taxes; T172/1698 "Economic Policy (Existing Preferences) 1930' for the continued resistance to tariffs; and IR113/21 "Labour Party's Surtax Scheme, 1926–27," and Grigg to Hopkins, 2 March 1931 in IR113/42 for opposition to that solution.

16 Skidelsky, *Politicians and the Slump*, 312–3, 369–71; IR63/132, memorandum to the Chancellor of the Exchequer from the Inland Revenue.

17 "Note on Taxation borne by the Wealthy," 10 August 1931, and Sir P. Thompson to Richard Hopkins, 10 August 1931, both in IR63/132. This same note appears in IR64/83, a file devoted to the general issue of "soaking the rich."

18 Hopkins, "Economy or Taxation," undated but apparently written in mid-August,

1931 in IR63/132; Memo to the Chancellor, undated and unsigned but most likely written by Warren Fisher, Hopkins, Grigg and A.J. Dyke shortly after 18 August 1931, in IR63/132; Warren Fisher, R. Hopkins, P.J. Grigg and A.J. Dyke to the Chancellor of the Exchequer, 18 August 1931, in IR63/132; and memo to the Chancellor on the taxation of the "rentier" in IR63/132.

19 Sprague's advocacy sparked protests from trade unionists which forced MacDonald to approach Montagu Norman about the propriety of the Bank's position. Norman was unmoved. See Boyce, *British Capitalism at the Crossroads*, 304-5.

20 Boyce, *British Capitalism at the Crossroads*, 339-55; Harrison and Harvey, cited in Boyce, 345, 347, 354; Skidelsky, *Politicians and the Slump*, 342-3.

21 Middleton, *Towards the Managed Economy*, 100.

22 Skidelsky, *Politicians and the Slump*, 360. The haggling within the Cabinet leading up to the formation of the National government can be followed in the Cabinet Minutes in CAB23/67, Cab 41 (31) to Cab 47 (31).

23 T172/1756,"Secretary's Notes of a Conversation between Sir Ernest Harvey and Mr. Peacock and Members of the Cabinet on Thursday, September 3rd, 1931 at 3 P.M." The secretary was Hankey.

24 Mallet and George, *British Budgets, 1921-33*, 366-75; "Income Tax, Sur-Tax and Death Duties. Comparison of Taxation as Increased by the Budget with Taxation before the War," Inland Revenue memo of September, 1931, in IR113/42; Short, "Politics of Personal Taxation," 292-3. Within the Cabinet Herbert Samuel seems to have been the main advocate for relief for industry. See Samuel to Grigg, 28 August 1931 and Grigg to Samuel, 31 August 1931, in IR113/42. On the sharp dip in capital spending by local authorities during 1932-5, see the memo prepared by the Economic Section of the Cabinet on "The Maintenance of Employment," 18 May 1943, in CAB87/13. The restrictions of the early 1930s were in addition to the normal control exercised by the granting or refusal of Ministry of Health sanction for local authority loans. The ministry operated a "blacklist" of local authorities that were not considered creditworthy. See Stephen Ward, *The Geography of Interwar Britain: The State and Uneven Development* (London: Routledge, 1988), 173-7. On restricting unemployment benefits to married women, see Jim Tomlinson, "Women as 'Anomalies': The Anomalies Regulations of 1931, Their Background and Implications," *Public Administration*, LXII (1982), 423-37.

25 Hicks, *Finance of British Government*, 265-77.

26 Forrest Capie, *Depression and Protection: Britain between the Wars* (London: Allen & Unwin, 1983), 105; Middleton, *Towards the Managed Economy*, 102.

27 Middleton, *Towards the Managed Economy*, 101-5. On the resistance to Keynes, see "Arguments against Unbalancing the Budget," unsigned memo from March or April, 1933; and notes by Fisher, Phillips, Hopkins and the Inland Revenue in T171/309. See also Frederick Phillips, "Mr Keynes' Articles," 21 March 1933 in T175/17, where Phillips conceded that Keynes was arguing not for an unbalanced budget but rather for "a speculative balancing of the Budget over a long term of future years without regard to the deficit produced in the early years of the period." He felt the optimistic expectations underlying such a "speculative balancing" were unfounded and unwise, however. Keynes' position was echoed by Harold Macmillan, Robert Horne and the so-called "Northern Group." For Hopkins" conclusion, see his note to Fergusson, 7 April 1933, in T171/309.

28 B.E.V. Sabine, *British Budgets in Peace and War, 1932-1945* (London: Allen & Unwin, 1970), chapters II-III; Middleton, *Towards the Managed Economy*, 136-40; Hicks, *Finance of British Government*, 129-31, 375; Report of the Committee on Local Expenditure (1932), Cmd. 4200 *Parliamentary Papers* (1932-3), XIV; Ken

Young, "Re-Reading the Municipal Progress: A Crisis Revisited," in Loughlin *et al.*, eds., *Half a Century of Municipal Decline*, 7-9.

29 Middleton, *Towards the Managed Economy*, 107-9, 115-20.

30 See memo by Thomas Inskip to the Treasury, 23 November 1937, cited in Robert Shay, *British Rearmament in the Thirties: Politics and Profits* (Princeton: Princeton University Press, 1977) 165, and more generally, 163-69, 189-93; Interim Report on Defence Expenditure in Future Years, 15 December 1937 by Sir Thomas Inskip, Minister for the Co-ordination of Defence, in CAB24/273, C.P. 316 (37); and Inskip's Final Report of 8 February 1938, C.P. 24 (38), in CAB24/274. The importance of Inskip's review of defence expenditure is discussed in G.C. Peden, *British Rearmament and the Treasury: 1932-1939* (Edinburgh: Scottish Academic Press, 1979), 10, 41-2, 64-5.

The pressure to rearm did force the Treasury to begin to think in somewhat broader terms about the economy, however, and to begin discussing it in the sorts of aggregates that would later come to distinguish Keynesian policy-making. The Treasury even moved so far as to compile an inventory of planned public works projects - something they had refused to do during the worst years of depression - in order to estimate the pressure of investment upon the nation's resources. As Middleton argues, however, these were highly pragmatic responses to the peculiar needs of the period of rearmament and did not signal a fundamental, or even partial, conversion to Keynesian ideas. See Middleton, *Towards the Planned Economy*, 118-20, 168-71.

31 *Manchester Guardian*, 21 April 1937, cited in Shay, *British Rearmament*, 149, and more generally, 147-55; Peden, *British Rearmament and the Treasury*, 87.

32 Peden, *British Rearmament and the Treasury*, 87-8; Shay, *British Rearmament*, 155-7; Middleton, *Towards the Managed Economy*, 179; Note by the Chancellor of the Exchequer, 16 March 1938, in T171/340; Sabine, *British Budgets in Peace and War*, chapter VI.

33 Hopkins to John Wood, 16 February 1937, in T175/96, cited in Peden, *British Rearmament and the Treasury*, 78, and more generally, 78-9; Hopkins note on expenditure, April, 1939, in T175/114.

34 Fisher to Simon, 3 January 1939, quoted in Peden, *British Rearmament and the Treasury*, 105; Alan Booth, *British Economic Policy, 1931-49* (London: Harvester Wheatsheaf, 1989), 35-8.

7 LABOUR AND THE STATE BETWEEN THE WARS

1 Ross McKibbin, *The Evolution of the Labour Party, 1910-1924* (Oxford: Oxford University Press, 1974), 107; "Labour's Call to the People," reprinted in F.W.S. Craig, ed., *British General Election Manifestos, 1900-1974* (London: Macmillan, 1975), 31—2.

2 W.R. Garside, *British Unemployment, 1919-1939* (Cambridge: Cambridge University Press, 1990); Alan Deacon, *In Search of the Scrounger: The Administration of Unemployment Insurance in Britain, 1920-1931* (London: Bell, 1976).

3 Noel Whiteside, "Social Welfare and Industrial Relations, 1914-1939," in Chris Wrigley, ed., *A History of British Industrial Relations*, Vol. II: *1914-1939* (Brighton: Harvester, 1987), 219; Leslie Hannah, *Inventing Retirement: The Development of Occupational Pensions in Britain* (Cambridge: Cambridge University Press, 1986), 31-2; Anne Crowther, *British Social Policy, 1914-1939* (London: Macmillan, 1988), 50-1.

4 N. Whiteside, "Private Agencies for Public Purposes: Some New Perspectives on Policy Making in Health Insurance between the Wars," *Journal of Social Policy*, XII (1983), 165-94; Jane Lewis, "Dealing with Dependency: State Practices and Social

Realities, 1870–1945," in Lewis, ed., *Women's Welfare/Women's Rights* (London: Croom Helm, 1983), 29; Lewis, *The Politics of Motherhood* (London: Croom Helm, 1980), 41–51.

5 Labour Party Annual Conference, *Report*, 1925, 100; P.A. Ryan, "Poplarism, 1894–1930," in Pat Thane, ed., *The Origins of British Social Policy* (London: Croom Helm, 1978), 70–80; James Gillespie, "Poplarism and Proletarianism: Unemployment and Labour politics in London, 1918–34," in David Feldman and Gareth Stedman Jones, eds, *Metropolis – London: Histories and Representations since 1800* (London: Routledge, 1989), 163–88.

6 Labour Party Annual Conference, *Report*, 1922, 173; Ralph Miliband, *Parliamentary Socialism* (New York: Monthly Review Press, 1964), 93–120; Labour Party Annual Conference, *Report*, 1923, 204, 179.

7 MacDonald, *A Policy for the Labour Party* (London: Leonard Parsons, 1920) 99; Labour Party Annual Conference *Report*, 1924, 106. How little reflection the decision to take office prompted on MacDonald's part is evident in the narrative of David Marquand, *Ramsay MacDonald* (London: Jonathan Cape, 1977), 297–9.

8 Crowther, *British Social Policy*, 56–7.

9 In *A Policy for the Labour Party*, MacDonald had spent considerable time arguing about the Labour party's fitness to govern in matters foreign and military. Likewise, when campaigning in 1924, he could not resist bragging about "a Labour Government that has met kings and rulers of the earth . . . this Labour Government that has met ambassadors, that has faced the rulers of Europe on terms of equality . . . as statesmen." Cited in Miliband, *Parliamentary Socialism*, 114. He also reacted violently against proposals made in 1925 by the party's International Advisory Committee designed to democratize the conduct of foreign policy by reorganizing the Foreign Office and the diplomatic service. See Marquand, *Ramsay MacDonald*, 416–18.

10 Labour Party Annual Conference, *Report*, 1925, 244ff. Bevin's resolution was defeated by 2,587,000 to 512,000 votes. Labour Party Annual Conference, *Report*, 1925, 102.

11 Walter Citrine, *Men and Work: An Autobiography* (London: Hutchinson, 1964), 238.

12 "Parliamentary Report," in the Labour Party Annual Conference, *Report*, 1922, 6-8; John Macnicol, *The Movement for Family Allowances, 1918-1945: A Study in Social Policy Development* (London: Heinemann, 1980); Bentley Gilbert, *British Social Policy, 1914-1939* (London: Batsford, 1970), 235–51; Susan Pedersen, "The Failure of Feminism in the Making of the British Welfare State," *Radical History Review*, 43 (Winter, 1989), 86–110.

13 Labour Party Annual Conference, *Report*, 1922, 5; *On the Dole or Off! What To Do with Britain's Workless: Report on the Prevention of Unemployment* (London, 1926); Alan Booth and Melvyn Pack, *Employment, Capital and Economic Policy: Great Britain, 1918-1939* (Oxford: Basil Blackwell, 1985), 27–8.

14 Oswald Mosley, *Revolution by Reason* (London: ILP Publications, 1925); H.N. Brailsford, John A. Hobson, A. Creech Jones and E.F. Wise, *The Living Wage* (London: ILP Publications, 1926); Booth and Pack, *Employment, Capital and Economic Policy*, 21–6; Labour Party Annual Conference, *Report*, 1928, 231–2; "Labour's Appeal to the Nation" (1929), in Craig, ed., *British General Election Manifestos*, 82.

15 *Britain's Industrial Future, being the Report of the Liberal Industrial Inquiry* (London: Ernest Benn, 1928); *We Can Conquer Unemployment: Mr Lloyd George's Pledge* (London: Cassell, 1929); Booth and Pack, *Employment, Capital and Economic Policy*, 35–54; Memoranda on Certain Proposals Relating to Unemployment, Cmd. 3331, *Parliamentary Papers* (1929).

16 See Keynes' articles on "How to Organise a Wave of Prosperity" in the *Evening Standard* in July, 1928; Peter Clarke, *The Keynesian Revolution in the Making, 1924-1936* (Oxford: Clarendon, 1988), 47-69; and G.C. Peden, "The 'Treasury View' on Public Works and Unemployment in the Interwar Period," *Economic History Review*, XXXVII (1984), 167-81. The crucial documents are in T172/2095, "Cure for Unemployment Memoranda of 1928 and 1929;" T175/26, "Unemployment Memoranda . . . 1928-1930;" and the Leith-Ross papers, T188/275. More specifically, see Hopkins memo of 31 January 1929, in T172/2095; Clarke, *Keynesian Revolution*, 54-8, and Garside, *British Unemployment*, 330, on the views of Joynson-Hicks and Steel-Maitland; Rodney Lowe, *Adjusting to Democracy* (Oxford: Clarendon, 1986), 191, 203-4, on the White Paper; and Grigg to Churchill, 2 March 1929, in T172/2095.

17 Warren Fisher, "Economic General Staff," 3 December 1929, in CAB58/15; Susan Howson and Donald Winch, *The Economic Advisory Council, 1930-1939* (Cambridge: Cambridge University Press, 1977), 17-29; R. Skidelsky, *Politicians and the Slump* (London: Macmillan, 1967), 169-82, 203-20; Clarke, *Keynesian Revolution*, 158; Skidelsky, *Oswald Mosley* (London: Macmillan, 1975), chapter 10. On the Macmillan Committee, see T172/1652 and T171/295; Booth and Pack, *Employment, Capital and Economic Policy*, 169-77; and Clarke, *Keynesian Revolution*, 103-61.

18 The Treasury and the Bank of England co-ordinated their testimony throughout the deliberations of the Macmillan Committee. See, for example, Harvey to Leith-Ross, 20 March 1931 in T188/275. See also Clarke, *Keynesian Revolution*, 148-56; Frederick Leith-Ross, "The Assumptions of Mr Keynes," 28 March 1930, cited in Clarke, 119; and the Treasury's note on "National Development and State Borrowing," July, 1930, reprinted in Skidelsky, *Politicians and the Slump*, 409-13.

19 Roger Middleton, "The Treasury in the 1930s: Political and Administrative Constraints to Acceptance of the 'New' Economics," *Oxford Economic Papers*, n.s. XXXIV (1982), 48-77; Garside, *British Unemployment*, 362-7; Ross McKibbin, "The Economic Policy of the Second Labour Government," *Past and Present*, 68 (August, 1975), 95-123; Skidelsky, *Politicians and the Slump*, 172-4; Alan Bullock, *The Life and Times of Ernest Bevin*, I (London: Heinemann, 1960), 501.

20 See Clarke, *Keynesian Revolution*, 288-92; Lowe, *Adjusting to Democracy*, 219-20; F. M. Miller, "The Unemployment Policy of the National Government, 1931-1936," *Historical Journal*, XIX (1976), 474; Booth and Pack, *Employment, Capital and Economic Policy*, 119-120; the Treasury memoranda in T160/688 and PREM1/183; "The New Deal and British Trade," 1935, in T188/117 (Leith-Ross Papers); and the Treasury memo of 18 July 1939 prepared in response to TUC concerns about unemployment, in T172/1917.

21 McKibbin, "Economic Policy of the Second Labour Government," 114; Stuart Ball, *Baldwin and the Conservative Party: The Crisis of 1929-1931* (New Haven, Yale University Press, 1988), 153-4; Philip Williamson, "A Bankers" Ramp? Financiers and the British Political Crisis of August 1931," *English Historical Review*, IC (1984), 770-806; Skidelsky, *Politicians and the Slump*, 380-2; R.W. Boyce, *British Capitalism at the Crossroads* (Cambridge: Cambridge University Press, 1987), *passim*; and Barbara Malament, "Philip Snowden and the Cabinet Deliberations of August 1931," *Bulletin of the Society for the Study of Labour History*, 41 (Autumn, 1980), 31-3.

22 What follows focuses on the more positive consequences of the post-1931 debate. It is also possible to argue that the experience of 1929-31 closed off policy options for the remainder of the 1930s. See Margaret Weir and Theda Skocpol, "State Structures and the Possibilities for 'Keynesian' Responses to the Great Depression in Sweden, Britain and the United States," in Peter Evans *et al.*, eds, *Bringing the*

State Back In (Cambridge: Cambridge University Press, 1985), 129; Peter Gour-evitch, *Politics in Hard Times* (Ithaca: Cornell University Press, 1987), 135–40; and Bradford Lee, "The Miscarriage of Necessity and Invention: Proto-Keynesianism and Democratic States in the 1930s," in Peter Hall, ed., *The Political Power of Economic Ideas: Keynesianism across Nations* (Princeton: Princeton University Press, 1989), 129–170.

23 See, for example, the speeches given to the Fabian Society and reprinted in *Where Stands Socialism To-Day?* (London: Rich & Cowan, 1933); Harold Laski, *The Crisis and the Constitution: 1931 and After* (London: Hogarth Press, 1932), 56; and Stafford Cripps, "Preface," in C. Addison *et al.*, *Problems of a Socialist Government* (London: Victor Gollancz, 1933), 16.

24 Cripps, "Can Socialism Come by Constitutional Methods?" in Addison *et al.*, *Problems of a Socialist Government*, 35–66.

25 Ernest Bevin and Colin Clark, "Reorganisation of Government Departments and Ministerial Functions," 22 January 1932, in Fabian Society Papers, J38/2, Nuffield College. I owe this reference to my colleague Peter Weiler, who also supplied me with a copy of the text.

26 On Attlee's reaction to the crisis of 1931, see Trevor Burridge, *Clement Attlee: A Political Biography* (London: Cape, 1985), 80–4. Attlee's memorandum on "The Reorganization of Government" was written some time in 1932 and is reprinted as Appendix III in Kenneth Harris, *Attlee* (New York: Norton, 1983), 589–95.

27 "Labour and Government," Labour Party Annual Conference, *Report*, 1933, 8-10, 166–8; Lewis Minkin, *The Labour Party Conference* (Manchester: Manchester University Press, 1980), 19; Hugh Dalton, "Draft for Policy Subcommittee on Finance and Trade," 15 March 1933, cited in Elizabeth Durbin, *New Jerusalems: The Labour Party and the Economics of Democratic Socialism* (London: Routledge & Kegan Paul, 1985), 88.

28 See the notes by Laski and Ellen Wilkinson appended to the Committee on Ministers' Powers Report (April, 1932), Cmd. 4060, *Parliamentary Papers* (1931–2), XII, 135–8; Durbin, *New Jerusalems*, 89; Ben Pimlott, *Labour and the Left in the 1930s* (Cambridge: Cambridge University Press, 1977).

29 Michael Newman, "Democracy versus Dictatorship: Labour's Role in the Struggle against British Fascism, 1933–1936," *History Workshop*, 5 (Spring, 1978), 67–88. For the changed view of British democracy see Cripps, *Democracy Up-To-Date* (London: Allen & Unwin, 1939); and Laski, "Government in Wartime," in Fabian Society, *Where Stands Democracy?* (London: Macmillan, 1940), 1–42. On Labour and local government, see J.S. Rowett, "The Labour Party and Local Government: Theory and Practice in the Inter-War Years," D. Phil. thesis, Oxford University, 1979, 245, 330–46; Herbert Morrison, *How Greater London Is Governed* (London: Lovat Dickson & Thompson, 1935); Ken Young, "Re-Reading the Municipal Progress: A Crisis Revisited," in M. Loughlin, M. D. Gelfand and Young, eds, *Half a Century of Municipal Decline, 1935-1985* (London: Allen & Unwin, 1985), 1–25; R. Lowe, *Adjusting to Democracy*, 135–67; and E. Briggs and A. Deacon, "The Creation of the Unemployment Assistance Board," *Policy and Politics*, II, 1 (1973).

30 Labour Party Conference, *Report* 1933, 14, 204–10; J. Cronin, *Labour and Society in Britain, 1918-1979* (London: Batsford, 1984), 102–4.

31 Booth and Pack, *Employment, Capital and Economic Policy*, 80–7, 95–122; Gary Cross, *A Quest for Time: The Reduction of Work in Britain and France, 1840-1940* (Berkeley: University of California Press, 1989), 216–22.

32 Durbin, *New Jerusalems*, 92–115.

33 Booth and Pack, *Employment, Capital and Economic Policy*, 145; Durbin, *New Jerusalems*, 245–48, 260–1; G.D.H. Cole, *Principles of Economic Planning*

(London: Macmillan, 1935); Cole, *The Machinery of Socialist Planning* (London: Hogarth Press, 1938); E.F.M. Durbin, *Problems of Economic Planning* (London: Routledge & Kegan Paul, 1949).
34 Geoffrey Foote, *The Labour Party's Political Thought: A History* (London: Croom Helm, 1985), 149–188.
35 "Labour's Home Policy," 1939, in *Report of the National Executive to the Labour Party Conference* (May, 1940), 95–9.

8 THE "PEOPLE'S WAR" AND THE TRANSFORMATION OF THE STATE

1 This was to be accomplished by means of the Stamp Survey, which grew out of the Economic Advisory Committee and was formed in the summer of 1939 to provide a "Survey of war plans in the economic and financial sphere." See Susan Howson and Donald Winch, *The Economic Advisory Council, 1930-1939* (Cambridge: Cambridge University Press, 1977), 151; R.S. Sayers, *Financial Policy, 1939-1945* (London: HMSO & Longmans, 1956), 153–5; and Russell Jones, *Wages and Employment Policy, 1936-1945* (London: Allen & Unwin, 1987), 15–16.
2 Sayers, *Financial Policy*, 34. The Treasury was also extremely complacent about its methods and procedures. Sir Warren Fisher set up an inquiry in October, 1936 on Treasury organization which concluded in February, 1938 that "After careful consideration we see no reason to recommend any drastic alteration in the present structure of the Treasury." See T199/50c.
3 Maurice Cowling, *The Impact of Hitler: British Politics and British Policy, 1933-1940* (Cambridge: Cambridge University Press, 1975), 355.
4 Keynes published a series of articles in *The Times* in November, 1939 that were later revised and put together as a little book, *How To Pay for the War* (London: Macmillan, 1940). At about the same time Evan Durbin published a book with the same title, *How To Pay for the War* (London: Routledge, 1939), presenting a Labour plan. *The Economist* did a famous series early in 1940 arguing that German war expenditure was greatly outpacing Britain's and calling for substantial increases in taxation. See also "Labour's Next Step: A Wartime Strategy", Fabian Tract, No. 252 (May, 1940). On the originality of Keynes' plan, see Tony Cutler, Karel Williams and John Williams, *Keynes, Beveridge and Beyond* (London: Routledge & Kegan Paul, 1986), 66–7. On the background to Durbin's essay, see Susan Howson, "The Origins of Cheaper Money, 1945–47," *Economic History Review*, XL, 3 (1987), 437.
5 Sayers, *Financial Policy*, 32; Memo "On 'Soaking the Rich'," 21 February 1940 in IR64/83; Frieda Wunderlich, *British Labor and the War* (New York: New School for Social Research, 1941), 50–6, 64.
6 J.M. Lee, *The Churchill Coalition, 1940-1945* (London: Batsford, 1980), 17.
7 Sayers, *Financial Policy*, 46–53.
8 Sayers, *Financial Policy*, 57; Hugh Molson to Churchill, 12 September 1940 and 17 August 1940, in PREM4/18/7, "Budgets July 1940–March 1945;" Sir Herbert Brittain, *The British Budgetary System* (London: Allen & Unwin, 1959), 31; The Sources of War Finance, an Analysis and Estimate of the National Income and Expenditure in 1938 and 1940, Cmd. 6261, *Parliamentary Papers* (1941).
9 B.E.V. Sabine, *British Budgets in Peace and War, 1932-1945* (London: Allen & Unwin, 1970), 181–201.
10 Wunderlich, *British Labor and the War*, 47; Labour Research Department, *The Keynes Plan - Its Danger to the Workers* (London: LRD, 1940).
11 Sayers, *Financial Policy*, 80–5; Sabine, *British Budgets*, 200–1; Churchill to Kingsley Wood, 19 February 1941, in PREM4/18/7; Russell Jones, *Wages and Employment Policy, 1936-1985* (London: Allen & Unwin, 1987), 15–19.
12 Alan Booth, "The 'Keynesian Revolution' in Economic Policy-Making," *Economic*

History Review, XXXVI (1983), 106–7; Booth, *British Economic Policy, 1931–49* (London: Harvester Wheatsheaf, 1989), 62–9; G.C. Peden, "Sir Richard Hopkins and the 'Keynesian Revolution' in Employment Policy, 1929–1945," *Economic History Review*, XXXVI (1983), 281–96; Meade to Lionel Robbins, 15 July 1943, in T230/66. On the Treasury's preference for pessimistic estimates, see Keynes" dissent to the paper, "Influences Affecting the Level of National Income," 25 June 1943, P.R. (43) 35, in CAB87/13. Kingsley Wood in fact used such estimates to restate the Treasury case, first made in January, 1943, against the commitments implied in the Beveridge Report. See Wood, "Postwar National Income and Taxation," 25 June 1943, P.R. (43) 63, in CAB87/13.

13   Mary Murphy, "England's Experience in Curbing Inflation through Fiscal Devices," in Marriner Eccles *et al.*, *Curbing Inflation Through Taxation* (New York: Tax Institute, 1944), 202; Jim Tomlinson, *Employment Policy: The Crucial Years 1939–1955* (Oxford: Clarendon, 1987), 24; José Harris, "Some Aspects of Social Policy in Britain during the Second World War," in W.J. Mommsen, ed., *The Emergence of the Welfare State in Britain and Germany* (London: Croom Helm, 1981), 247–62; Harold Laski, "Government in Wartime," in Fabian Society, *Where Stands Democracy?* (London: Macmillan, 1940), 7. The contrast between the constraints imposed on policy by the debt after the First World War and the relative equanimity with which it was dealt during and after the Second World War can be seen from the deliberations of the National Debt Enquiry committee, which met during 1945. See T230/94 and the extensive references in the diary of James Meade (Meade Papers, LSE).

14   Ian McLaine, *Ministry of Morale: Home Front Morale and the Ministry of Information in the Second World War* (London, 1979); Correlli Barnett, *The Audit of War: The Illusion and Reality of Britain as a Great Nation* (London: Macmillan, 1986), 22, 31–3; and Paul Addison, *The Road to 1945* (London: Quartet, 1977), 125–6, 219–24.

15   *Report of the National Executive to the Labour Party Conference*, May, 1940, 95–9; Attlee, cited in Addison, *Road to 1945*, 121–2. See also Addison more generally, 122–6, 167.

16   Social Insurance and Allied Services, Cmd. 6404, *Parliamentary Papers* (1942–3), VI; José Harris, *William Beveridge: A Biography* (Oxford: Clarendon, 1977), 378–428; Addison, *Road to 1945*, 211–28.

17   On popular reactions to the report, see Addison, *Road to 1945*, 217–19; on the more mixed response of "organized opinion," see PREM4/89/2/Pt 2; and on official reactions, see T172/2093. See also J. Harris, "Political Ideas and the Debate on State Welfare, 1940–1945," in Harold Smith, ed., *War and Social Change: British Society in the Second World War* (Manchester: Manchester University Press, 1986), 248–9.

18   Harry Pelling, "The Impact of the War on the Labour Party," in Smith, ed., *War and Social Change*, 129–48; Stephen Brooke, "Revisionists and Fundamentalists: The Labour Party and Economic Policy during the Second World War," *Historical Journal*, XXXII, 1 (1989), 157–75; E. Durbin, "Keynes, the British Labour Party and the Economics of Democratic Socialism," in O.F. Hamonda and J.N. Smithin, eds., *Keynes and Public Policy after Fifty Years*, I (New York: New York University Press, 1988), 39–40; Kevin Jefferys, *The Churchill Coalition and Wartime Politics, 1940–1945* (Manchester: Manchester University Press, 1990); Harris, "Debate on State Welfare," 251; and Harris, *William Beveridge*, 400–1, 415. The debate on family allowances can be followed in the Labour Party Annual Conference *Report*, 1941, 166–69, 189–93; Labour Party Annual Conference *Report*, 1942, 137–7; and John Macnicol, *The Movement for Family Allowances 1918–1945* (London: Heinemann, 1980), chapter 7. The employers' spokesman was John Boyd, writing to Forbes Watson on 18 January 1943 and cited in F. Honigsbaum,

"The Interwar Health Insurance Scheme: A Rejoinder," *Journal of Social Policy*, XII, 2 (1984), 522.

19 The National Council of Labour, representing both the Labour party and the Trades Union Congress, publicly supported the plan in December, 1942. The NCL also offered a point-by-point comparison between Beveridge's recommendations, the position of the government and their own position. They did not reject a single item in Beveridge's plan, but merely added a couple of qualifications. See the Labour Party Annual Conference *Report*, 1943, 5, 20–6.

20 On deliberations inside the government, see in particular Kevin Jefferys, ed., *Labour and the Wartime Coalition: The Diary of James Chuter Ede, 1941–1945* (London: Historians" Press, 1987), chapter 8; and, more generally, Pat Thane, *The Foundations of the Welfare State* (London: Longman, 1982), 252–3.

21 Kevin Jefferys, "British Politics and Social Policy during the Second World War," *Historical Journal*, XXX, 1 (1987), 123–44; Meade, "Internal Measures for the Prevention of General Unemployment," in CAB87/54, reprinted in Susan Howson, ed., *The Collected Papers of James Meade*, Vol. I, (London: Unwin & Hyman, 1988), 171–83; Peden, "Sir Richard Hopkins and the 'Keynesian Revolution' "; Alan Booth, "The War and the White Paper," in S. Glynn and Booth, eds, *The Road to Full Employment* (London: Allen & Unwin, 1987), 175–95; Russell Jones, *Wages and Employment Policy*, 20–30; R. MacLeod, "The Promise of Full Employment," in Smith, *War and Social Change*, 78–100; and Jim Tomlinson, *Employment Policy: The Crucial Years, 1939–1955* (Oxford: Clarendon, 1987), 45–79. See the White Paper on Employment Policy (May, 1944), Cmd. 6527, *Parliamentary Papers* (1943–4), VIII.

22 Tomlinson, *Employment Policy*, 48–9; "The Maintenance of Employment, Prefatory Note by the Treasury" (October, 1943) in CAB87/63.

23 "The Maintenance of Employment. Memorandum by the Economic Section of the War Cabinet Secretariat," P.R. (43) 26, 18 May 1943, in CAB87/13; Tomlinson, *Employment Policy*, 49–57.

24 William Beveridge, *Full Employment in a Free Society* (London: Allen & Unwin, 1944).

25 Booth, "The War and the White Paper," 186–9; Richard Hopkins, 10 May 1944, quoted in Tomlinson, *Employment Policy*, 59; Keynes, quoted in Booth, 184; and Cutler *et al.*, *Keynes, Beveridge and Beyond*, 71.

26 Trades Union Congress, *Interim Report on Post-War Reconstruction* (London: TUC, 1944). For some of the disagreements, see James Meade's critique, "Sir William Beveridge's 'Full Employment in a Free Society' and the White Paper on Employment Policy," 1 December, 1944, in CAB123/229, CAB124/83 and T230/16 and reprinted in *The Collected Papers of James Meade*, 233–64.

27 Beveridge Papers, IXa 15, Full Employment Investigation, Evidence.

28 Beveridge, *Full Employment in a Free Society*, 175–80.

29 See Meade, "Sir William Beveridge's 'Full Employment' and the White Paper," *Collected Papers*, 256–57. Beveridge was defended in a memo by R.C. Tress, "Sir William Beveridge on Full Employment in a Free Society, the Government on Employment Policy, and Mr Meade on Both," 8 December 1944, in CAB124/831. Tress did not, however, specifically defend Beveridge's position on the machinery of government. Among officials Meade's views were endorsed by John Jewkes and by Norman Brook, who had the memo widely circulated throughout Whitehall in January, 1945. See notes by Brook and Jewkes in CAB124/831 and by Edward Bridges and Lord Woolton in PREM4/96/8.

30 J.M. Lee, *Reviewing the Machinery of Government: An Essay on the Anderson Committee and its Successors* (London: privately published, 1977); Ivor Jennings, *Parliament Must Be Reformed: A Programme for Democratic Government*

(London: Kegan Paul, 1941), 57–8; letters by Lords Ampthill, Strabolgi and Salisbury and by Hugh Molson, MP to Churchill, in PREM4/8/6; Hankey, commenting on the report on the Treasury to the Machinery of Government Committee, 1943, and Gilbert's response, in PREM8/17 and T199/78.

31 Lee, *Reviewing the Machinery of Government*, 8–19; Richard Chapman and J.R. Greenaway, *The Dynamics of Administrative Reform* (London: Croom Helm, 1980), 126–30; Chapman, *Ethics in the British Civil Service* (London: Routledge, 1988), 191–4.

32 D.N. Chester *et al.*, eds, *The Organization of British Central Government, 1914-1964* (London: Allen & Unwin, 1968), 94–105.

33 "Functions of the Cabinet Secretariat. Historical Memo," June, 1944, in T230/90; "War Cabinet Secretariat. Functions and Organisation of the Economic Section, 1939–1940," in CAB21/940; David Butt, "Notes on the History of the Economic Section," in T230/283, Part II: and Alec Cairncross and Nita Watts, *The Economic Section, 1939-1961: A Study in Economic Advising* (London: Routledge, 1989), 10–39. On the prewar background and controversies, see CAB58/15, which depicts the efforts by the Treasury to limit the role of economists in government; "Committee on the Future Organisation of the Economic Advisory Committee, 1938," in CAB58/16; and Howson and Winch, *Economic Advisory Council*, 147–8.

34 On these innovations, see Alan Booth, "Economic Advice at the Centre of British Government, 1939–1941," *Historical Journal*, XXIX, 3 (1986), 655–75; D.N. Chester, "The Central Machinery for Economic Policy," in Chester, ed., *Lessons of the War Economy* (Cambridge: Cambridge University Press, 1951), 5–33; CAB21/1579; Lee, *Churchill Coalition*, 84.

35 Lee, *Churchill Coalition*, 98–101; Max Nicholson, *The System: The Misgovernment of Modern Britain* (New York: McGraw-Hill, 1967), 279, 292, 412–4.

36 Lee, *Churchill Coalition*, 85–97; Keith Middlemas, *Power, Competition and the State*, Vol. I: *Britain in Search of Balance, 1940-1961* (Stanford: Hoover Institution, 1986), 23, 29–30.

37 Durbin, n.d., quoted in Brooke, "Revisionists and Fundamentalists," 164.

38 PREM4/8/7; Bridges to Churchill, 26 August 1942, and Churchill to Bridges, 27 August, 1942, Laski to Churchill, 1 October 1942 and Churchill to Laski, 10 October 1942, in PREM4/63/2; Middlemas, *Power, Competition and the State*, 77–83; Lee, *Reviewing the Machinery of Government*, 11–19. Cripps" original plan was for "another Haldane," but Anderson convinced him that it should be an inside inquiry. The phrase about "official silence" comes from the LSE journal devoted to reconstruction, *Agenda* (May, 1944). The nearest equivalent to a final report was Anderson's lecture to the Royal Institute of Public Administration, on 4 December, 1945, which appeared as "The Machinery of Government," *Public Administration*, XXIV, 3 (Autumn, 1946), 147–56.

39 See the memo on superintending ministries in CAB21/1998, and Bridges" impatient reaction in his letter to Norman Brook of 18 February 1943: "I am sick to death of the word 'co-ordinate;' Keynes to Lionel Robbins, 1 February 1943, in T230/283; Lee, *Reviewing the Machinery of Government*, 29, 95–6; entries for 8 February and 4 November 1943 in *The Second World War Diary of Hugh Dalton, 1940-1945* (London: Jonathan Cape, 1986), 551–2, 663–4; Bevin to Anderson, 22 May 1943 and the accompanying memorandum from the Ministry of Labour on "Post-War Responsibility for Employment Policy," the unsigned response (possibly by Norman Brook) of 15 June 1943, and the response contained in James Meade's note to Anderson of 24 June 1943, in CAB123/229; and the Attlee memo of 31 December 1942, in PREM8/17.

40 B.D. Fraser, R.M.J. Harris and E.C.S. Wade, "The Role of the Treasury," 27 August 1943, in PREM4/8/6.
41 Bridges to Robbins, 21 January 1943, in T230/283; "Report on the Centre of the Government Machine," to which was attached as an Appendix Lionel Robbins' "Notes on the Role of the Economist in the Future Machinery of Government," in T199/78 and also in T222/75; Attlee to Morrison, 9 November 1945, in PREM8/17; and, on Labour's subsequent evaluation of the Committee's work, see the report of the meeting of 18 October 1945, MG (45), 10th Meeting, in T222/75.
42 The Conservative critic was Leo Amery. See CAB120/228, "Reorganization of the War Office, 1940–1943;" and the Memorandum by Anthony Eden, "Proposals for the Reform of the Foreign Service," November, 1942, W.P. (42) 538, in PREM4/35/5. On the interwar background, see David Dilks, "The British Foreign Office between the Wars," in B.J. McKercher and D.J. Moss, eds, *Shadow and Substance in British Foreign Policy*, II: *1895–1939* (Edmonton: University of Alberta Press, 1984).
43 See Bevin's memo on "The Diplomatic Service," n.d., and Dalton's response to Bevin, 22 December 1940, in CAB127/209; Alan Bullock, *Ernest Bevin: Foreign Secretary, 1945–1951* (New York: Norton, 1983), 73, 96; and Peter Weiler, *British Labor and the Cold War* (Stanford: Stanford University Press, 1988).
44 Eden, "Proposals for the Reform of the Foreign Service."
45 The final form of the reforms was decided at a meeting on 7 January 1943. See Bridges to Churchill, 3 December 1942 and 10 December 1942 and Bridges' memo "Reform of the Foreign Service," 16 December 1942, and Eden, "Proposals for the Reform of the Foreign Service," in PREM4/35/5; and Attlee's memo on the "Application of Democratic Principles in Government," 11 May 1943, W.P. (43) 199, in CAB118/32.
46 "Mr Churchill's Declaration of Policy to the Electors," in F.W.S. Craig, ed., *British General Election Manifestos, 1900–1974* (London: Macmillan, 1975), 113–23.

9 TOWARDS THE "LIBERAL–SOCIALIST" STATE, 1945–51

1 Anthony King, "Overload: Problems of Governing in the 1970s," *Political Studies*, XXII, 2–3 (1975), 163; Keith Middlemas, *Power, Competition and the State* Vol. I: *Britain in Search of Balance, 1940–1961* (Stanford: Hoover Institution, 1986), 91–2.
2 The most comprehensive account is Kenneth Morgan, *Labour in Power, 1945–1952* (Oxford: Clarendon, 1984), 142–73. See also Jörgen Hess, "The Social Policy of the Attlee Government," in W.J. Mommsen, ed., *The Emergence of the Welfare State in Britain and Germany* (London: Croom Helm, 1981), 296–314; and, for a brief but reliable account, G.C. Peden, *British Economic and Social Policy: Lloyd George to Margaret Thatcher* (Oxford: Philip Allan, 1985), 152–9.
3 The doctors came around in part due to Bevan's reassurances in April, 1948, in part due to the work on behalf of the new system by doctors associated with the Royal Colleges and in part because the scheme proved so popular with their patients. See Charles Webster, *The Health Services since the War* (London: HMSO, 1988); Webster, "Conflict and Consensus: Explaining the British Health Service," *Twentieth Century British History*, I, 2 (1990), 115–51; Morgan, *Labour in Power*, 158–60; and Harold Perkin, *The Rise of Professional Society: England since 1880* (London: Routledge, 1989), 346–7.
4 Centre for Contemporary Studies, *Unpopular Education: Schooling and Social Democracy in England since 1944* (London: Hutchinson, 1981), 59–62; "Let Us Face the Future" (1945), in F.W.S. Craig, ed., *British General Election Manifestos, 1900–1974* (London: Macmillan, 1975), 128–9; Paul Addison, *The Road to 1945* (London: Quartet, 1977), 267; Morgan, *Labour in Power*, 167; and Peden, *Economic and Social Policy*, 157–8.

5 On the nationalization of the Bank, see T241/5. On the pre-history, see Sidney Pollard, "The Nationalisation of the Banks: The Chequered History of a Socialist Proposal," in D. Martin and D. Rubinstein, eds, *Ideology and the Labour Movement* (London: Croom Helm, 1979), 167–90; Morgan, *Labour in Power*, 94–110.

6 Steven Tolliday, *Business, Banking and Politics: The Case of British Steel, 1918–1939* (Cambridge, MA: Harvard University Press, 1987); Morgan, *Labour in Power*, 110–21.

7 T.H. Marshall, *Citizenship and Social Class* (Cambridge: Cambridge University Press, 1950); Carole Pateman, "The Patriarchal Welfare State," in Amy Gutman, ed., *Democracy and the Welfare State* (Princeton: Princeton University Press, 1988), 231–60; Pat Thane, *The Foundations of the Welfare State* (London: Longman, 1982), 249–50; Denise Riley, *War in the Nursery* (London: Virago, 1983); Barry Jones and Michael Keating, *Labour and the British State* (Oxford: Clarendon, 1985), 60–3; Bernard Donoughue and G.W. Jones, *Herbert Morrison: Portrait of a Politician* (London: Weidenfeld and Nicolson, 1973), 140–50, 186–7; Elizabeth Durbin, *New Jerusalems: The Labour Party and the Economics of Democratic Socialism* (London: Routledge & Kegan Paul, 1985), 161–8, 186–94, 260–1, 271–6; Herbert Morrison *et al.*, *Can Planning Be Democratic?* (London: Routledge, 1944); CAB124/928, "Workers" Assistance in the Management of the Socialised Industries," especially George Isaacs' 28 March 1946 Memo, S.I. (M) (46) 16; R. Pryke, *Public Enterprise in Practice* (London: MacGibbon & Kee, 1971); and *The Nationalized Industries* (Oxford: Martin Robertson, 1981).

8 Peden, *Economic and Social Policy*, 154–5; Hess, "Social Policy of the Attlee Government," 304–7; Asa Briggs, "The Social Services," in G.D.N. Worswick and P.H. Ady, eds., *The British Economy, 1945-1950* (Oxford: Clarendon, 1952), 370, 373–7.

9 In January, 1946 the government announced their intention of continuing the wartime arrangements. See the report of the 21 January 1946 meeting of the Ministerial Economic Planning Committee, MEP (46), 1, in CAB134/503; and the record of the 18 October 1945 meeting between Cripps, Morrison and Dalton, MG (45), 10 in T222/75; and, for some of the prior discussion, CAB124/890. See also Peter Hennessy, *Cabinet* (Oxford: Blackwell, 1986), 37–44; R.S. Barker, "Civil Service Attitudes and the Economic Planning of the Attlee Government," *Journal of Contemporary History*, XXI (1986), 473–6; and D.N. Chester, "Machinery of Government and Planning," in Worswick and Ady, *The British Economy*, 336–54.

10 In his diary James Meade refers favourably to Bridges' support for employment policy, in contrast to Wilfrid Eady who, as Meade put it, "remains the real menace to the work of the Economic Section," and to Bernard Gilbert who, again according to Meade, "just does not believe in employment policy." See Meade diary entries for 27 May, 3 June and 23 September 1945, Meade Papers 1/4. On Bridges' position more generally, see Richard Chapman, *Ethics in the British Civil Service* (London: Routledge, 1988), esp. 28–33; Peter Hennessy, *Whitehall* (London: Secker & Warburg, 1989), 138–45, 149–50; and Morgan, *Labor in Power*, 87–8.

11 J.P.R. Maud to Bridges, 25 August 1945, and Bridges' memo on the machinery of planning of 19 September 1945, in CAB124/890; diary entry for 3 June 1945, Meade Papers 1/4; Maud to the Lord President, 9 October 1945, in T222/75; W.S. Murrie to Bridges, n.d., in CAB124/890; Samuel Beer, *Treasury Control* (Oxford: Clarendon, 1957), chapter 1; Lord Bridges, *The Treasury* (London: Allen & Unwin, 1964), 89–103; Bridges to Leslie Rowan, 18 July 1947 and Rowan to Attlee, 24 July 1947, in PREM8/642. On the meeting of officials, which took place on Saturday, 2 March 1946, see Hennessy, *Whitehall*, 121–5; on its effects, see Chapman, *Ethics in the British Civil Service*, 198–9.

12 CAB134/503, "Ministerial Economic Planning Committee, 1946-47." Cripps tried unsuccessfully in July, 1945 to have the Economic Section attached to the Board of Trade, but Morrison refused. See Morrison to Cripps, 31 July 1945 and also Bridges to John Woods, 21 August 1945, in CAB124/890. On the changing role of the Economic Section, see Alec Cairncross and Nita Watts, *The Economic Section, 1939-1961: A Study of Economic Advising* (London: Routledge, 1989), 113-31; and Cairncross, *Years of Recovery: British Economic Policy, 1945-1951* (London: Methuen, 1985), 47-52.

13 For the debates that did occur, see Jim Tomlinson, *Employment Policy: The Crucial Years, 1939-1955* (Oxford: Clarendon, 1987), chapter 5.

14 This was how Meade described the choice to Herbert Morrison. See Meade's diary entry for 1 September 1945, Meade Papers, 1/4.

15 Diary of James Meade, entries for 26 August and 1 September 1945, Meade Papers 1/4.

16 The positions of Keynes, Robinson, Meade and Dalton are outlined in Susan Howson, " 'Socialist' Monetary Policy: Monetary Thought in the Labour Party in the 1940s," *History of Political Economy*, XX, 4 (1988), 543-64. See also Ben Pimlott, *Hugh Dalton* (London: Cape, 1985), 461-5; Susan Howson, "The Origins of Cheaper Money, 1945-1947," *Economic History Review*, XL (August, 1987); Alan Booth, "The 'Keynesian Revolution' in Economic Policy-Making," *Economic History Review*, XXXVI (1983), 103-23; and *British Economic Policy, 1931-49* (London: Harvester Wheatsheaf, 1989); Jim Tomlinson, *Employment Policy*, 106-21; Neil Rollings, "British Budgetary Policy, 1945-1954: A 'Keynesian Revolution' ?" *Economic History Review*, XLI (1988), 283-98; diary entry for 16 July 1945, Meade Papers, 1/4.

17 Morgan, *Labour in Power*, 330-58; Roger Eatwell, *The 1945-1951 Labour Governments* (London: Batsford, 1979); Jacques Leruez, *Economic Planning and Politics in Britain* (Oxford: Martin Robertson, 1975), 45-52.

18 A series of other minor changes, designed to reduce expenditure, were also introduced. See C.P. 237, "Administrative Measures for the Emergency," 22 August 1947, in CAB129/20.

19 Bridges to Dalton, 23 September 1947, cited in Booth, "The 'Keynesian Revolution' in Economic Policy-Making," 122; memo on budgetary policy by Robert Hall, 16 March 1950, in CAB124/1167; Morgan, *Labour in Power*, 348; Pimlott, *Hugh Dalton*, 522-3.

20 Pimlott, *Hugh Dalton*, 524-48; Chester, "Machinery of Government and Planning,' 348-9; Edward Bridges, "Proposals for Strengthening the Staff for Economic Planning," 6 March 1947, in CAB124/1081; Economic Planning Committee, 7 March 1947, GEN169 (47), 2nd Mtg., PREM8/642; Morrison to Bridges, 6 July 1947, cited in Donoughue and Jones, *Herbert Morrison*, 407, and more generally, 405-8; Rowan to Attlee, 24 July 1947, PREM8/647; Edwin Plowden, *An Industrialist in the Treasury: The Post-War Years* (London: Andre Deutsch, 1989), 18; Norman Brook to Attlee, 4 September 1947, in PREM8/422.

21 Norman Brook to John Woods, 7 December 1948, in CAB21/2220; Plowden, *Industrialist in the Treasury*, 17; Pimlott, *Hugh Dalton*, 520; Cairncross, *Years of Recovery*, 137; Sir Richard "Otto" Clarke, *Anglo-American Economic Collaboration in War and Peace, 1942-1949*, edited by Alec Cairncross (Oxford: Clarendon, 1982), 79-84; Michael Hogan, *The Marshall Plan: America, Britain, and the Reconstruction of Western Europe, 1947-1952* (Cambridge: Cambridge University Press, 1987), 27-53; Alan Milward, *The Reconstruction of Western Europe, 1945-1951* (London: Methuen, 1984), chapters 1-3; Bridges' memo on "Further American Aid," 17 October 1945, in BT91/7; Alan Bullock, *Ernest Bevin: Foreign Secretary*

(New York: Norton, 1983), 404–27; T. Brett, S. Gilliatt and A. Pople, "Planned Trade, Labour Party Policy and US Intervention," *History Workshop*, 13 (Spring, 1982), 130–42.

22 "Interdepartment Organisation for Handling Balance of Payments Questions, 1947" in PREM8/493; Norman Brook, "Organisation for Economic Planning," O.N. (48), 6th, 11 February 1948, in CAB21/2220; memo by Attlee, 19 March 1948, EPC (48) 21st, and note from Brook to Attlee, 23 March 1948, in PREM8/770; Clarke, *Anglo-American Collaboration*, 190–200; Chancellor of the Exchequer, "European Recovery Programme," 22 December 1947, C.P. (47) 340, in CAB129/22; T238/1 on the Treasury's work in setting up the machinery for the Marshall Plan; Peter Weiler, *British Labour and the Cold War* (Stanford: Stanford University Press, 1988); CAB134/216, "Economic Policy Committee, 1948;" Plowden, *Industrialist in the Treasury*, 41–51; Clarke, "Marshall Proposals. Alternative Action in the Event of a Breakdown, 1947," in T229/136; "Economic Consequences of Receiving No European Recovery Programme Aid," 23 June 1948, C.P. (48) 161, in CAB129/88; Cairncross and Watts, *Economic Section*, 147, 176, 181–2; Brook to Attlee, 2 June 1948 and Brook, "European Recovery Programme: Committee Organisation," 3 June 1948, C.P. (48), 137, in PREM8/769; Brook to John H. Woods, 7 December 1948, in CAB21/2220; Cabinet Conclusions 1948, 20 (2), 8 March 1948, excerpt from C.P. (48) 75, in CAB128/12; "Treasury Administration and Modification of Economic Surveys and Long-Term Programme," in T199/234; "CEPS Long-term Programme Working Group," in T229/199.

23 See the FBI statement, "Industry and the Way to Recovery," 27 August 1947, and Plowden's brief for the meeting with Federation representatives on 5 September, in T229/63; Clarke, *Anglo-American Economic Collaboration*; the statement by Will Clayton, delivered in a meeting with British Cabinet members on 25 June 1947 and the *General Report* of the Committee on European Economic Co-operation, both cited in C.C.S. Newton, "The Sterling Crisis of 1947 and the British Response to the Marshall Plan," *Economic History Review*, XXXVII (1984), 395–7, 404.

24 Clarke, *Anglo-American Collaboration*, 201–10; Hogan, *Marshall Plan*, 109–14, 179–185, 225–35, 301–30; David Goldsworthy, *Colonial Issues in British Politics, 1945–1961* (Oxford: Clarendon, 1971), 18; J.M. Lee, *Colonial Development and Good Government* (Oxford: Clarendon, 1967), 111–27; David Fieldhouse, "The Labour Governments and the Empire-Commonwealth, 1945–51," in Ritchie Ovendale, ed., *The Foreign Policy of the Labour Governments, 1945–1951* (Leicester: Leicester University Press, 1984), 83–120; Morgan, *Labour in Power*, 200–202.

25 Bevin elaborated his vision in a conversation with Dalton in October 1948. See the entry for 15 October 1948 in the *Political Diary of Hugh Dalton*, 443. For a broader discussion, see P.S. Gupta, *Imperialism and the British Labour Movement, 1914–1964* (London: Macmillan, 1975), 304–25.

26 Jim Tomlinson, "Industrial Democracy and the Labour Government, 1945–1951," *Brunel University, Discussion Papers in Economics*, No. 8702, 1987; Anthony Carew, *Labour under the Marshall Plan* (Manchester: Manchester University Press, 1987).

27 This was the conclusion of the Control of Investment Committee appointed in 1949, cited in Tomlinson, *Employment Policy*, 101, and more generally, 83–102.

28 Middlemas, *Power, Competition and the State*, 141–2, 165; Howson, " 'Socialist' Monetary Policy," 558–9.

29 Gilbert to Edward Bridges, 20 March 1945, cited in Tomlinson, *Employment Policy*, 81–2; Alan Booth, "The Second World War and the Origins of Modern Regional

Policy," *Economy and Society*, 11 (1982), 1–21; and Michael Fogarty, "The Location of Industry," in Worswick and Ady, *British Economy*, 261–70; and, for the interwar background, Carol Heim, "Interwar Responses to Regional Decline," in Bernard Elbaum and William Lazonick, eds, *The Decline of the British Economy* (Oxford: Clarendon, 1986), 240–65; Stephen Ward, *The Geography of Interwar Britain: The State and Uneven Development* (London: Routledge, 1988); and W.R. Garside, *British Unemployment, 1919–1939* (Cambridge: Cambridge University Press, 1990), 240–77; Sidney Pollard, *The Development of the British Economy, 1914–1967* (New York: St Martin's, 1969), 385–6; R. MacLeod, "The Promise of Full Employment," in Harold Smith, ed., *War and Social Change: British Society in the Second World War* (Manchester: Manchester University Press, 1986), 92; Board of Trade, "The Long Term Prospects of British Industry," 23 June 1945, in CAB87/14; Correlli Barnett, *The Audit of War* (London: Macmillan, 1986), 55–7; L. Rostas, *Comparative Productivity of British and American Industry* (Cambridge: Cambridge University Press, 1948).

30 Alec Cairncross and Barry Eichengreen, *Sterling in Decline: The Devaluations of 1931, 1949 and 1967* (Oxford: Basil Blackwell, 1983), 111–55; Cairncross, *Years of Recovery*, 165–211; Scott Newton, "The 1949 Sterling Crisis and British Policy Towards European Integration," *Review of International Studies*, XI, 3 (1985), 171–5.

31 See the entry for 28 June 1949 in Philip Williams, ed., *The Diary of Hugh Gaitskell, 1945–1956* (London: Cape, 1983), 116; P. Williams, *Hugh Gaitskell. A Political Biography* (London: Cape, 1979), 195–203; the unsigned memo, apparently by a Treasury official, of 23 June 1949 in PREM8/976; and the "Draft Report of the Working Group on Wages Policy and Devaluation," 6 September 1949, in T229/213.

32 See the records of the committee on "Wages Policy Following Devaluation," in T229/213; Cairncross and Eichengreen, *Sterling in Decline*, 134–9; entry for 3 August 1949, *Diary of Hugh Gaitskell*, 130; Douglas Jay, *Change and Fortune: A Political Record* (London: Hutchinson, 1980); entry for 19 July 1949 by Hugh Dalton in Ben Pimlott, ed., *The Political Diary of Hugh Dalton: 1918–1940, 1945–1960* (London: Cape, 1986), 453–5.

33 Cairncross, *Years of Recovery*, 25–8, 154; Cairncross and Eichengreen, *Sterling in Decline*, 151–5; Hogan, *Marshall Plan*, 368–72. Cf. Newton, "The 1949 Sterling Crisis," 179–81; Jim Tomlinson, *Public Policy and the Economy since 1900* (Oxford: Clarendon, 1990), 234–7.

34 Hall to Plowden and Nicholson, 27 September 1950, in CAB124/1167; and on rearmament see the entry for 30 April 1951 in Alec Cairncross, ed., *The Robert Hall Diaries, 1947–1953* (London: Unwin & Hyman, 1989), 155–6.

35 On PAYE see T171/366 and T171/1992; on Dalton's thinking, see Dalton to Bridges, "Next Year's Budget," 20 November 1945, in IR63/171. On the "gap" see the Cabinet discussion of the *Economic Survey 1947*, Cabinet Conclusions, C. C. 7 (2) and C. C. 8 (2), 16 January 1947, CAB128/9, during which the gap was discussed in terms of a shortage of 630,000 workers. See also Pimlott, *Hugh Dalton*, 452–5; Cairncross, *Years of Recovery*, 422–3; J.C.R. Dow, *The Management of the British Economy, 1945–1960* (Cambridge: Cambridge University Press, 1964), 19–20; B.E.V. Sabine, *A History of Income Tax* (London: Allen & Unwin, 1966), 207–11.

36 Dow, *Management of the British Economy*, 27–8, 38, 47–8, 198–9. Even the Federation of British Industries had come around by 1946 to accepting the priority of closing the inflationary gap through high taxes and welcomed Dalton's decision to "abandon the aim of achieving a Budget balance rigidly year by year, but rather to achieve this objective over a number of years." This did not, however, prevent

them from opposing the continuation of excess profits tax. See the submission of the FBI to the Chancellor, 10 January 1946, in IR63/171.

37 See the report of the meeting of the joint deputation of the Federation of British Industries and the Association of British Chambers of Commerce to the Chancellor, 4 March 1943, in T172/2003; the "Evidence of Association of British Chambers of Commerce and Federation of British Industries to the Committee of the Board of Inland Revenue on Post-War Taxation," August, 1943; the reports of the meetings of 15 October and 5 November 1943 between BIR officials and representatives of the FBI and ABCC; and the submission of the National Farmers Union of 31 December 1943, in IR63/169, "Income Tax Bill 1945." On Keynes' intentions, see the memo (undated but presumably from March, 1944) from Hopkins to the Chancellor, in IR63/169; also B.E.V. Sabine, *British Budgets in Peace and War, 1932-1945* (London: Allen and Unwin, 1970), 248–9; A.R. Ilersic, *Government Finance and Fiscal Policy in Post-War Britain* (London: Staples, 1955), 135–46; C.M. 65 (4), 10 November 1949, CAB128/16.

38 The Radcliffe committee, as the Royal Commission was known, published a series of three reports. See the Final Report of the Royal Commission on the Taxation of Profits and Income (June 1955), Cmd. 9474, *Parliamentary Papers* (1955–6) XXVII, especially the "Memorandum of Dissent" by Labour's representatives, Nicholas Kaldor, George Woodcock and H.L. Bullock. (354–424) On the background, see Kaldor's "Introduction" to his *Reports on Taxation*, I: *Papers Relating to the United Kingdom* (New York: Holmes and Meier, 1980), vii–x. On setting up the committee, see PREM8/1182; T171/427; and the Cabinet discussion reported in C. M. 50 (4), 25 July 1950, CAB128/18.

39 Robert Hall to Edwin Plowden, 18 May 1950, in T171/427; unsigned memo to Bridges, 28 June 1950, apparently from an official in the Board of Trade, in T171/427.

40 R.F. Bretherton, "Taxation and the Control of Investment by Companies," 7 November 1950, in T229/340.

41 See, in particular, records of the Government Organisation Committee; especially the minutes for 5 November 1947, G.O.C. (47) 1st, and for 27 May 1948, G.O.C. (48) 2nd, T222/592; memo by Woods, 14 July 1948, in T222/504. The assumption of Treasury predominance was key to the committee's deliberations. As Woods wrote to Norman Brook on 8 December 1948, "I am of course very conscious of the attitude of some ministers towards further concentration of power in the hands of the Treasury. But I had better say straight out that, in my judgment, while the thing has in fact happened by a series of what one might call historical accidents, we had better now face the fact, and accept it, that the Treasury is the leading Department *in economic policy generally*. This is, of course, a big subject . . . But if the Treasury Organisation Committee is to do its job, it has to make an assumption on this point; and . . . this is, in fact, the assumption on which we are working." See Woods to Brook, 8 December 1948, CAB21/2220; and also T.L. Rowan, "Treasury Organisation," 18 October 1948, T222/504.

42 Plowden to Bridges on 8 July 1947, cited in Neil Rollings, "British Budgetary Policy, 1945–1954: A 'Keynesian Revolution'?, *Economic History Review*, XLI, 2 (1988), 283–98; Bridges to Plowden, 24 July 1947, T229/208; Norman Brook, "Organisation for Economic Planning," O.N. (48) 6, 11 February 1948 and the annex to the memo: "Duties of the Economic Secretary, Treasury," in CAB21/2220; T.O.C. (48) 3rd, 16 September 1948, and T.L. Rowan's memorandum on "Treasury Organization," 18 October 1948, in T222/504; "Interim Report," 17 February 1949, T.O.C. (49) 3, T222/510; "Treasury Administration and Modifications of Economic Surveys and Long-Term Programme," T199/234.

43 Cripps, "Review of the Machinery of Government," M.G. (49) 3rd, 30 November 1949, PREM8/1443; G.O.C. (49) 4th, 14 December 1949, T222/592; L. Petch to D. Allen, 18 February 1950, T229/272; Allen, "The Essential Functions of Government in the Economic Field," in T222/338.

44 Economic Organisation Working Group, Second Interim Report: "Organisation for Discharging the Major Economic Responsibilities of Government," September 1951, in T222/346; "The Major Responsibilities of the Treasury," 17 November 1950, and "The Major Activities of Government," 16 June 1950, T238/62; memo of 10 July 1951 by L. Petch, in T273/188.

45 See "The Investment Programme," appendix to memo on "The Work of the Central Economic Planning Staff," May, 1951, in CAB21/2220; the memo of 14 April 1950 by H.A. Turner, in T229/272; Allen's memo on "Economic Planning," drafted in late 1949, in T229/208; "Treasury Delegation Committee Report," T.D.C. (51) 3, 11 December 1951, T222/1068; Middlemas, *Power, Competition and the State*, 193–96. The committee's report was actually never circulated, for it was completed on the eve of the Conservative general election victory and officials seem to have felt that the new government would not have welcomed such a report at the outset of their term of office. See the report of the meeting of the reconstituted Steering Committee on the Economic Organization Enquiry, G.O.C. (SC) (52) 2, 27 June 1952, CAB134/906.

46 Memorandum by Hugh Gaitskell, "Economic Planning and Liberalisation," E.P.C. (50) 9, 7 January 1950, CAB134/225; G.D.N. Worswick, "Direct Controls," and P. Ady, "Britain and Overseas Development," in Worswick and P. Ady, *The British Economy*, 278-312, 554; Dow, *The Management of the British Economy*, 144–77; and Cairncross, *Years of Recovery*, 333–53.

47 Cairncross, *Years of Recovery*, 399–403; Cairncross and Nita Watts, *The Economic Section, 1939-1961: A Study in Economic Advising* (London: Routledge, 1989), 323–31; W. Arthur Lewis, "The Prospect before Us," *Manchester School* (May, 1948), quoted in Keith Hutchinson, *The Decline and Fall of British Capitalism* (London: Cape, 1951), 313.

48 Prior to 1948 the government was concerned with wages but relied largely upon exhortation. This took the form of setting up the tripartite National Joint Advisory Committee, of publishing the White Paper, the Statement on the Economic Considerations Affecting Relations between Employers and Workers (Cmd. 7018) in January, 1947, and of more general propaganda. See, in particular, the discussions from 1947 reported in T238/65, "National Wages Policy, 1947–50."

49 See T229/213, "Wages Policy Following Devaluation;" report of the meeting held on 6 February 1951 between Gaitskell and TUC leaders, in T172/2033, "Discussions with TUC Representatives on Wages and Other Papers on Wages Policy, 1947–51;" Russell Jones, *Wages and Employment Policy, 1936-1985* (London: Allen & Unwin, 1987), 34–47; Cairncross, *Years of Recovery*, 399–408; and, on 1950-1, Middlemas, *Power, Competition and the State*, 188–92.

50 The paper, which was drafted in consultation with Douglas Jay, is in CAB134/225.

51 Harold Wilson, "The State and Private Industry," 4 May 1950, CAB124/1200. Wilson's position is discussed in Middlemas, *Power, Competition and the State*, 181–4; and in David Edgerton, "Liberal Militarism and the British State," *New Left Review*, 185 (January–February, 1991), 138–69.

52 See the reports of the separate meetings of junior and senior ministers on Wilson's paper, both of which seem to have taken place on 17 May, and also Wilson's note to Attlee of 14 July, in CAB124/1200.

53 Report by Marcus Fleming on the 11th Session of the UN Economic and Social

Council, August, 1950, in T230/230, quoted in Tomlinson, *Employment Policy*, 125.

54 See, for example, Fleming's report on discussions over full employment at the UN in New York, E.P.C. (50), 32, 4 March 1950, CAB134/225. Fleming argued that "As regards the U.S. domestic full employment policies, the impression left on me by my talks was reassuring so far as the *will* to maintain employment is concerned but less reassuring as regards the *power* to maintain the degree of stability which we would regard as satisfactory."

55 Max Nicholson to the Lord President, 8 March 1951, T230/230; Tomlinson, *Employment Policy*, 122–30.

56 Tomlinson, *Employment Policy*, 130–7. The decision to drop the bill was made at the 9 February 1951 meeting of the Committee on the Economic Planning and Full Employment Bill, G.E.N. 343 (51) 2nd Mtg., T229/267.

57 Kenneth Morgan, *Labour in Power*; Ben Pimlott, *Hugh Dalton*, 498–500; Peter Weiler, *British Labor and the Cold War* (Stanford: Stanford University Press, 1988), 21–2; Wm Roger Louis, *The British Empire in the Middle East, 1945–1951* (Oxford: Oxford University Press, 1984), 50.

58 On the setting up of the new department, see the *New Statesman and Nation*, 12 October 1946; T199/73; DEFE7/811; Harold Parker, "The Development of the Functions of the Ministry of Defence since 1946,' 18 April 1953, DEFE7/556; D. N. Chester, ed., *The Organization of British Central Government, 1914–1964* (London: Allen & Unwin, 1968), 207–48, 314–21. On its functioning, see the report of the "Inter-Service Working Party on the Shape and Size of the Armed Forces," chaired by Lord Harwood, DEFE7/592; and "Machinery for Defence Planning," unsigned Ministry of Defence memo, 23 March 1950, DEFE7/593. On Cripps' efforts to limit spending, see the minutes of the Defence Committee for late 1949: in particular, D.O. (49) 19th, 19 October 1949, and D.O. (49) 22nd, 25 November 1949, CAB131/8. On the dissatisfaction of the chiefs of staff with Harwood, see C.O.S. (49) 77th, 25 May 1949; also C.O.S. (49) 214th, 16 June 1949; and on Alexander's acquiescence to the position of the chiefs of staff, D.O. (49) 48th, 21 June 1949; in DEFE7/592. On Churchill's silly intervention of 10 May 1949, see DEFE7/560; and on the Conservatives' criticisms in March, 1950, see T225/75, "Defence Estimates, 1950–1." On the actual level of spending, see Cairncross, *Years of Recovery*, 212. The major qualification to this conclusion about declining spending is, of course, the secret decision to build the atomic bomb. On this see Margaret Gowing, *Independence and Deterrence*, 2 vols. (London: Macmillan, 1974); Morgan, *Labour in Power*; Trevor Burridge, *Clement Attlee: A Political Biography* (London: Cape, 1985), 234–47; and Peter Hennessy, *Cabinet* (Oxford: Blackwell, 1986), 123–34.

59 Cairncross, *Years of Recovery*, 214–16, 228–33; "Size and Shape of the Armed Forces, 1951–54," D.O. (50) 81st, 12 October 1950, and "The Finance of Defence," joint memo by Ernest Bevin and Hugh Gaitskell, D.O. (50) 91st, 23 October 1950, both in CAB131/9; Gaitskell, "Economic Implications of the Defence Proposals," in CAB129/44.

60 See Bevin and Gaitskell, "The Finance of Defence;" and T225/76, "Defence Budget in Event of Cessation of American Aid."

61 Dow, *Management of the British Economy*, 58–9; Cairncross and Watts, *The Economic Section*, 252–6; Philip Williams, *Hugh Gaitskell: A Political Biography* (London: Cape, 1979), 249–62; Cairncross, *Years of Recovery*, 230; Norman Brook, "Official Committees Dealing with Defence and Economic Policy," E.S. (50) 1st, 17 October 1950, CAB21/2368.

10 CENTRING THE POSTWAR SETTLEMENT

1 In his review of election addresses from 1951 David Butler uncovered virtually as many endorsements of full employment from Conservative candidates (69 per cent) as from Labour (74 per cent). See David Butler, *The British General Election of 1951* (London: Macmillan, 1952), 53–6.

2 The most authoritative discussion of the strengths and weaknesses of the model is Sir Norman Chester, *The Nationalisation of British Industry, 1945–51* (London: HMSO, 1975), 383–466, 1034–49. See also Kenneth O. Morgan, "The Rise and Fall of Public Ownership in Britain," in J.W.M. Bean, ed., *The Political Culture of Modern Britain* (London: Hamish Hamilton, 1987), 262–76.

3 R.A. Butler, *The Art of the Possible* (London: Hamish Hamilton, 1971), 126; Andrew Gamble, *The Conservative Nation* (London: Routledge & Kegan Paul, 1974), 40–1.

4 Hartmut Kopsch, "The Approach of the Conservative Party to Social Policy during World War II," Ph.D thesis, University of London, 1974, 70–2.

5 John Ramsden, *The Making of Conservative Party Policy: The Conservative Research Department since 1929* (London: Longman, 1980), 103–15.

6 Ramsden, *Making of Conservative Party Policy*, 113–14.

7 "This is the Road," 1950, reprinted in F.W.S. Craig, ed., *British General Election Manifestos, 1900–1974* (London: Macmillan, 1975), 139–52.

8 Ramsden, *Making of Conservative Party Policy*, 161.

9 The Liberal vote dropped from 2.6 million in 1950 to 730,000, a loss of almost 1.9 million. David Butler, *The British General Election of 1951*, 242; J. Cronin, *Labour and Society in Britain, 1918–1979* (London: Batsford, 1984), 144–5.

10 Paul Addison, "Churchill in British Politics," in Bean, *The Political Culture of Modern Britain*, 253.

11 Churchill's difficulties with the Treasury went back at least to his tenure as Chancellor of the Exchequer and his stormy relationship with Warren Fisher. See T199/415, "Relations between the Permanent Secretary and the Chancellor of the Exchequer, 1924–1926;" and Lord Woolton, 25 January 1954, cited in Anthony Seldon, *Churchill's Indian Summer: The Conservative Government, 1951–55* (London: Hodder & Stoughton, 1981), 110.

12 Peter Hennessey, *Whitehall* (London: Secker Warburg, 1989), 138–52; CAB134/906, "Steering Committee on Economic Organisation Enquiry, 1952–53" minutes of meeting of 27 June 1952, G.O.C. (S.C.) (52) 2.

13 See the memo by Brook in CAB21/2654, "Papers Prepared on the Assumption that a Conservative Government Was Formed after the General Election October 1951;" and also Alec Cairncross, ed., *The Robert Hall Diaries, 1947–1953* (London: Unwin Hyman, 1989), entry for 30 April 1951, 155–6.

14 Seldon, *Churchill's Indian Summer*, 102–6.

15 Seldon, *Churchill's Indian Summer*, 167.

16 *Robert Hall Diaries*, entry for 25 October 1951, 175. Bridges and William Armstrong first conveyed news of an impending financial crisis to Butler over lunch at the Athenaeum. "Their story," Butler later recalled, "was of blood draining from the system and a collapse greater than had been foretold in 1931." See Butler, *The Art of the Possible* (Harmondsworth: Penguin, 1973), 158–9; and also the memo by David Butt, 13 March 1952, in T230/242.

17 "The Economic Position: Analysis and Remedies. Memorandum by the Chancellor of the Exchequer," 31 October 1951, C. (51) 1, CAB129/48.

18 See Thomas Padmore to Norman Brook, 19 February 1952, and the memo by the Paymaster General, 5 March 1952, in CAB21/2223; also T230/242; Alec Cairncross, *Years of Recovery: British Economic Policy, 1945–51* (London: Methuen,

1985), 245; and the entry for 27 November 1951 in the *Robert Hall Diaries*, 184. Hall went on in his diary to note perceptively the political implications of the Bank's, and the officials", actions and the obstacles to their achievement. "The whole incident," he wrote, "was very disturbing and shows how silly some of them are. If they are not careful it will be 1931 and another Bankers' ramp. But there is much more economics on the labour side, and much more confidence and militancy on the TUC side, now than then. I cannot see that labour will meekly accept the view that because the experts say this will restore confidence the workers must accept a large cut in their standard of living as a result, and not ask for more wages, which is what they will certainly do."

19 Edwin Plowden, *An Industrialist in the Treasury: The Post-War Years* (London: Andre Deutsch, 1989), 143–61; entries for 20, 22, 23 and 29 February and 4 March in the *Robert Hall Diaries*, 204–7; Eden to Churchill, 23 February 1952, and Butler to Churchill, 25 February 1952, in PREM11/127; Alec Cairncross and Nita Watts, *The Economic Section, 1939-1961: A Study in Economic Advising* (London: Routledge, 1989), 304; Keith Middlemas, *Power, Competition and the State*, I: *Britain in Search of Balance, 1940-1961* (Stanford: Hoover Institution Press, 1986), 203; K. Morgan, *The People's Peace* (Oxford: Oxford University Press, 1990), 119–22. His subsequent opposition notwithstanding, Hall was at first attracted to the plan and wrote on 20 February that, "It certainly looks a great deal better when one thinks of alternatives."

20 Henry Roseveare, *The Treasury: Evolution of a British Institution* (New York: Columbia University Press, 1969), 322.

21 See J.C.R. Dow, *The Management of the British Economy, 1945-60* (Cambridge: Cambridge University Press, 1964), 72–5, 140, 198–200; CAB124/1167 on industry's reaction to the budget; Cairncross and Watts, *Economic Section*, 257–61; the memo of 16 September 1952 by Bernard Gilbert in T171/413.

22 Bernard Gilbert, "Food Subsidies and Social Payments," 6 February 1952, B.C. (52) 14, PREM11/138; Cairncross, *Years of Recovery*, 241; T171/409, "Budget, 1952, Vol. II;" Neil Rollings, "British Budgetary Policy, 1945-54: A 'Keynesian Revolution' ?" *Economic History Review*, XLI, (1988), 283–98; Robert Hall, "Note on Economic Policy," 15 August 1952, T230/328.

23 I.M.D. Little, "Fiscal Policy," in G.D.N. Worswick and P.H. Ady, eds, *The British Economy in the Nineteen-Fifties* (Oxford: Clarendon, 1962), 236. Little was a member of the Economic Section from 1953–5.

24 Peter Thorneycroft, *Hansard*, 15 April 1957; Cairncross and Watts, *Economic Section*, 262; "Taxation and Incentives," 8 November 1952, T230/328; *Financial Times*, 6 November 1952; C.R. Ross to J.C.R. Dow, 27 January 1953, T230/328; Hall, "Economic Prospects for 1953," 4 December 1952, B.C. (52) 27, T171/413, also his "The Economic and Budgetary Problem in 1953," 9 February 1953, summarized in Cairncross and Watts, *Economic Section*, 262.

25 Governor of the Bank of England to Bridges and the Chancellor of the Exchequer, 25 March 1953, T171/413.

26 Dow, *Managment of the British Economy*, 75, 198–203; B.E.V. Sabine, *A History of Income Tax* (London: Allen & Unwin, 1966), 226–7.

27 Among the pressures were the regular representations made to the Chancellor by industrial organizations. See, for example, the reports of the deputations from the FBI (11 December 1952), the Association of British Chambers of Commerce (10 December 1952), the Engineering Industries Association (30 December 1952) and the National Union of Manufacturers (8 January 1953), in T171/413.

28 Bridges to Butler, 3 October 1952; Butler to Churchill, 8 October 1952; Churchill to Butler, 13 October 1952; in T171/413; Butler to Churchill, 6 October 1952,

PREM11/658; Butler to Bridges, 22 November 1952, T199/236; Butler to Chur-
chill, 28 January 1953, PREM11/658.
See the report of Thorneycroft's statement of 10 February 1953 in C.C. (53) 6th,
PREM11/658.

29 "The Economic Situation," memorandum by the Chancellor of the Exchequer, 24
July 1953, C. (53), 211, PREM11/658; *The Times*, 16–18 July 1953; H.A. Copeman
to B. Trend, 20 July 1953, in T229/463; Cairncross and Watts, *Economic Section*,
262–4, who give the quotation from the Budget Committee meeting of 1 March
1954; and Dow, *Management of the British Economy*, 204–9.

30 Cherwell to Churchill, 29 January 1954, PREM11/653; Woolton, "Government
Methods of Financing and Effects of Taxation," 21 January 1954, C. (54), 22,
PREM11/658 and Butler's response, 2 March 1954, C. (54), 83; and the report from
the Cabinet meeting of 3 March 1954, C.C. (54) 14th, excerpted in PREM11/658.

31 T227/256, "Swinton Committee on Civil Expenditure, 1954;" Hall, "The Economic
Situation and Prospects," 5 April 1955, T171/459, cited in Cairncross and Watts,
Economic Section, 271; Middlemas, *Power, Competition and the State*, 269; and
Bridges speaking to a meeting of officials held on 16 December 1954, cited in
Cairncross and Watts, *Economic Section*, 266–7.

32 Dow, *Management of the British Economy*, 198–9. The April 1955 budget was
popular and did seem to sway some voters. See Richard Rose and Terence Karran,
Taxation By Political Inertia (London: Allen & Unwin, 1987), 170.

33 Minutes of the Economic Policy Committee, E.P. (55), 5th, 4 July 1955, CAB134/
1226; PREM11/888; Samuel Brittan, *Steering the Economy: The Role of the
Treasury* (Harmondsworth: Penguin, 1971), 200–3; Dow, *Management of the
British Economy*, 78–80; and Cairncross and Watts, *Economic Section*, 271–4.

34 Hennessy, *Whitehall*, 153; *Robert Hall Diaries*, entries for 4, 5, 7, 26 and 27 March
1951, 206–8, 214; Rollings, "British Budgetary Policy;" J.C.R. Dow to Robert Hall,
30 June 1954, T230/267; Plowden, *An Industrialist in the Treasury*, 161; T229/417,
and on Hall's relationship with Clarke, Cairncross and Watts, *Economic Section*,
154.

35 Cairncross and Watts, *Economic Section*, 154–61; Dow, notes for talk in 1953 at
Manchester University, in T230/283; Hall to Robbins, 19 June 1953; Robbins to
Hall, 22 June 1953; Meade to Hall, 26 June 1953; in T230/283; Samuel Beer,
Treasury Control (Oxford: Clarendon, 1957).

36 Dow to Hall, 30 June 1954, T230/267.

37 The report of Swinton's Employment Committee was submitted to Cabinet in
November, 1952 and discussed in December. See the excerpt from the Cabinet
minutes, C.C. (52) 106th, 18 December 1952, PREM11/13.

38 The key document in the discussion was the note of 3 February 1953 by the
Economic Section on "Measures to Maintain Employment." For the note and the
discussion around it, see CAB134/890. On the overall mix of policy devices under
the Conservatives, see Jim Tomlinson, *Employment Policy: The Crucial Years,
1939–1955* (Oxford: Clarendon, 1987), 144, 151–5.

39 On the favourable international context, see Tomlinson, *Employment Policy*, 143.

40 Royal Commission on the Taxation of Profits and Income, Final Report, Cmd. 9474
(June, 1955), *Parliamentary Papers*, XXVII. For an evaluation of the Commission's
work, see G.D.N. Worswick, "The Royal Commission on the Taxation of Profits
and Income," *Economic Journal*, LXVI (June, 1956), 370–7; and A.R. Prest's article
of the same title in *Economica*, n.s., XXIII (November, 1956), 366–74.

41 Tomlinson, *Employment Policy*, 145, is thus surely correct in arguing that, "Central
to Conservative concern with budgetary policy was a desire to reduce both taxation
and expenditure," and that "fiscal policy was as much about the search for public
expenditure economies as it was about the fiscal balance."

42 Hennessy, *Whitehall*, 143; Seldon, *Churchill's Indian Summer*, 107–14; Royal Commission on the Civil Service, Report, Cmd. 9613 (November, 1955); Richard Chapman and J.R. Greenaway, *The Dynamics of Administrative Reform* (London: Croom Helm, 1980), 167–8.

43 DEFE7/665, "Progress of the Rearmament Programme, 1951–53;" *White Paper on Defence*, 1952, Cmd. 8475; report of the Defence Committee meeting of 9 July 1952 in DEFE7/678.

44 C.O.S. (52) 150th mtg., 28 October 1952, DEFE7/678; D. (52) 11th mtg, 5 November 1952, CAB131/12; G.P. Humphreys-Davies to Antony Head, 17 December 1953, T225/350; "Report by the Sub-Committee of the Conservative Finance Committee, 1956 . . . on Economies in Defence Expenditure," in T225/350; Head to Butler, 10 December 1953; Humphreys-Davies to Bancroft, 11 December 1953; Bridges to Humphreys-Davies, 15 December 1953; Humphreys-Davies to Head, 17 December 1953; also in T225/350.

45 Alan Peacock and Jack Wiseman, *The Growth of Public Expenditure in the United Kingdom* (Princeton: Princeton University Press, 1961), 52–1, 190.

46 See Margaret Gowing, *Independence and Deterrence: Britain and Atomic Energy, 1945-52*, Vol. I: *Policy Making* (London: Macmillan, 1974); Churchill to Cherwell, 15 November 1951, cited in Peter Hennessy, *Cabinet* (Oxford: Basil Blackwell, 1986), 134; Trevor Burridge, *Clement Attlee: A Political Biography* (London: Cape, 1985), 234–47.

47 Seldon, *Churchill's Indian Summer*, 334; Cabinet minutes for 26 July 1954, C.C. (54) 48th, CAB128/27, cited in Hennessy, *Cabinet*, 140; White Paper on Defence (1955), Cmd. 9391 *Parliamentary Papers* (1954–5), X; Middlemas, *Power, Competition and the State*, 269; David Edgerton, "Liberal Militarism and the British State," *New Left Review*, 185 (January–February, 1991), 138–69.

48 Brook to Bridges, 21 April 1950, CAB21/1626. Support for holding down expenditure on social services was nearly unanimous among officials. Even Robert Hall, who had fought hard against the mandarins over budgetary and monetary policy, agreed on the need to cut social expenditure. Thus, after his old antagonist on economic policy, Otto Clarke, had been placed in charge of the social services at the Treasury in late 1953, Hall recorded that "he and I have become fellow conspirators against the increase in Social Services." See the entry for 30 December, 1953 in the *Robert Hall Diaries*, 281.

49 Iain Macleod and Enoch Powell, *The Social Services - Needs and Means* (London: Conservative Political Centre, 1949, 1954); Macleod and A. Maude, eds, *One Nation: A Tory Approach to Social Problems* (London: Conservative Political Centre, 1950); Powell, "Conservatives and Social Services," *Political Quarterly*, XXIV (1952), 156–66; and Timothy Raison, *Tories and the Welfare State: A History of Conservative Social Policy since the Second World War* (London: Macmillan, 1990), 15–41; Richard Titmuss, "The Social Division of Welfare: Some Reflections on the Search for Equity," (1955) in *Essays on "The Welfare State"* (New Haven: Yale University Press, 1959); *Sunday Times*, 20 January 1952, quoted in Seldon, *Churchill's Indian Summer*, 245; *British Medical Journal*, 2 December 1950, cited in Titmuss, "The National Health Service in England: Some Aspects of Structure," in *Essays on "The Welfare State"*, 148.

50 Report of the Committee of Enquiry into the cost of the National Health Service (Guillebaud Report) (1956), Cmd. 9663 *Parliamentary Papers* (1955–6), XX. The figures had been compiled by Brian Abel-Smith and Richard Titmuss. See, in addition to the *Report*, Abel-Smith and Titmuss, *The Cost of the National Health Service in England and Wales* (Cambridge: Cambridge University Press, 1956), esp. 54. For a fuller discussion of the committee and its report, see Titmuss, "The

National Health Service in England," 147–51; T.E. Chester, "The Guillebaud Report," *Public Administration*, XXXIV (1956); and Charles Webster, *The Health Services since the War* (London: HMSO, 1988), 204–11.

51 Peacock and Wiseman, *Growth of Public Expenditure*, 92; Centre for Contemporary Cultural Studies, *Unpopular Education: Schooling and Social Democracy in England since 1944* (London: Hutchinson, 1981), 192.

52 A.R. Ilersic, "Relief for Ratepayers," in Ralph Harris, ed., *Freedom or Free-for-all? Essays in Welfare, Trade and Choice* (London: Institute of Economic Affairs, 1965), Volume 3 of the Hobart Papers, 263–319; Richard Jackman, "Local Government Finance," in M. Loughlin *et al.*, eds, *Half a Century of Municipal Decline, 1935–1985* (London: Allen & Unwin, 1985), 156; Ken Young, *Local Politics and the Rise of Party* (Leicester: Leicester University Press, 1975), 195–212; John Gyford, "The Politicization of Local Government," in *Half a Century of Municipal Decline*, 84–9.

53 "Conservative Manifesto 1951," in Craig, *British General Election Manifestos*, 172; Peacock and Wiseman, *Growth of Public Expenditure*, 184–5, 190–1; Seldon, *Churchill's Indian Summer*, 244–294. As a proportion of GNP, social service spending dropped from 17.5 per cent in 1952 to 16.3 per cent in 1955.

54 See PREM11/658, "Government Economies, 1954–5;" and T227/256, "Swinton Committee on Civil Expenditure, 1954."

55 Monckton, cited in Middlemas, *Power, Competition and the State*, 257.

56 CAB134/874, "Emergency Legislation Committee. Working Party on Economic Controls;" Margaret Hall, "The Consumer Sector," and Paul Streeten, "Commercial Policy," in Worswick and Ady, *British Economy*, 86–90, 439; Dow, *Management of the British Economy*, 149–50, 160, 174; BT91/4, "Board of Trade Responsibility for Distribution of Industry, 1954–5."

57 Middlemas, *Power, Competition and the State*, 217.

58 P.D. Henderson, "Government and Industry," in Worswick and Ady, *British Economy*, 332–4.

59 Kathleen Burk, *The First Privatisation: The Politicians, the City and the Denationalisation of Steel* (London: The Historians' Press, 1988); Richard Pryke, *Public Enterprise in Practice: The British Experience of Nationalization over Two Decades* (London: MacGibbon & Kee, 1971), 31; Labour Party, *Challenge to Britain* (London: 1953); Middlemas, *Power, Competition and the State*, 223; Philip Williams, *Hugh Gaitskell. A Political Biography* (London: Jonathan Cape, 1979), 318; D.L. Munby, "The Nationalized Industries," in Worswick and Ady, *British Economy*, 376–84.

60 Pryke, *Public Enterprise in Practice*, 36–57; Munby, "The Nationalized Industries," 383–6, 426–7; and, on the setting up of the Select Committee, CAB124/1202. See also the White Paper on "The Financial and Economic Obligations of Nationalised Industries," Cmnd. 1337 (1961), which was largely a response to the reports of the Select Committee.

61 Middlemas, *Power, Competition and the State*, 238–40; Nigel Harris, *Competition and the Corporate Society: British Conservatives, The State and Industry, 1945–1964* (London: Methuen, 1972), 220–7; Seldon, *Churchill's Indian Summer*, 185; Christina Fulop, "Revolution in Retailing," in Ralph Harris, ed., *Ancient or Modern? Essays in Economic Efficiency and Growth*, Hobart Papers, 2 (London: Institute of Economic Affairs, 1964), 94–8.

62 Department of Employment and Productivity, *British Labour Statistics. Historical Abstract, 1888–1968* (London: HMSO, 1971).

63 *Robert Hall Diaries*, entry for 9 March 1953, 269. Hall did concede later, however,

that "although I don't think there is any real inflation in the system, there isn't as much deflation as we thought." See the entry for 30 December 1953, 282.

64 CAB134/936, "Cabinet Home Affairs Committee, Workers" Charter, 1952."
65 Churchill's position was noted in Lord Woolton's diary entry for 13 December 1954 and cited in Seldon, *Churchill's Indian Summer*, 200.
66 Middlemas, *Power, Competition and the State*, 257–64.
67 Russell Jones, *Wages and Employment Policy, 1936–1985* (London: Allen & Unwin, 1987), 50–3; T230/300, "National Wages Policy and Full Employment Policy, 1954–55;" The Economic Implications of Full Employment, Cmd. 9725, *Parliamentary Papers* (1955–6), XXXVI; Middlemas, *Power, Competition and the State*, 278.

11 DECLINE TO THATCHER

1 On Treasury concerns, see Rodney Lowe, "Resignation at the Treasury: the Social Services Committee and the Failure to Reform the Welfare State, 1955–1957," *Journal of Social Policy*, XVIII (1989), 505–26; on businessmen, see Keith Middlemas, *Power, Competition and the State*, Vol. I: *Britain in Search of Balance, 1940–1961* (Stanford: Hoover Institution Press, 1986), 236–7, 242–3; and on economists and growth, see T.W. Hutchinson, *Economics and Economic Policy in Britain, 1946–1966* (London: Allen & Unwin, 1968), 125–61.
2 Andrew Shonfield, *British Economic Policy since the War* (Harmondsworth: Penguin, 1958), 224; Samuel Brittan, *Steering the Economy: The Role of the Treasury* (Harmondsworth: Penguin, 1970), 206; Alec Cairncross and Nita Watts, *The Economic Section, 1939–1961: A Study in Economic Advising* (London: Routledge, 1989), 274–5; Lowe, "Resignation at the Treasury," esp. 508–17.
3 H.A. Clegg and R. Adams, *The Employers' Challenge* (Oxford: Oxford University Press, 1957); Middlemas, *Power, Competition and the State*, 312, 388; Alistair Horne, *Harold Macmillan*, Vol. II: *1957–1986* (New York: Viking, 1989), 66.
4 Thorneycroft to Macmillan, 30 July 1957, in PREM11/2306; Brittan, *Steering the Economy*, 207–17; Cairncross and Watts, *Economic Section*, 226–30.
5 "The 1958/59 Civil Estimates. Memorandum by the Chancellor of the Exchequer," 19 December 1957, in PREM11/2306; Cabinet Conclusions for 5 January 1958, C.C. (58), 3rd, CAB128/32 (Part I).
6 On the politics and economics behind the 1959 budget and election, see T171/496 and PREM11/2654.
7 Middlemas, *Power, Competition and the State*, 242.
8 See T233/1677, and Hutchinson, *Economics and Economic Policy*, 125–30.
9 Lionel Robbins, *The Balance of Payments*, Stamp Memorial Lecture, 1951, quoted in Hutchinson, *Economics and Economic Policy*, 104; A.W. Phillips, "The Relation between Unemployment and the Rate of Change of Money Wages in the United Kingdom, 1861–1957," *Economica*, XXV (November, 1958).
10 Robert Hall, "Economic outlook – preliminary appraisal," 13 December 1957, cited in Cairncross and Watts, *Economic Section*, 278; Russell Jones, *Wages and Employment Policy, 1936–1985* (London: Allen & Unwin, 1987), 53–4.
11 Shonfield, *British Economic Policy since the War*, 243–7; Sidney Pollard, *The Wasting of the British Economy* (New York: St Martin's, 1982), 22–30, 37–47; Thomas Balogh, "The Apotheosis of the Dilettante," in Hugh Thomas, ed., *The Establishment* (London: Anthony Blond, 1959), 83–126; Geoffrey K. Fry, *Statesmen in Disguise* (London: Macmillan, 1969), 232–5.
12 The term "Establishment," with its predominantly negative connotations, achieved wide currency after Henry Fairlie used it in his column in the *Spectator*, 23 September 1955, on the reaction of the "establishment" to Burgess' and Maclean's escape to Moscow.

13 Among many examples, see Anthony Sampson, *The Anatomy of Britain* (London: Hodder & Stoughton, 1962); Brian Chapman, *British Government Observed* (London: Allen & Unwin, 1963); *The Administrators: The Reform of the Civil Service*, Fabian Tract No. 355 (London: Fabian Society, 1964); and the follow-up to the first effort – Hugh Thomas, ed., *Crisis in the Civil Service* (London: Anthony Blond, 1968). For an earlier, more ironic treatment, see C.H. Sisson, *The Spirit of British Administration* (London: Faber, 1952). On Radcliffe, Plowden and the list, see the entertaining account in Peter Hennessy, *Whitehall* (London: Secker & Warburg, 1989), 546–58, 565–8.

14 Report of the 20 March 1956 meeting between the Chancellor and the group of MPs led by Robert Boothby, in T233/1686; Report of the Committee on the Working of the Monetary System (1959), Cmnd. 827 *Parliamentary Papers* (1958–9), XVII; T233/1404, on the Treasury's handling of the Radcliffe Committee; Cairncross and Watts, *Economic Section*, 223–6; Hutchinson, *Economics and Economic Policy*, 150–61; Brittan, *Steering the Economy*, 83–5, 156–7.

15 T133/1640, "Select Committee on Estimates, 1957–8, Treasury Control of Expenditure, Preparation of Treasury Observations;" B.D. Fraser to Thomas Padmore, 22 June 1959, in T233/1710; Control of Public Expenditure, Cmd. 1432, *Parliamentary Papers* (1960–1), XX; Richard Chapman and J. R. Greenaway, *The Dynamics of Administrative Reform* (London: Croom Helm, 1980), 135–6; Hennessy, *Whitehall*, 177–9; Leo Pliatzky, *Getting and Spending: Public Expenditure, Employment and Inflation* (Oxford: Basil Blackwell, 1984), esp. 44; Richard Clarke, *Public Expenditure Management and Control: The Development of the Public Expenditure Survey Committee* (London: Macmillan, 1978), 25–6; Keith Middlemas, *Power, Competition and the State*, Vol. II: *Threats to the Postwar Settlement: Britain, 1961–74* (London: Macmillan, 1990), 29–30; Hugh Heclo and Aaron Wildavsky, *The Private Government of Public Money*, 2nd edn, (London: Macmillan, 1981), xiii.

16 Jacques Leruez, *Economic Planning and Politics in Britain* (Oxford: Martin Robertson, 1975), 84–95; Brittan, *Steering the Economy*, 242–5; Federation of British Industry, *The Next Five Years: Report of the Brighton Conference* (November, 1960).

17 Jones, *Wages and Employment Policy*, 61–2.

18 Peter Hall, *Governing the Economy: The Politics of State Intervention in Britain and France* (New York: Oxford University Press, 1986), 86–7.

19 Clarke, *Public Expenditure Management and Control*.

20 Cairncross, in the "Symposium: 1967 Devaluation," *Contemporary Record*, I, 4 (Winter, 1988), 46; Harold Lever on the Treasury, quoted in Hennessy, *Whitehall*, 182; Macleod, speaking in the Commons on 3 November 1965, cited in Leruez, *Economic Planning and Politics*, 179; Middlemas, *Power, Competition and the State*, II, 103–6, 119–22.

21 Hall, *Governing the Economy*, 88–9; Middlemas, *Power, Competition and the State*, II, 157–63, 165–8, 171–3; Douglas Hague and Geoffrey Wilkinson, *The IRC – An Experiment in Industrial Intervention* (London: Allen & Unwin, 1983).

22 Peter Kellner and Lord Crowther-Hunt, *The Civil Servants: An Inquiry into Britain's Ruling Class* (London: Macdonald Futura, 1980); Middlemas, *Power, Competition and the State*, II, 204–6; Fry, *Statesmen in Disguise*, 251–426; Hennessy, *Whitehall*, 190–208.

23 Alec Cairncross and Barry Eichengreen, *Sterling in Decline* (Oxford: Basil Blackwell, 1983), 156–217; Middlemas, *Power, Competition and the State*, II, 113–19, 189–94; Kathleen Burk, "Chronology," in the "Symposium: Devaluation 1967," and Kenneth Morgan's contribution to the "Symposium: The Labour Party's

Record in Office," *Contemporary Record* (April, 1990), 22–3. Morgan here appears to rely upon material in Clive Ponting's *Breach of Promise: Labour in Power, 1964–70* (London: Hamish, Hamilton, 1989).

24 Jones, *Wages and Employment Policy*, 66–75; Leruez, *Economic Planning and Politics*, 198–209.

25 See the White Paper on The Reorganisation of Central Government, Cmnd. 4506, (1970); and Hennessy, *Whitehall*, 210–13, 220–36.

26 Jones, *Wages and Employment Policy*, 84–98.

27 Ivor Crewe, Bo Sarvlik and James Alt, "Partisan Dealignment in Britain, 1964–74," *British Journal of Political Science*, VII (1977), 129–90; Bob Jessop, "The Transformation of the State in Post-war Britain," in R. Scase, ed., *The State in Western Europe* (New York: St Martin's, 1980), 38–47; Paul Sacks, "State Structure and the Asymmetrical Society: An Approach to Public Policy in Britain," *Comparative Politics* (1980), 349–76; Peter Hall, "The State and Economic Decline," in B. Elbaum and W. Lazonick, eds, *The Decline of the British Economy* (Oxford: Clarendon, 1986), 266–302.

28 Samuel Beer, *Britain against Itself: The Political Contradictions of Collectivism* (New York: Norton, 1982), 69; Jim Tomlinson, *Public Policy and the Economy since 1900* (Oxford: Clarendon, 1990), 252–3; and Leruez, *Economic Planning and Politics*, 231–4; Michael Foot, quoted in the *Guardian*, 3 October 1973 and cited in David Coates, *Labour in Power? A Study of the Labour Government, 1974–1979* (London: Longman, 1980), 6.

29 Coates, *Labour in Power?*, 230–8. Even its supporters now concede that the external dimensions of the "alternative economic strategy" were seriously deficient. See Nicholas Costello, Jonathan Michie and Seumas Milne, *Beyond the Casino Economy* (London: Verso, 1989).

30 Hennessy, *Whitehall*, 243–50, 261–7. Far less judicious and more interesting reading than the English Committee report was Brian Sedgemore's alternative draft, the main points of which would reappear in his book, *The Secret Constitution* (London: Hodder & Stoughton, 1980).

31 Coates, *Labour in Power?*, 86–146.

32 Joel Barnett, *Inside the Treasury* (London: Andre Deutsch, 1982), 31–47; Peter Browning, *The Treasury and Economic Policy, 1964–1985* (London: Longman, 1986), 59–135; Jones, *Wages and Employment Policy*, 105–7.

33 Cairncross and Watts, *Economic Section*, 280–1; Leruez, *Economic Planning and Politics*, 91; Peter Flora, *State, Economy and Society in Western Europe, 1815–1975* (Frankfurt a. M.: Campus Verlag, 1983), 440; and M. Kogan, "The Politics of Public Expenditure," *British Journal of Political Science*, VII (1977), 401–32.

34 Ann Robinson and Cedric Sandford, *Tax Policy-Making in the United Kingdom: A Study of Rationality, Ideology and Politics* (London: Heinemann, 1983), 5, 9, 24–33, 98–99; Jones, *Wages and Employment Policy*, 81; K. Langley, *Capital Gains Taxation*, Fabian Research Series No. 150 (London: Fabian Society, 1952); Bruce Millan, *Taxes for a Prosperous Society*, Fabian Research Series No. 234 (London: Fabian Society, 1963); Jebs (pseud.), *Personal Taxation*, Fabian Research Series No. 255 (London: Fabian Society, 1966); James Callaghan, 11 November 1964, House of Commons Debates, cited in Robinson and Sandford, 13; Richard Rose and Terence Karran, *Taxation by Political Inertia: Financing the Growth of Government in Britain* (London: Allen & Unwin, 1987), 157–67.

35 See "A Better Tomorrow" (1970) in F.W.S. Craig, ed., *British General Election Manifestos, 1900–1974* (London: Macmillan, 1975), 327; Flora, *State, Economy and Society*, 339; Barnett, *Inside the Treasury*, 32–3; Rose and Karran, *Taxation by Political Inertia*, 117–18; and, on the capital transfer tax and the wealth tax

proposals, Robinson and Sandford, *Tax Policy-Making*, 38–43, 48–51.

36 By the late 1970s and early 1980s workers were paying on average 9 per cent of earnings for national insurance. See Howard Glennerster, *Paying for Welfare* (Oxford: Basil Blackwell, 1985), 218–23.

37 The most extensive contemporary evaluation of the tax system was the report of the Meade Committee, *The Structure and Reform of Direct Taxation* (London: Allen & Unwin and the Institute of Fiscal Studies, 1978). See also J.A. Kay and M.A. King, *The British Tax System*, 3rd edn (Oxford: Oxford University Press, 1983). On local taxes, see Richard Jackman, "Local Government Finance," in M. Loughlin *et al.*, eds, *Half a Century of Municipal Decline, 1935-1985* (London: Allen & Unwin, 1985), 144–68; and Bryan Keith-Lucas and Peter Richards, *A History of Local Government in the Twentieth Century* (London: Allen & Unwin, 1978), 127–53; Alan Alexander, "Structure, Centralization and the Position of Local Government," in Loughlin, *Half a Century of Municipal Decline*, 59–61; and Alan Sked and Chris Cook, *Post-War Britain: A Political History* (Harmondsworth: Penguin, 1984), 269–70. The Ken Livingstone quote comes from Jackman, 157.

38 Rudolf Klein, "Public Expenditure in an Inflationary World," in Leon Lindberg and Charles Maier, eds, *The Politics of Inflation and Economic Stagnation* (Washington, DC: Brookings Institution, 1985), 204; H. Glennerster, "Social Service Spending in a Hostile Environment," in C. Hood and M. Wright, eds., *Big Government in Hard Times* (Oxford: Martin Robertson, 1981), 172, 175; P. Esam *et al.*, *Who's To Benefit? A Radical Review of the Social Security System* (London: Verso, 1985); Paul Wilding, *Socialism and Professionalism*, Fabian Tract No. 473 (London: Fabian Society, 1981); Wilding, *Professional Power and Social Welfare* (London: Routledge & Kegan Paul, 1982); Harold Perkin, *The Rise of Professional Society: England since 1880* (London: Routledge, 1989), 475–6; Abram de Swaan, *In Care of the State* (Oxford: Oxford University Press, 1983), 230–44; Paul Johnson, "Some Historical Dimensions of the Welfare State Crisis," *Journal of Social Policy*, XV, 4 (October, 1986), 443–65; David Harris, *Justifying State Welfare: The New Right versus the Old Left* (Oxford: Basil Blackwell, 1987); Stephen Davies, *Beveridge Revisited: New Foundations for Tomorrow's Welfare* (London: Centre for Policy Studies, 1986); P. Alcock, "Welfare State – Safety Net or Poverty Trap," *Marxism Today* (July, 1985), 9–15.

39 Even so, public opinion was never especially Thatcherite on the issue. See Peter Taylor-Gooby, "The Future of the British Welfare State: Public Attitudes, Citizenship, and Social Policy under the Conservative governments of the 1980s," *European Sociological Review*, IV, 1 (1988), 1–17.

40 Hennessy, *Whitehall*, 419–25. The creation of the DHSS was a Labour innovation, but a similar reorganization had been proposed by Iain Macleod in the late 1950s. It was quashed, however, by Norman Brook. See PREM11/2722.

41 Nicholas Deakin, "Local Government and Social Policy," in Loughlin, *Half a Century of Municipal Decline*, 211–12; Eileen Younghusband, *Social Work in Britain: 1950-1975* (London: Allen & Unwin, 1978), 227–45; Leslie Hannah, *Inventing Retirement* (Cambridge: Cambridge University Press, 1986), 55–62; PREM11/2760 on pensions policy; Richard Parry, "United Kingdom," in Peter Flora, ed., *Growth to Limits: The West European Welfare States since World War II*, Vol. II: *Germany, United Kingdom, Ireland, Italy* (New York: de Gruyter, 1988), 161; Michael Hill, *Understanding Social Policy*, 3rd edn (Oxford: Basil Blackwell, 1988), 28–39; A.H. Halsey, "Schools," and "Higher Education," in Halsey, ed., *British Social Trends since 1900* (London: Macmillan, 1988), 226–67, 268–96; Patrick Dunleavy, "The Urban Basis of Political Alignment: Social Class, Domestic Property Ownership, and State Intervention in Consumption Processes," *British*

Journal of Political Science, IX (1979); Tomlinson, *Public Policy and the Economy*, 264-7; Leruez, *Economic Planning and Politics*, 156-63, 187-91; Hall, *Governing the Economy*, 52, 89; G.C. Peden, *British Social and Economic Policy: Lloyd George to Margaret Thatcher* (London: Philip Allan, 1985), 197-202; Sked and Cook, *Post-War Britain*, 207-9, 241-2, 252.

42   Glennerster, *Paying for Welfare*, 239; Julia Parker and Catriona Mirrlees, "Welfare," in Halsey, *British Social Trends since 1900*, 505, 510-1; Parry, "United Kingdom," 188-190. Parry calculates the value of child and family allowances differerently from Parker and Mirrlees, showing a decline rather than an increase, but overall the estimates concur.

43   Robinson and Sandford, *Tax Policy-Making*, 70-80; Vito Tanzi et al., *Taxation: A Radical Approach* (London: Institute of Economic Affairs, 1970).

44   Leo Pliatzky, *The Treasury under Mrs Thatcher* (Oxford: Basil Blackwell, 1989), 7-9; Barnett, *Inside the Treasury*, 77-8; Hennessy, *Whitehall*, 251-2, 260.

45   Amid the steadily growing literature, see especially Dennis Kavanagh, *Thatcherism and British Politics: The End of Consensus?* (Oxford: Oxford University Press, 1987); D. Kavanagh and A. Seldon, eds., *The Thatcher Effect* (Oxford: Clarendon, 1989); Martin Holmes, *Thatcherism: Scope and Limits, 1983-87* (New York: St Martin's, 1989); Peter Riddell, *The Thatcher Decade* (Oxford: Basil Blackwell, 1989); Stuart Hall and Martin Jacques, eds., *The Politics of Thatcherism* (London: Lawrence & Wishart, 1983); Bob Jessop et al., *Thatcherism: A Tale of Two Nations* (Oxford: Polity, 1989); Andrew Gamble, *The Free Economy and the Strong State: The Politics of Thatcherism* (Durham, NC: Duke University Press, 1988); J. Krieger, *Reagan, Thatcher and the Politics of Decline* (New York: Oxford University Press, 1986), 223-46; J. Bulpitt, "The Discipline of the New Democracy: Mrs Thatcher's Domestic Statecraft,' *Political Studies*, XXXIV (1986), 19-39; S.E. Finer, "Thatcherism in British Political History," in K. Minogue and M. Biddiss, eds, *Thatcherism: Personality and Politics* (London: Macmillan, 1987); Peter Jenkins, *Mrs Thatcher's Revolution* (Cambridge, Mass.: Harvard University Press, 1988); and Hugo Young, *The Iron Lady: A Biography of Mrs Thatcher* (New York: Farrar, Strauss & Giroux, 1989).

46   On taxes, see A.G. Jordan and J.J. Richardson, *British Politics and the Policy Process: An Arena Approach* (London: Allen & Unwin, 1987), 215; on expenditure and state intervention, Ray Robinson, "Restructuring the Welfare State: An Analysis of Public Expenditure, 1979/80-1984/85," *Journal of Social Policy*, XV (1986), 1-21; Julian Le Grand and David Winter, "The Middle Classes and the Defence of the British Welfare State," in R. Goodin and Le Grand, eds, *Not Only the Poor: The Middle Classes and the Welfare State* (London: Allen & Unwin, 1987), 147-68; Norman Flynn, "The 'New Right' and Social Policy," *Policy and Politics*, XVII, 2 (April, 1989), 97-109; Paul Pierson, "Cutting Against the Grain: Reagan, Thatcher and the Politics of Welfare State Retrenchment," Ph.D Thesis, Yale University, 1989; Aidan Kelly, "An End to Incrementalism? The Impact of Expenditure Restraint on Social Services Budgets, 1979-1986," *Journal of Social Policy*, XVIII (1989), 187-210; Tomlinson, *Public Policy and the Economy since 1900*, 323; Timothy Raison, *The Tories and the Welfare State* (London: Macmillan, 1990), 107ff; Andrew Dilnot and Ian Walker, eds, *The Economics of Social Security* (Oxford: Oxford University Press, 1989); John Hills, ed., *The State of Welfare: The Welfare State in Britain since 1974* (Oxford: Oxford Clarendon, 1990); and P. Dunleavy, "The United Kingdom: Paradoxes of an Ungrounded Statism," in Francis Castles, ed., *The Comparative History of Public Policy* (Oxford: Oxford University Press, 1989), 281-3. On law and order and the government's softness towards police, see K.D. Ewing and C.A. Gearty, *Freedom under Thatcher:*

Civil Liberties in Modern Britain (Oxford: Oxford University Press, 1990); Ian Taylor, "Law and Order, Moral Order: The Changing Rhetorics of the Thatcher Government," *Socialist Register 1987*, 297–331; Patrick Dunleavy, "The Architecture of the British Central State, Part II: Empirical Findings," *Public Administration*, LXVII, 4 (Winter, 1989), 414–15; Gamble, *The Free Economy and the Strong State*; and Jim Bulpitt, *Territory and Power in the United Kingdom* (Manchester: Manchester University Press, 1983).

47 The distinction between "despotic" and "infrastructural" power derives from Michael Mann, "The Autonomous Power of the State: Its Origins, Mechanisms and Results," *European Journal of Sociology*, XXV (1984), 185–213. Mann employs a different, but closely related, set of distinctions in *The Sources of Social Power*, Vol. I: *A History of Power from the Beginning to A.D. 1760* (Cambridge: Cambridge University Press, 1986).

48 See, in particular, the arguments in the March, 1985 White Paper, Employment: The Challenge of the Nation, Cmnd. 9474, *Parliamentary Paper* (1984–5), L, which are pointedly contrasted with those of the 1944 White Paper by Jim Tomlinson in *Employment Policy: The Crucial Years, 1939–1955* (Oxford: Clarendon, 1987), 160–75.

49 On the demoralization of the civil service in the early Thatcher years, see Michael Lee, "Whitehall and Retrenchment," in Hood and Wright, *Big Government in Hard Times*, 35–55.

50 Kavanagh, *Thatcherism and British Politics*, 289–90; Peter Hennessy, "Mrs Thatcher's Poodle? The Civil Service since 1979," *Contemporary Record*, II, 2 (Summer, 1988), 2–4; and *Whitehall*, 587–682; William Plowden, "The Treasury: Continuity and Change," *Contemporary Record*, II, 3 (Autumn, 1988), 26; Pliatzky, *The Treasury under Mrs Thatcher*; Colin Thain, "The Treasury: Its Evolving Role since 1979," *Contemporary Record* (April, 1990), 17–19; and Thain and Maurice Wright, "Coping with Difficulty: The Treasury and Public Expenditure, 1976–1989," *Policy and Politics*, XVIII, 1 (January, 1990), 1–15.

51 C. Veljanovski, *Selling the State: Privatization in Britain* (London: Weidenfeld & Nicolson, 1987); J. Le Grand and R. Robinson, eds, *Privatisation and the Welfare State* (London: Allen & Unwin, 1983); S. Brittan, "The Politics and Economics of Privatisation," *Political Quarterly*, LV (1984), 109–28; and C. Leys, "Thatcherism and British Manufacturing," *New Left Review*, 151 (1985), 5–25.

52 B. Barry, "Does Democracy Cause Inflation? Political Ideas of Some Economists," in L. Lindberg and C. Maier, eds, *The Politics of Inflation and Economic Stagnation*, 317.

Index